NINE LIVES

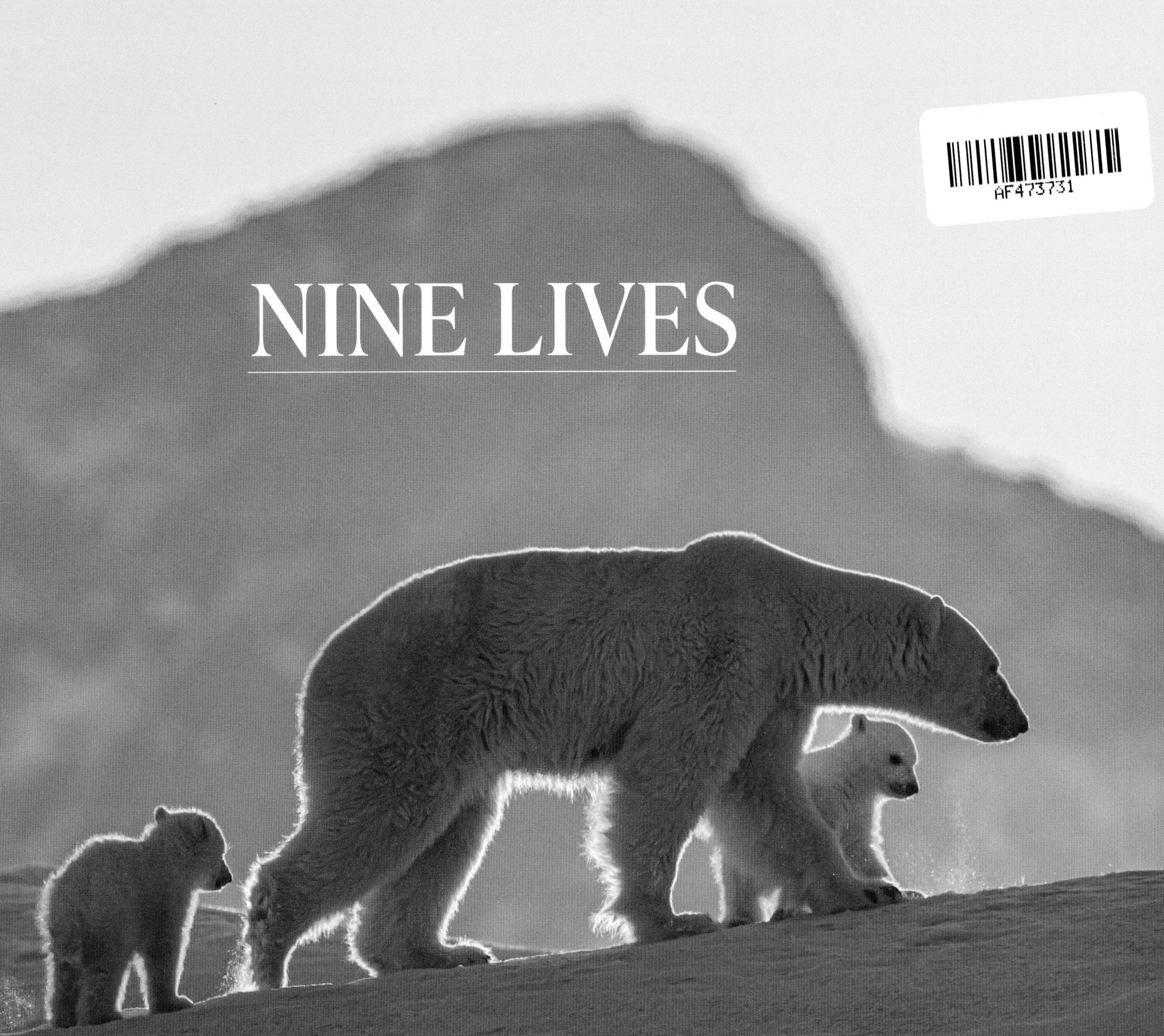

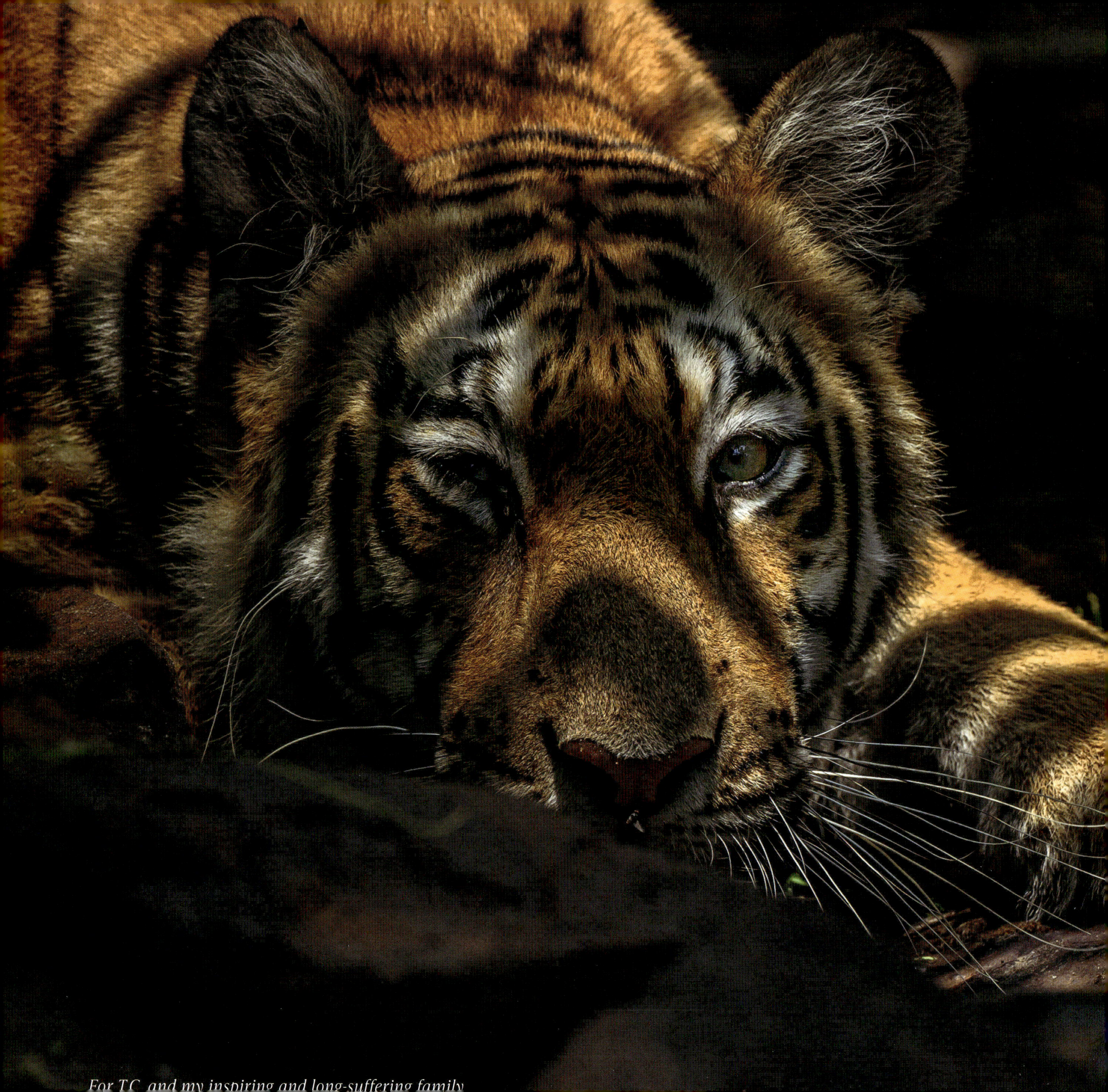

For TC, and my inspiring and long-suffering family

NINE LIVES

One photographer,
nine persecuted species

PAUL
GOLDSTEIN

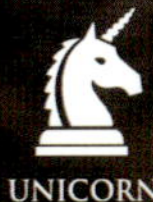
UNICORN

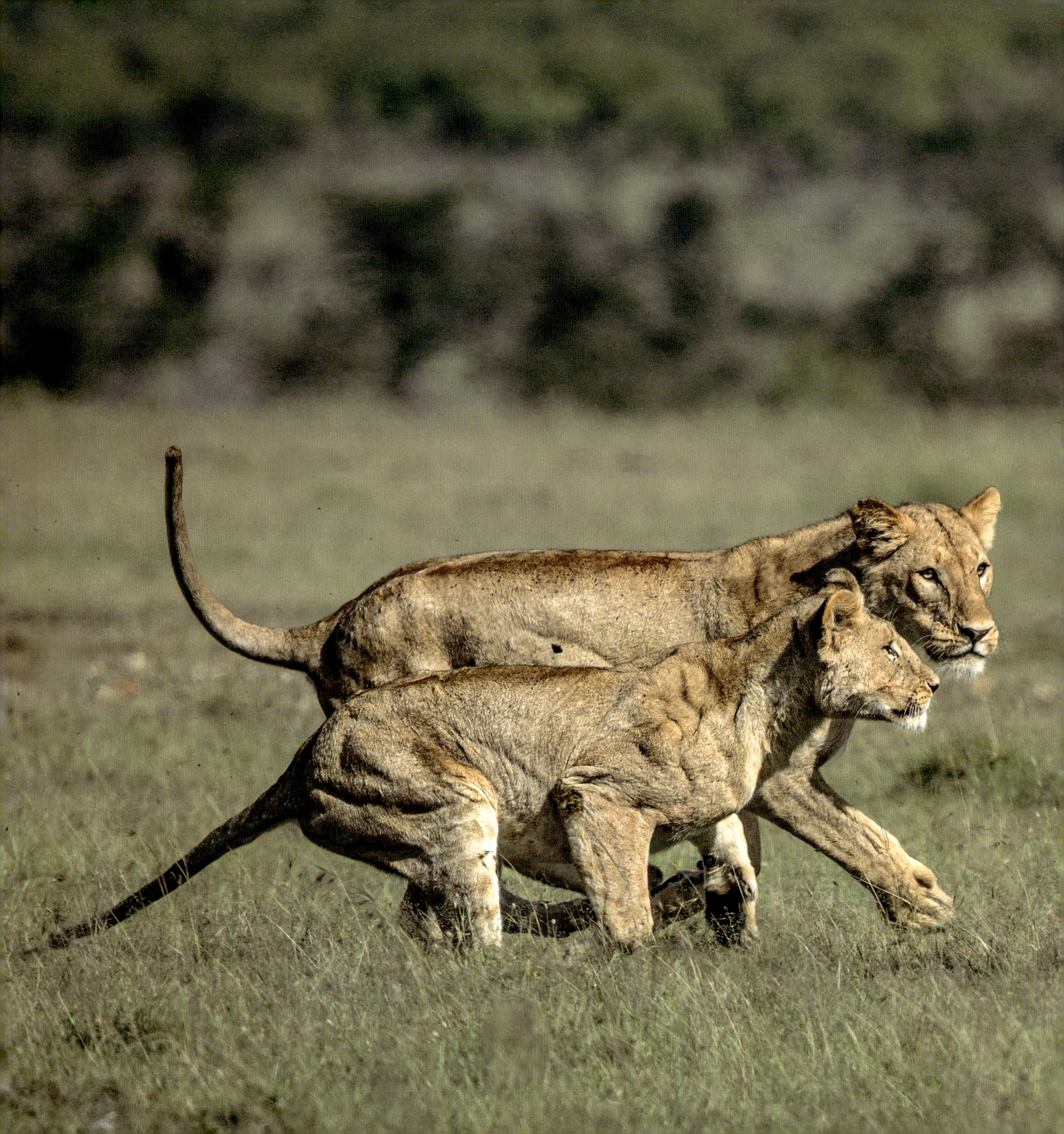

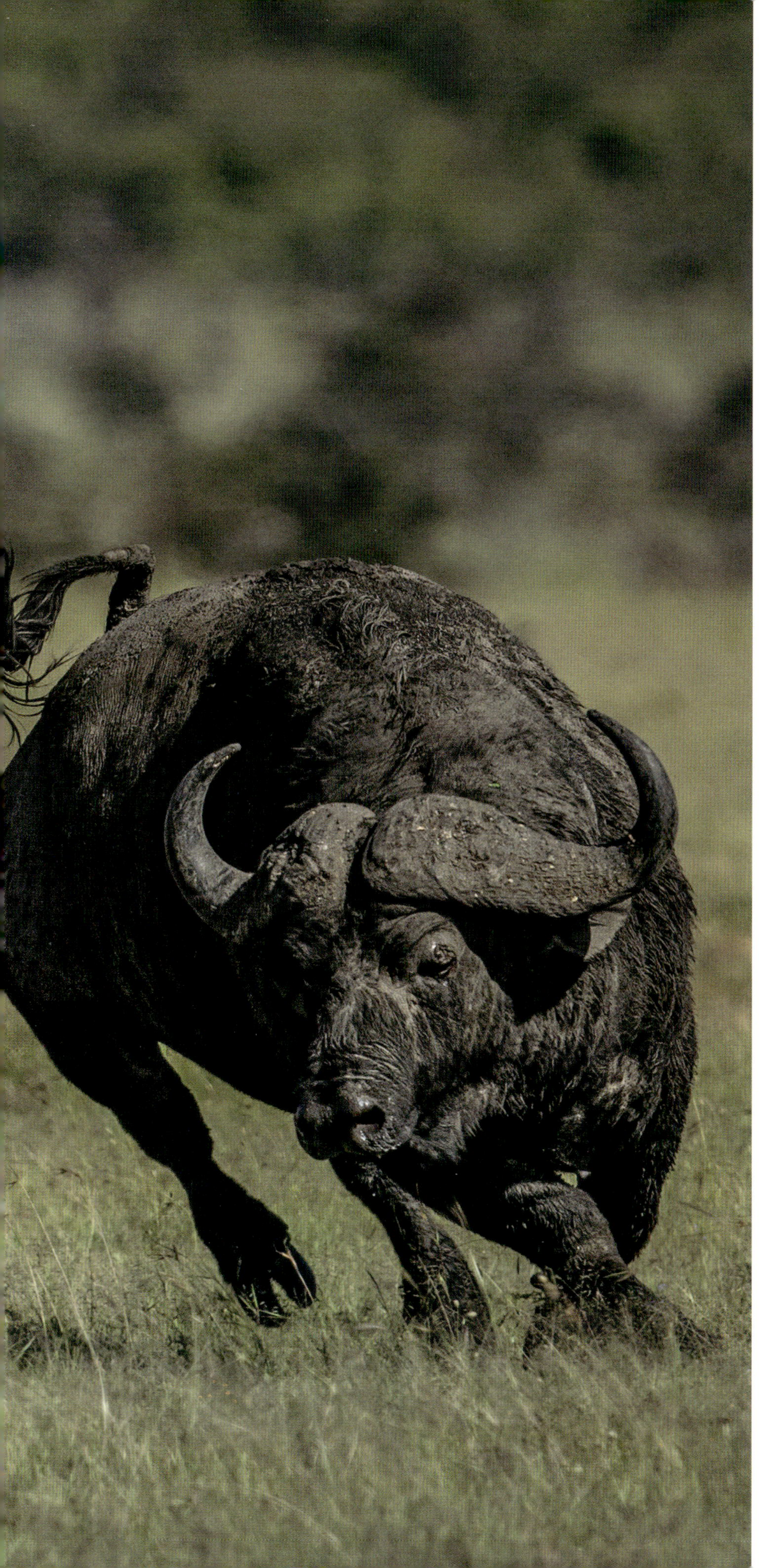

CONTENTS

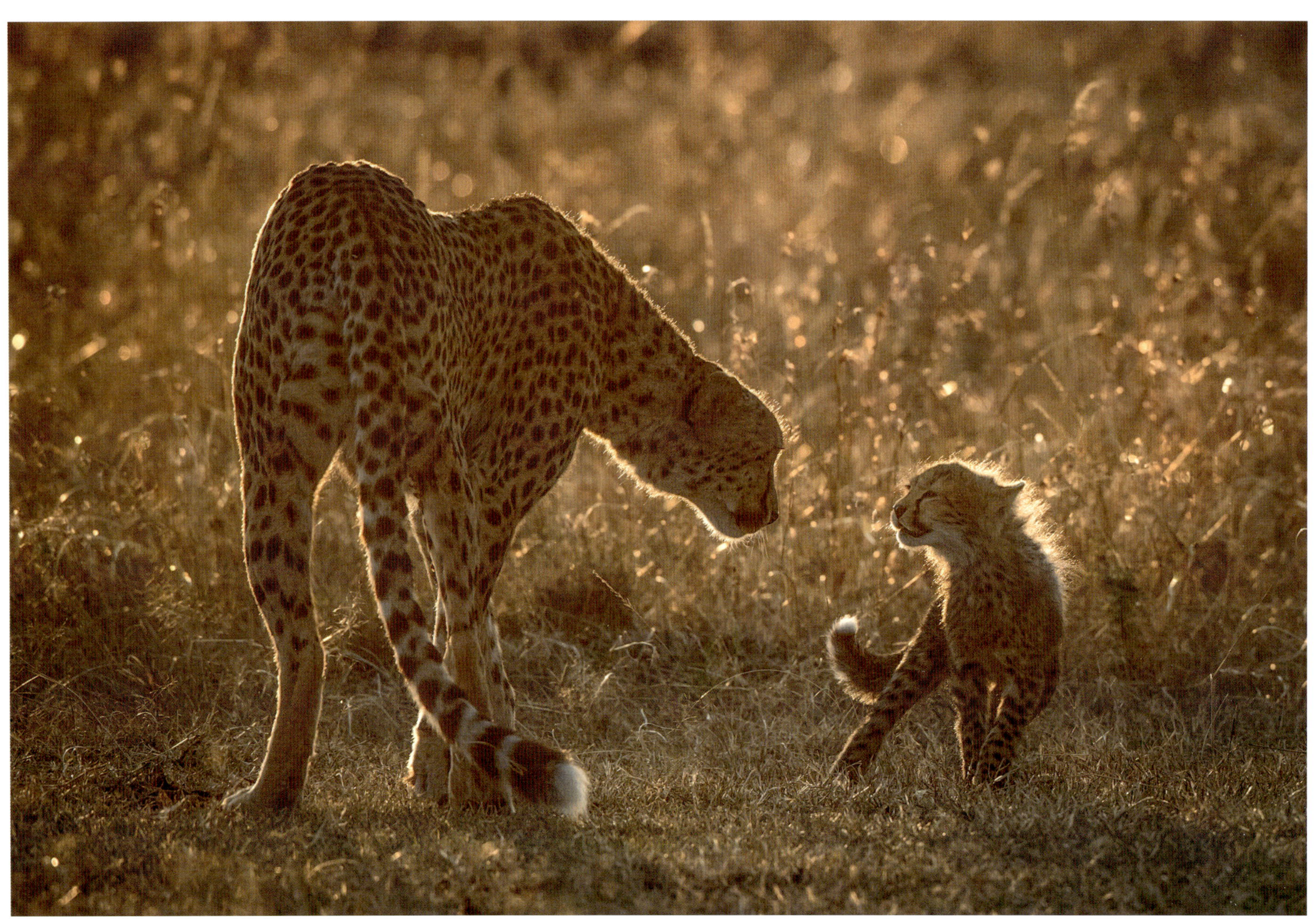

FOREWORD

CHRIS PACKHAM

I first met Paul twenty years ago on an ice ship in Antarctica. My initial thought was, 'Well he's not going to be able to keep that energy level up for more than a couple of days, and, if he does, what will we do?' He did. It was at times exhausting but always exhilarating. No one I have ever met works as hard, for as long, to make sure everyone gets the thrill. And because of this surging energy, many might call him Marmite – and I do understand this. But when he pauses for breath he's actually incredibly perceptive and sensitive to people's thoughts, and it's this combination which makes him such a successful guide with such a huge following.

He is a force of nature and of course nature is what he cares about most. Anyone who completes fifty marathons in a huge and heavy tiger suit clearly cares about those endangered cats; his stitched-up body wears the legacy of those gruelling miles. But this determined zeal is aligned with his photographic passions – he goes to absurd physical lengths to try and get 'that' perfect shot, which he knows full well (and I constantly remind him) he will never actually get. But what really drives him to get up and get moving is inspiring others to improve their skills. *The Times* asserted that 'no-one will drag you up the photographic ladder quicker'. I think that's right but only if you are robust; he has little time for sugar-coating anyone's out of focus, poorly composed snaps.

Unlike almost any other wildlife photographer and guide, Paul has considerable invested commitment. He and his close friend Greg Monson started Kicheche Camp in Kenya with five staff, zero electricity and long-drop toilets. They now have four camps and over 200 staff, renewable energy and a dining table to die for. They were instrumental in setting up the unique conservancies in and around the Mara, a method of conservation other countries should rapidly learn from. And notably Kicheche has a very high repeat business level, having not sold out to either venture capitalists or ethically questionable larger companies. I have stayed there several times. The accommodation, the food, the staff are outstanding, but critically it has the greatest density of the greatest diversity of visible wildlife anywhere I have ever visited. It's the best – end of.

Paul's photography is distinctive. He is ambitious with no fear of failure, is a bit of a purist, treats his gear with reckless abuse and spends too little time perfecting the art of processing his images. But he delivers – his pictures are okay/good/sometimes exceptional. I once scored one with an unprecedented 7.2/10. I like to keep him on his toes. He has won many awards, some even merited!

I have worked with Paul on three continents and I've typically arrived tired and fed up with fighting the world's decay. It never takes him long to re-invigorate and re-align my creative side and he always makes me laugh. In fact, he is very good at making people laugh, being an accomplished raconteur with an admirable memory for hilarious detail. Buried beneath the bustle, burlesque and bravado, he cares about the same things I do and is driven enough to do something about it.

Paul is not welcomed in some countries; something he typically wears as a badge of honour. He has faced death threats after speaking the truth about abject injustices and will not compromise those truths before power. I like that. *The Sunday Times* described him as 'impossibly vivacious and having psychotic gusto'. Fair and rare – so good by me. He has an opinion on pretty much everything, says he has never touched a drop or a drug and won't even countenance coffee, but a scalding pot of English Breakfast is his elixir. In conclusion, he's not everyone's cup of this, that or any other tea, but he's made a great deal of difference to the world's creatures, both two-legged and four. Long may he continue.

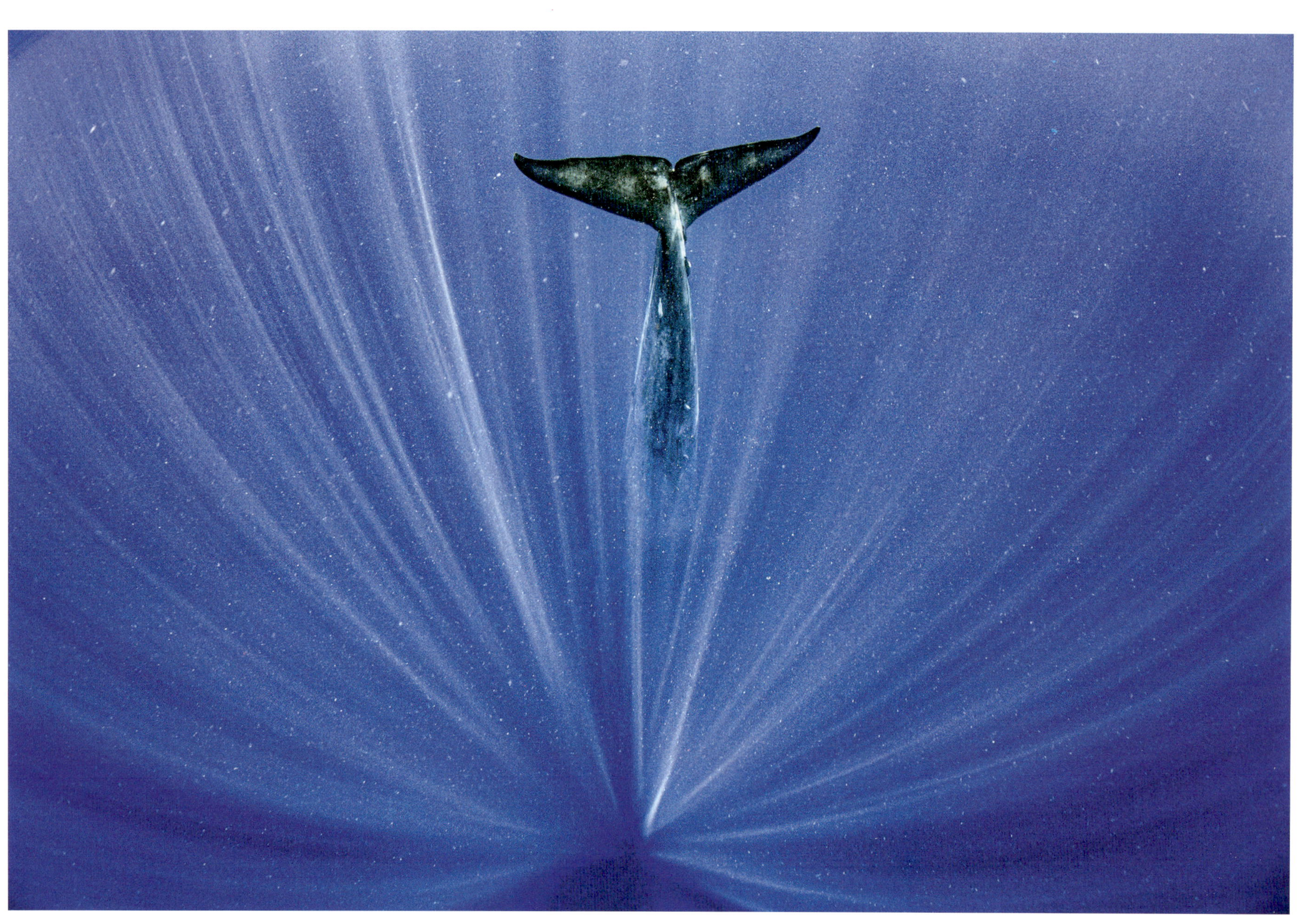

INTRODUCTION

PAUL GOLDSTEIN

In the time it took to type this page, an elephant will have been poached, its body joining a rotting collection of butchered carcasses across Africa and beyond. All species in these pages are either threatened, vulnerable or endangered, except one; they are by no means the only ones, just the ones I have spent the most time with. Photographing them has been a big part of my life over the past thiry-five years and has filled me with joy and despair, frustration and inspiration. Raising funds for them has left indelible scars on me physically, and many would claim mentally.

We only have one go with the planet's inhabitants and much of that credit has been abused and exploited, but the faunal Rubicon has not been crossed, yet. However, animals have only so many Praetorians who understand that these species' value is worth so much more alive in the plains, forests and mountains than on the poacher's slab or in the despicable wet market's stalls.

The time for tears and wringing of hands is long past. It is not enough just to admire, care or pimp online; this faunal house needs to be put in order and many shells need to be broken along the way.

Meetings or conferences won't save them, nor will fund-raising alone, however critical, but turning rage into effective monetised pragmatism just might … I hope these pages elicit this passion as you leaf through them. Many of the pictures have required months or even years of tortuous research, weapons-grade patience and monstrous frustrations… but none of this comes close to the suffering some of these species still, shamefully, endure.

Tourism (my background) has always had a role to play, bringing vital hard currency and crucial prying eyes that deter the faunal bandits that prey on these priceless species. But tourism has to feel reciprocity from both sides; too often animals are exploited and pillaged by greed-head politicians who think more of their murky, stinking pockets than the welfare of the species and indeed the many thousands who depend on them. Likewise, in areas in Asia, particularly with tigers, glutinous and rancid layers of bureaucracy, as well as Byzantine regulations, hamper both animal and tourist alike. A combination of jobs for life and a motto seemingly decreed by out-of-touch knuckleheads of 'we're not happy till you're not happy' does untold and unnecessary damage.

The trophy business is not the answer: for years the comfortable and cloying 'if the game can pay, the game can stay' mantra was echoed across the wilderness by desperately 'brave' thumb-dicked hunters, claiming their ordnance actually helps conservation. There may be a miniscule bat squeak of reason here, but essentially these butchers are just trying to legitimise their wanton craving for slaughter. They sicken me.

When an animal, like the blue whale opposite, becomes a meal ticket to thousands, not just a corpulent handful, it will have both a future and a legacy. When greed and the stinking pus of corruption is permitted to rule, it will have neither. These perpetrators of poaching, trophy hunting and mismanagement, as well the misinformed and rapacious end-users, have blood on their hands, two-legged and four. Thankfully, there are many heroes out there – the priceless custodians of this book's characters. A shame that we need them.

With prey decline, human conflict at an all-time high and a still rampant trade in wildlife, the King of the Jungle is officially classed as vulnerable. As lion habits fragment across Africa, so do their prey areas; perhaps more critically it means their populations become indelibly separated, reducing their genetic diversity.

If you thought for a moment that poaching was more dedicated to spotted and striped creatures, think again. The consumptive trade in lion bones flourishes as the Asian demand for tiger bone substitutes and other body parts increases. These 'products' are claimed to have curative values. They don't, they never have, but somehow the ludicrous nature of 'traditional' medicine and fertility still hold water.

African governments don't help though: poaching may be illegal in South Africa but somehow they permit 1,600 lion skeletons to be exported from 'captive breeding' centres. It is an outrageous negligence and just incentivises poaching. 'Legal' lion products or illegal ones, it makes little difference to the unscrupulous Asian traders and none at all to the misguided butchers who consume them. Likewise, if anyone believes the funds generated from these sales or indeed from the desert elephant permits in Namibia go to fund conservation, they need to take a long hard look in the mirror.

I can't remember the last time my canvas walls were not pierced by the curmudgeonly rumble and groan of a lion. It is a sound that excites, scares and humbles at the same time. Imagine the plains with the volume turned off.

LION

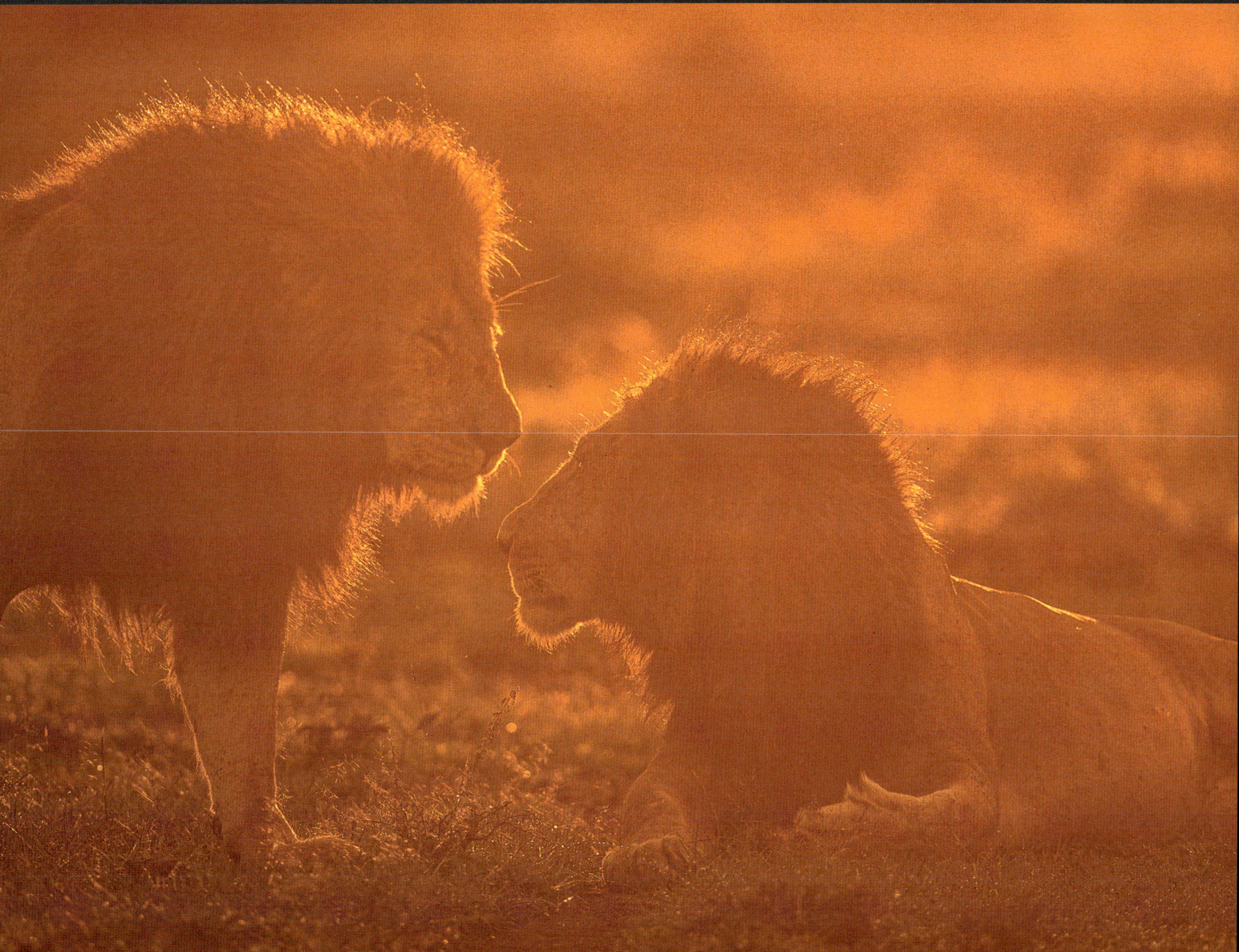

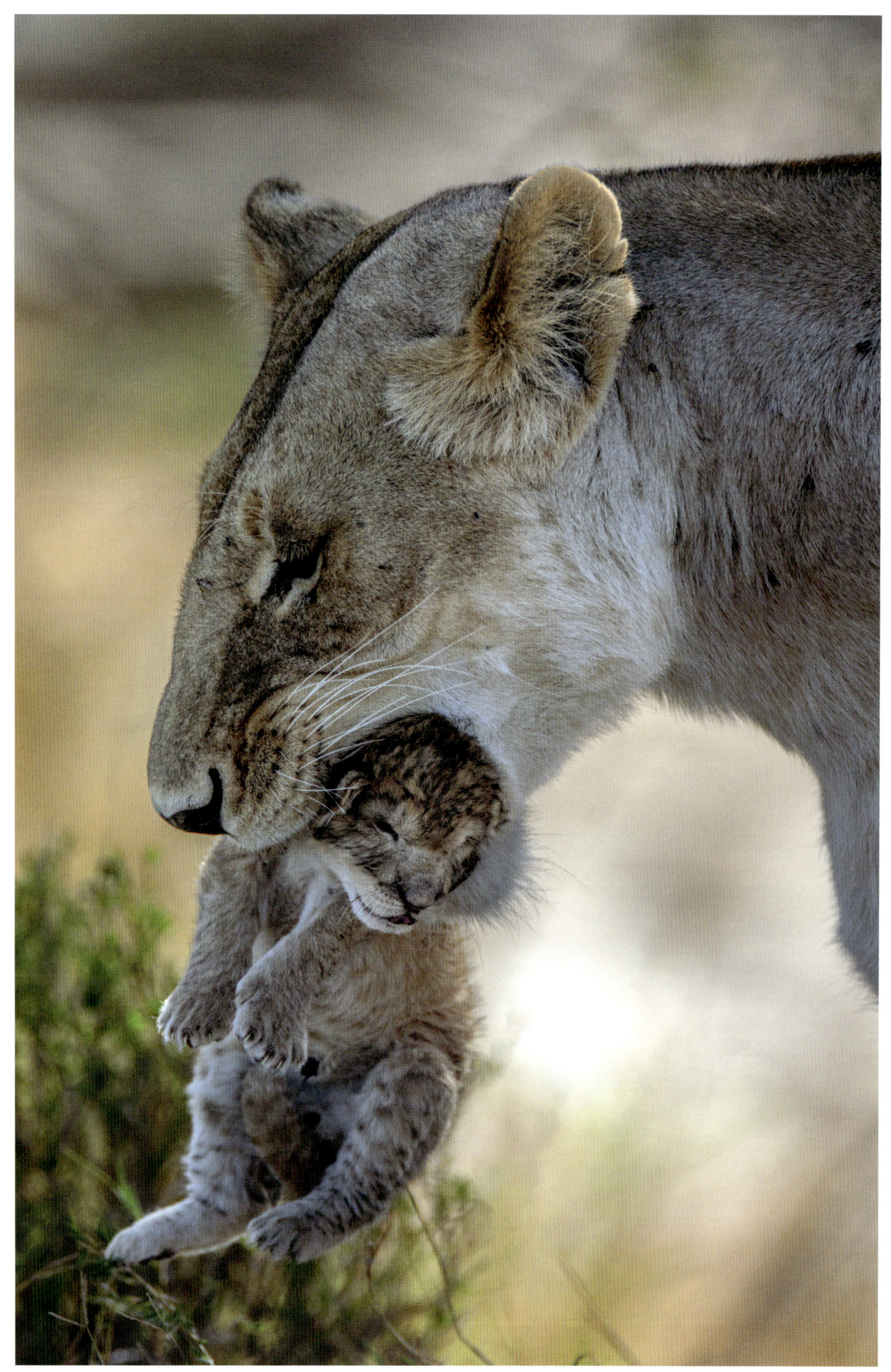

Young cubs face many perils, but for this one the danger came from the mother herself. It appeared that she had lost the rest of her brood and this youngster, only ten days old, was not worth the bother. When I took this I was unaware, as she tenderly lifted her but then despite protestations, refused to open her optics. We saw the body a few days later. Pious and patronising 'experts' will say 'this is nature' or 'survival of the fittest', the same pilgrims who claim we should never interfere… I defy them to watch this unfold unmoved.

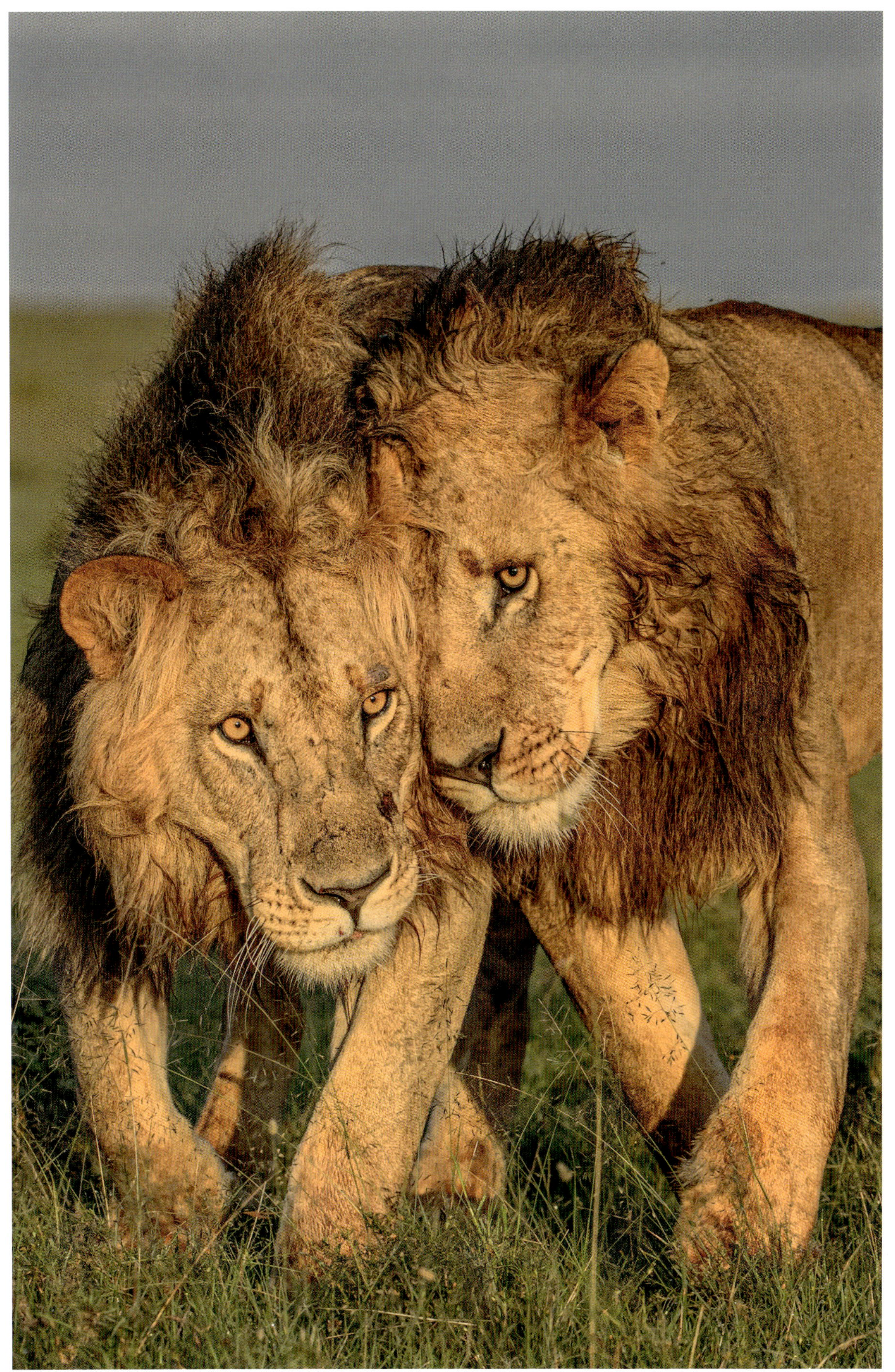

Finding active male lions is hard enough, but two alpha males is extremely challenging. These were two Olare Conservancy males strolling across the plains together, essentially saying: 'This is our house.' They were also looking for somewhere to sleep for the day. James Nampaso, with his leonine genes and years of plains pedigree, knew precisely where to position way out in front of them. Asante James.

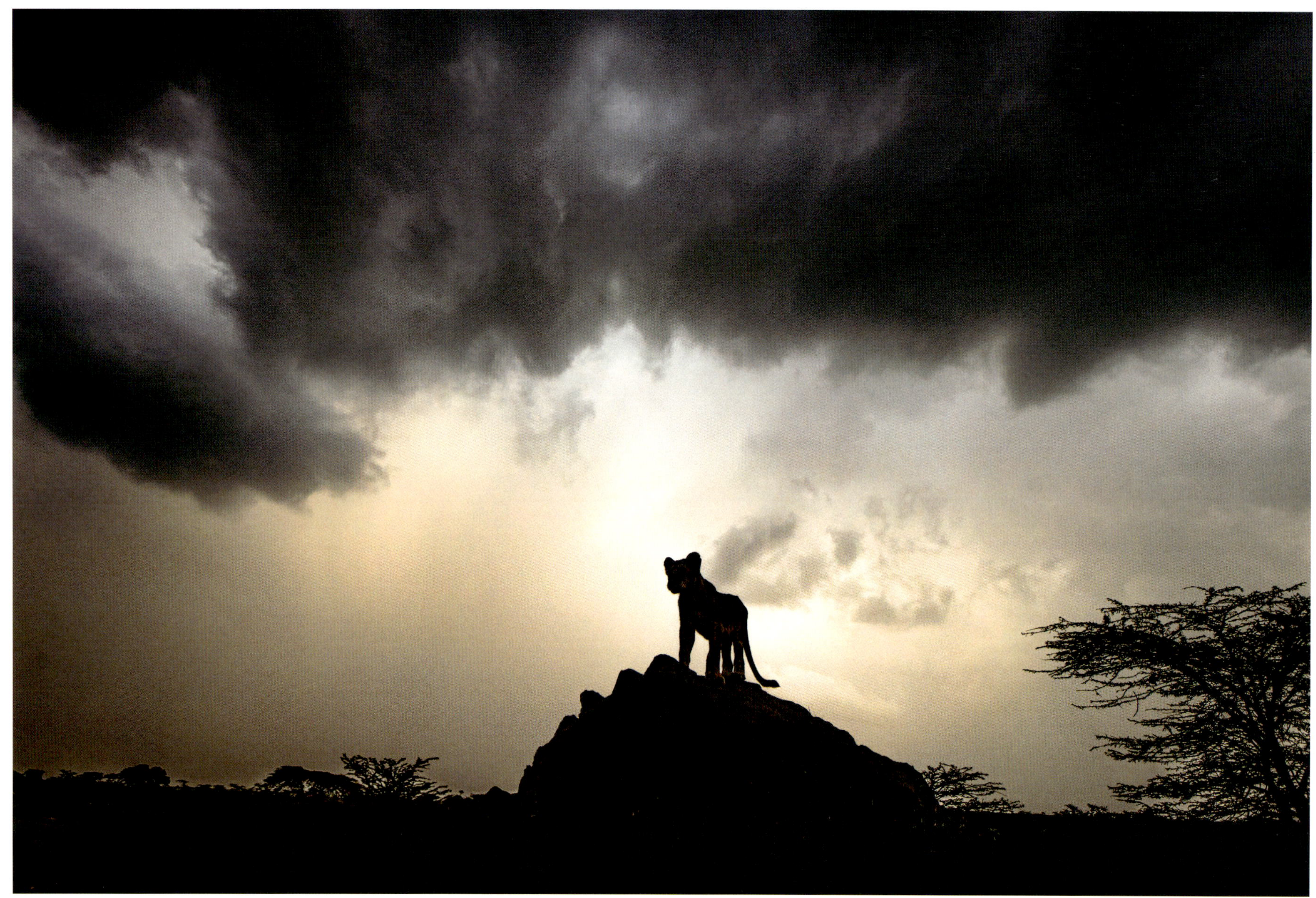

'Don't chase the prize' has been my photographic mantra for over thirty years. Gamble: pick a long position, do your research (the key to any half-decent image or indeed safari) and if it fails … it's only a photograph. The whole of the Enkoyanai pride were waking up from their matinee slumbers. My eyes were on the sky, not the lions, as it was cloudy, dark and dramatic, yet the whole canvas was almost criminally filled with clutter. Positioning right next to the only clean background – a smooth termite mound – we waited, enjoying the scene. Around 90 minutes later this youngster pulled his *Lion King* pose and a 14mm lens appropriately underexposed did the rest. Pressing the shutter is only 5 per cent of the job. Asante James. Again.

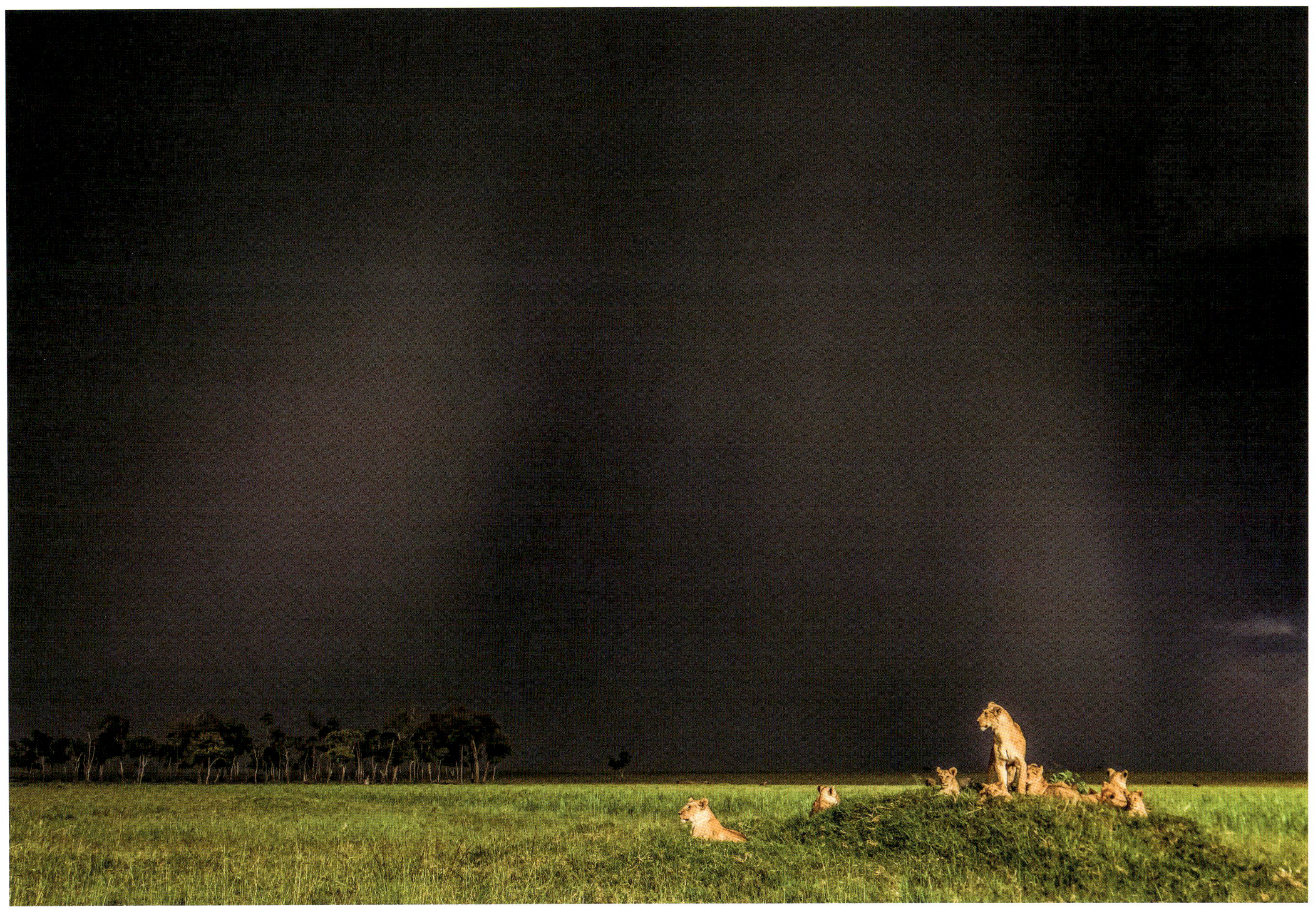

‘Mkubwa Paul, we may be getting very wet,’ was Patrick Koriata’s rueful warning. He knew full well we weren’t going anywhere. We did get wet, drenched in fact, but did we care? By positioning early, as with the previous image, a wide-angle lens could capture the intensity of the storm while the sun was still evident. Longest or widest is normally the deal here and the Rift Valley *never* has a dull afternoon sky. Sorry Patrick for turning a one hour journey into three … not that sorry.

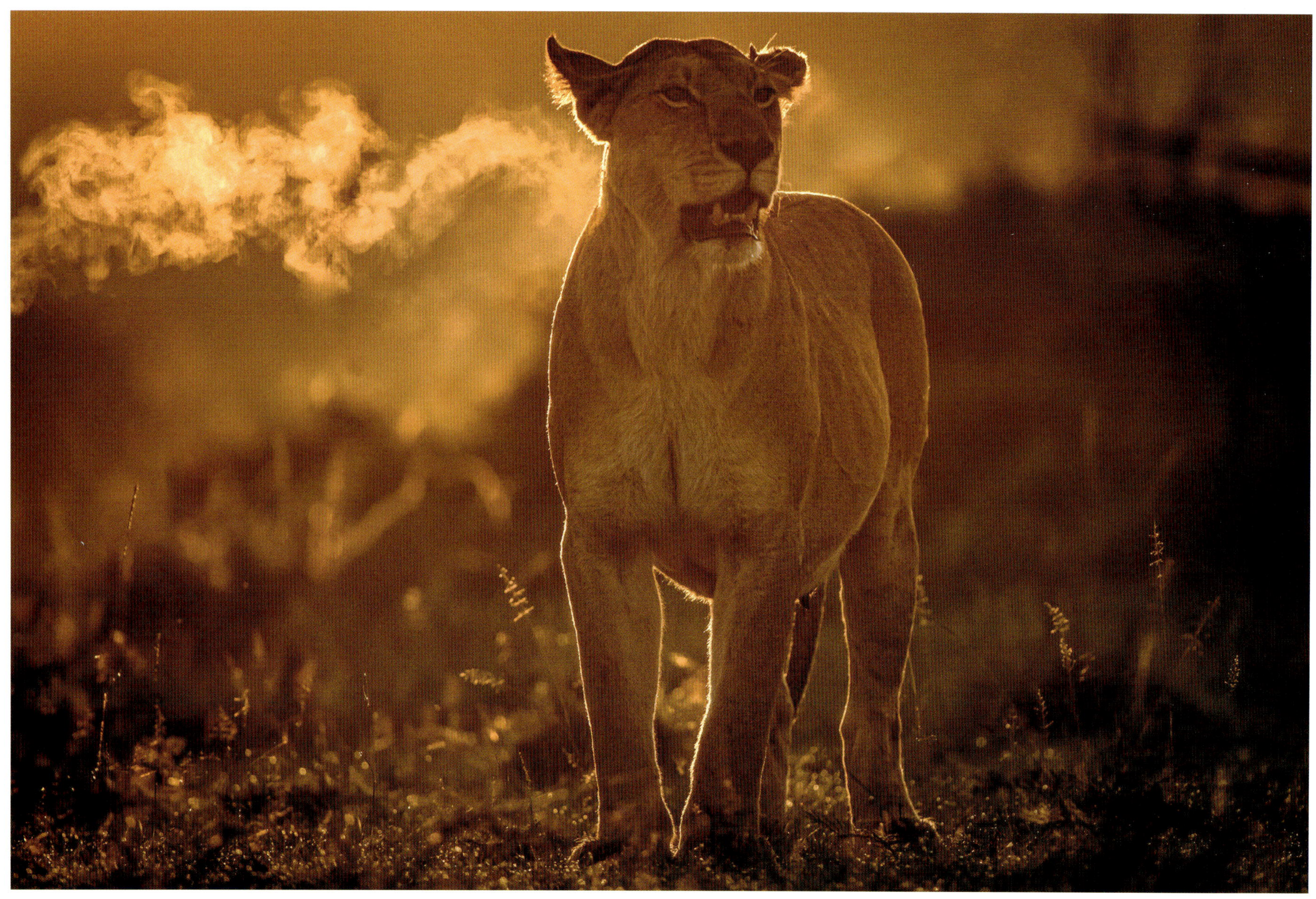

It takes a bit to leave a mother panting into a nasturtium sunrise as she tends her cubs. However, this was one of those gambles and one Charles Wandero and I have done a few times. Driving 15 minutes away from them, as we looked to cross the river, was not universally popular but imagine the 'crossing' taken from the south bank not the north? A gamble and a result, a good one; we'd seen mum constantly looking north, so it was a calculated one too. They aren't always.

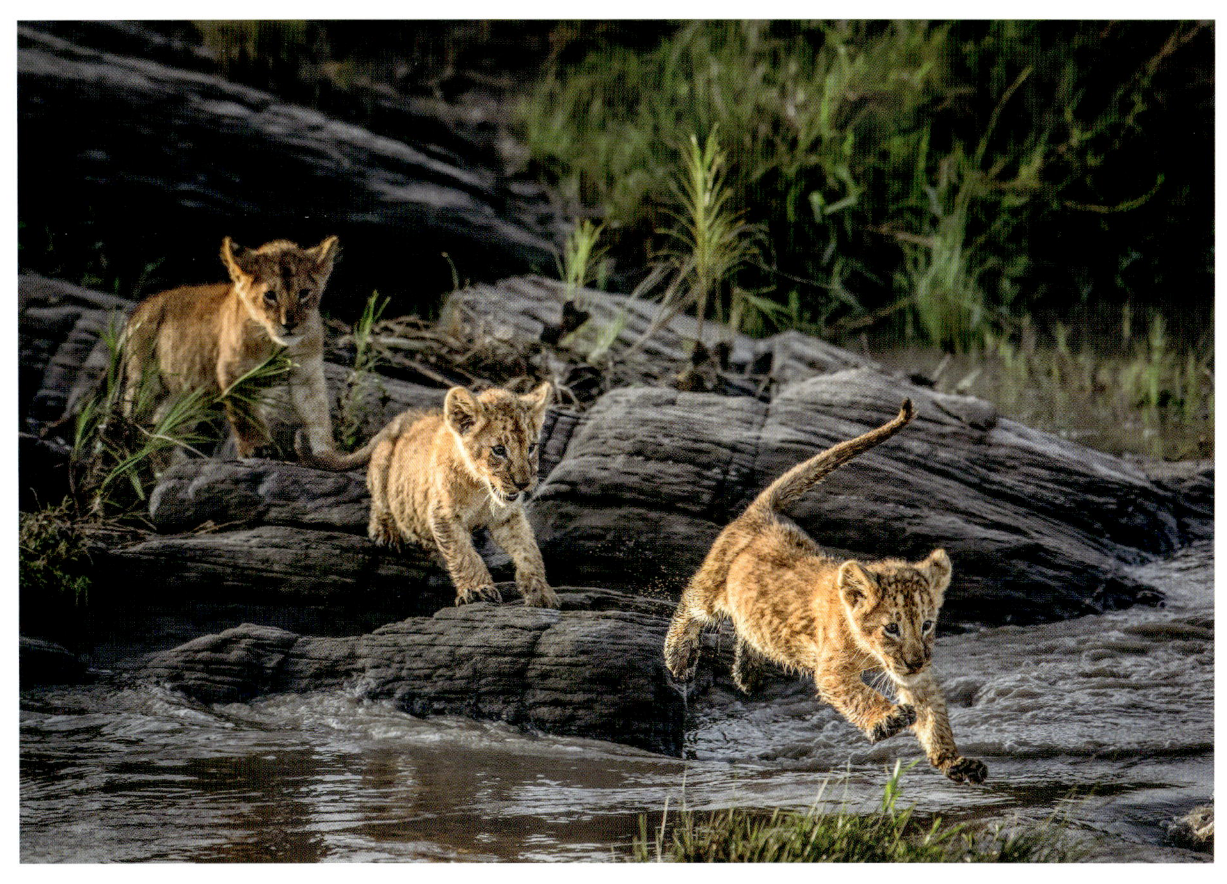

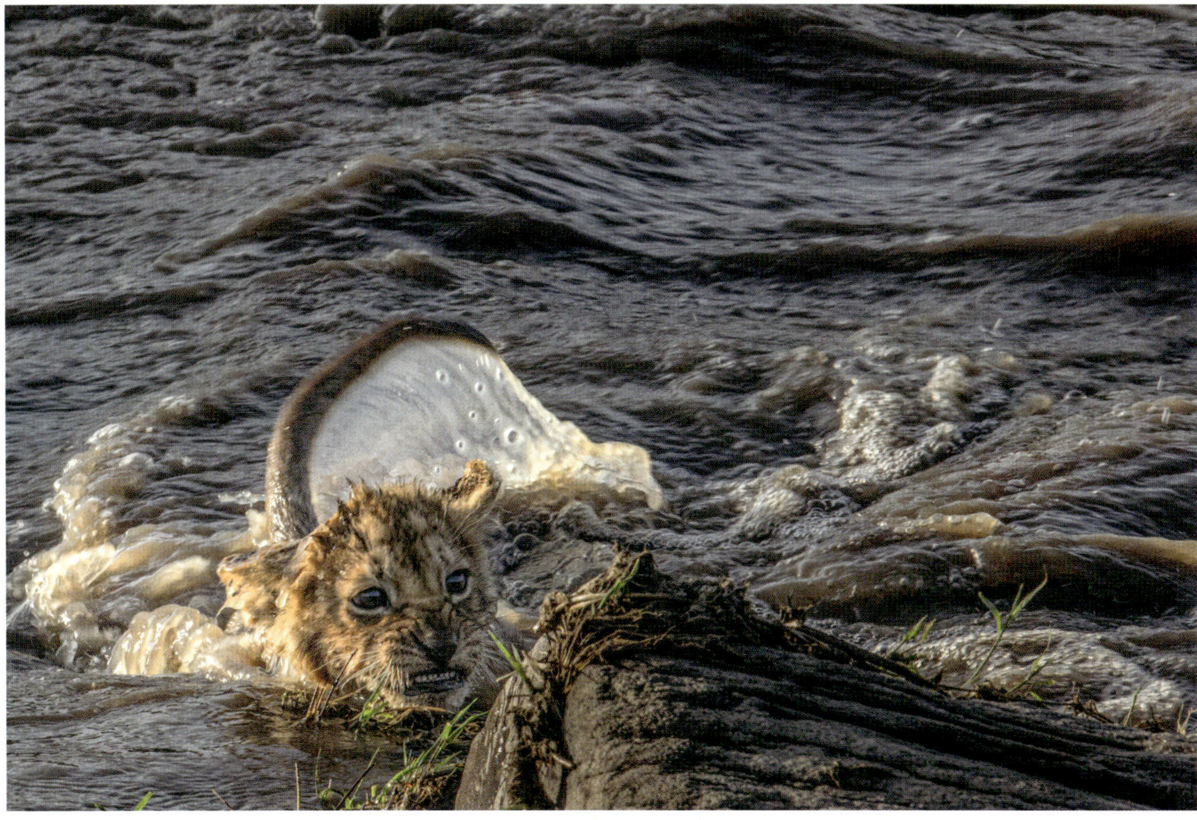

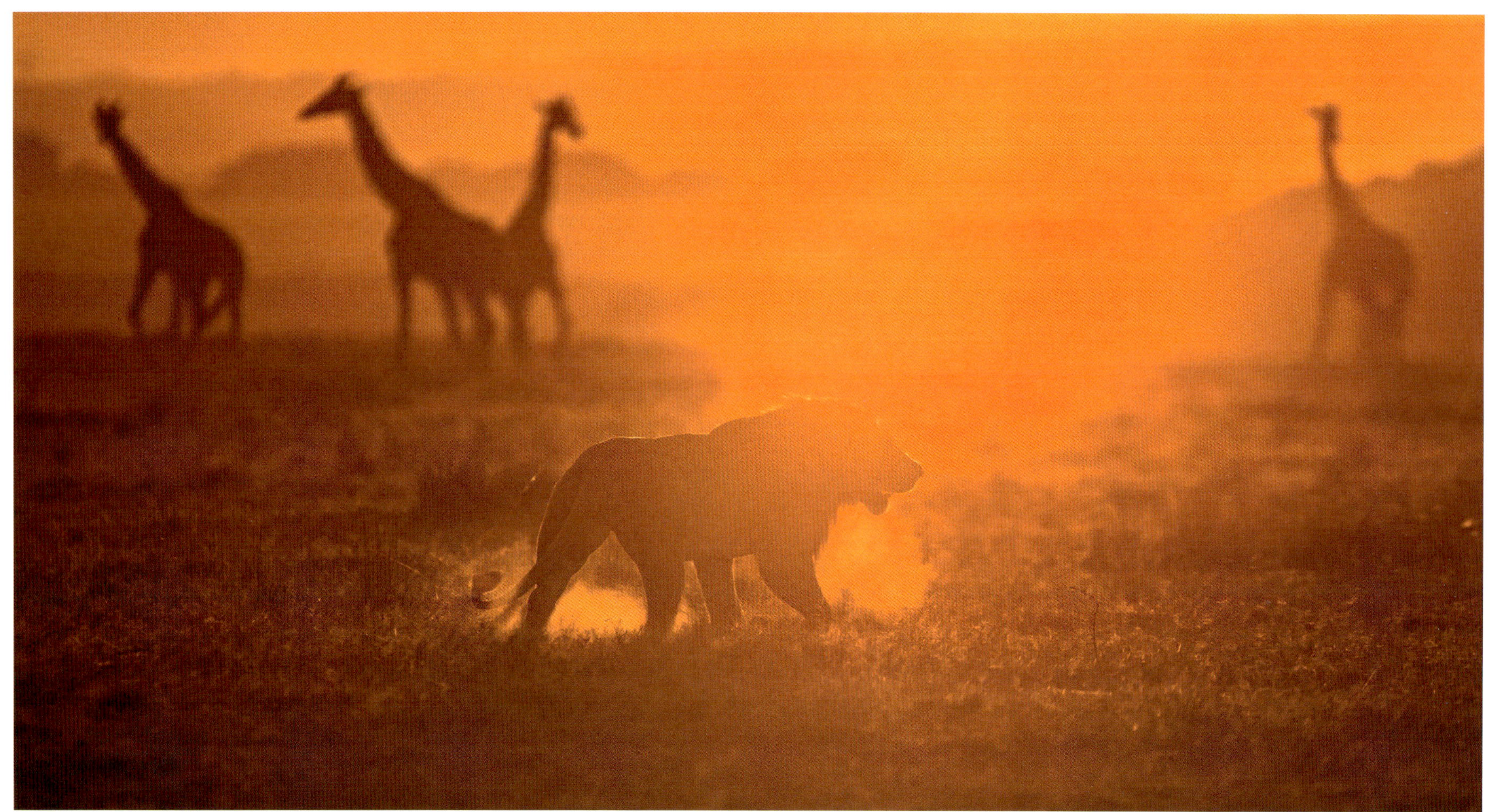

Thousands of times I've woken up in the dark hoping for a clear sky. Frequently the Mara Conservancies deliver with the light, but not the subject, or vice versa. This is how it should be, as nature intended; we wouldn't do it if it were easy. Lions were fighting hyenas over a giraffe calf that the hyenas they had recently pulled down. They then fought off this young male. 1,500 metres often produces mist and breath and this sort of scenario showed the conservancies at their very best. This was taken during the Covid-19 pandemic, when thankfully some people still jumped through the ridiculous and absurd hoops to get their safari fix.

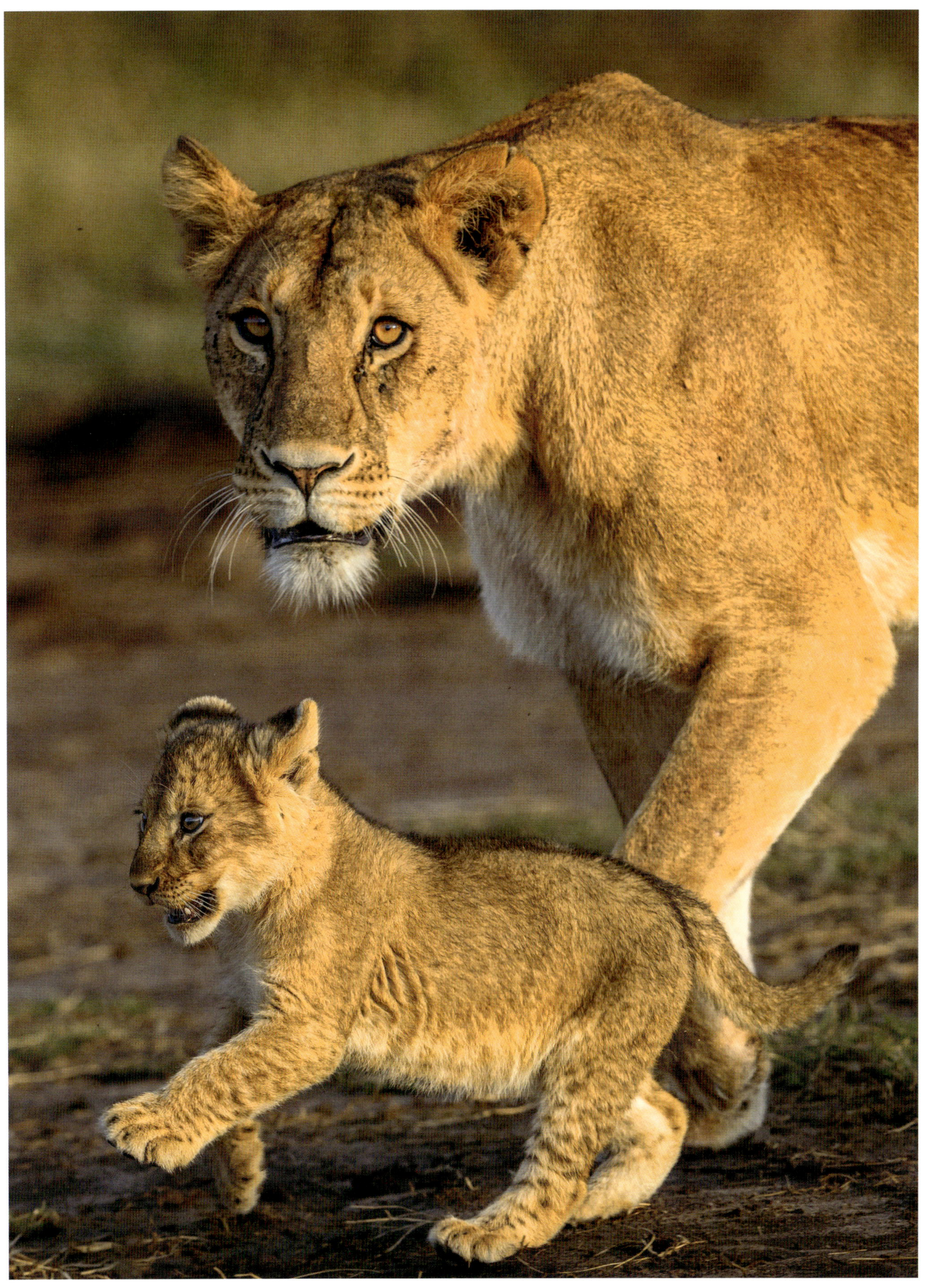

Mums rarely like to have their youngsters out for long after sunrise. This was all about finding, positioning and then taking. Thanks Vivian.

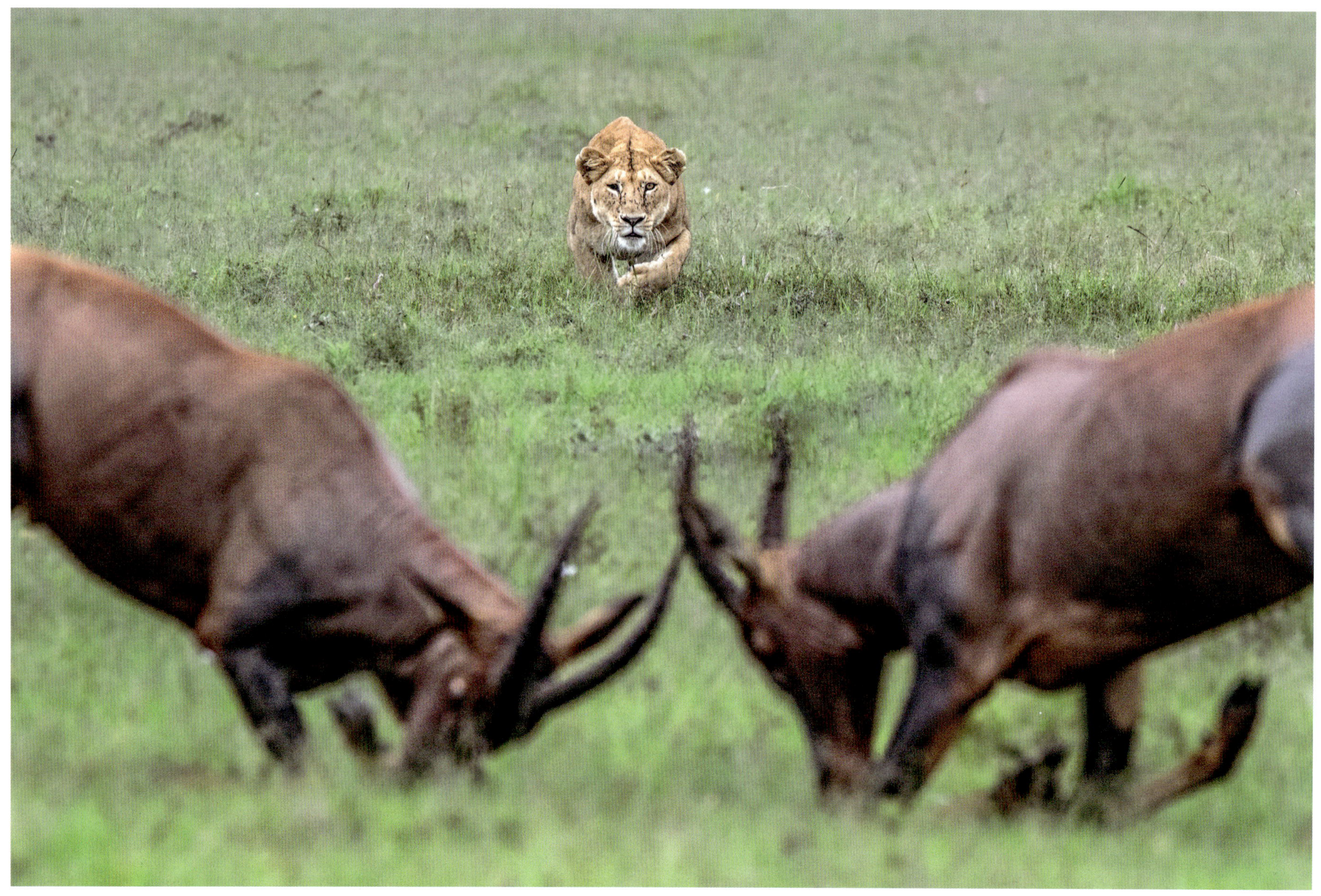

Predators will often wake when they hear the brittle clattering of horns. This one-eyed lioness had made warthogs her quarry of choice, but here was attracted by these two topi bulls. In open grass she was never going to succeed but it was fascinating to watch her advance every time the topis' heads dropped. There were no crowds (it's a conservancy) and it was all about continually positioning and repositioning and closing the aperture down a touch just to keep the topis honest.

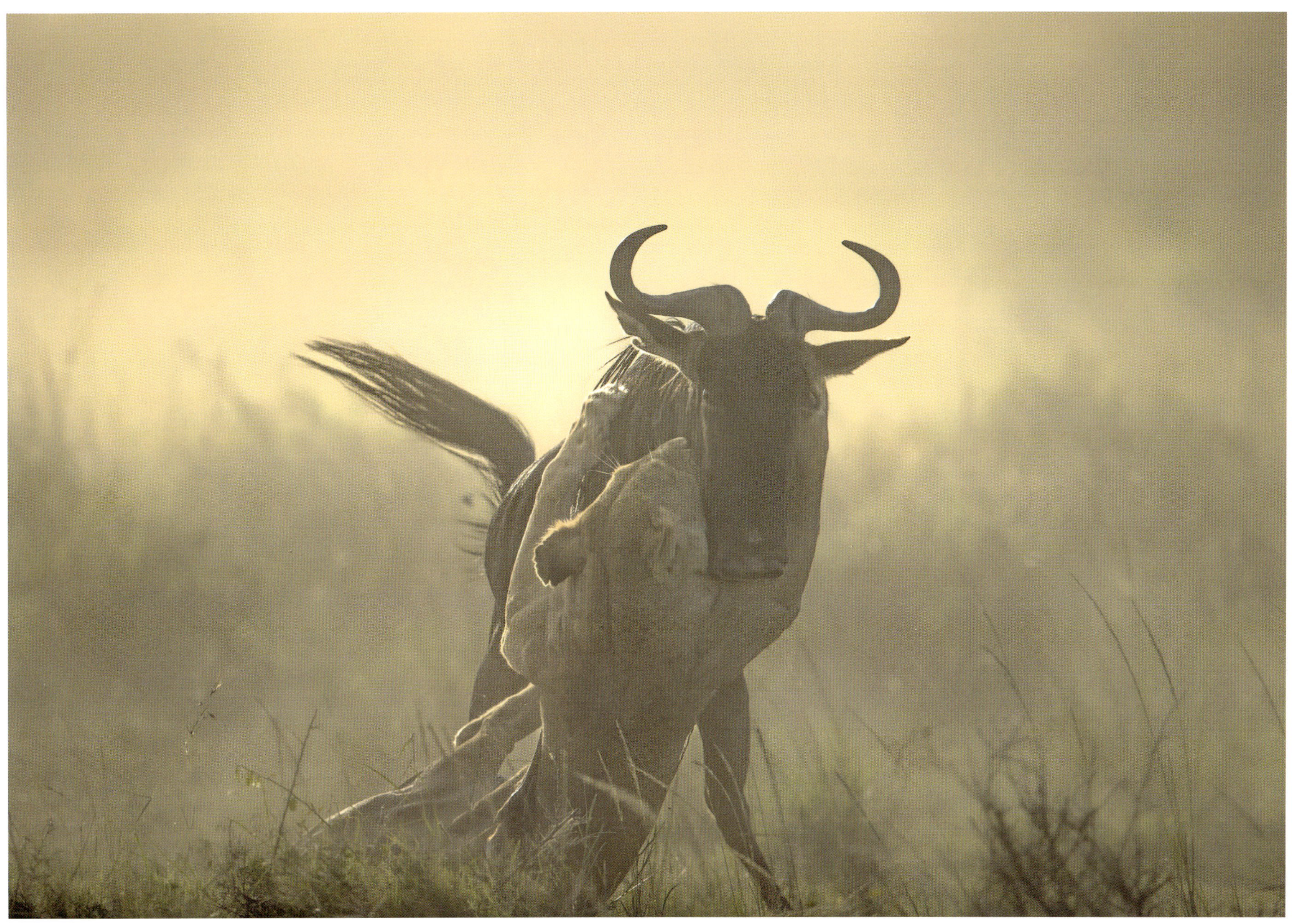

Praise to you Esther; just marvelous driving on a hot afternoon. Several hours watching sleeping lions in the middle of Olare Conservancy is no hardship but the faunal thermometer rose dramatically when a line of wildebeest cantered over the bone-dry soil to drink. The lioness had chosen a stallion and the rest of the pride just looked on from their gallery atop a termite mound. After a long struggle the gnu prevailed and the pride went hungry. They really can be amateurs sometimes.

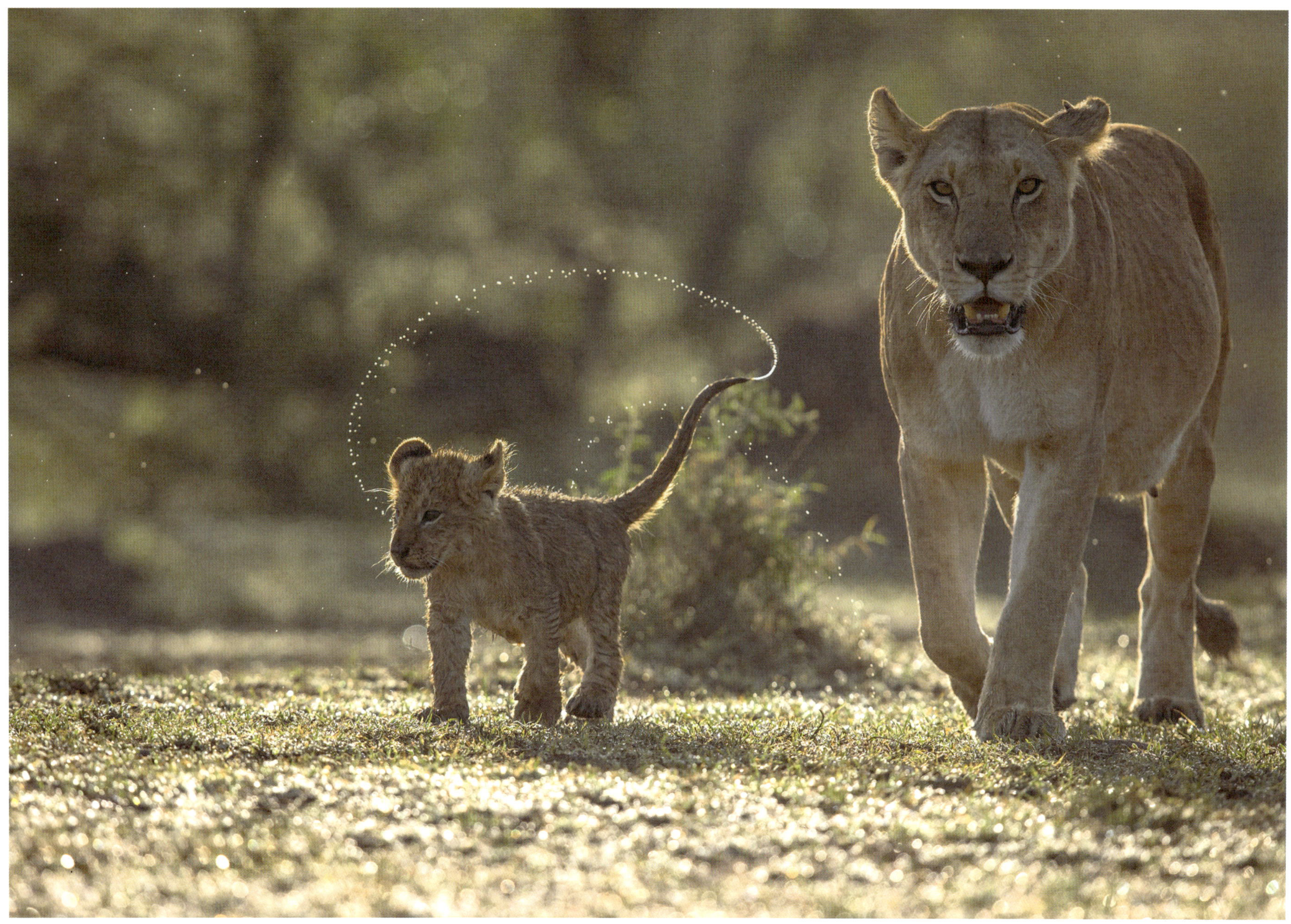

Plenty of dew on the ground always makes the background more interesting, and this youngster had just crossed a stream. Positioning is everything here and when you can drive off-road and there are vehicle limits, it makes everything easier.

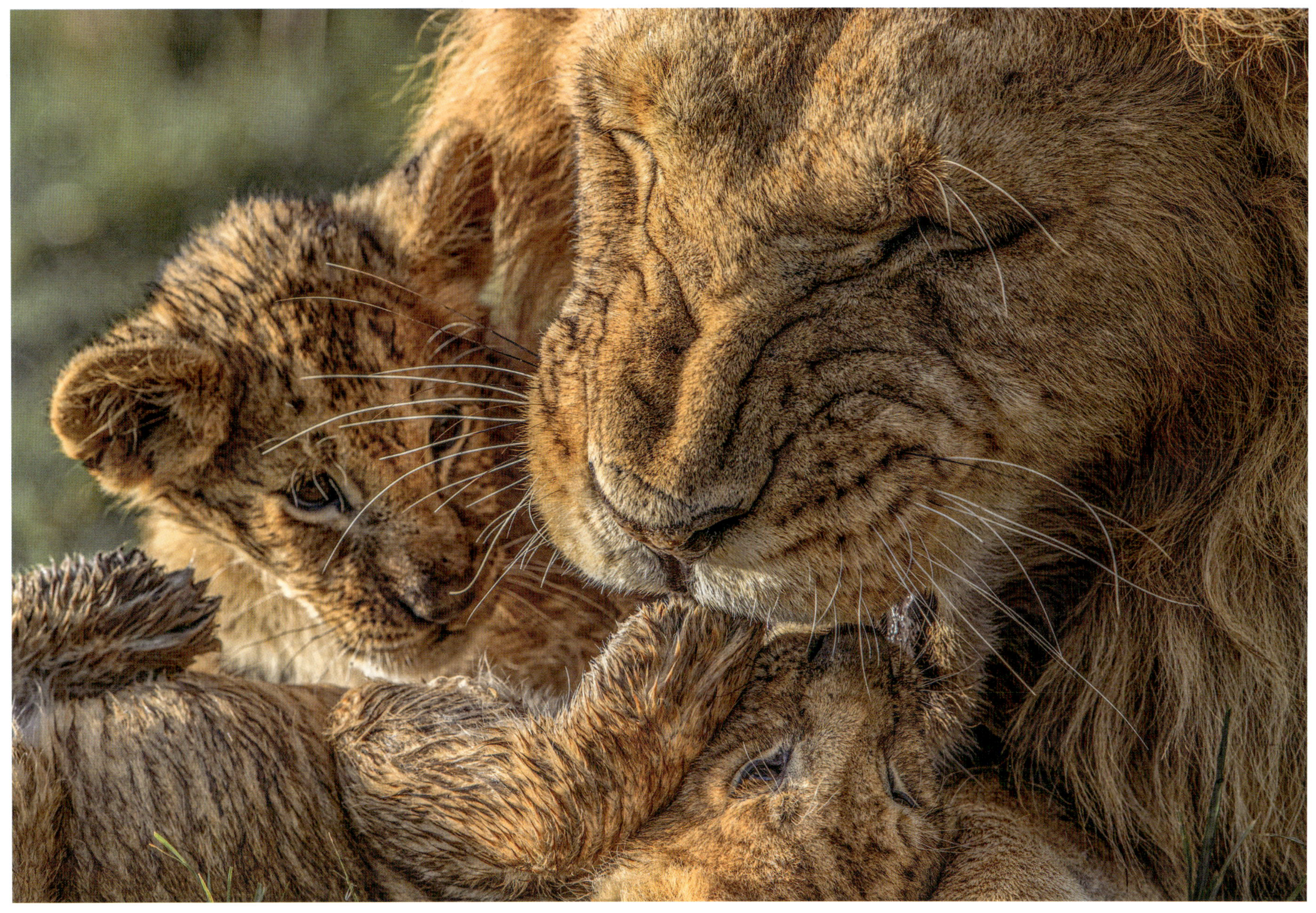

It is rare to see a pride male indulge his young brood, so this was a thrill. The long lens just cuts out any clutter or distraction. They were tolerated for around five minutes.

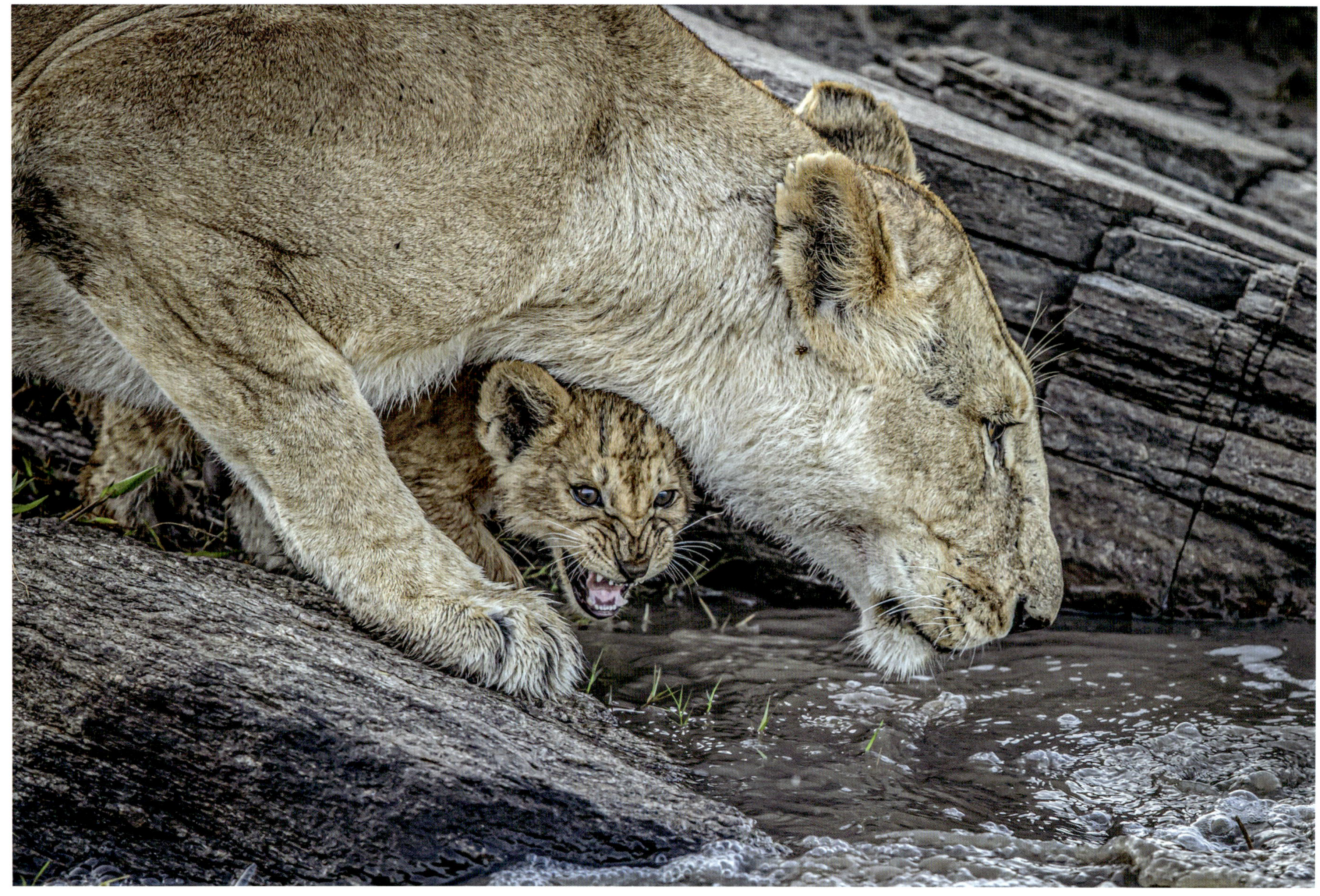

The mother needed to drink but the cub was just a little spooked by the water. I closed right in with 800mm+ as this was the teeth of the photograph and I knew that pose would only be momentary. Granite, cats, water – a decent early morning trinity.

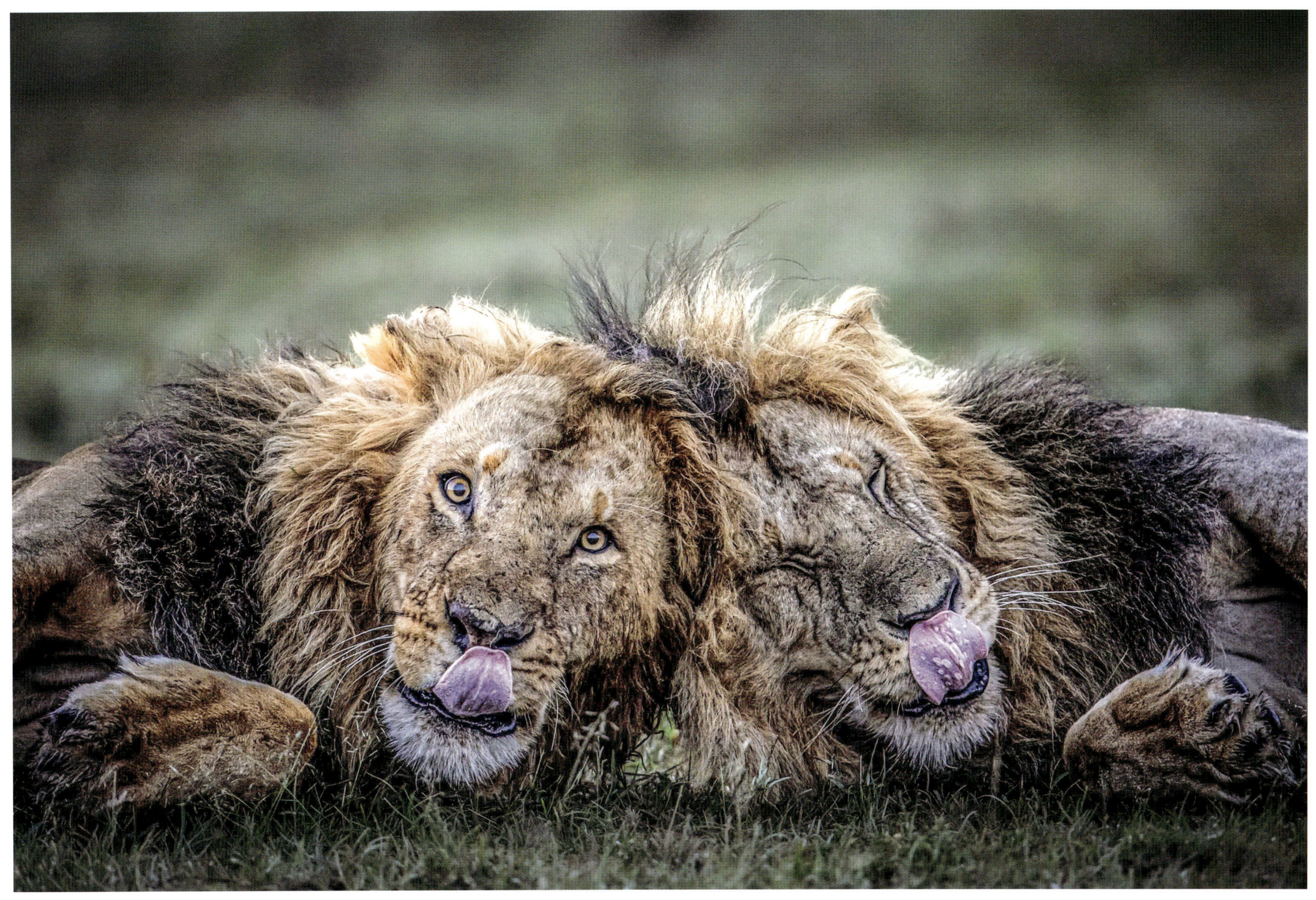

Symmetry is one of the things we crave as photographers, and this is so close, but unfortunately the right-hand male (an animal that had killed one of our fabled leopards a year before) just couldn't be bothered to open its eyes. 4/10 at best.*

*I've given one 7. This century.

ONE

TWO

THREE

FOUR

FIVE

SIX

SEVEN

EIGHT

NINE

I have spent months and months glued to precision optics searching distant icescapes searching, frequently in vain, for an ivory blob. The visceral thrill in locating a polar bear is almost narcotic level. And, like any unshakable addiction, the lure and seduction has never dimmed, perhaps has even increased. There has never been a moment, when observing one quartering vast hectares of pack ice, when I don't think just how challenging their environment is: putting food on the table is a Herculean task and the precarious equilibrium of global warming probably affects no animal more than this.

Truffling ashore for birds and eggs is the behavioural pattern of a scavenger, not an apex predator. Polar bears need ice – big pans of ice – to catch their favourite prey: seals. Human-generated greenhouse gases are warming the seas and the atmosphere, and the ice is either vanishing or freezing over much later and melting earlier. The table not only becomes bare but denning sites are also affected. If we continue with these emissions at this level, in fifty years' time there may only be bears at the North Pole.

What is equally worrying is that the thawing of permafrost could release bacteria and viruses that have been previously locked into the tundra: sinister toxins that the bear will have no defence against.

For those who deny climate change, saying it is cyclical, their argument is not only tired, it is also absurd. Hundreds of years ago our atmosphere was not being poisoned by toxins thrown upwards with impunity, particularly by China, who lead this dubious league table by a scandalous distance. They sadly have more sinister connections to this animal's potential demise, and people who think there is no skin trade in these bears need to wake up. Fast.

In Canada there are warehouses with hundreds of bear carcasses. In a Chinese market they can fetch as much as $100,000. Anyone who romantically thinks they are protected because of the 1973 ban in Norway is misguided. They are still only listed as Appendix 2 in the CITES (Convention on International Trade in Endangered Species of Wild Fauna and Flora) list – that vast talking shop that purports to look after species. Huge efforts to uplist them in the 2013 conference (in Bangkok…) fell on deaf ears. Yet, Norway trades in bear pelts, maybe not slaughtered on their shores but from Russia and elsewhere. There are ghastly menageries of coiffured furs in Bergen and Tromsø, yet their complicit government blames *tourists* for their demise, introducing ridiculous 500-metre viewing rulings. Somehow this trade in bears is legal. It stinks and it is sad that it has taken the superb 'Trade Secret' documentary to highlight their scandalous hypocrisy and also the practices of the WWF (World Wildlife Fund) who seem to care about the unholy trinity of brand, image and revenue streams more than protection.

Each time I spend time with bears – particularly when I see them struggling to find a meal – I think of these damning statistics and my horror at the complicity of supposedly paragon organisations. Photographing them has become almost a crusade and the crackle of excitement with a confirmed sighting, often miles away, will never dim.

POLAR BEAR

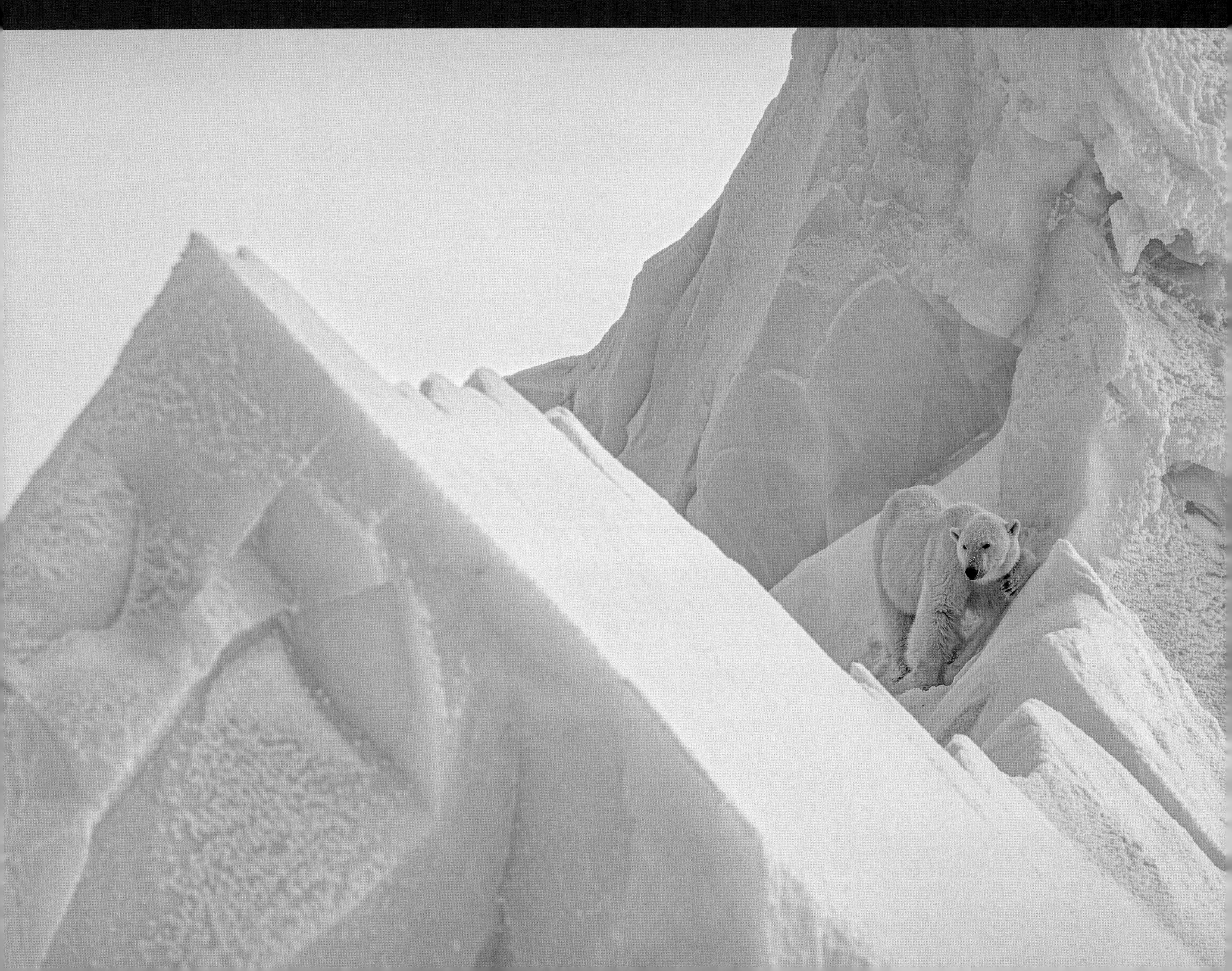

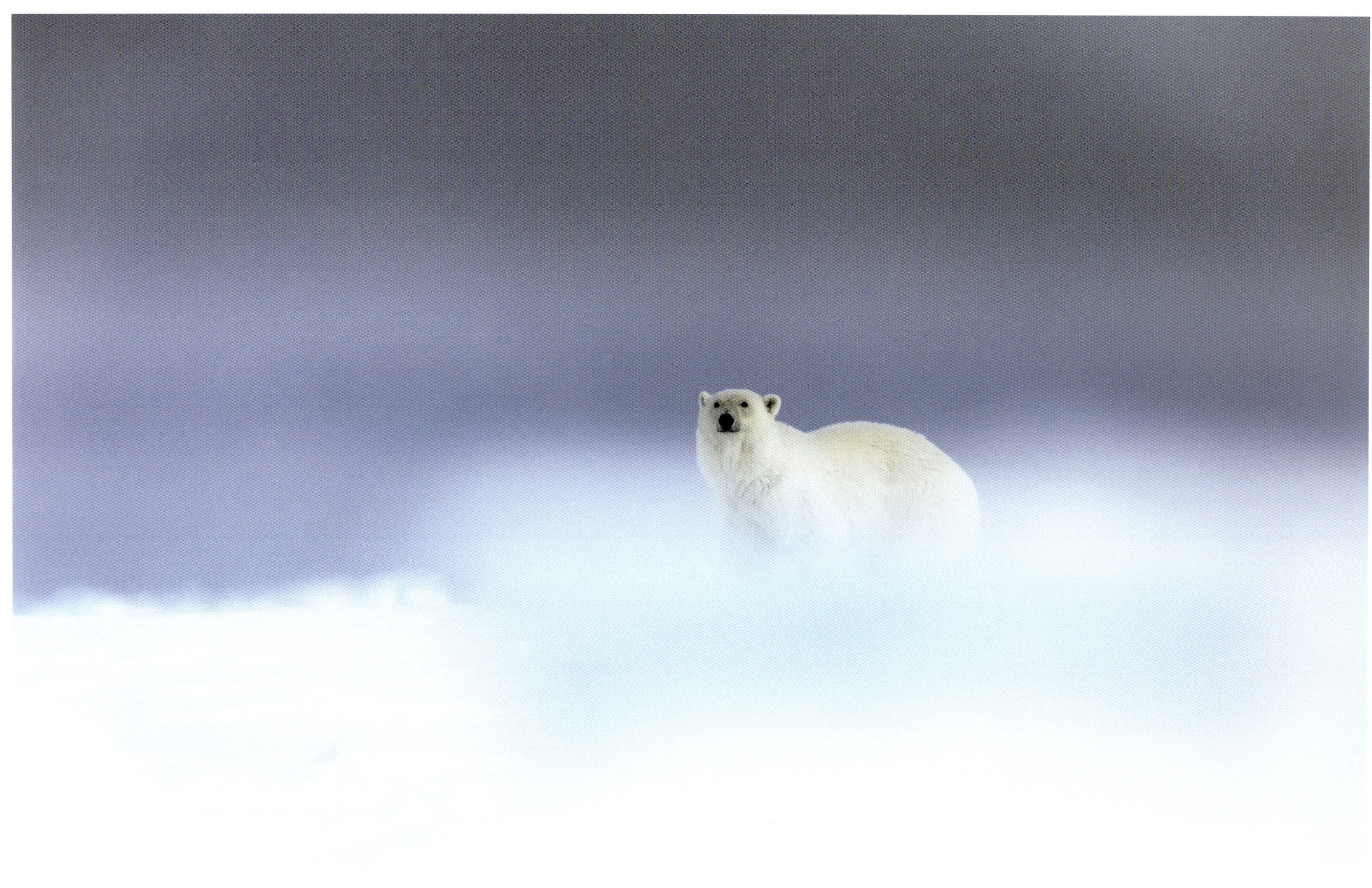

I have waited a long time for the situation to be right to try this, and a Baffin snowscape in 15 below zero proved perfect. I crawled forward and dusted a snow drift off a big slab of cobalt-blue ice, then lay down and photographed across and through it and the surrounding snow. There really is nowhere like it in spring.

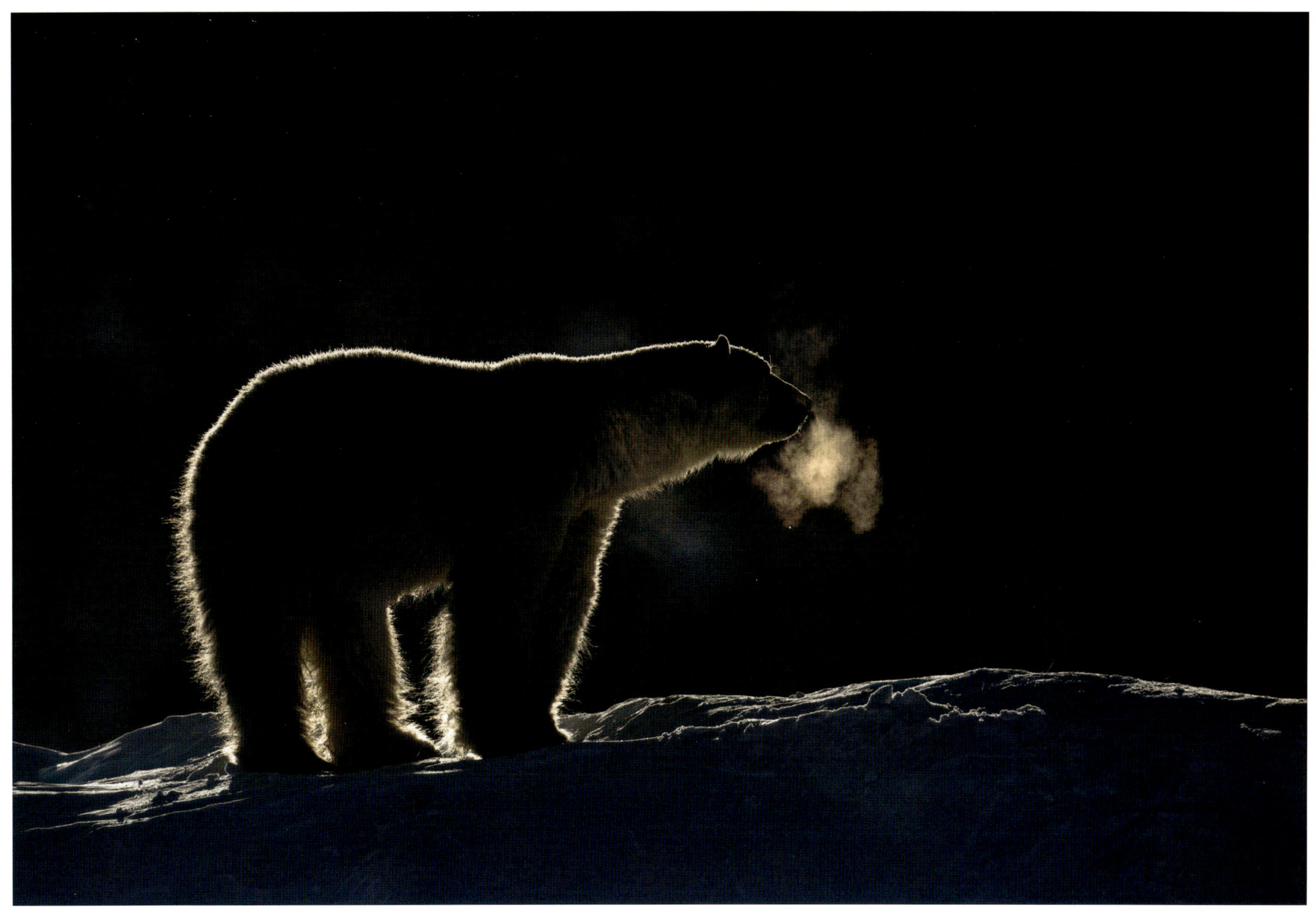

My current favourite bear image. I took one similar in Spitsbergen, Norway in 2011 but it wasn't this cold in their Arctic summer. Here it was searingly so, as the bear rose from its matinee slumbers. I had planned this sort of picture for years, positioning directly in line with a late sun but with a dark mountain behind. Three stops under took care of the rest. A magnificent animal that is still being rabidly traded despite the 'traditional' (that word again) excuses pedalled out disguising their slaughter.

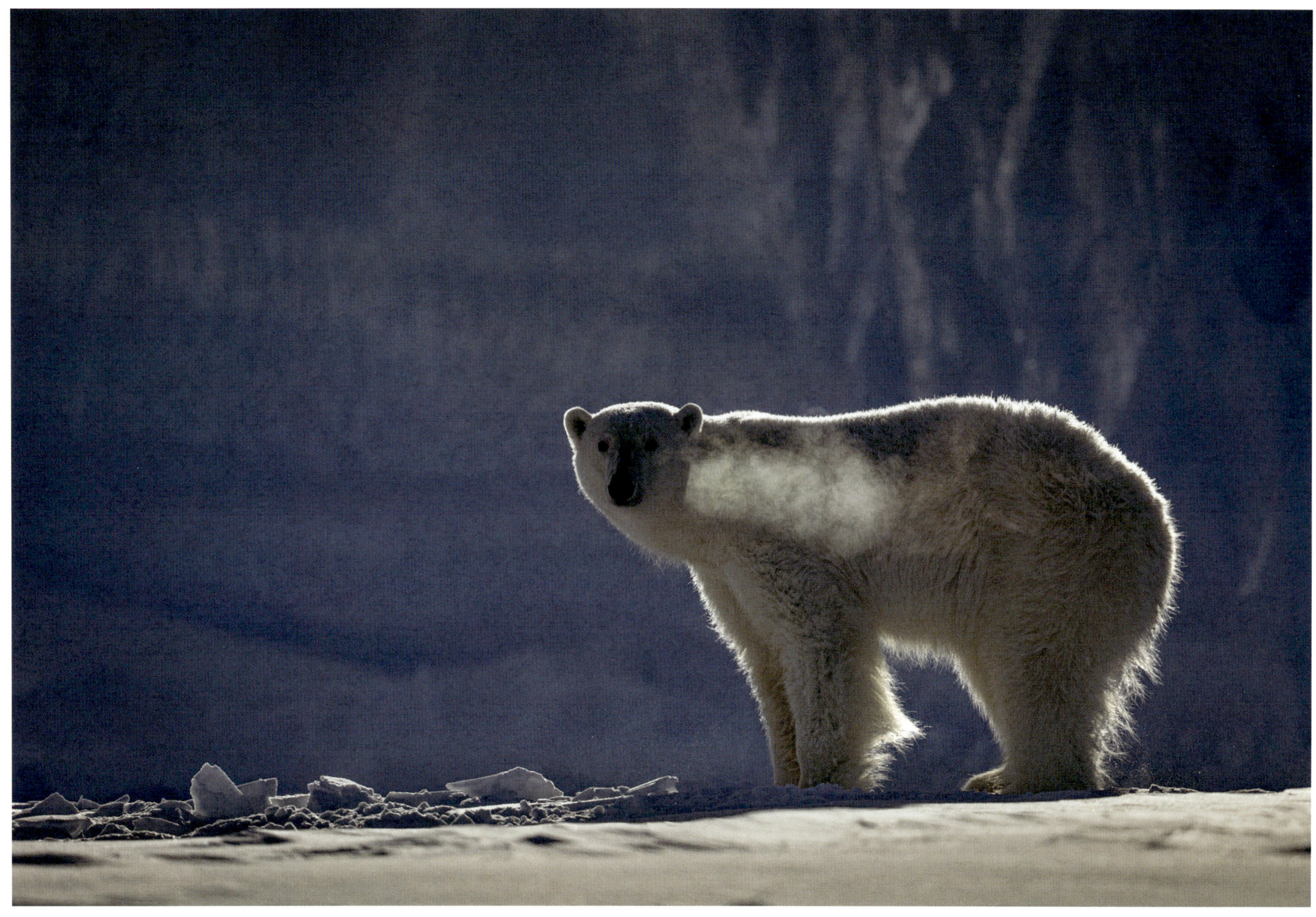

Blue background, biting cold, backlit with breath.
It took my breath away too.

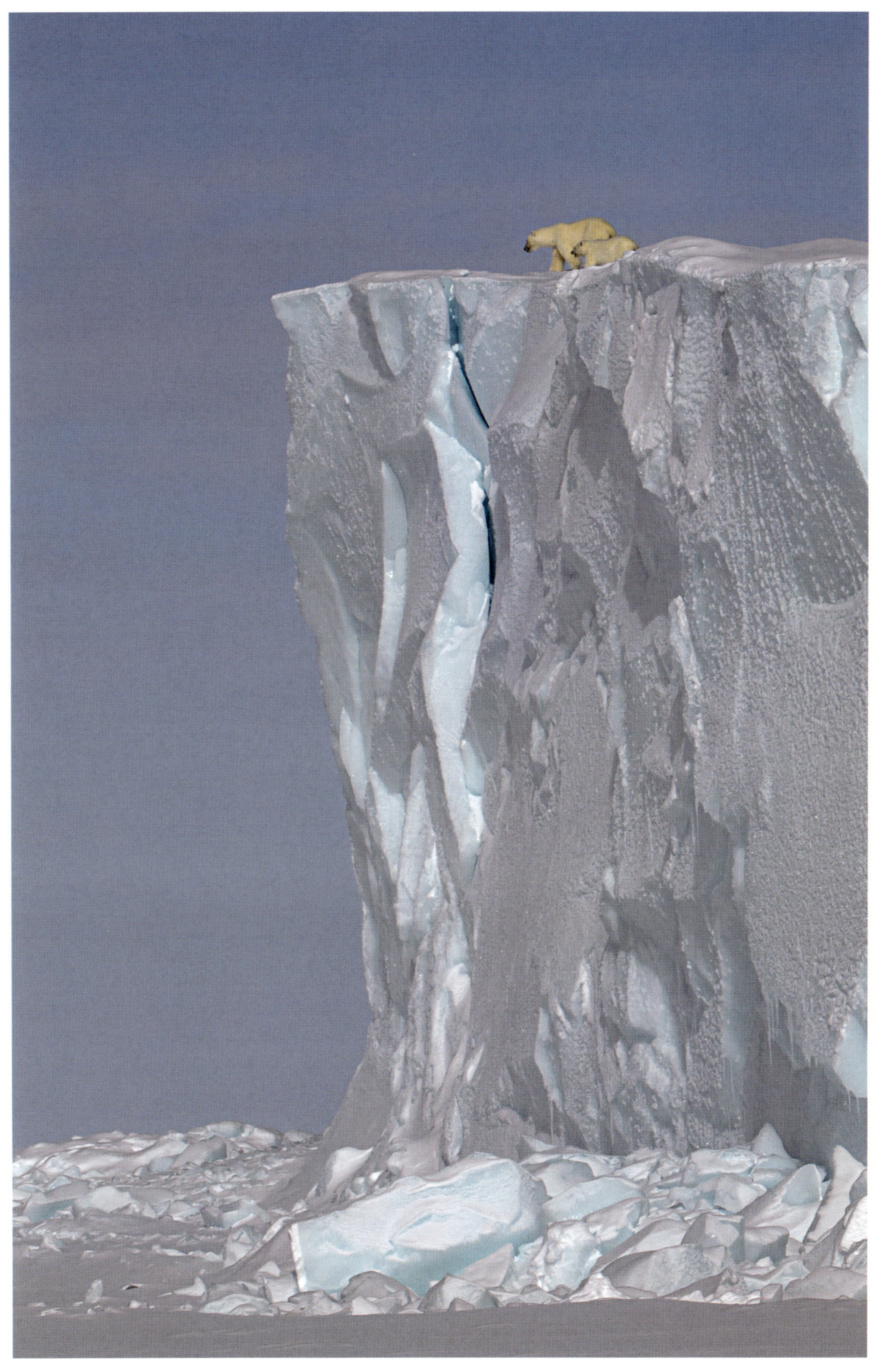

This was a real heart in the mouth moment as a mother led her yearling to the edge of a towering grounded iceberg. Bears have plenty to worry about: hunting is still practised in Canada and putting food on the table is a constant challenge, so losing them through a misjudgement would have been a catastrophic fall from grace.

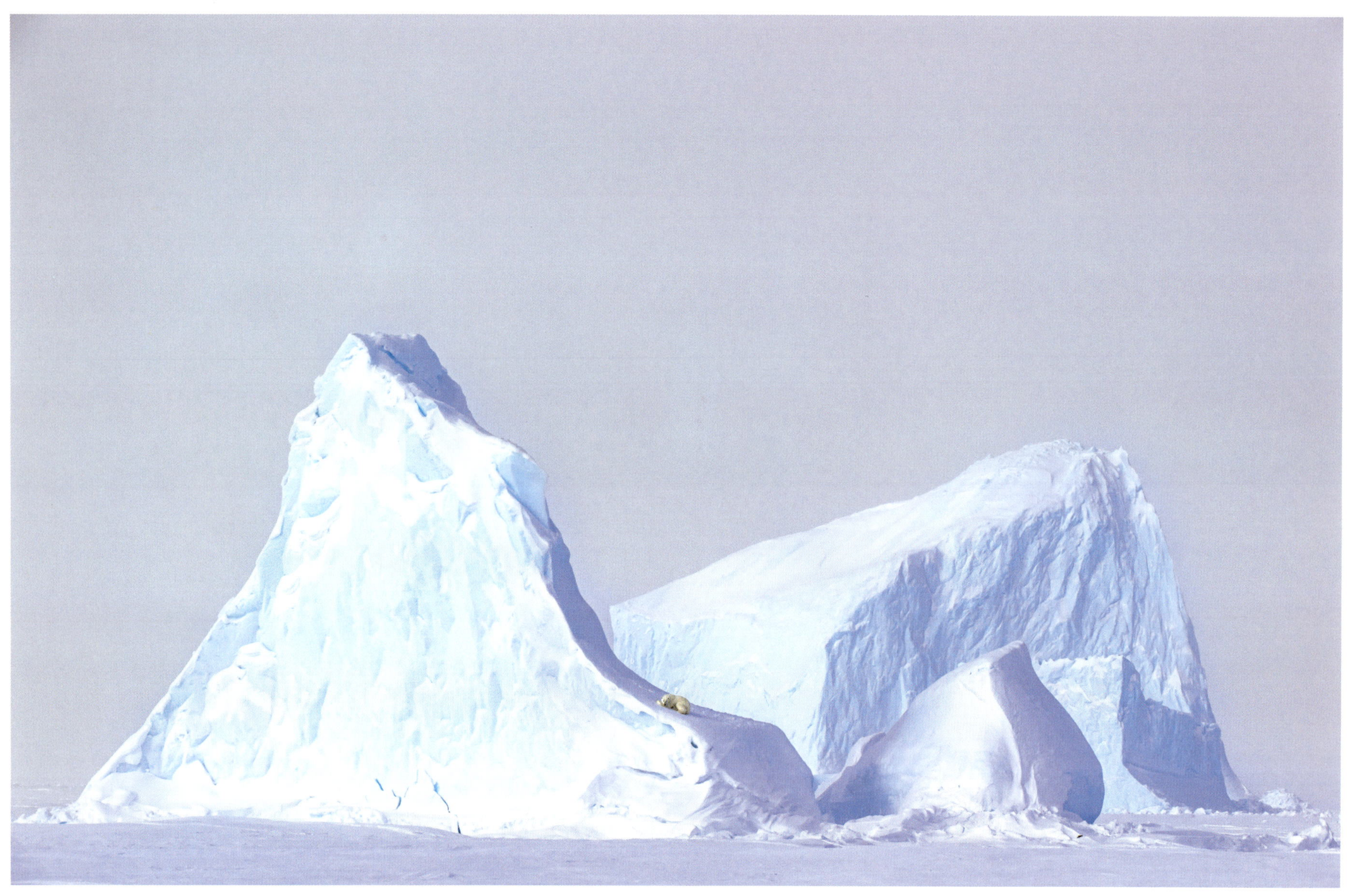

It is the purity of a frozen Baffin that makes this particular morning one of my best ever. We had been pissed around by an airline that cared little for us (and not for the first time, despite their eye-watering prices) and having chartered a small plane we managed to Skidoo into camp – a canvas dwelling on a frozen fjord. This male was on the nearby grounded berg in sight of my tent. After half an hour, we left to some protestations but Jay, a dear friend and the most remarkable Inuit I have ever met, conjured up a single parent family fresh from the den. The rest of the day was unbelievable … make that bearly believable.

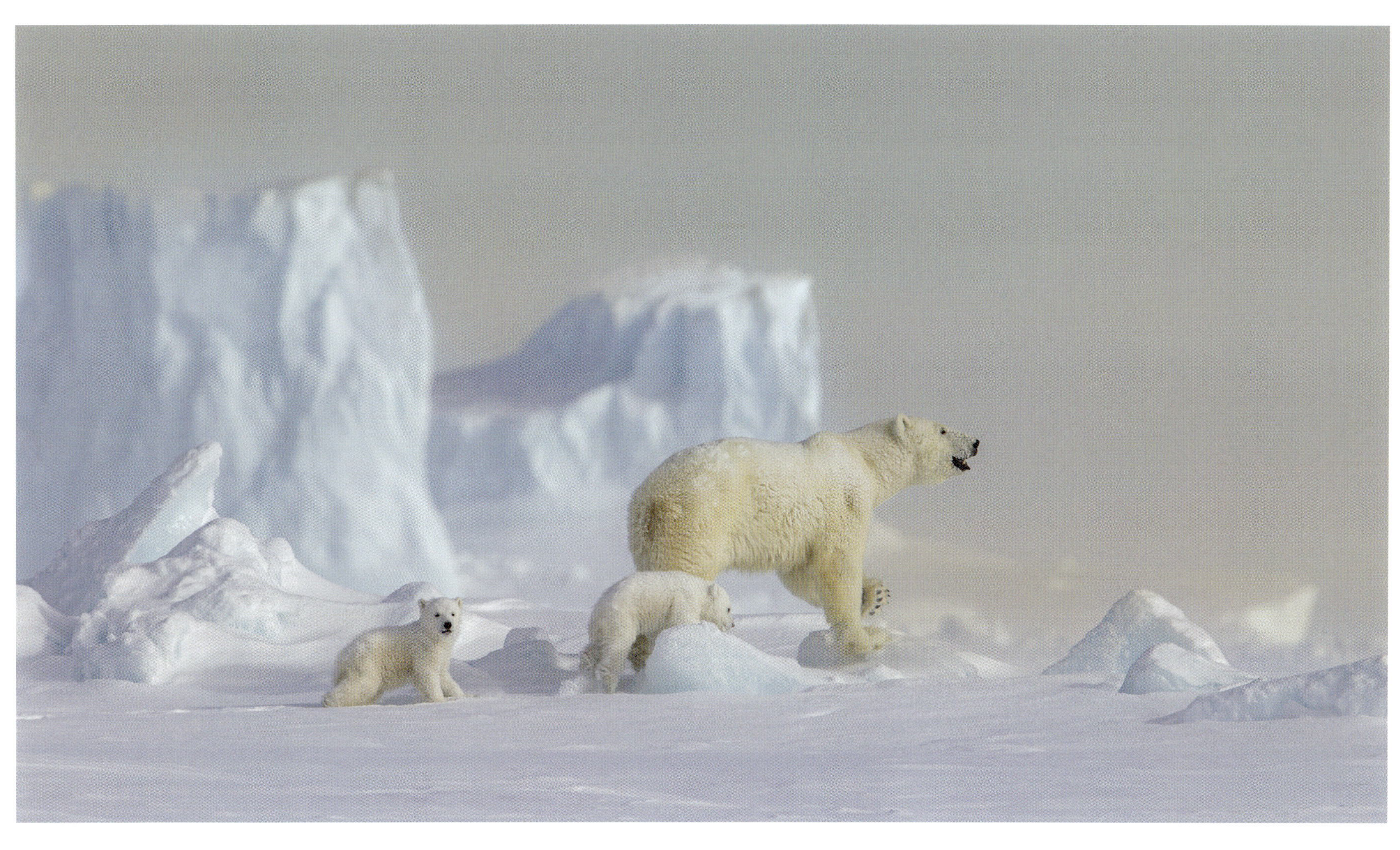

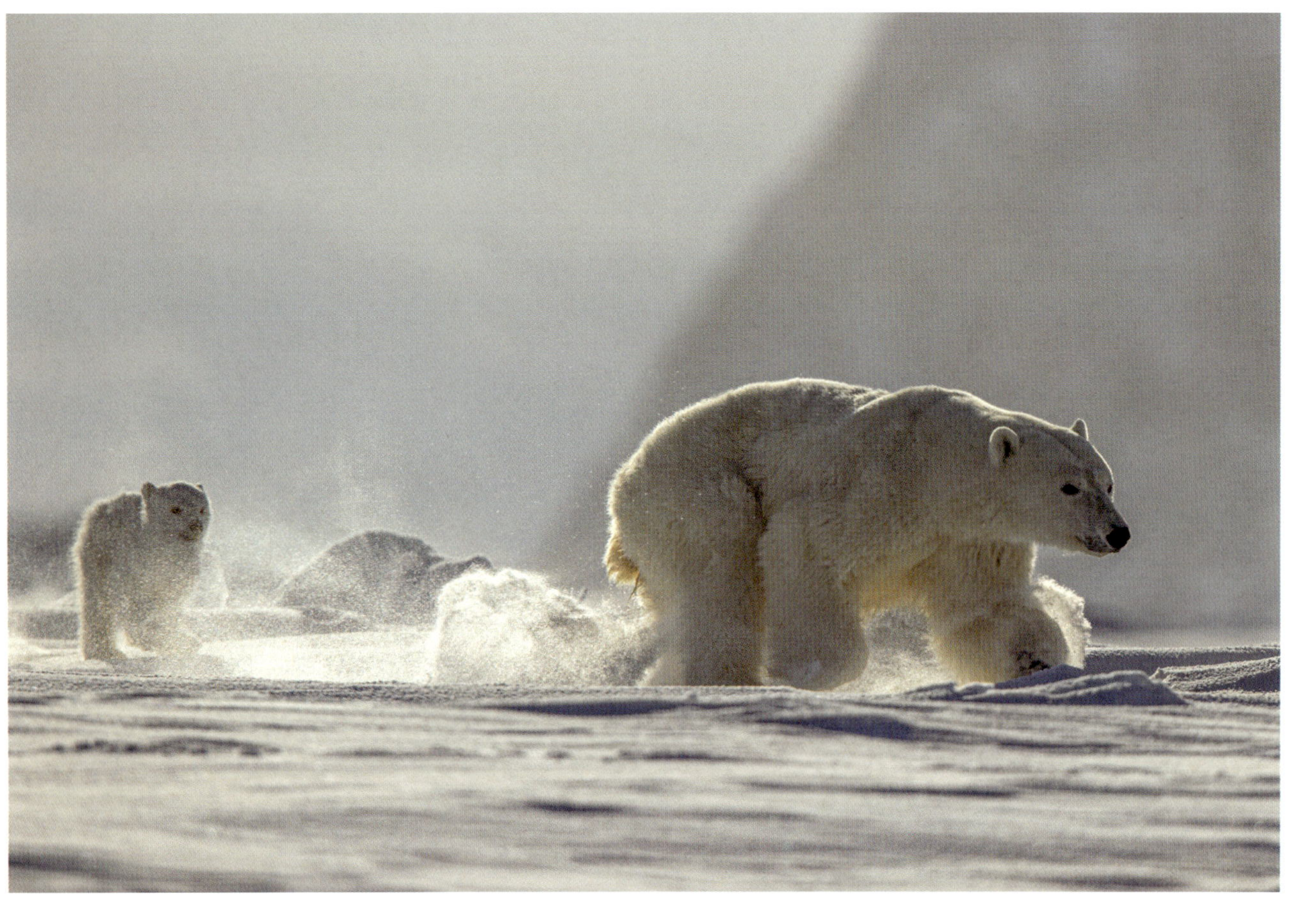

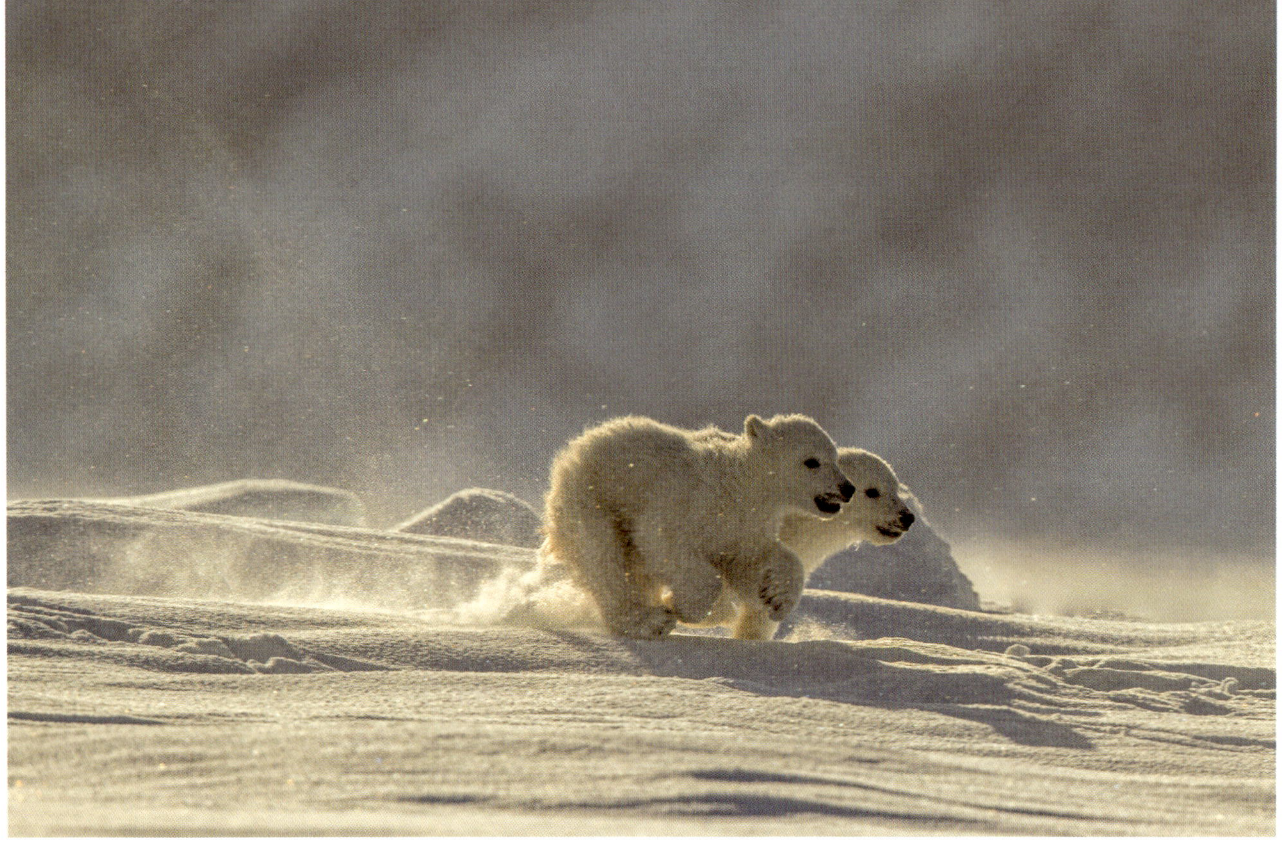

Spending time – quality time – with any species is the faunal grail; spending it in a well-managed conservancy or a remote and often savage wilderness ups the stakes even more.

Low down on the ice we began a long vigil. I love guiding here, working with utterly committed people. Seeing tears on guests' faces, good tears and in this case tears that immediately froze and grouted to cheeks, is the consummate reward. Thanks Jay, thanks Jaime, thanks team.

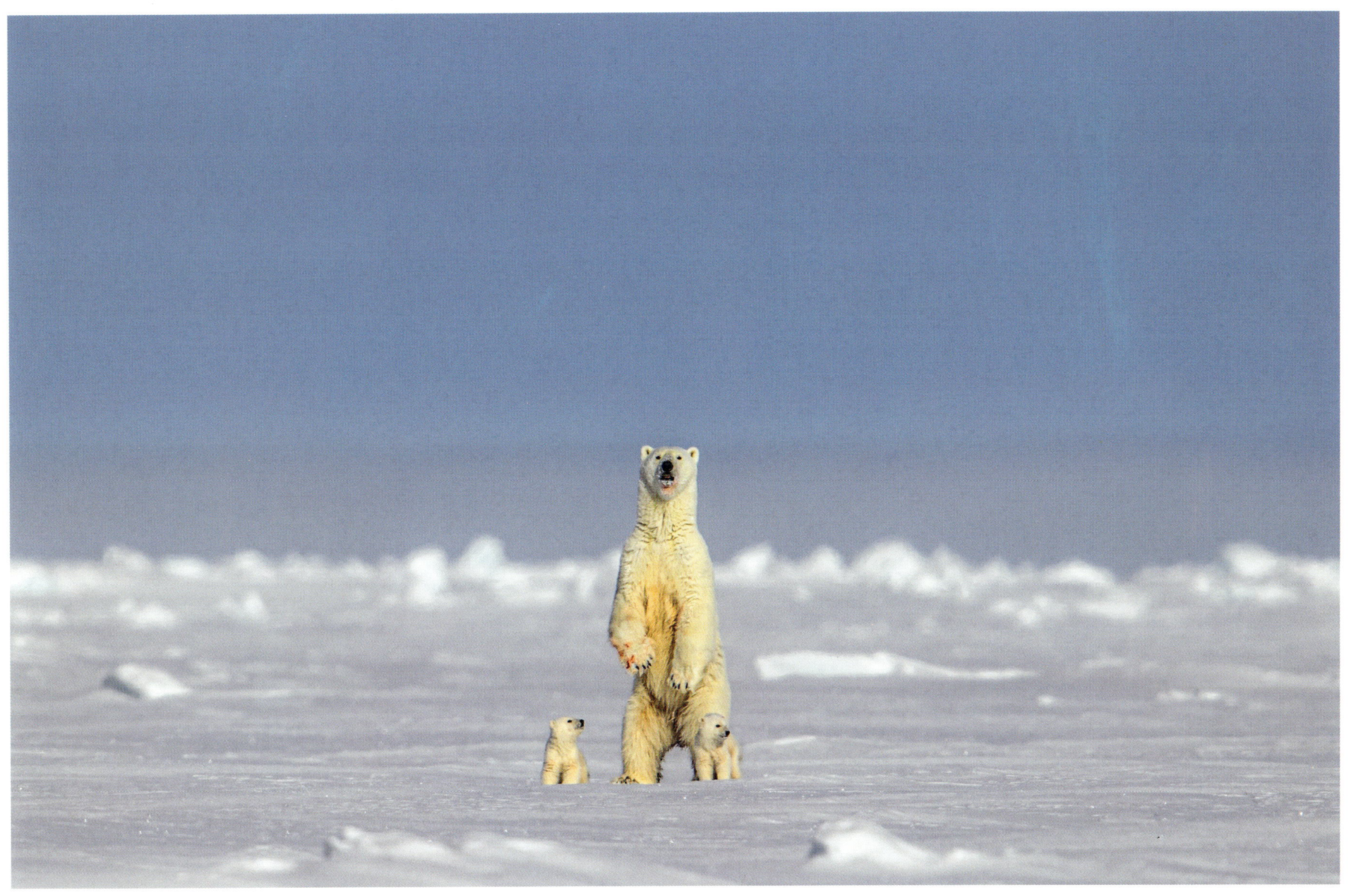

Stand and deliver: I have said for thirty years or more that wildlife viewing is *never* about numbers. These mainstream demeaning brays are both boorish and misguided. It is about moments, precious ones, and if protracted even better. This one lasted less than three seconds as this recently fed mother examined her adoring gallery before deciding these Gore-Tex-clad down-filled pilgrims were not for her. We were 150 yards out, motionless and utterly ecstatic. It was the final morning but no fat ladies were singing anywhere I could see above the Arctic Circle.

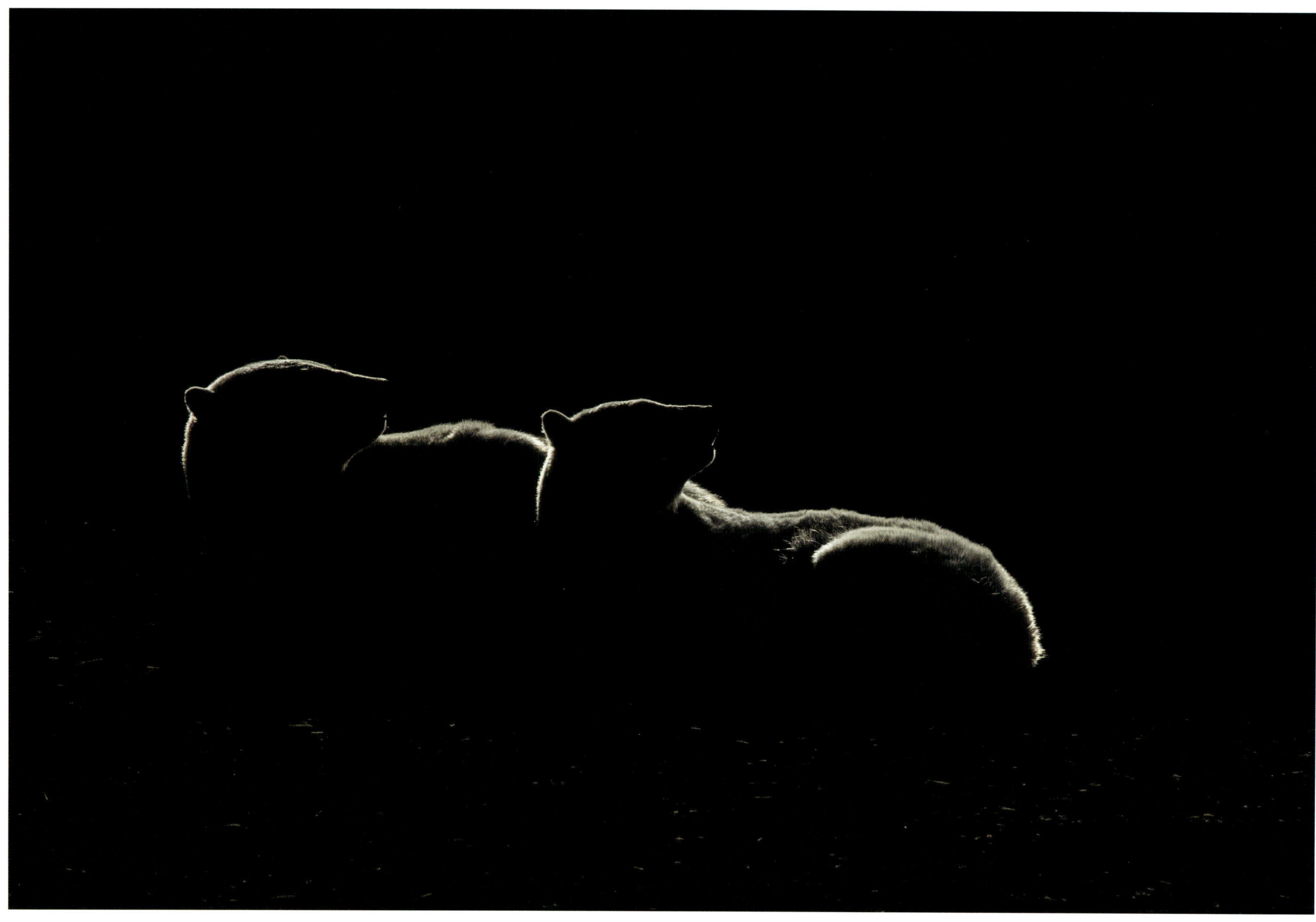

I remember the guide I was working with saying the most excursions he had ever done in a day was a miserly three. That changed that day in Spitsbergen, north of the Monaco Glacier. We slept when the bears slept and with 24-hour daylight we managed five Zodiac journeys. It was incredible and this photograph was taken towards midnight when the still bright sun lazily dropped a few degrees towards the horizon. Ridiculous and meaningless rules have compromised Spitsbergen and bear encounters.

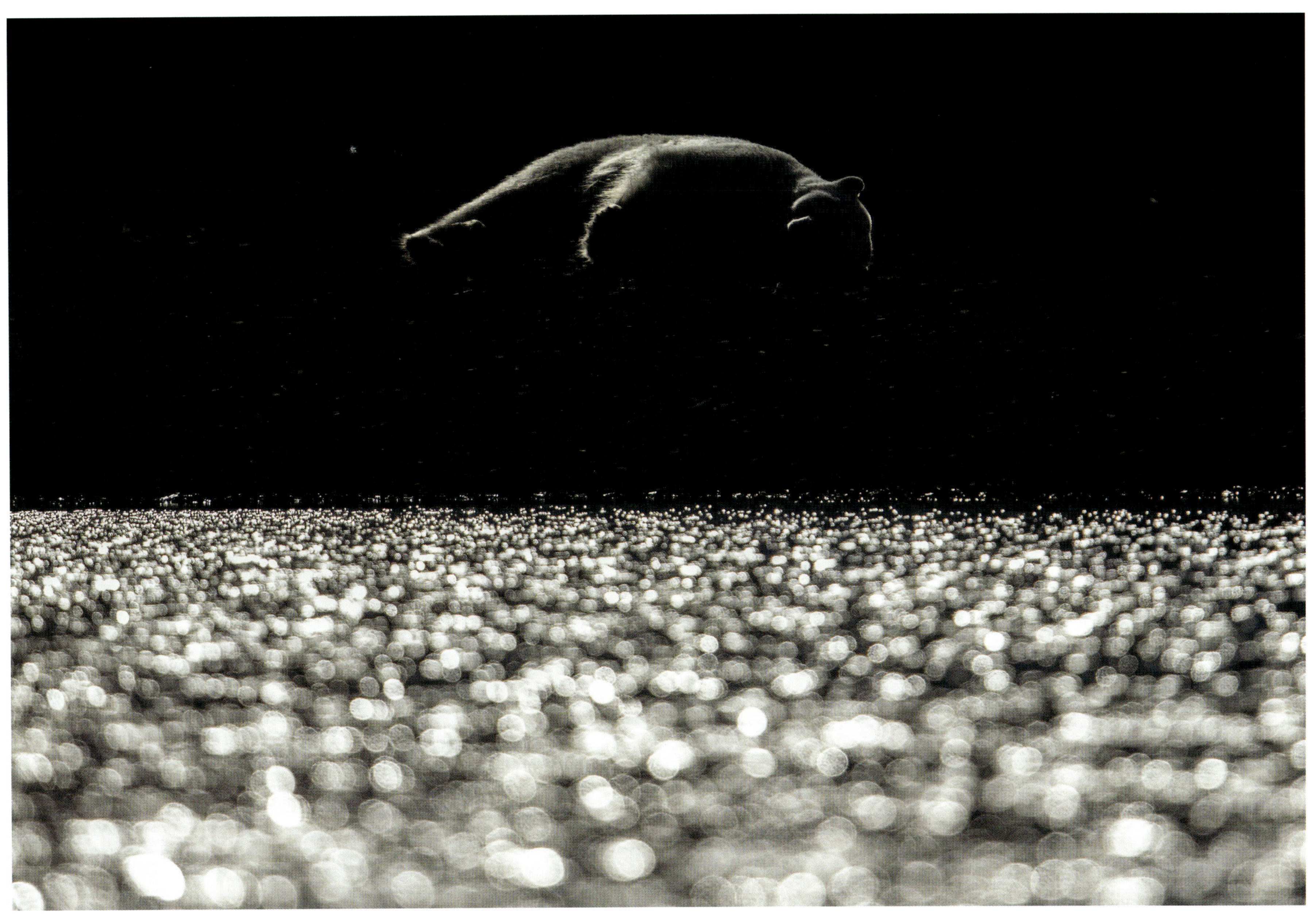

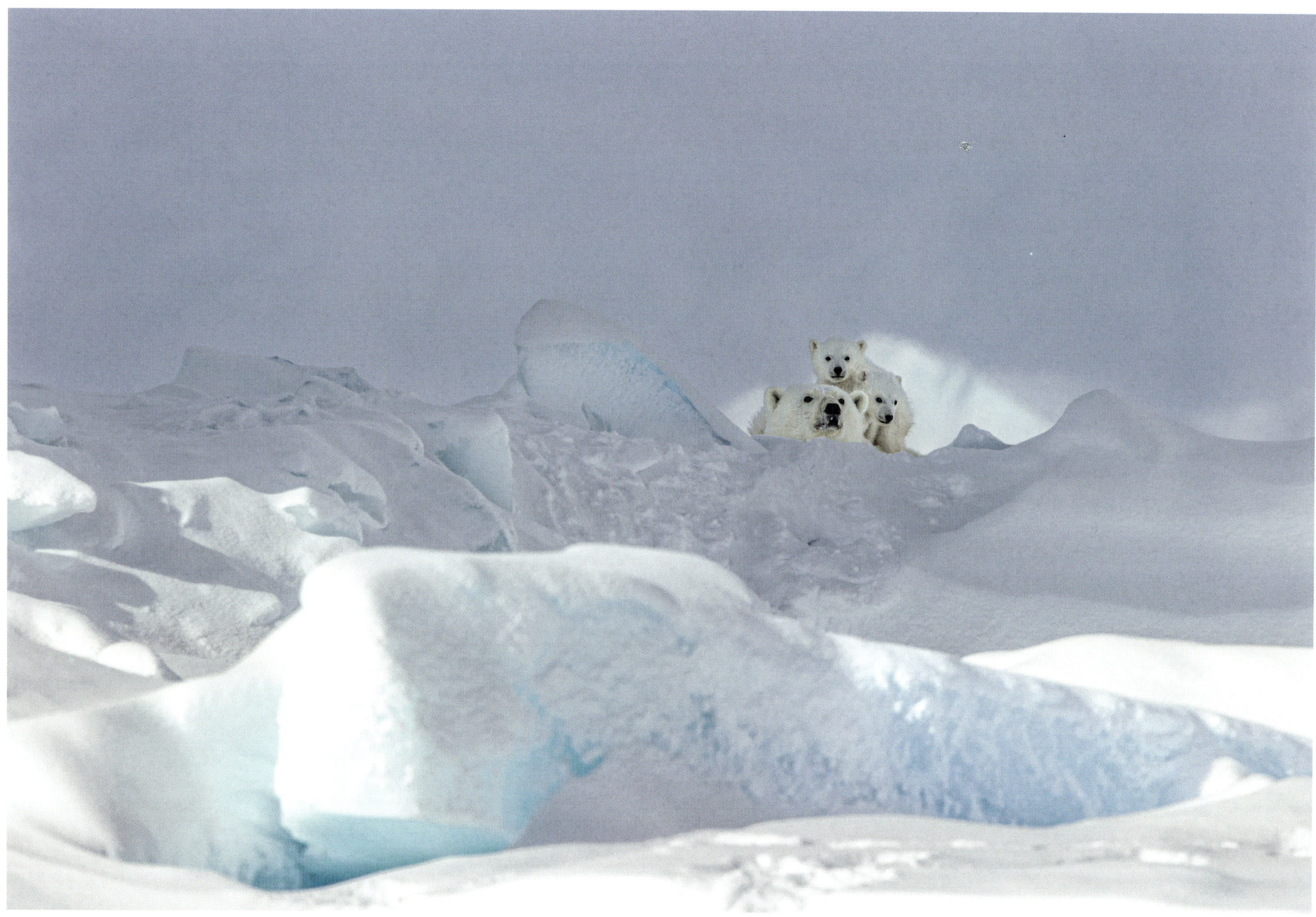

That evening, contemplating frost nip after the coldest day I'd ever experienced, an Inuit rolled into camp after a three-hour skidoo ride in the dark from the nearest settlement, wondering if we wanted any char – he had about a dozen of these stiff, but delicious, Arctic fish in a bag over his shoulder. No face protection and a snout seemingly glued to his lip… Hard. As. Nails. But what a day; this moment of a piggy-backing mother was one of a few highlights.

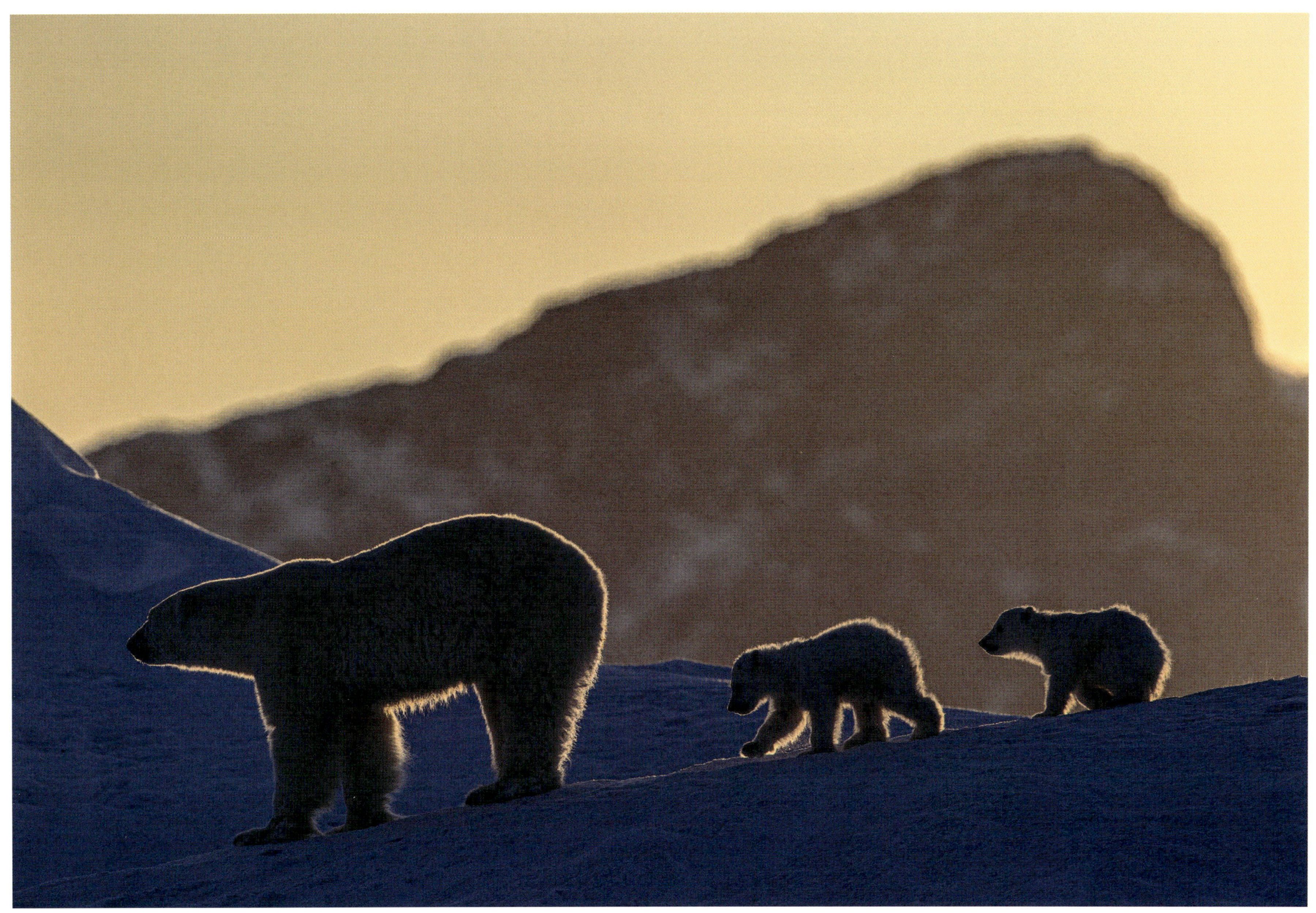

The final movement to a whole Arctic opera. A mother and two virtual newborns backlit on an iceberg as the sun dropped. In minus 25. Faunal nirvana … well, not far off it, and a dear friend and client said it was her best day ever. She still does.

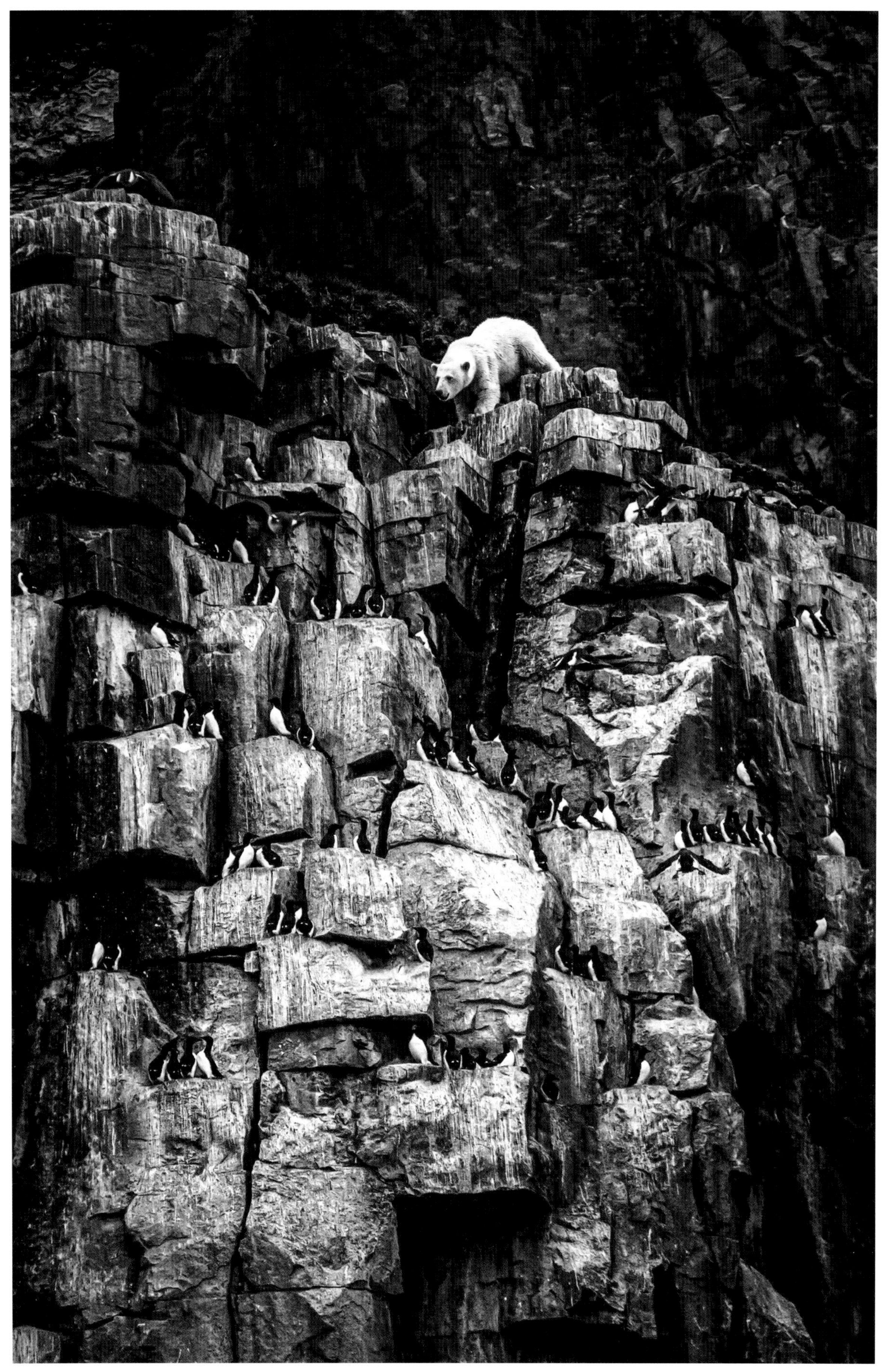

A top three wildlife moment ever but also a sobering one. A rudely early excursion to the prime avian real estate at Alkefillet in Spitsbergen. Following an industrial breakfast I felt we should have another go at this unique ornithological amphitheatre. Nine people stayed on board. Error. Big one. The radio call of 'Paul, bear' was met with derision but she wasn't kidding. A young bear then made several flash climbs up these vertical columns on the hunt for fledglings and eggs. Bears need big pans of ice to hunt, so although their climbing skills may supersede those of Messner and Hillary, this is not their larder. For 90 minutes it tried in vain to augment its diet unsuccessfully. It was a thin young bear of around three years. There was little ice that year and there are glaciers here that have retreated over 2 km in the last twenty years. Those who deny climate change need to get a hold of themselves.

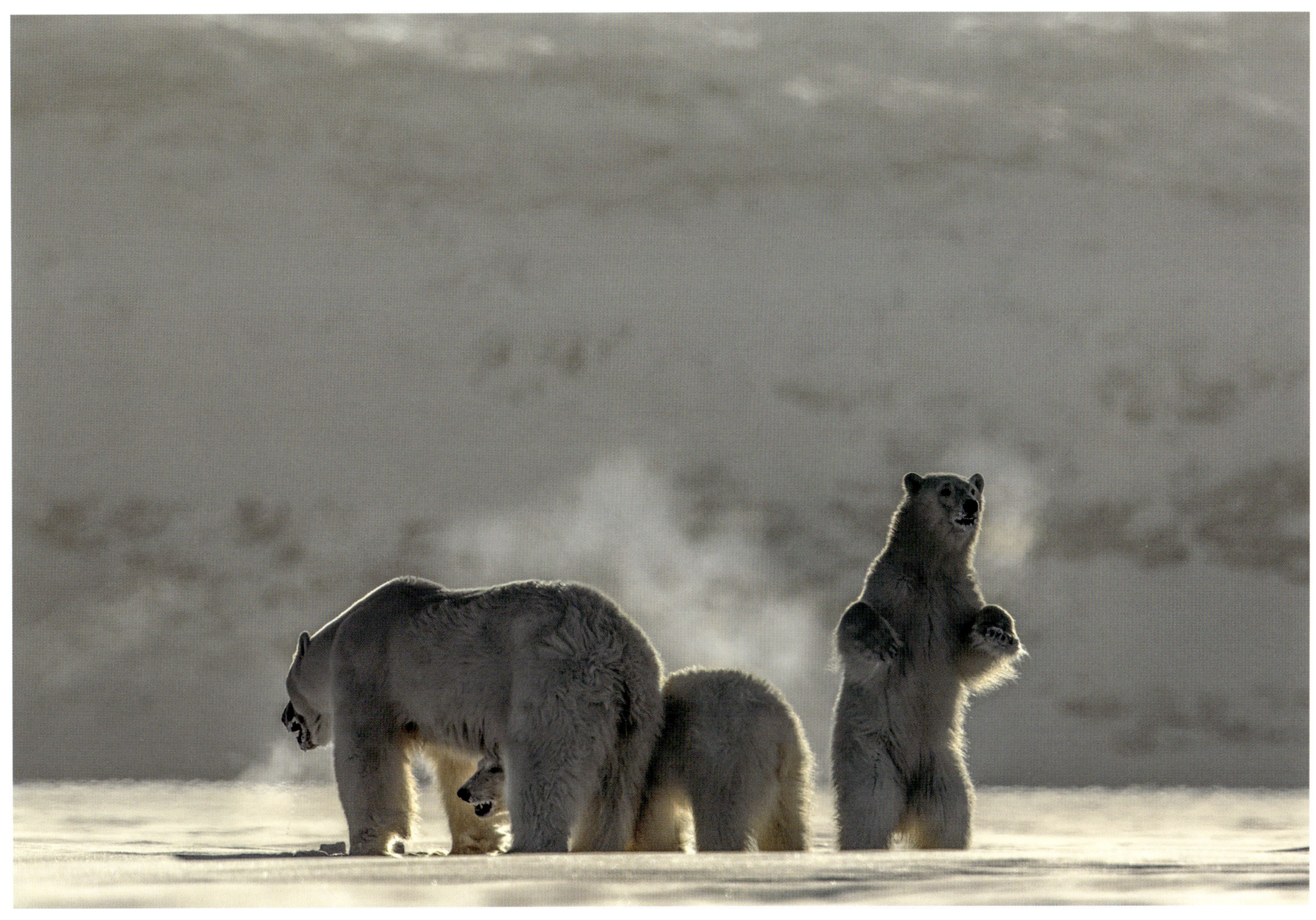

A good photo is normally 70 per cent background, 20 per cent subject and then, hopefully, something else. The steam rising off the bodies was that vital and enigmatic ingredient. Thanks Team AK, thanks Jay.

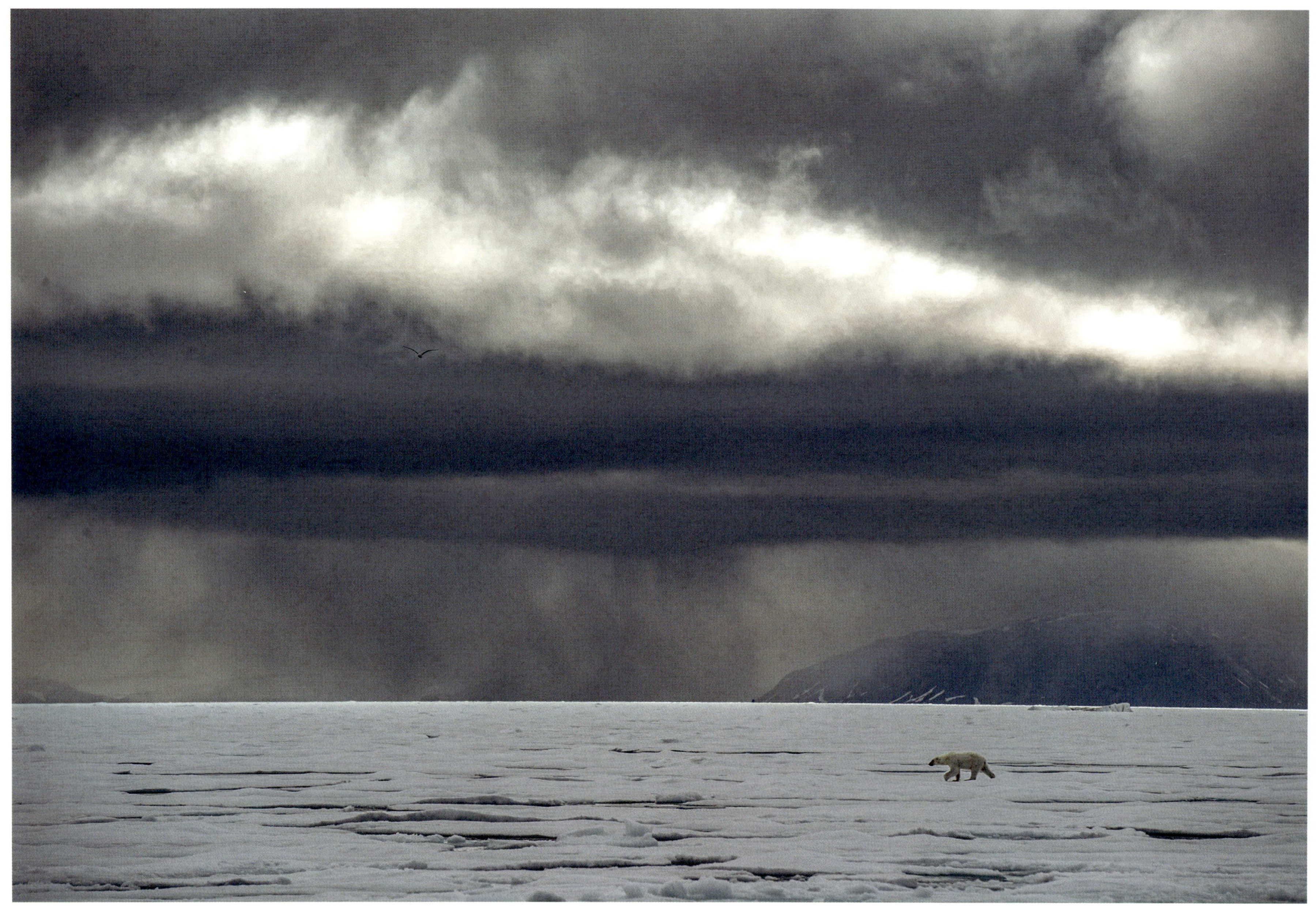

This patchwork, or even mosaic, of ice appears most frequently in Spitsbergen. It is close to a polar narcotic and to gain class A status it requires a vital ingredient … these moments are worked hard for, over long hours and the bears work even harder: diligently quartering the ice for some pinniped sushi. It is magical.

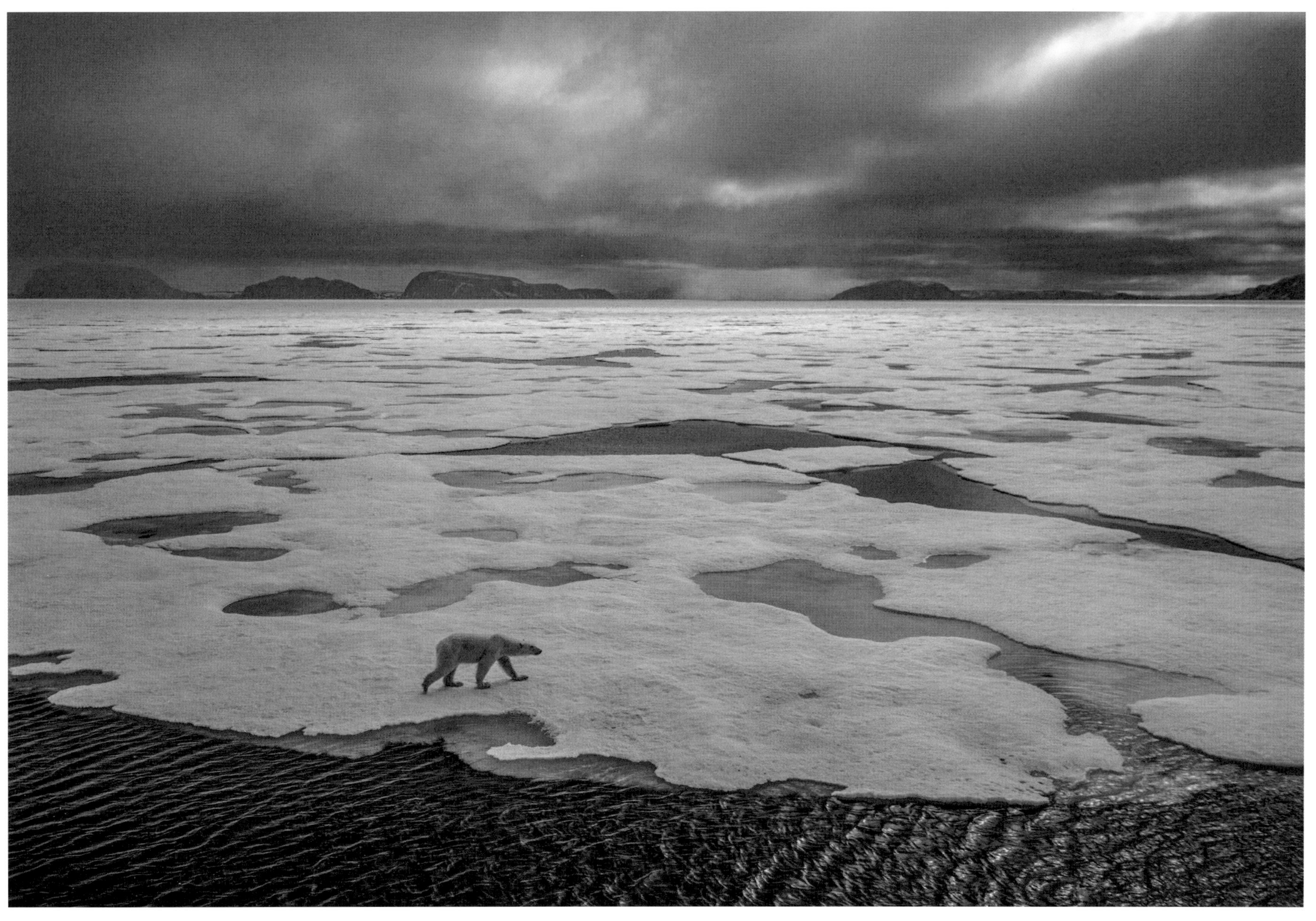

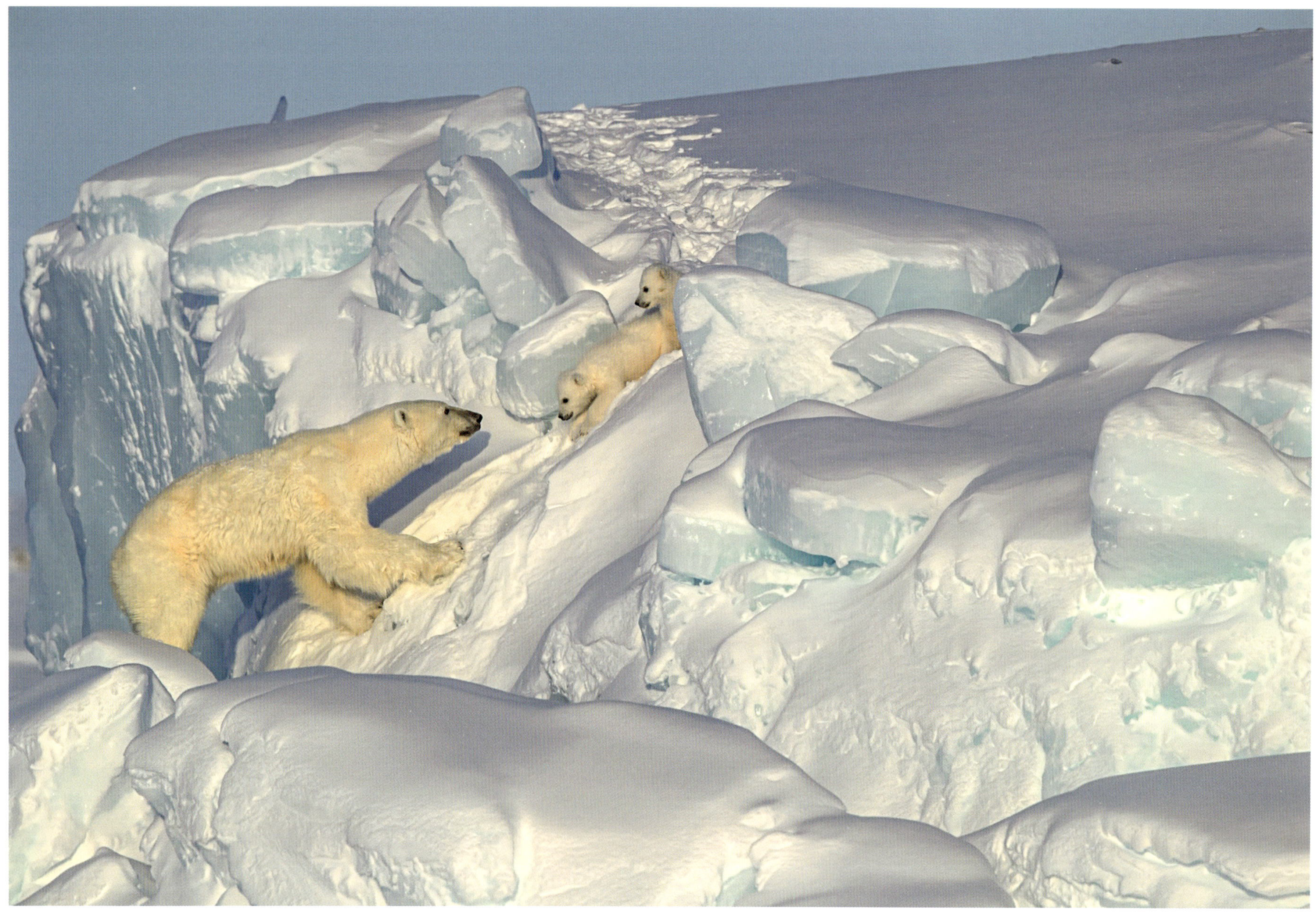

Ice dramas: a whole day with a single parent family is towards the top of my wildlife moments. Likewise, watching a yearling take on a vertiginous flash climb searching for its mother. These animals are still hunted, still traded and still worn. It sickens me and anyone who wants to throw the 'tradition' argument at me would do so at their peril.

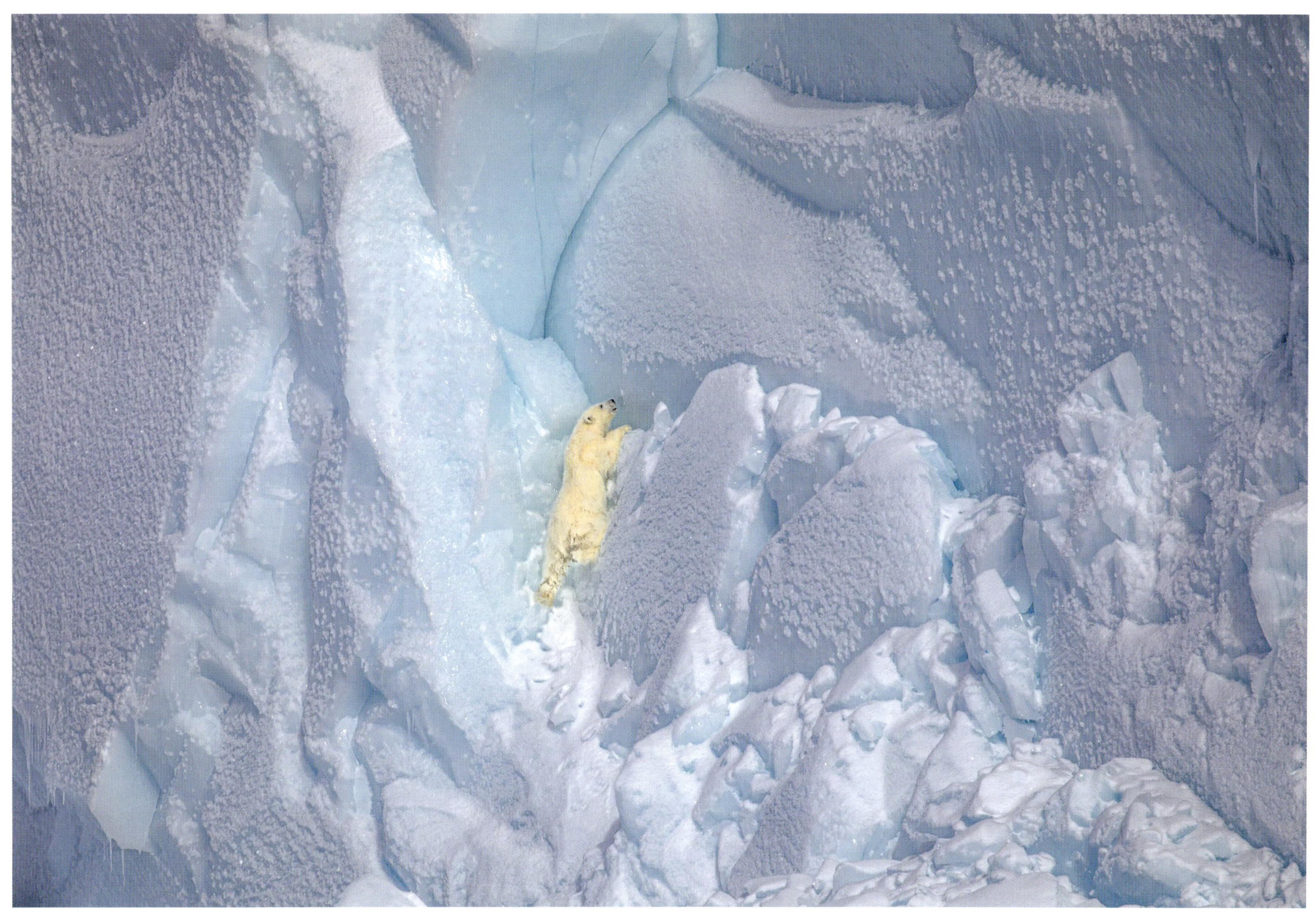

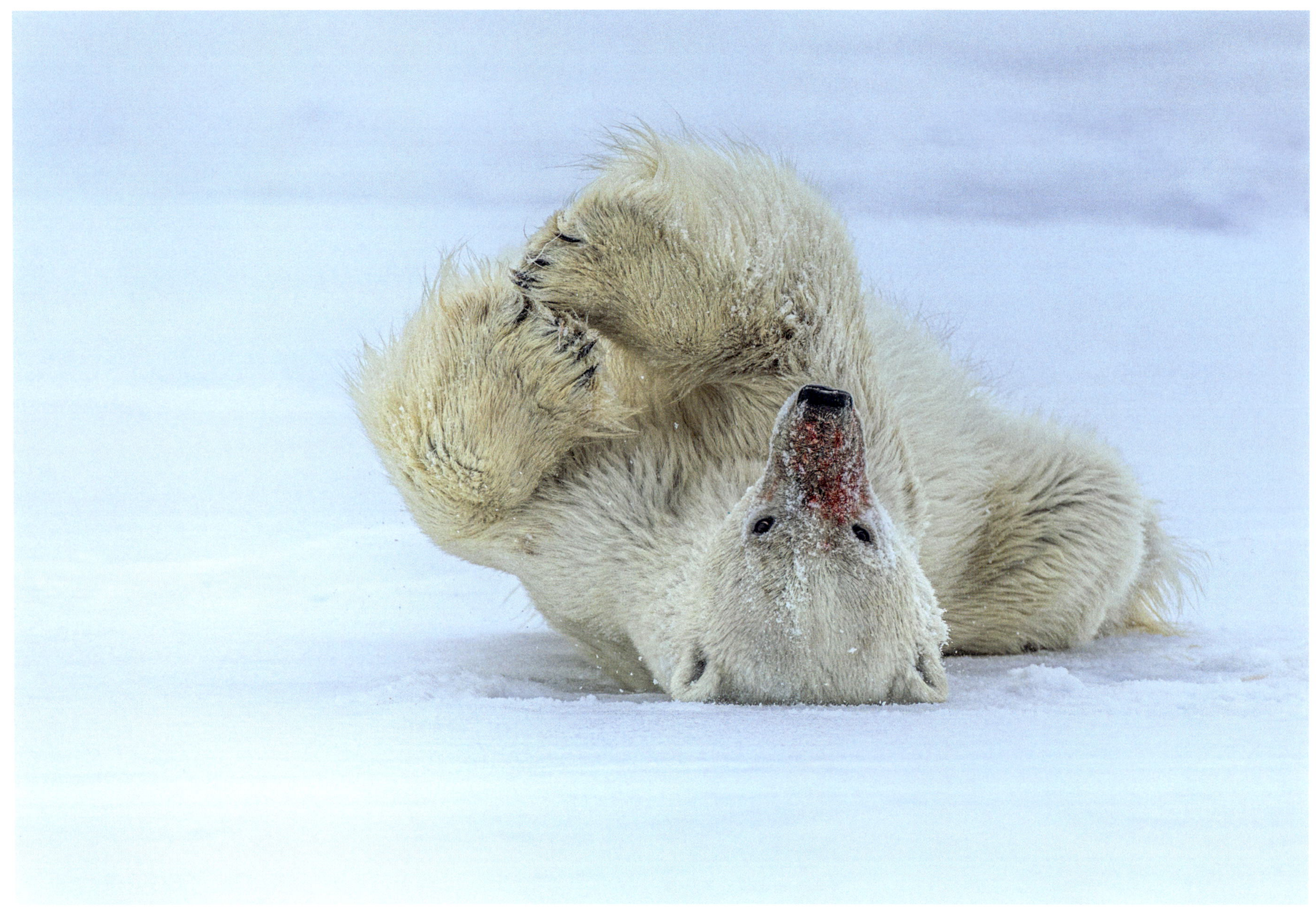

The Norwegian officials looking to augment their empty, sensitive wardrobe on their national CV have introduced ludicrous distance regulations for polar bears. Meanwhile, they butcher and frankly abuse seals and whales with impunity. This was outside their pathetic coastal water borders and deep into the sea ice. When you find a bear like this, you go to bear time: you sleep when they do – 24 hour daylight, 24 hour clock – as nature intended.

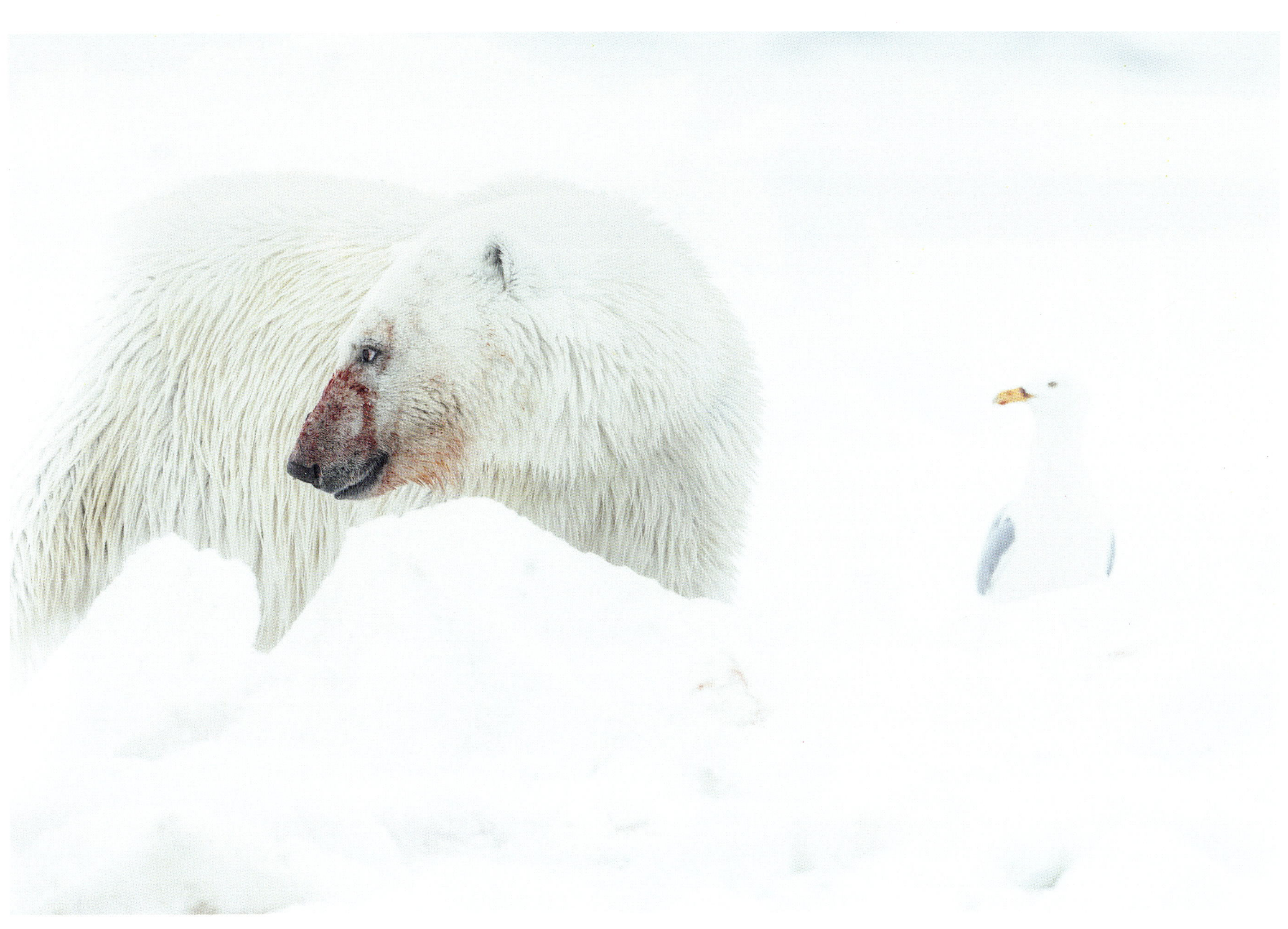

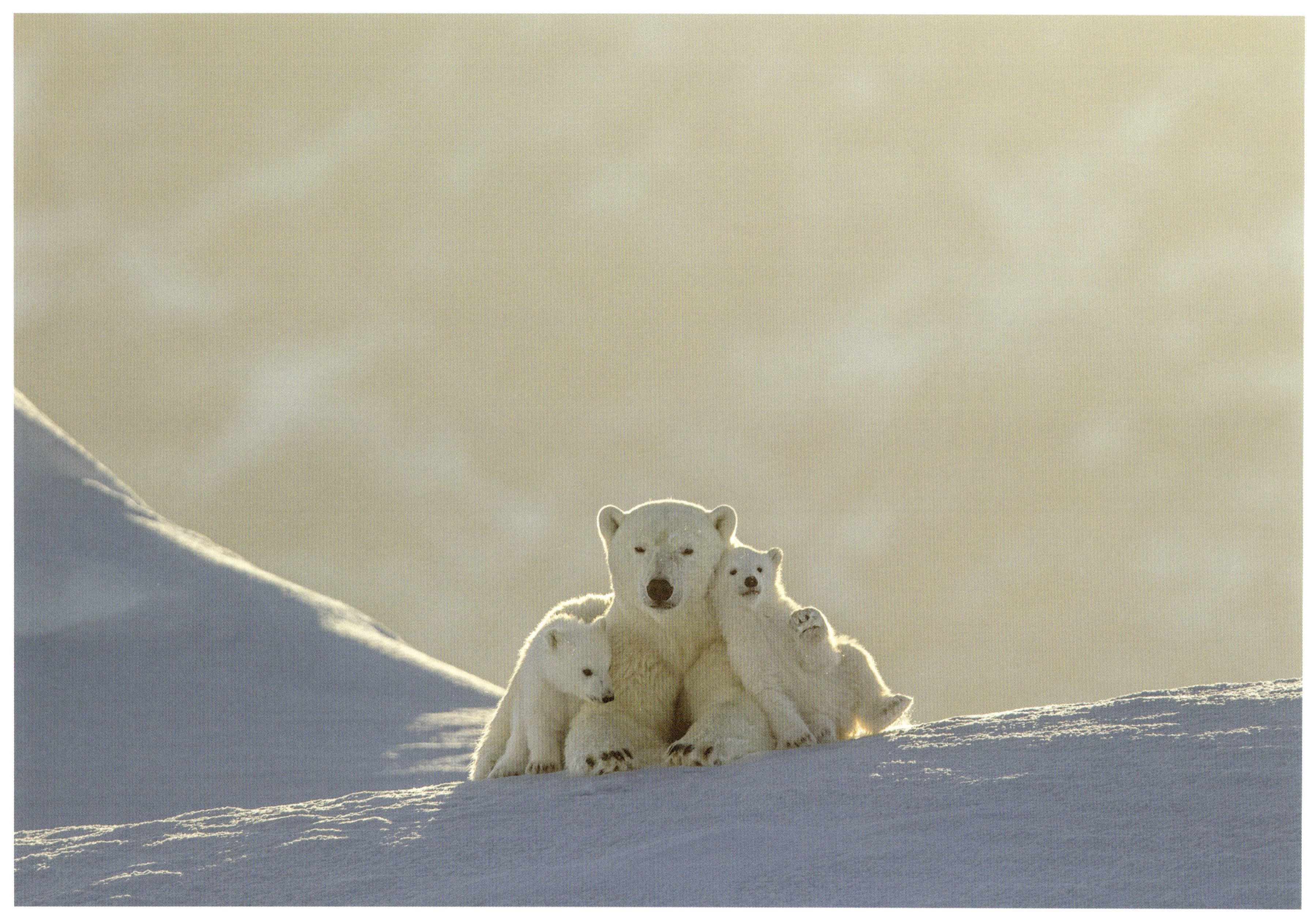

Two hours, three bears on a grounded berg, backlit.
No further words necessary except thanks Graham,
thanks Jay.

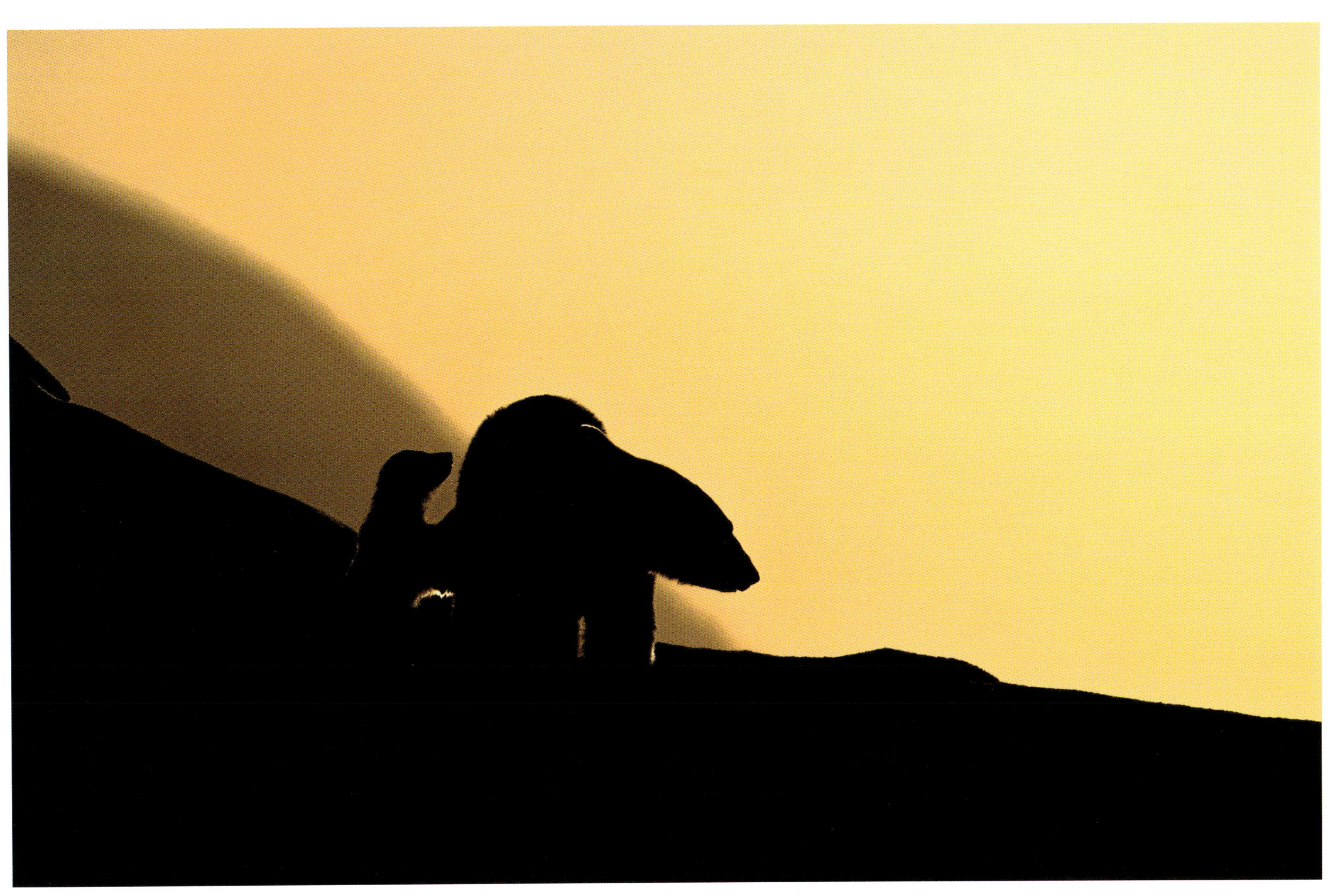

ONE
TWO
THREE
FOUR
FIVE
SIX
SEVEN
EIGHT
NINE

Three or four an hour are killed, their tusks, despite new laws on ivory, seemingly as sought-after as ever. There are numerous loopholes, even in the UK, to bypass the supposed restrictions and there is an awful lot of anguish, but the bodies keep tumbling to the African earth. The booty from this macabre harvest benefits comparatively few: the Janjaweed in Sudan, the dealers in China and Vietnam and the wet markets and clinics that bogusly claim medical benefit where there is none. Trinkets and jewellery add to the ghoulish crop. 90 per cent of African elephants have been lost in the last one hundred years. As many as 20,000 are killed each year; it's just not sustainable in our lifetime, nor our children's. Tougher laws, tougher sentencing and a candid exposure of the countries that are underwriting this slaughter would also help. But it is a complicated one – almost everywhere elephants live, humans do, and in ever-growing numbers. This presents huge challenges but the thought of these animals being shot for 'sport' is shameful, with the huge bucks financing this grisly pastime rarely correctly appropriated.

It is not just African elephants; Asian ones are killed also to fuel this dreadful demand. However, until the end users are publicly shamed and disgraced for their countless violations and the poaching ring kingpins put away for grown-up sentences, little will change despite some indescribably brave guardians. Those who desire ivory in Hong Kong and China have little knowledge of the genesis of their desire – many believe tusks grow back naturally.

Once the animal is killed and the tusks untimely ripped from the cranium, the rest of the elephant is abandoned as waste. If there are calves, they are also abandoned, their mother's slaughtered body next to them. They have zero chance in the wild, so a single bullet can destroy two generations.

Stocks of 'legal' ivory should have run out in 2004; this has not happened, the forms altered, the expiry dates tampered with. Also, scandalously, the 2008 sale of ivory, with the WWF seal of approval, was responsible for restarting and legitimising the trade. It was a ludicrous decision and a sinister one, and those responsible have the blood of one-third of Africa's elephants on their hands.

There are areas like Kenya conservancies where elephants live comparatively well. Tourism is the great protector: countless eyes and properly appropriated fees (always the key to conservation of a species) deter the poachers better than any other measures.

But the demand is still rampant for this 'traditional' product. When the desire and purchasing ceases, so does the poaching. It is a rancid, stinking business and it is not slowing down. Consider this: Namibia only has a couple of hundred desert elephants. They eke out an existence in the northeast of the country, in desperately challenging, arid conditions. They are not a subspecies even though their legs are longer, the legacy of dwelling in sand for so long. Each year five licenses are given by the government to shoot five breeding bulls. It is just unspeakable. When corrupt greed-heads hold the power, there is little hope for elephants, or frankly for us.

Of all the words in the English language, 'traditional' may well be the most damaging.

ELEPHANT

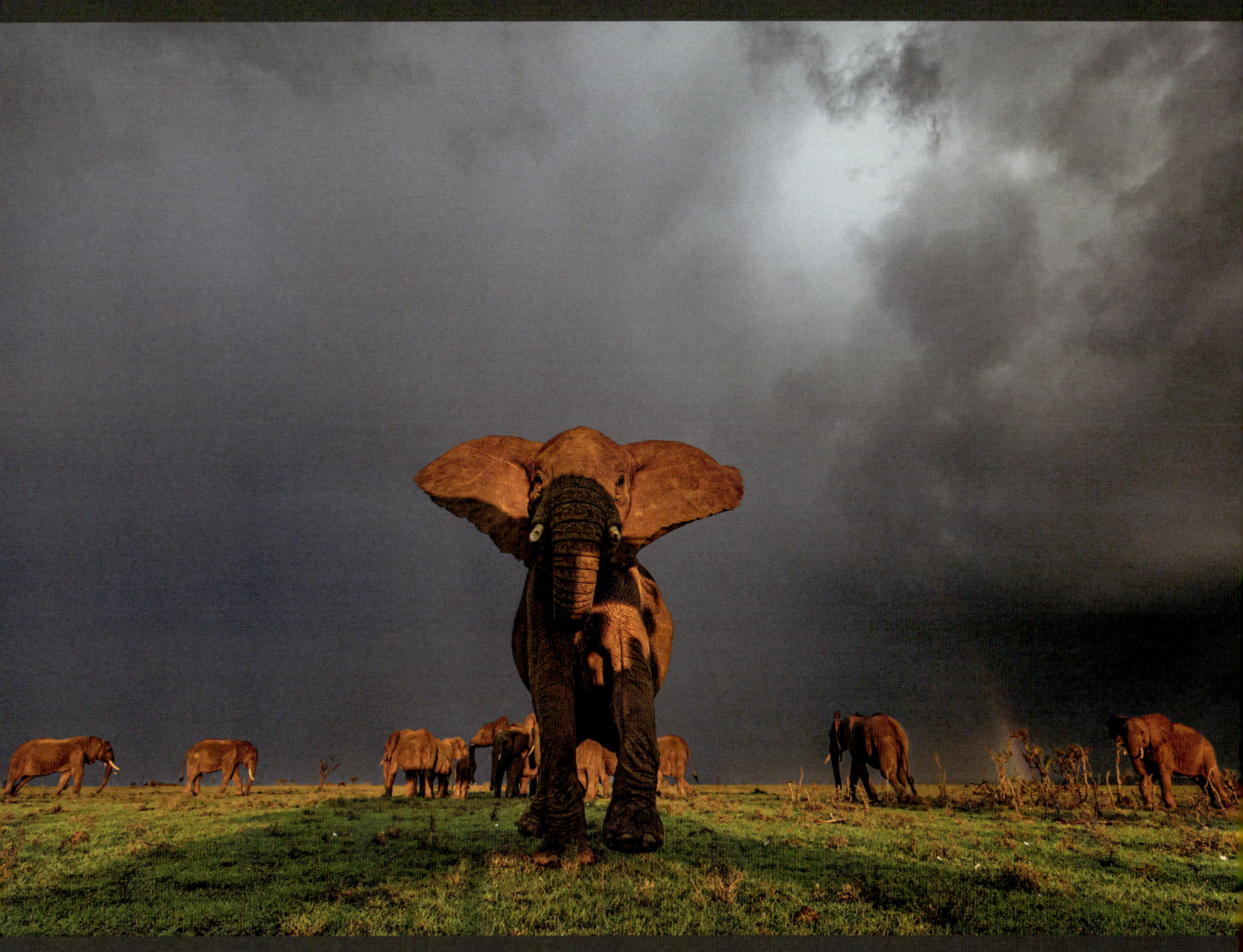

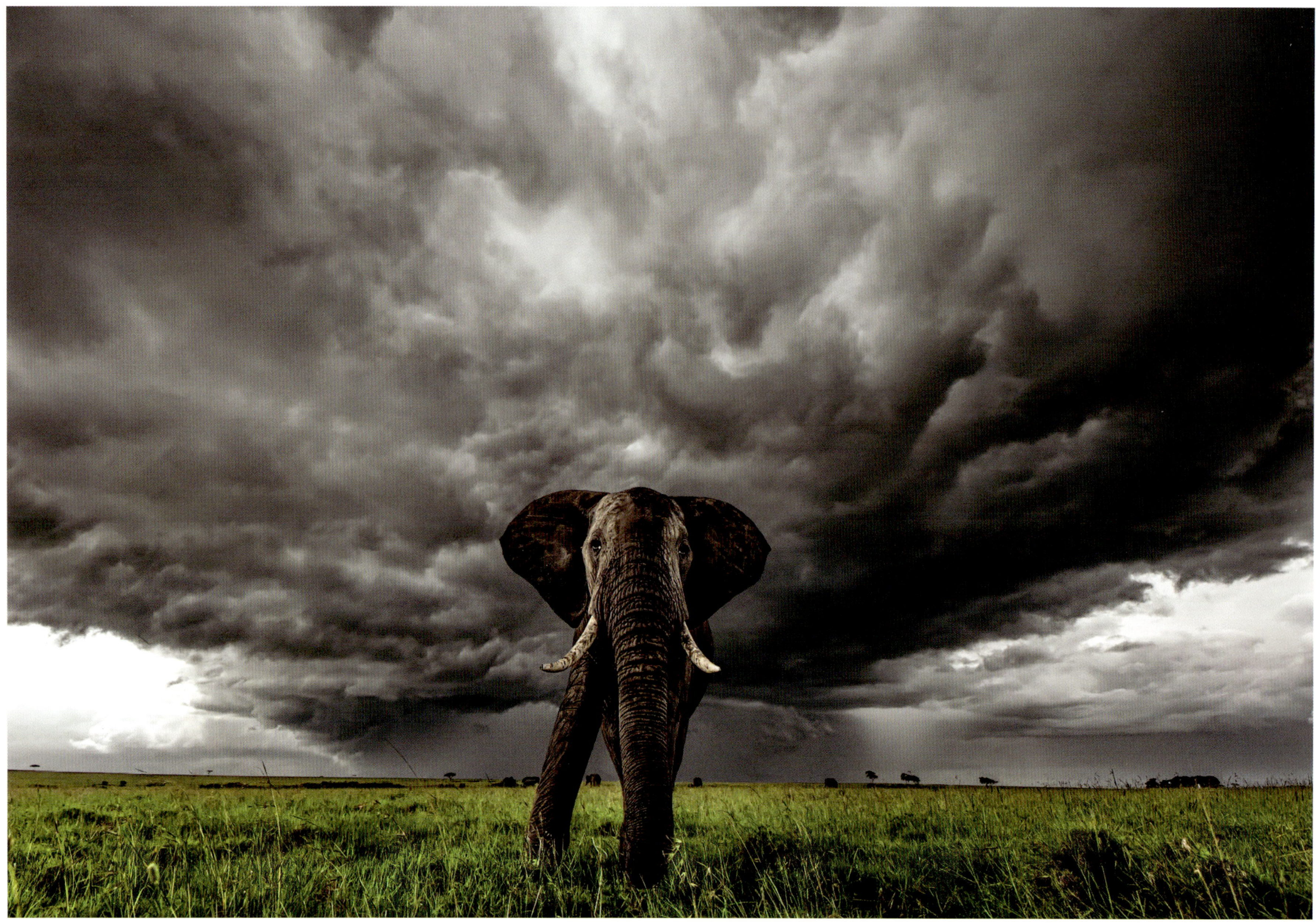

The sound of an elephant brushing through nutritious knee-high oat grass is a bush overture unlike any other. Combine it with the groan of the wildebeest and the elephants' often indignant trumpeting and you have both woodwind and brass of the bush orchestra. A long and patient approach from downwind makes these encounters possible, armed with the widest of lenses. There is nowhere better in Africa for this than Mara North Conservancy.

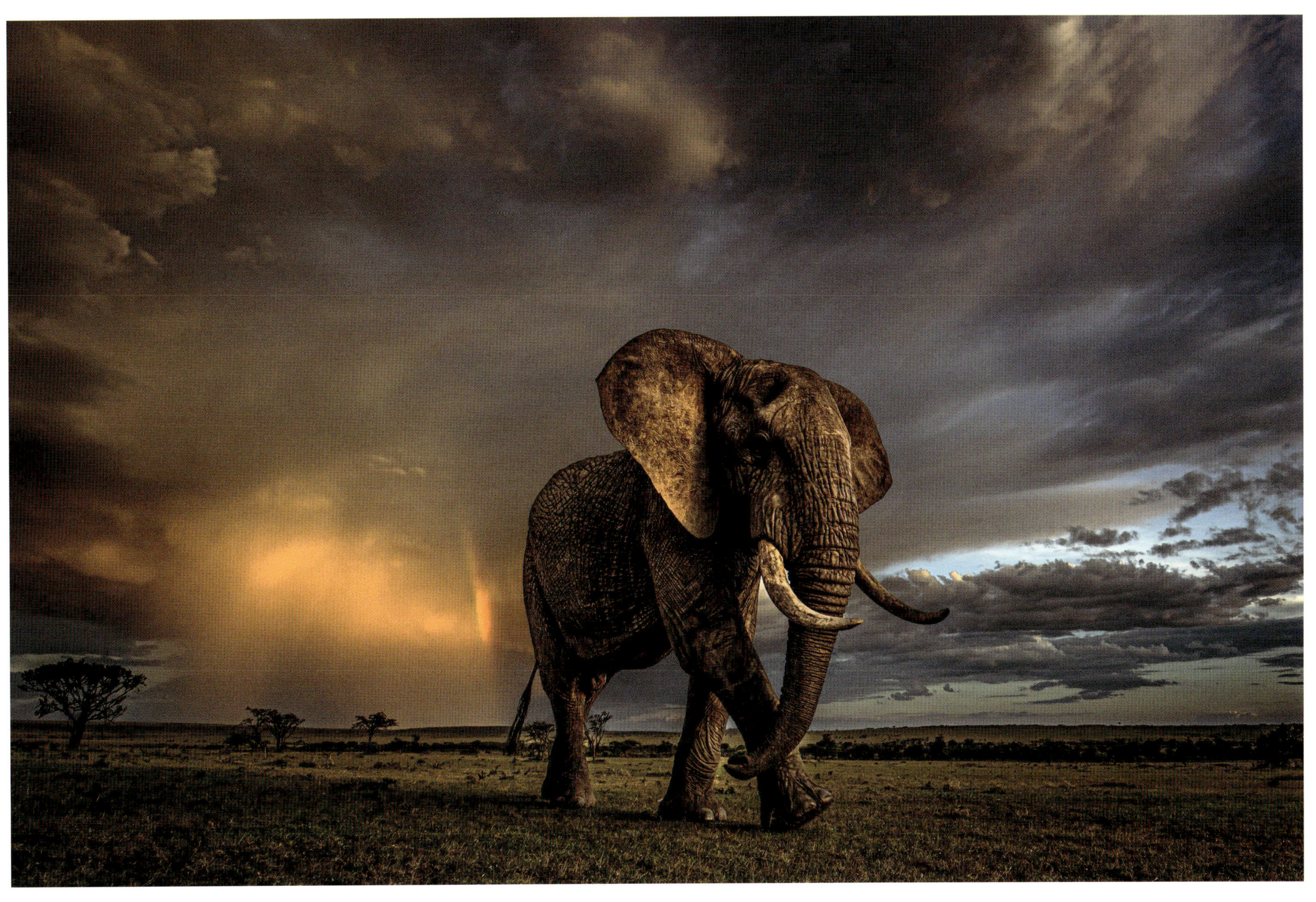

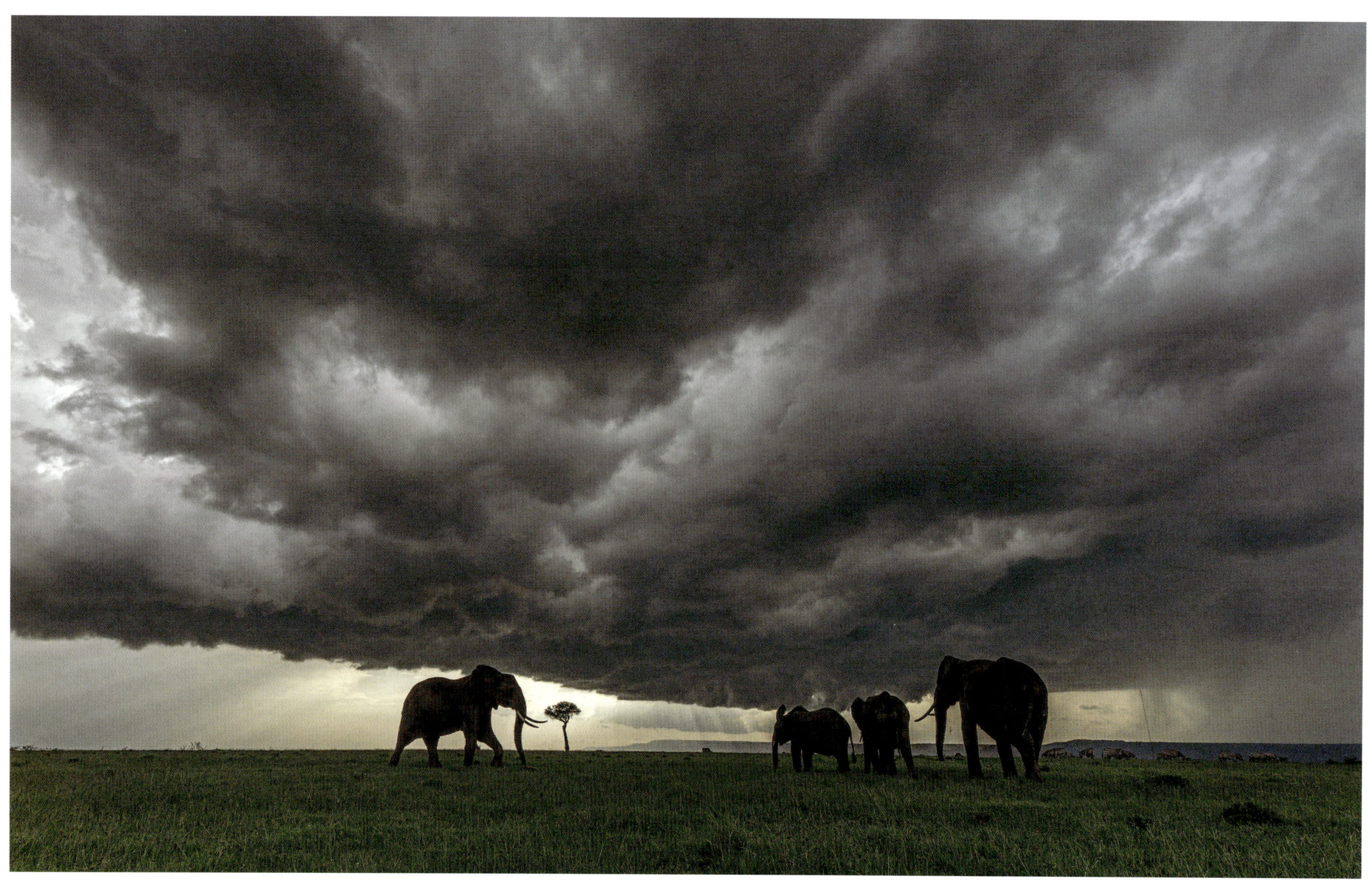

Mara North Conservancy again … peerless.

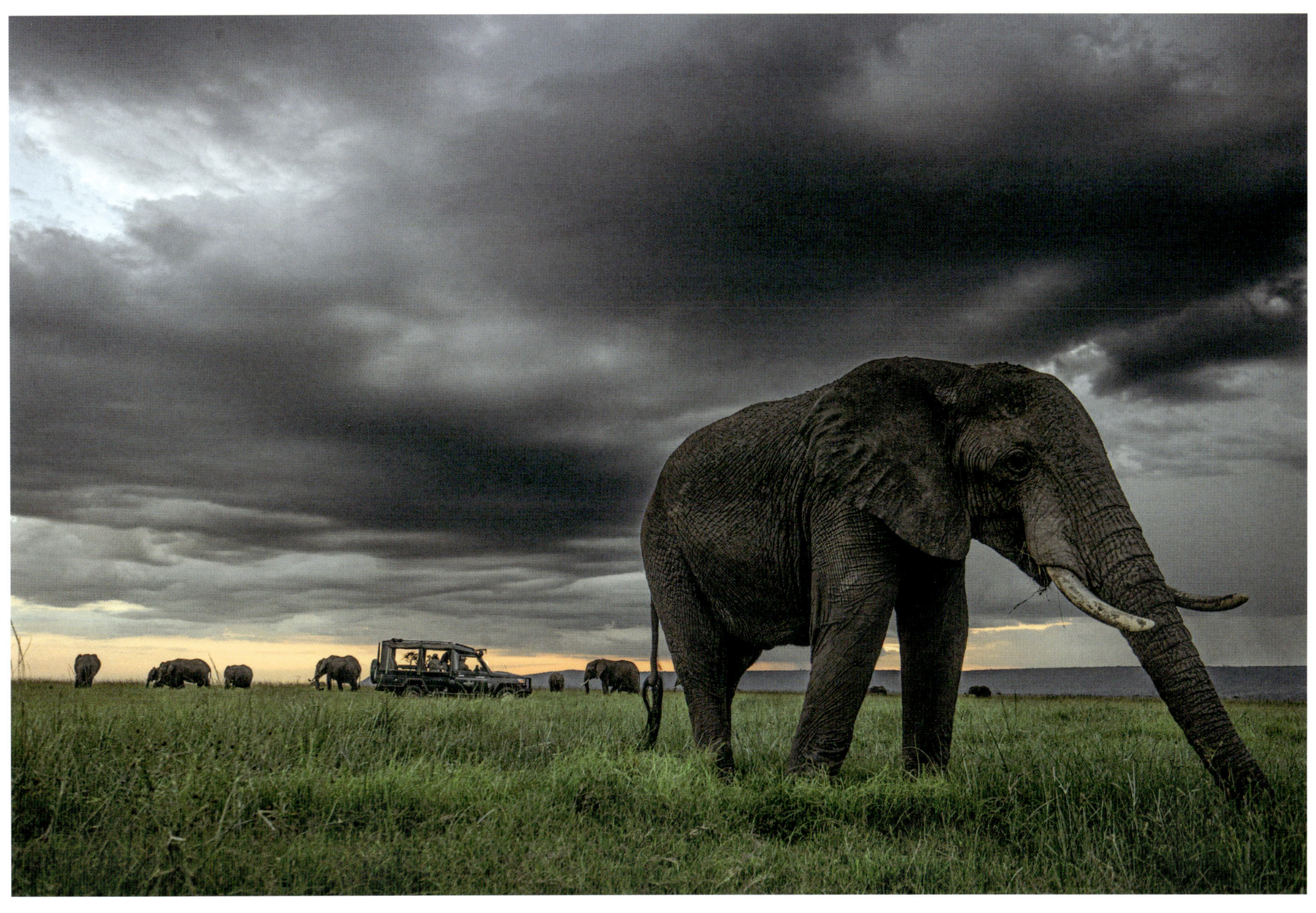

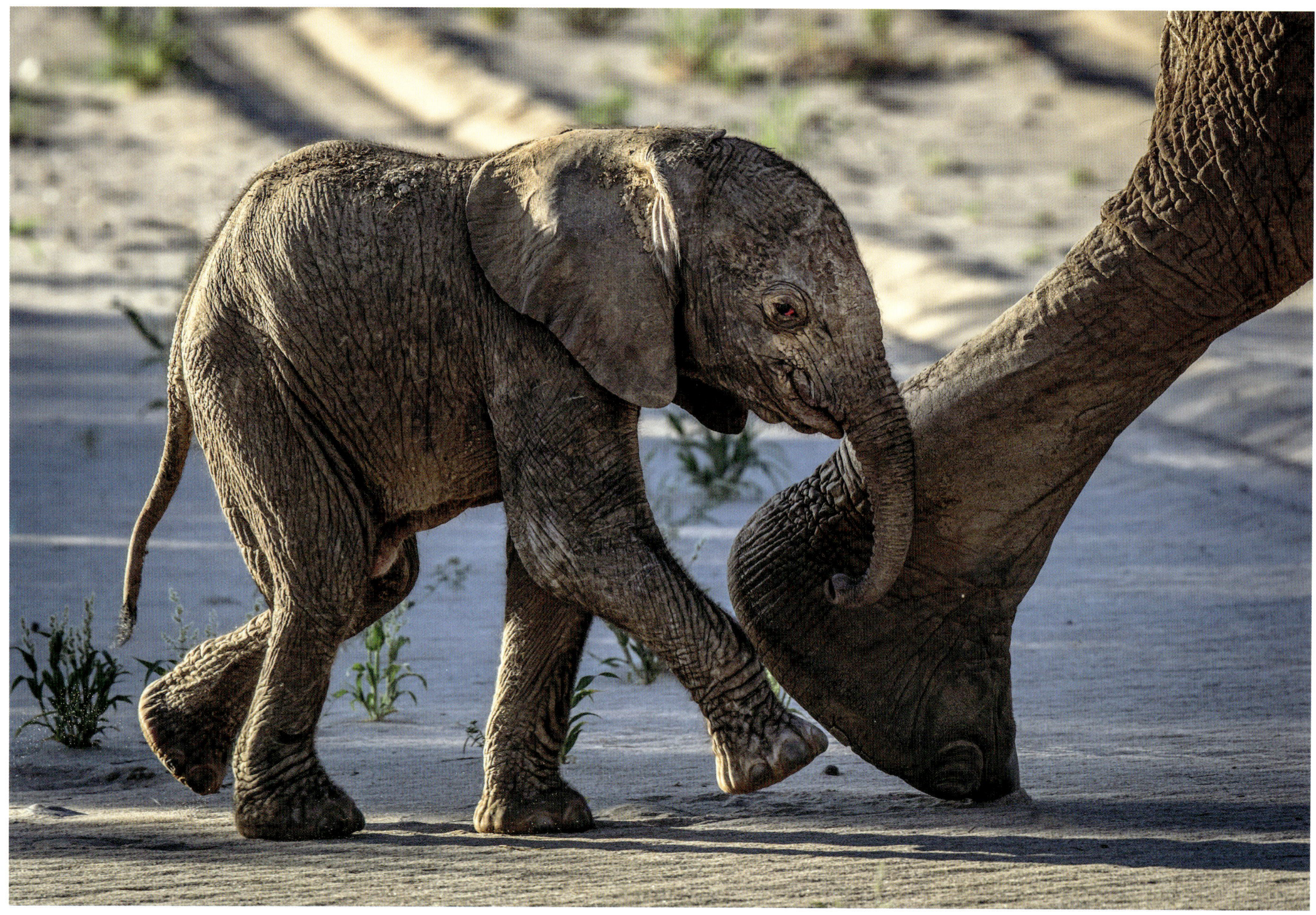

This was the youngest Namibian desert elephant either my guide Durr or I had ever seen. It tottered along on spindly legs, only a few days old. It is dauntingly hard for these elephants to eke out a living in these often abominably harsh conditions. A recent documentary charted the demise of one such calf as the drought took its toll. Nobody interfered; perhaps they should have done, particularly when these vanishing pachyderms are down to a few hundred. They did, however, manage to construct a pitifully anthropomorphic name for the doomed beast. Desert elephant numbers aren't helped by permits still being issued from the capital for them to be shot. For sport…

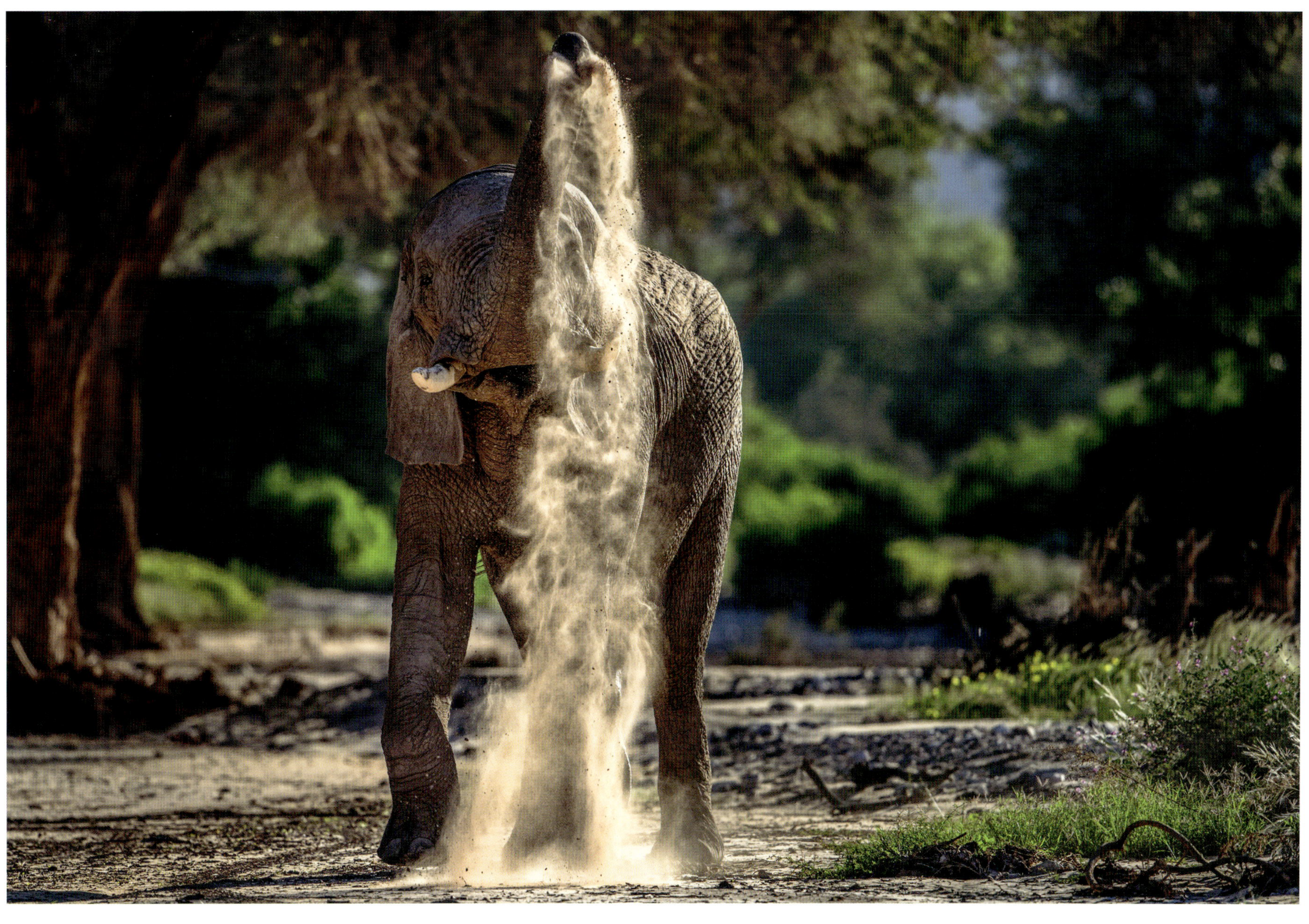

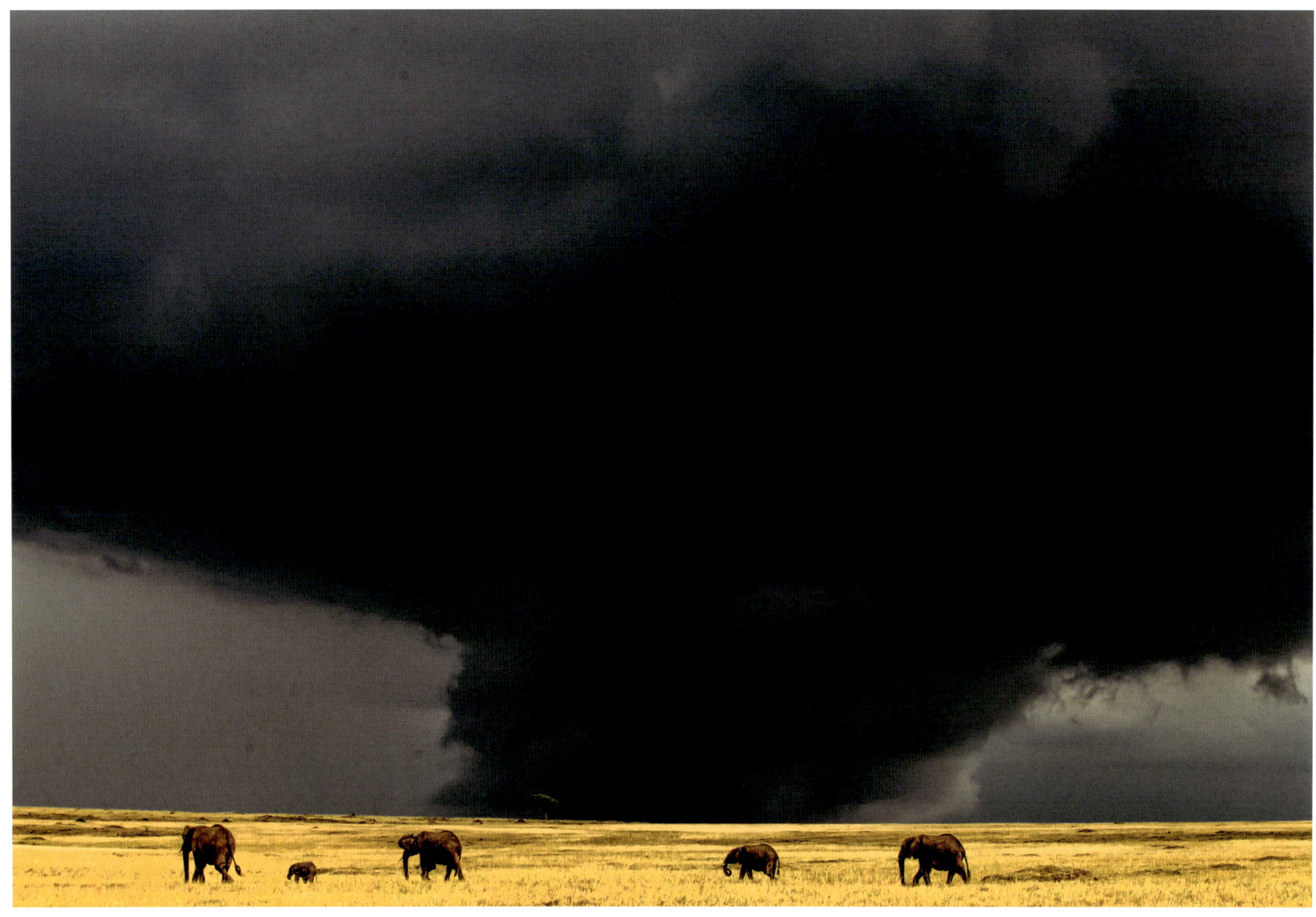

The Masai Mara / Serengeti ecosystem has the most dramatic skies in the world. Period. Not only are they spectacular but they occur almost every day. When photographing you need a big subject. Both these images required long and studious approaches. It was intoxicating and I must thank Charles Wandero for feeling the same as me that afternoon. Asante Mkubwa.

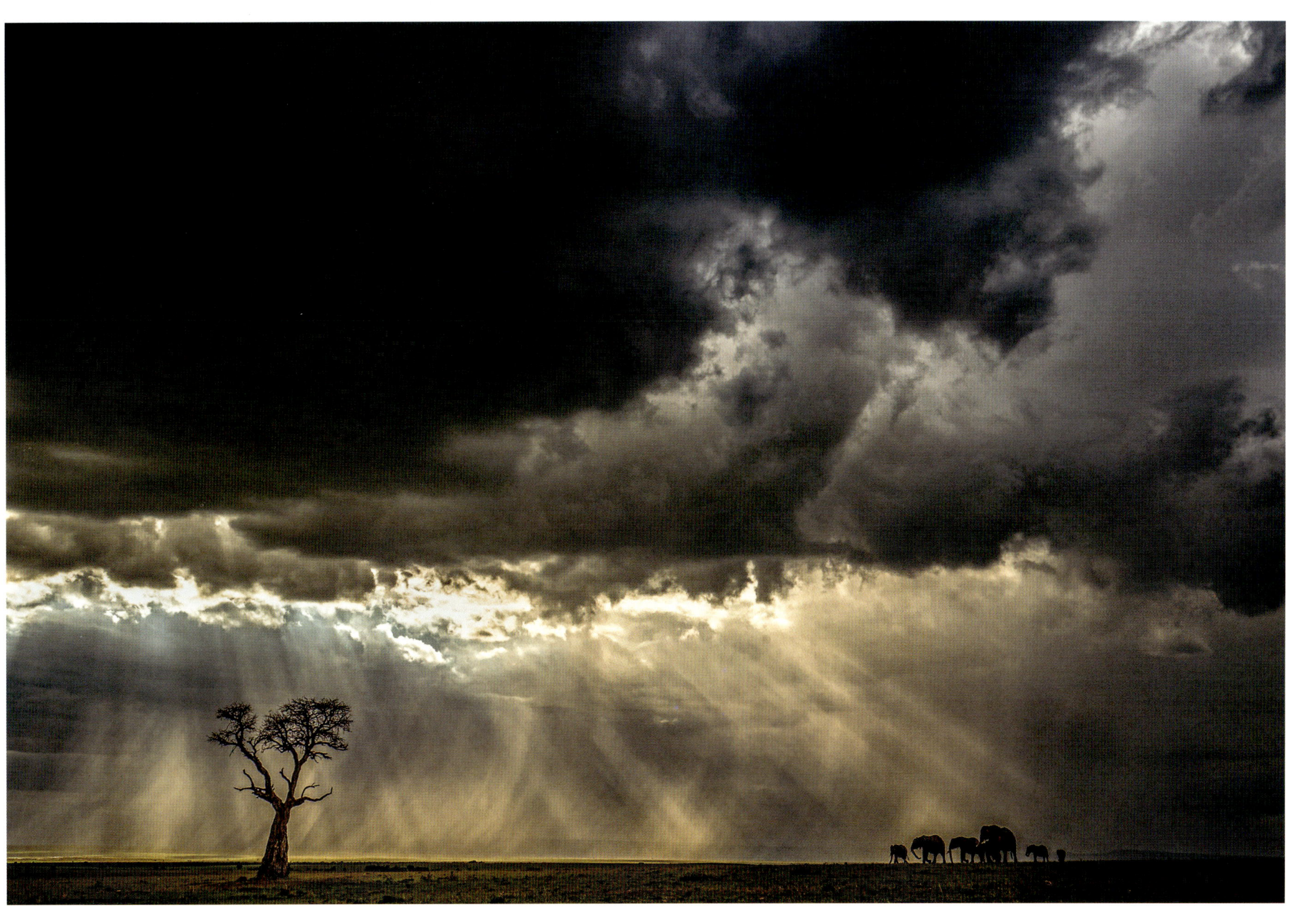

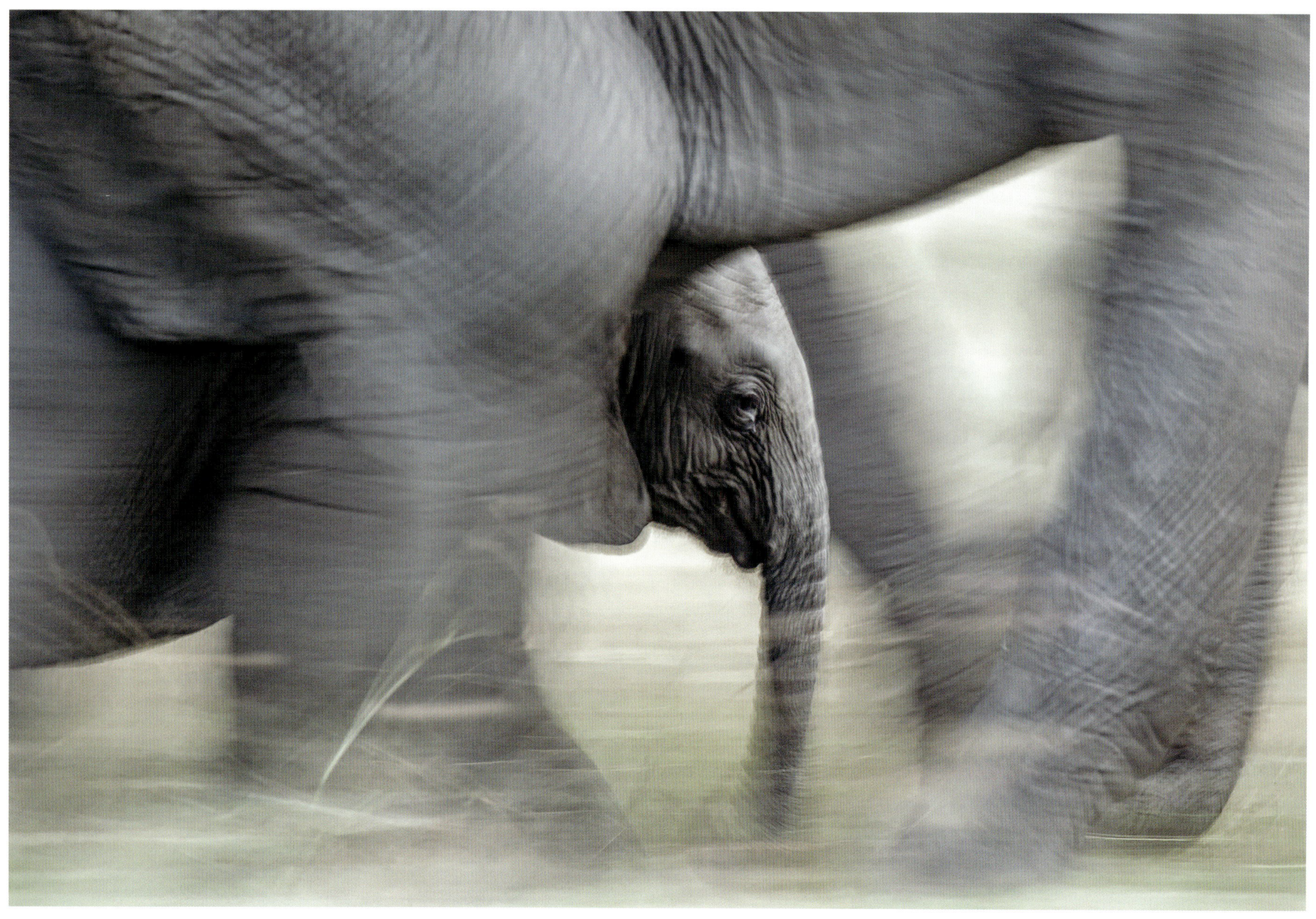

A tiny calf in Olare Conservancy late in the day, photo taken at a quarter of a second. When they can fit beneath their mums, you know they are under three months. Any elephant sighting is a good sighting, particularly when you think what they still endure.

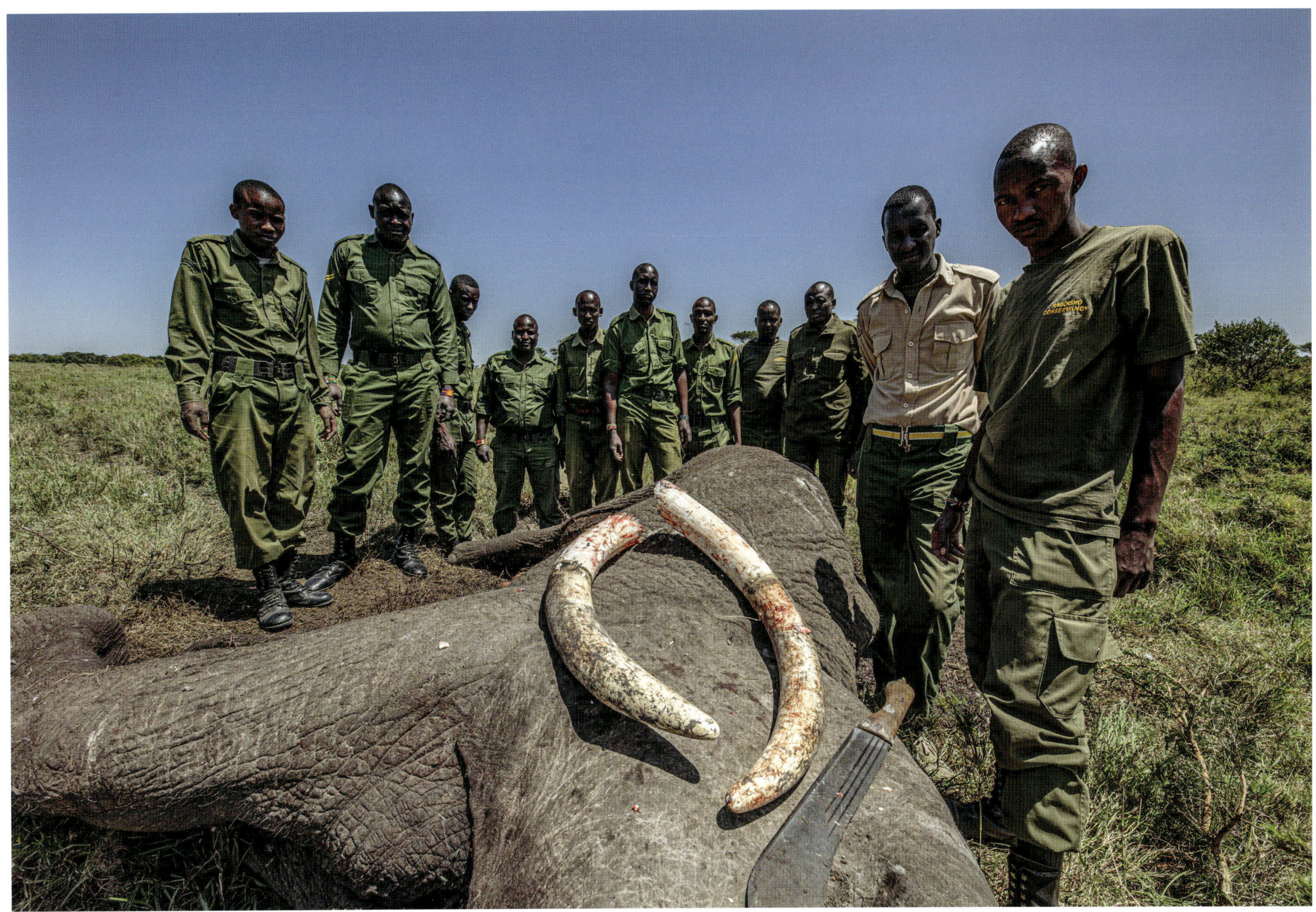

Sobering, distressing but also, in this case, natural. A conservancy emptied by the absurd restrictions of Covid – an illness that barely touched Kenya physically yet bankrupted its tourism – except a few guests who jumped through numerous Byzantine hoops to get their safari fix. Mid-morning and a swirling cloud of vultures blocked the sun momentarily, signifying a large kill. This was no kill but a recently deceased elephant, possibly from anthrax. The rangers were alerted and they showed up, sensitively but dispassionately removing the ivory – it was taken to the Kenya Wildlife Service in Nairobi. They posed for me over the carcass, knowing I was upset. I was unsure whether I should be photographing. However, this was not the poacher's bullet, it was not for the trinket stores in China and elsewhere, it was a natural death; many are not. Its remains were for the hyenas, hundreds of them.

ONE
TWO
THREE
FOUR
FIVE
SIX
SEVEN
EIGHT
NINE

As a youngster on my first safari in the mid '80s I saw a leopard elegantly descend from a fallen acacia tree and dance off into the dust and haze of a parched Amboseli National Park. I was hooked. Obsessed would be a more accurate term. I waited another eight years to see another in the wild as the skin trade was leaving a permanent scar on this cat's future. For many years I would drive hours just on the off-chance of a fleeting glimpse of one of their tails, but fortunately the Mara Conservancies have changed all that. Proper guardianship and appropriated fees, as well as diligent auditing, off-road driving and vehicle limits would make a difference to any wilderness.

The animal's enigmatic nature and elusiveness have helped keep it off the most persecuted list, but now it appears it faces fresh dangers. Tigers are becoming more challenging to hunt and are increasingly better protected. Leopards are easier to find and without impregnable barricades around them. They are becoming a common substitute for tiger body parts in the international market, being deliberately mis-labelled so they can slake the wanton and craven desires for 'traditional' (that word again) medicine, luxury trinkets and trophies. Over 12,000 were poached and traded in the three years during Covid and they have been wiped out from 75 per cent of their natural habitat across Africa, Asia and the Middle East.

Africa is not without blame, and the anodyne and piss-weak laws concerning captive breeding of cats in South Africa has helped fuel this scandalous trade. YouTube has clips of 'brave' hunters shooting baited leopards off branches. They should burn.

Nothing raises the plains pulse like the report of a leopard; many safari fans openly admit narcotic-like addictions with this dappled assassin. They are as enigmatic as they are beautiful and I've often wondered, does anyone really think they look better as a rug than prostrated on a gnarled branch? Exactly.

▷ Give me fever: I had driven for twelve years past this mature fever tree, never seeing a leopard. Patience isn't a virtue, it's a must. Finally, one afternoon it delivered, with Fig, a leopard unlike any I've ever known. Background, subject and something else – the mostly impossible trinity – in this case the gnarled diamond of trunk delivered. Conservancy game viewing from the highest table. She barely moved for half an hour; one guest of mine took over 400 images … that few?

LEOPARD

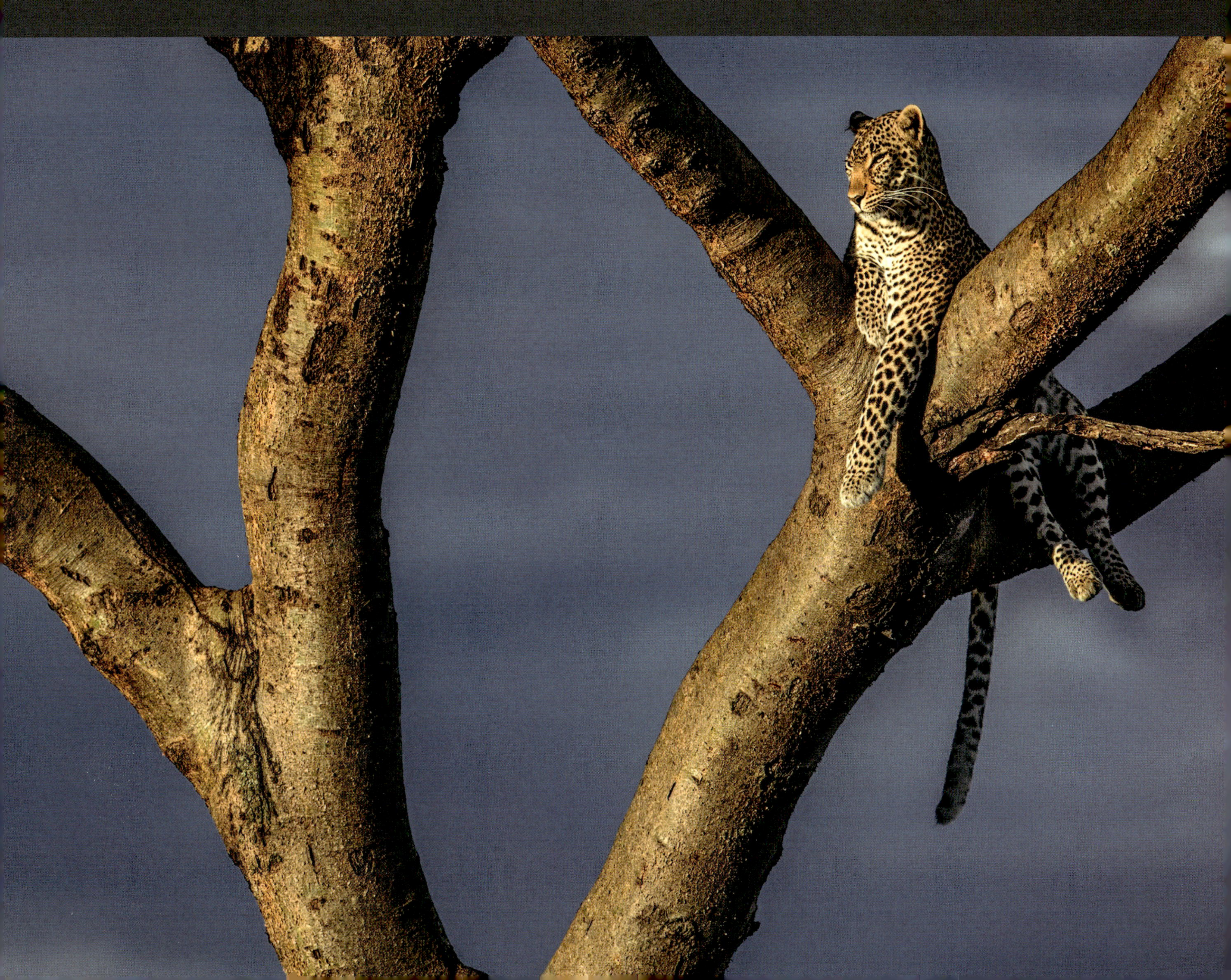

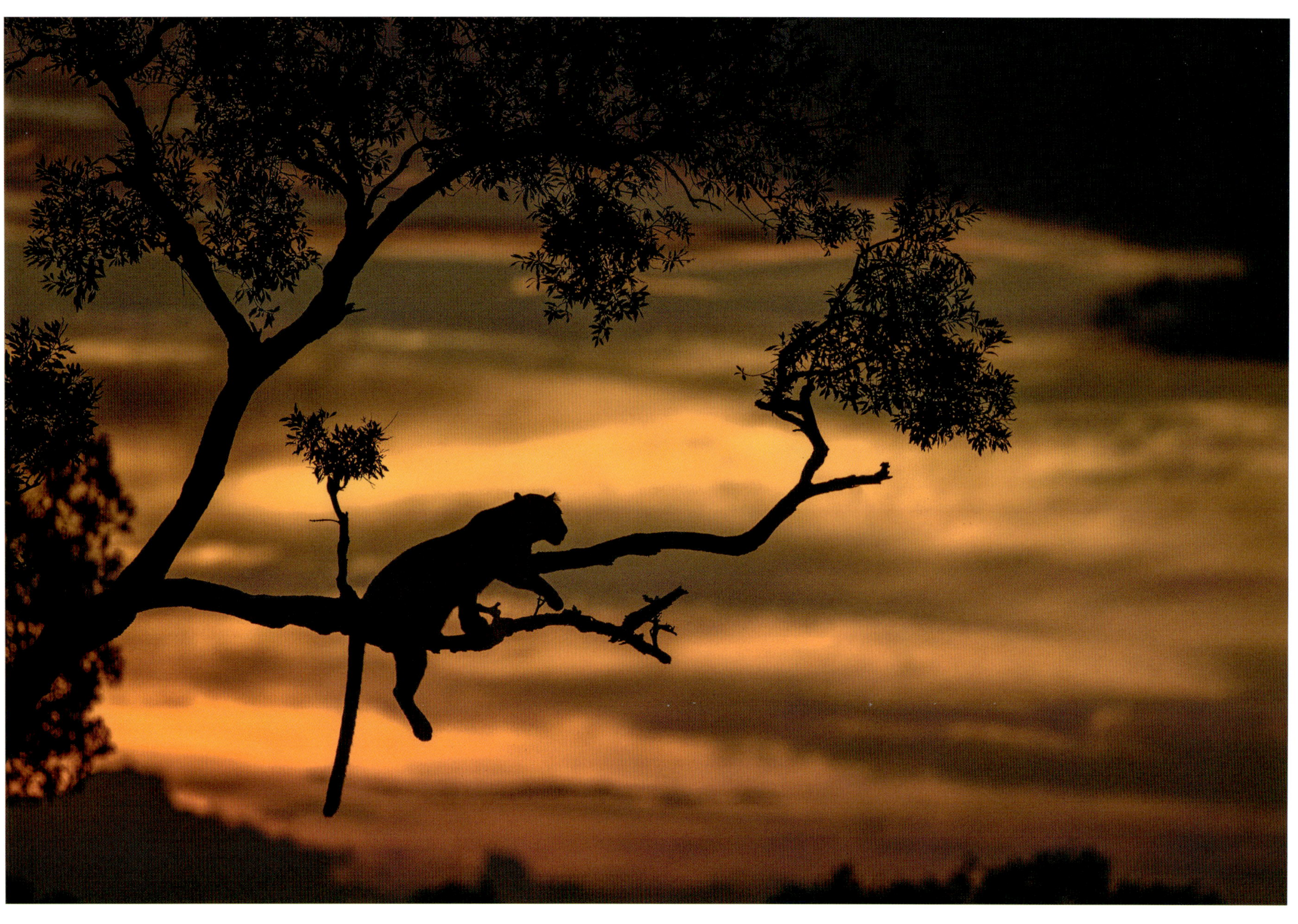

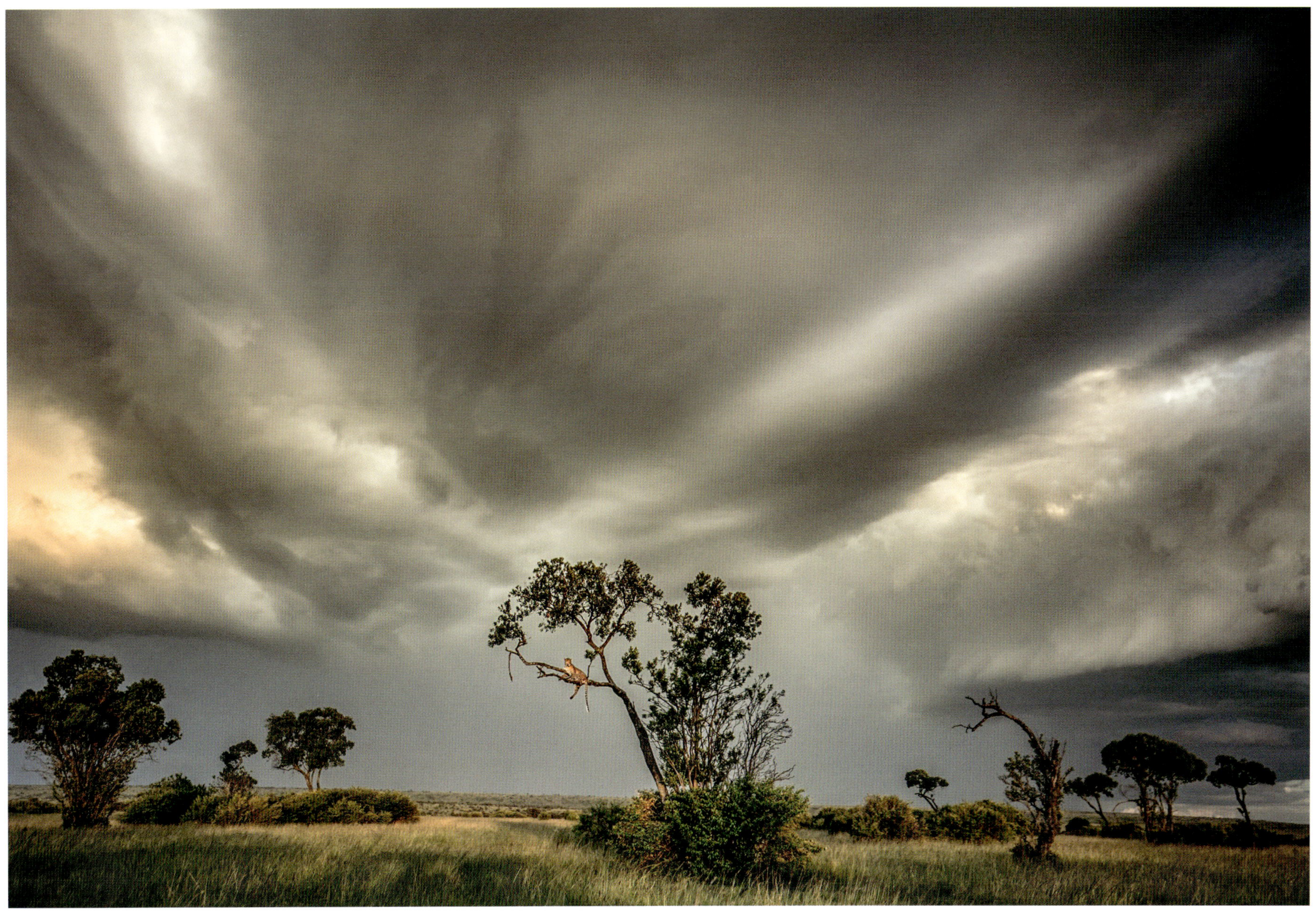

During Covid the grass was high not just because of El Niño in 2020/21 but because deploying and managing the cows to keep it down was challenging without money and manpower. I was guiding two wonderful Swiss guests who didn't tell us they were in the business, realising how parlous everything was. They paid full price and a sole-use vehicle … immeasurably classy. That afternoon all the Swiss banks couldn't have delivered such a bounty. Patrick Koriata somehow found this leopard and it obliged him by clambering up the nearest tree. Then the storm began. Just before the heavens opened and the rare lenticulars ganged up, we drove to the other side to try a sunset image; for a second I stopped with my wide angle. We nearly drowned on the return to Bush Camp. Asante Patrick, not for the first time.

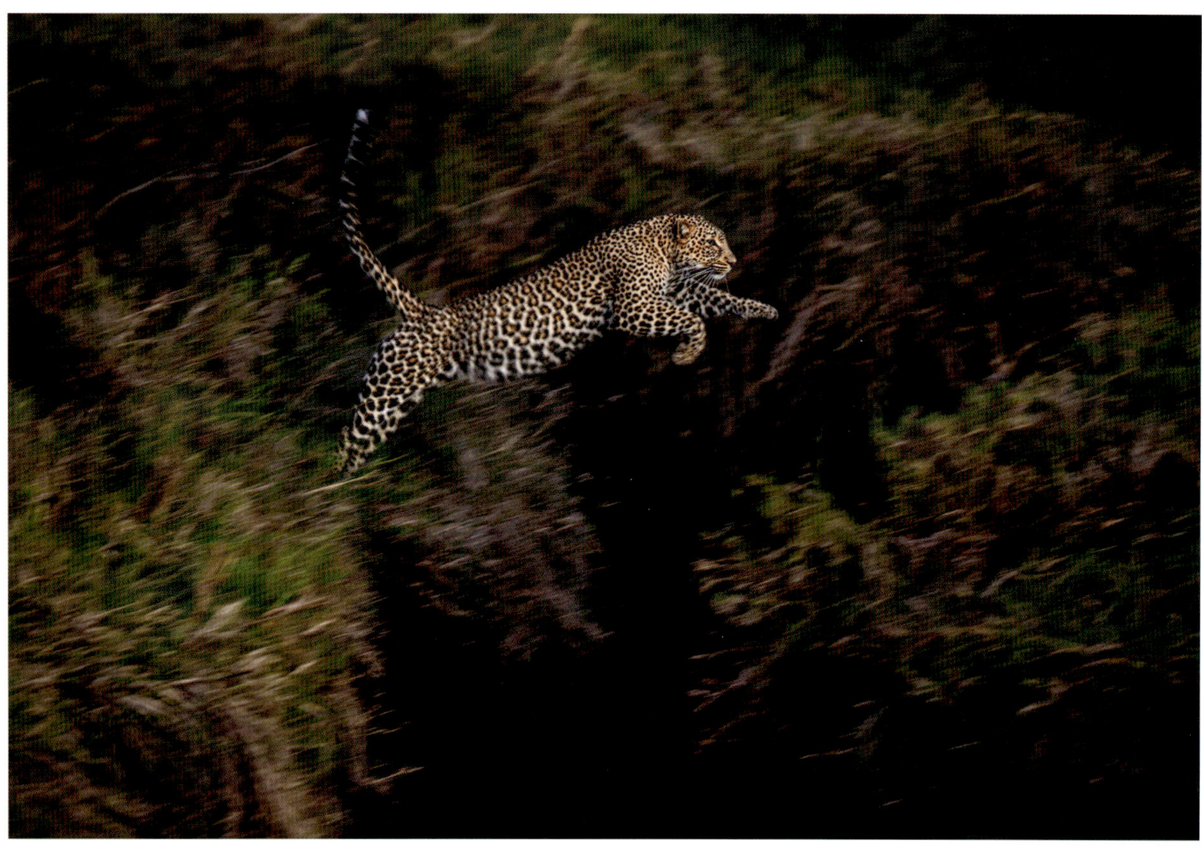

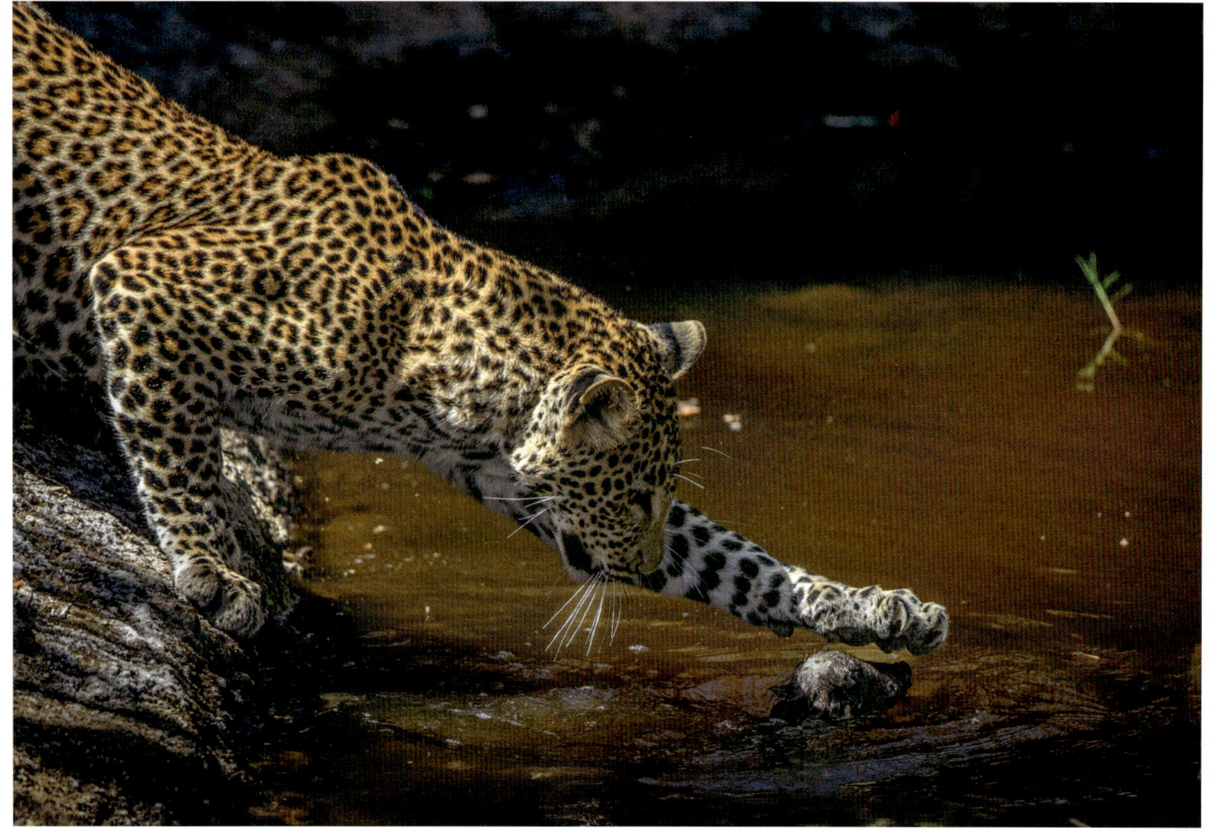

Action is the stiffest currency with cats, particularly the oft catatonic leopard. A slow shutter speed catching one leaping over a river is one thing, but a young male chasing piglets down a burrow and then into the water before being bullied off by the outraged sow (who then lost one of the youngsters to lions) was a remarkably foolish first hunt.

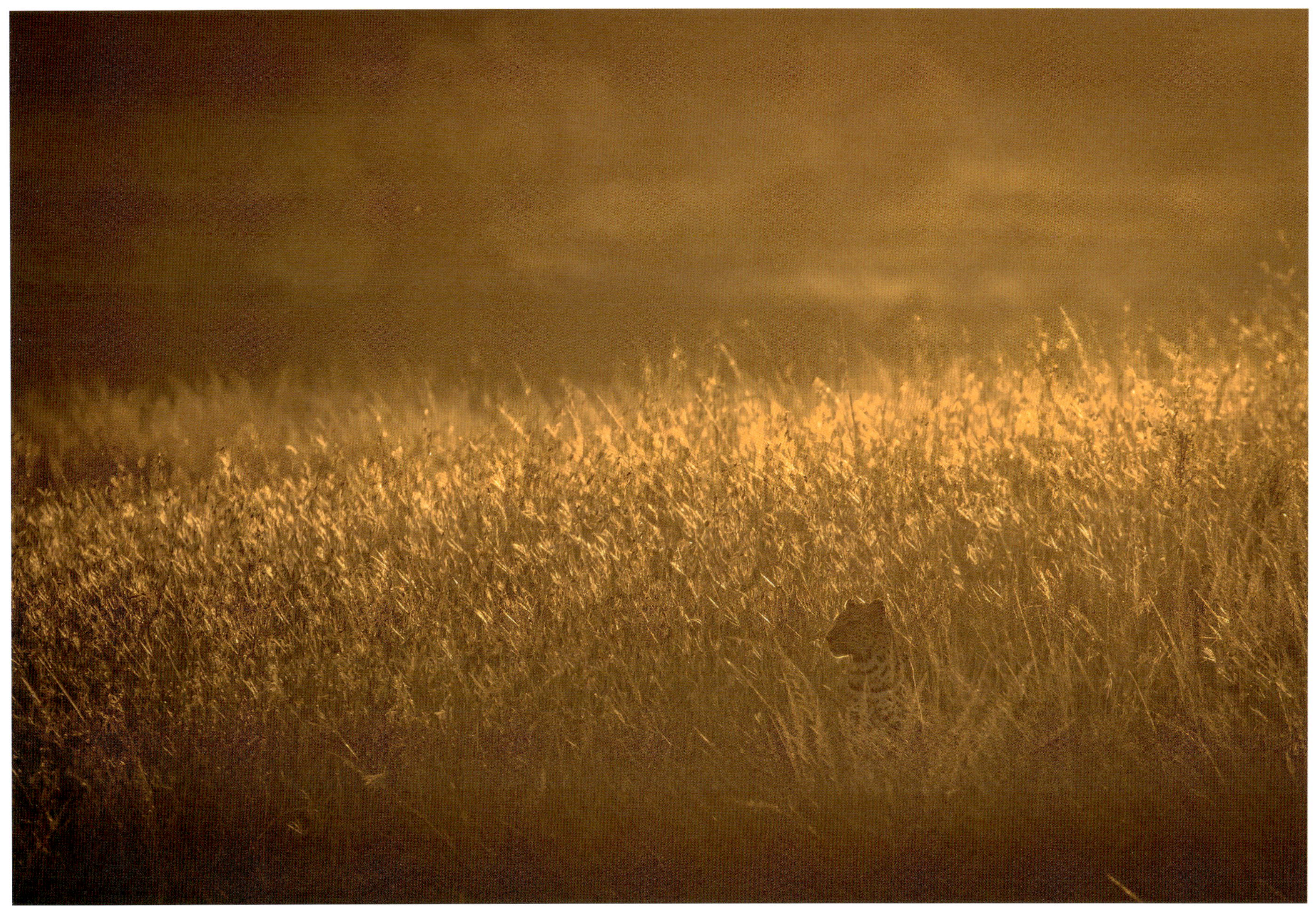

Field of gold: a late Mara North matinee with a leopard that refuses to go quietly. Nalangu is now seventeen, a remarkable age for a leopard; again, a testimony to conservancies and what they stand for.

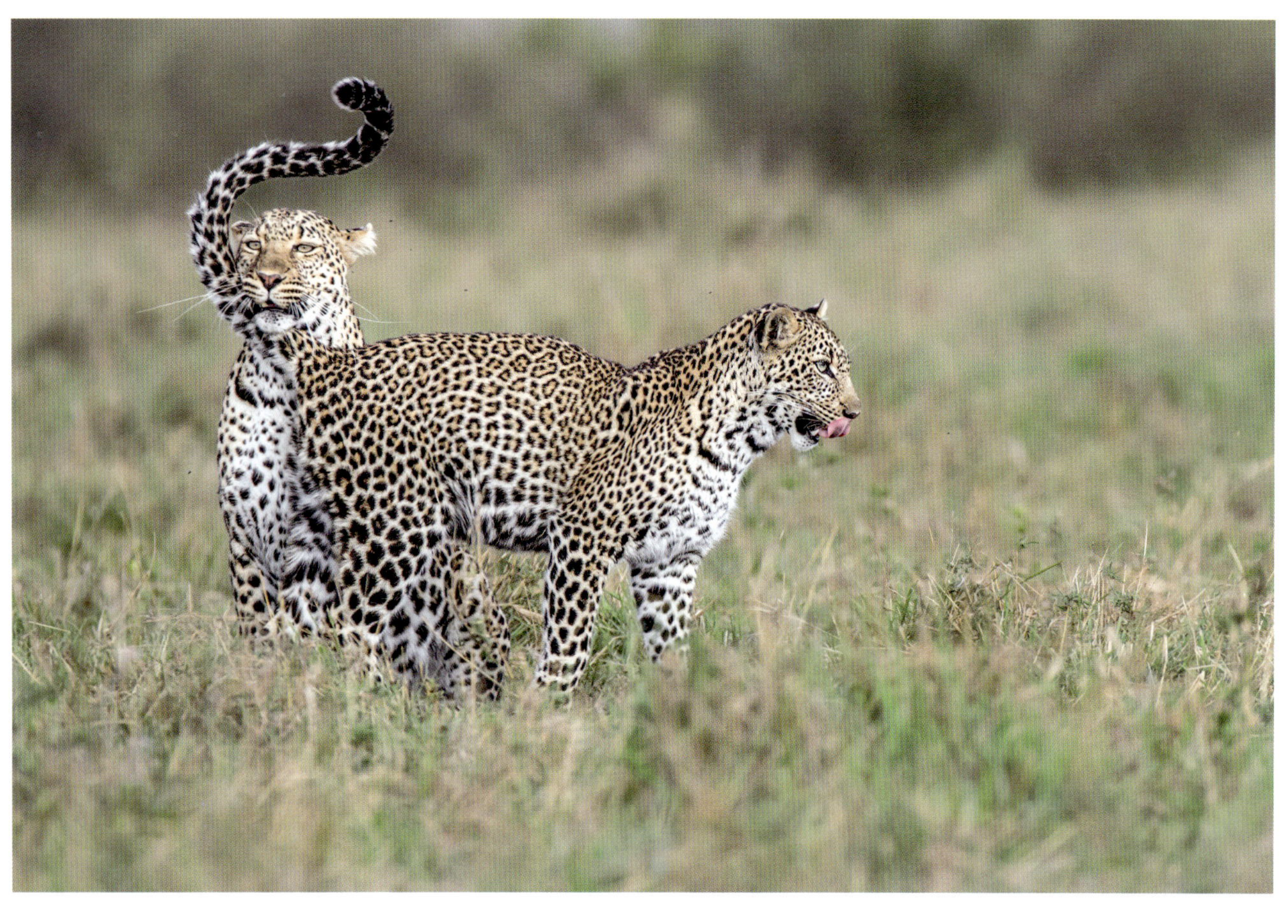

Trick of the tail: a gorgeous intimate moment deep in the Masai Mara reserve during Covid when we had virtually the whole place to ourselves, as whole economies were butchered by ludicrous and cynical travel and health warnings.

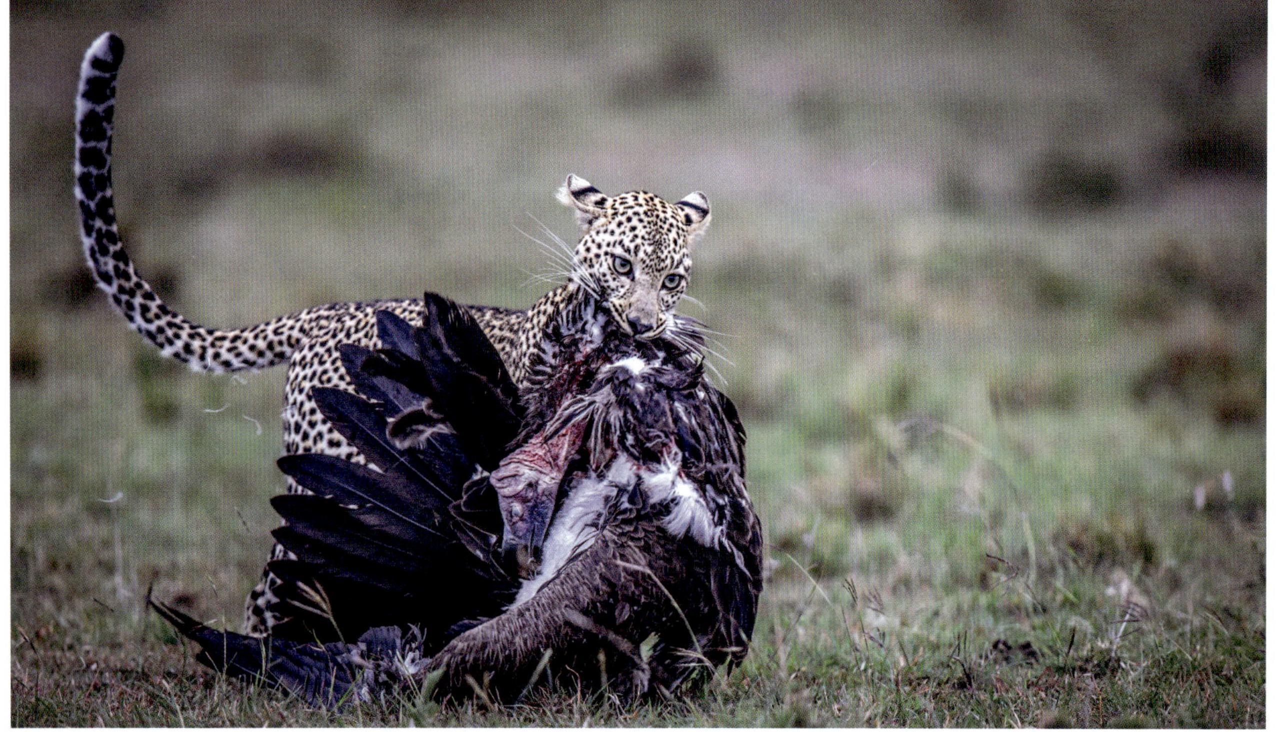

A young leopard dashing up a whistling thorn to grab a lappet-faced vulture is not only unheard of, it is also absurd. There was no way in the world this fastidious cat was going to eat this scavenger and it proved the case, but it showcased the cat's hunting DNA. Sometimes, rarely though, record shots are permissible … I have checked with friends all over Africa and the internet to see examples of this behaviour, but so far it appears unique. Good job James, even better job Sapit.

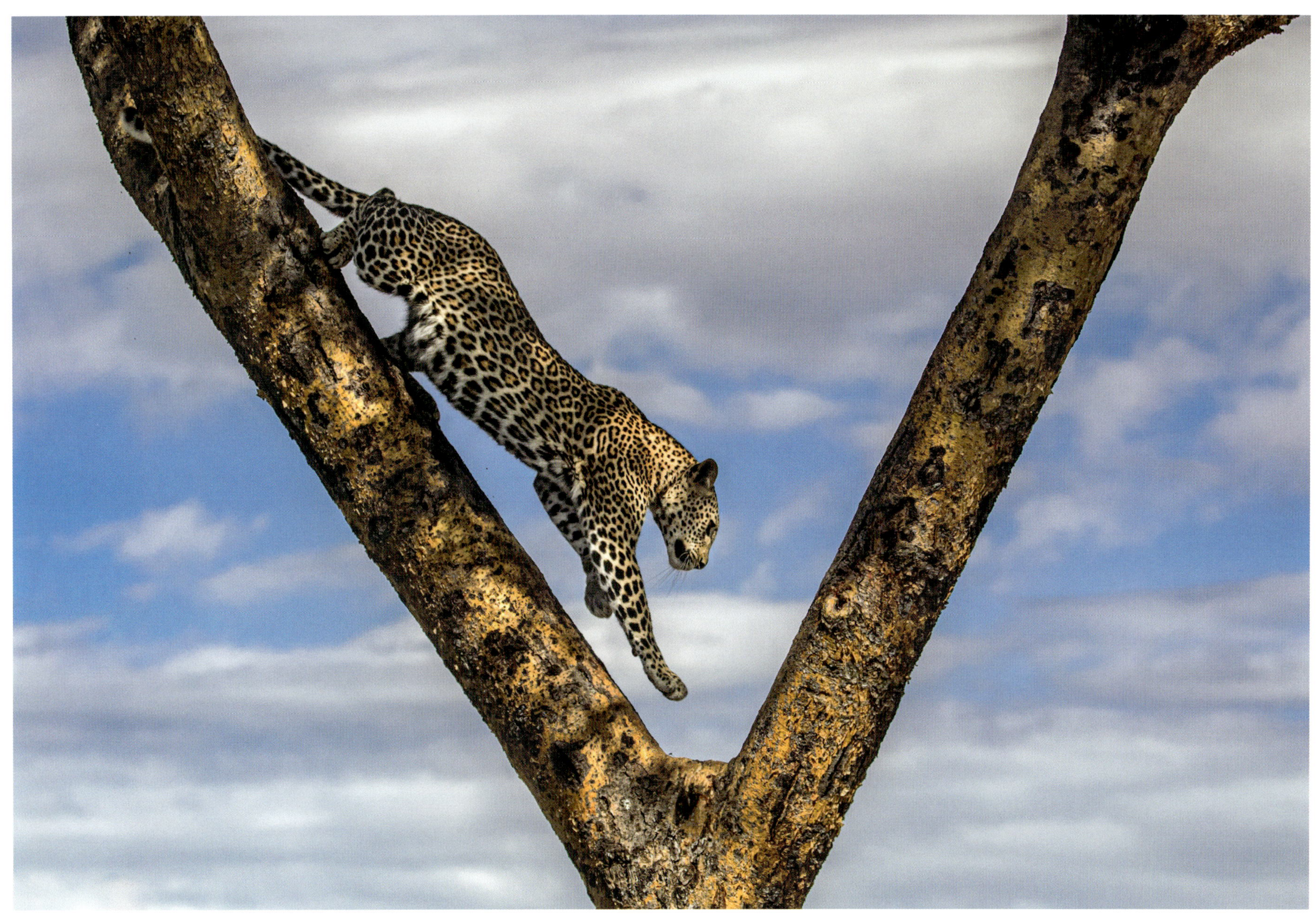

'Unique' is a childishly over-used and almost always erroneously employed epithet. Not here. I'd never seen a leopard up this perfect fever tree until Tito duly obliged. Two days later elephants pushed this down, hence 'unique' … probably.

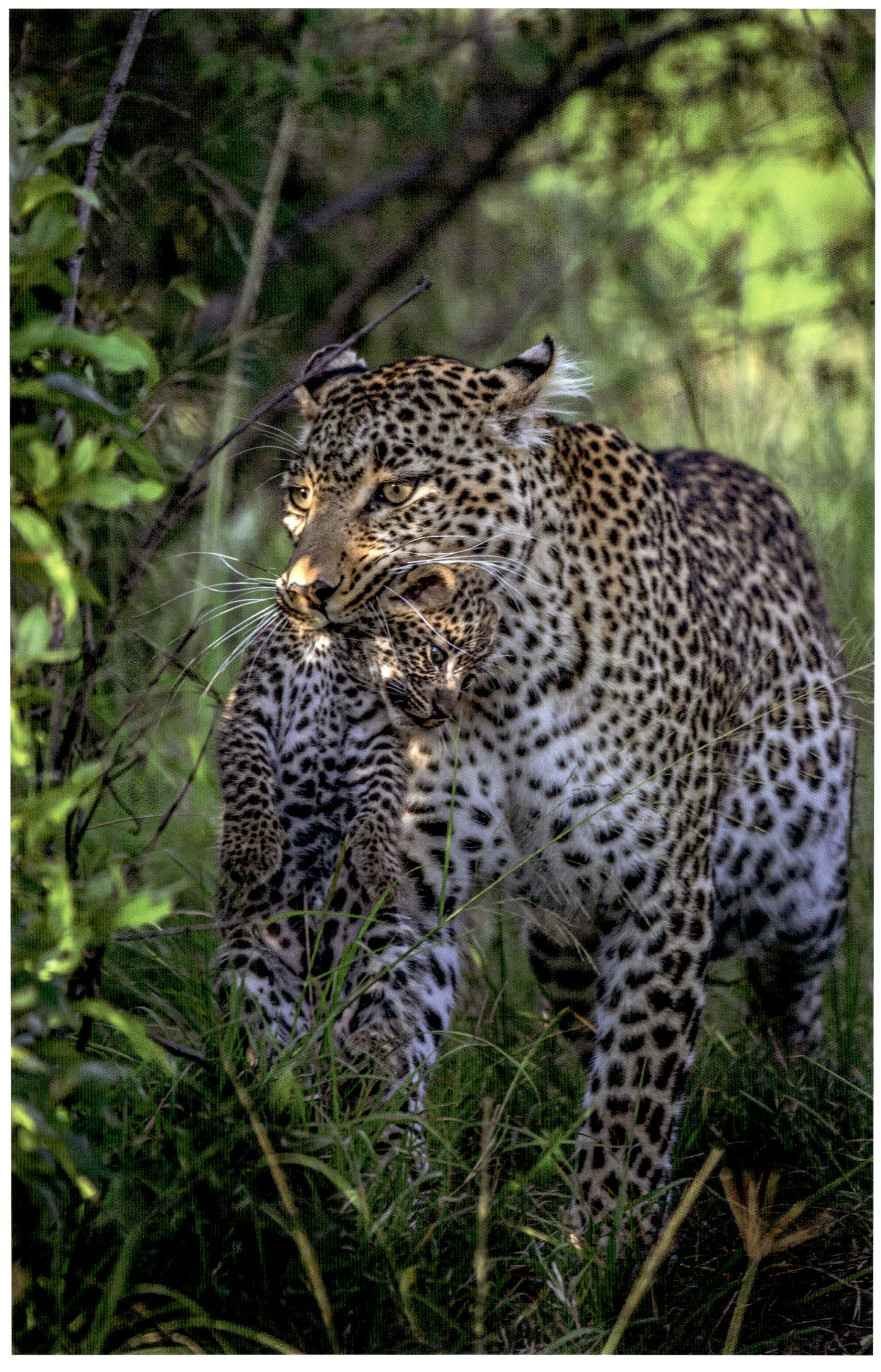

Carry-on baggage:
Boxing Day 2020 –
of course I remember it!

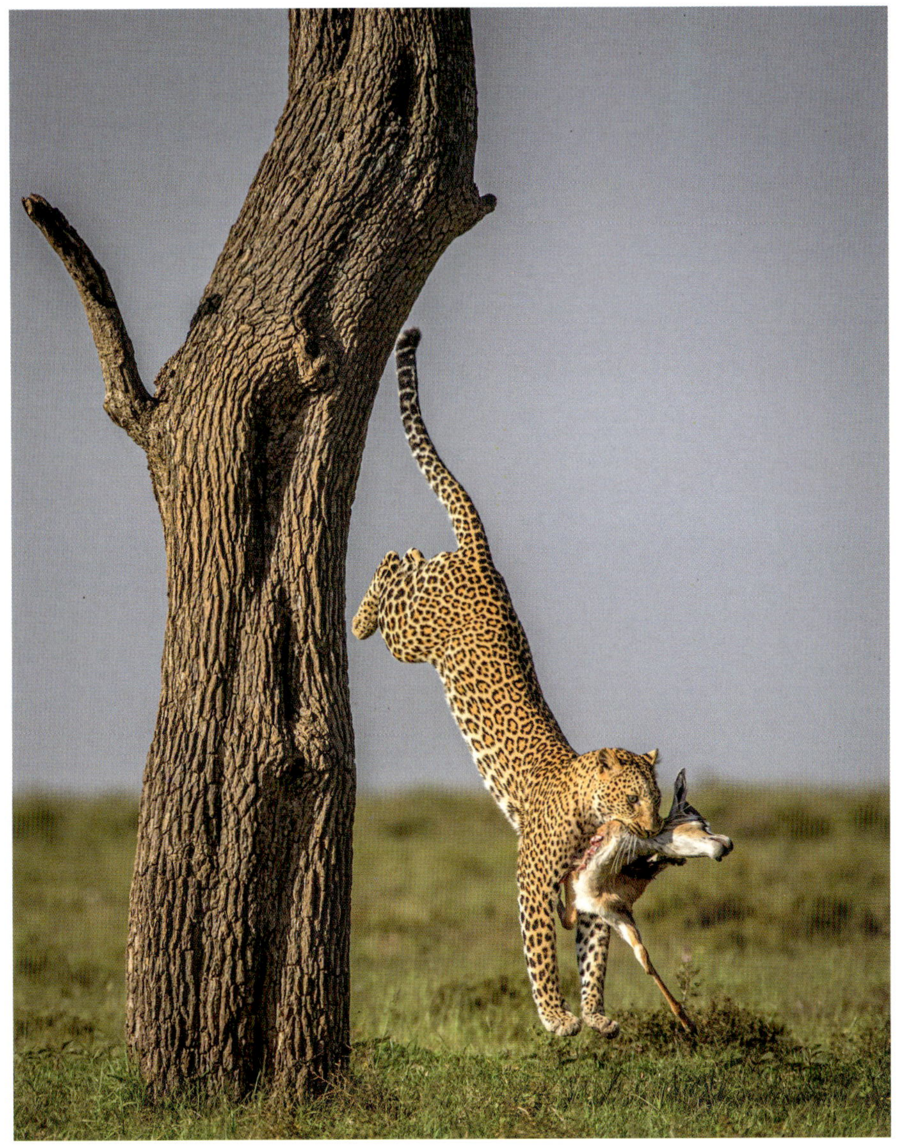

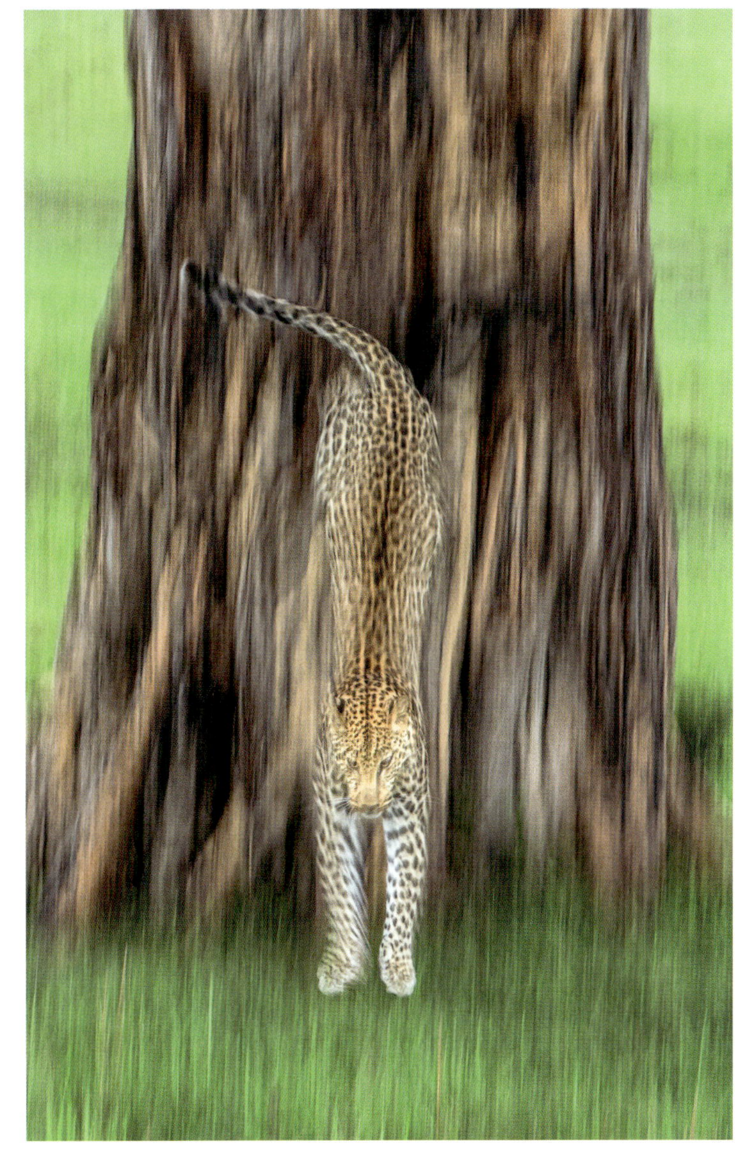

Descent of a woman: the previous evening we'd lost Fig, a favourite daughter, favourite leopard and put bluntly a whole conservancy's meal ticket. She was killed by a male lion whilst feeding in a gully. Would I have stepped in if I'd been there? An emphatic yes. Anyone who wants to piously preach (and on TV they love this sanctimonious bilge) about never getting involved and wants to argue with me on this, bring it on. We have caused 95 per cent of these animals' problems so surely we should redress the balance for our past trespasses? It was like losing a member of the family. I have never seen my guides so distressed, nor guests. This was the following morning: a younger female moving her breakfast down an open acacia. It helped salve the grief we and thousands of others, who let us know, were feeling. Spotted cats in tourism areas for wildlife are the most viable commodity by far. And Fig was so much more than a commodity.

Merci Florian and Sonia. Not once but twice these two French Olympians arrived during Covid. This fig tree has perhaps the most appealing trunk in the whole conservancy. For two hours we watched this young leopard with his larder in the leafy crown. He had three separate dishes. Finally, as it got dark he descended, hence the very slow speed.

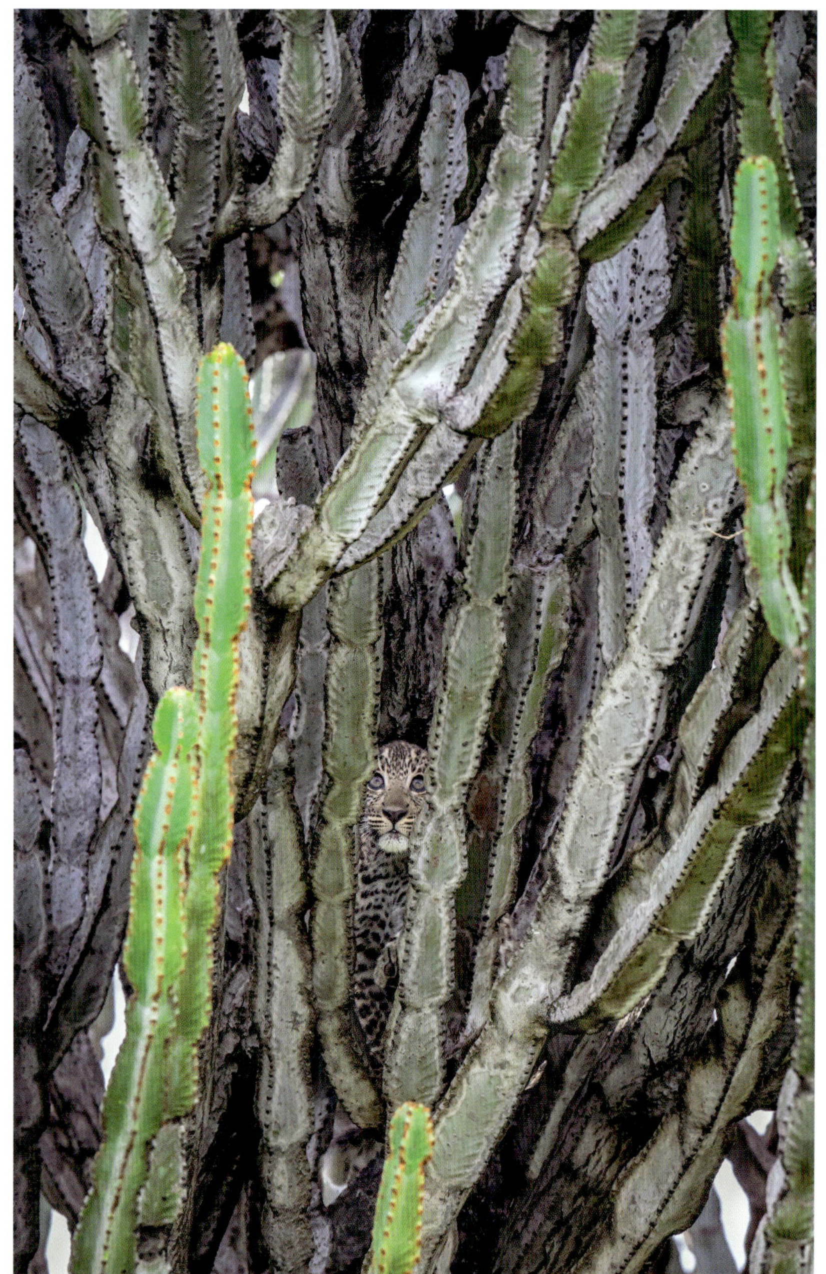

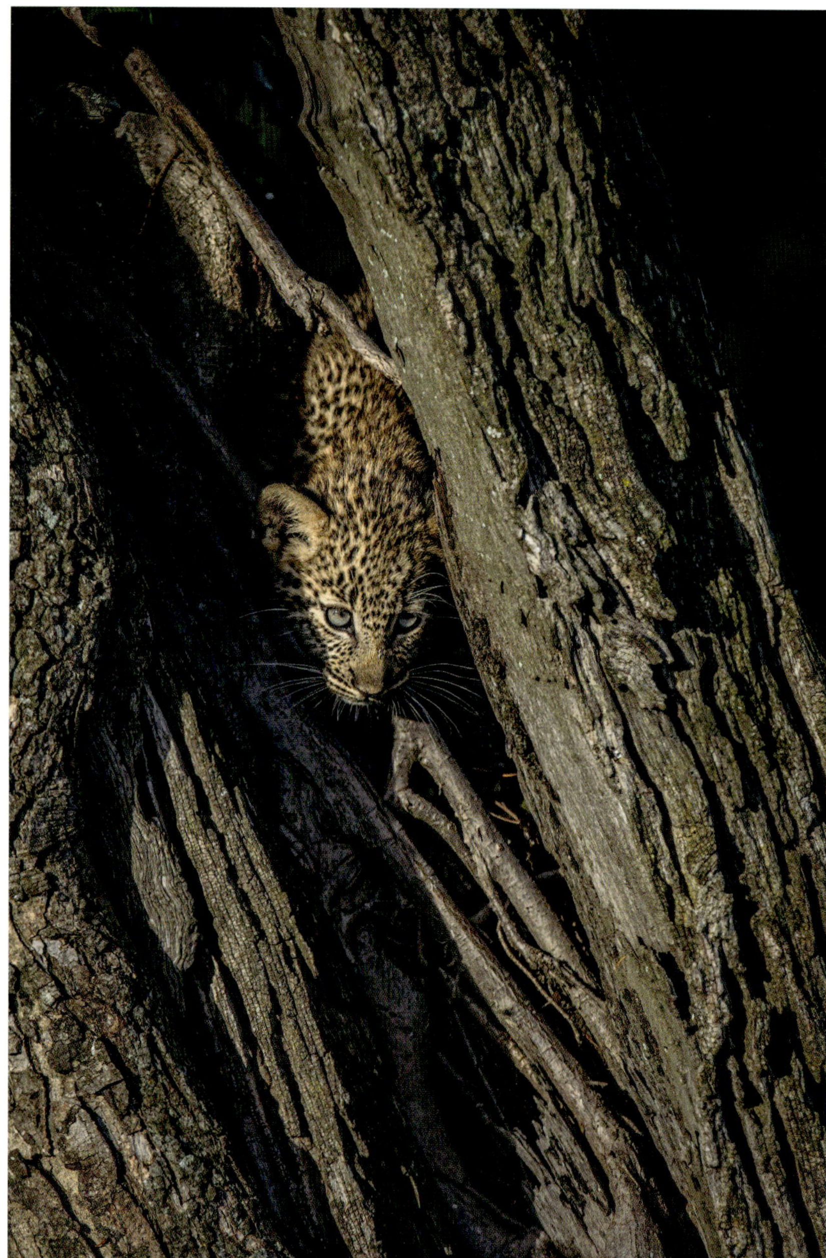

It is both ludicrous and indeed absurd to chuck human reactions and idiosyncrasies on to the animal kingdom. Tito, a fabled leopard in this part of Olare Conservancy, was prostrated on a branch nearby as her young cub was marooned in a giant euphorbia cactus. For two hours. One or two guests – who had perhaps not fully swallowed the faunal code – suggested this was poor motherhood. It was anything but. The cub finally tumbled down onto a croton bush. They have to learn. When I hear the often understandable emotions and concern for a creature, I smile; when I hear advice given (often with that Shoreditch bray), normally from Hugo, Arabella or Tobias, to hunting predators I openly laugh.

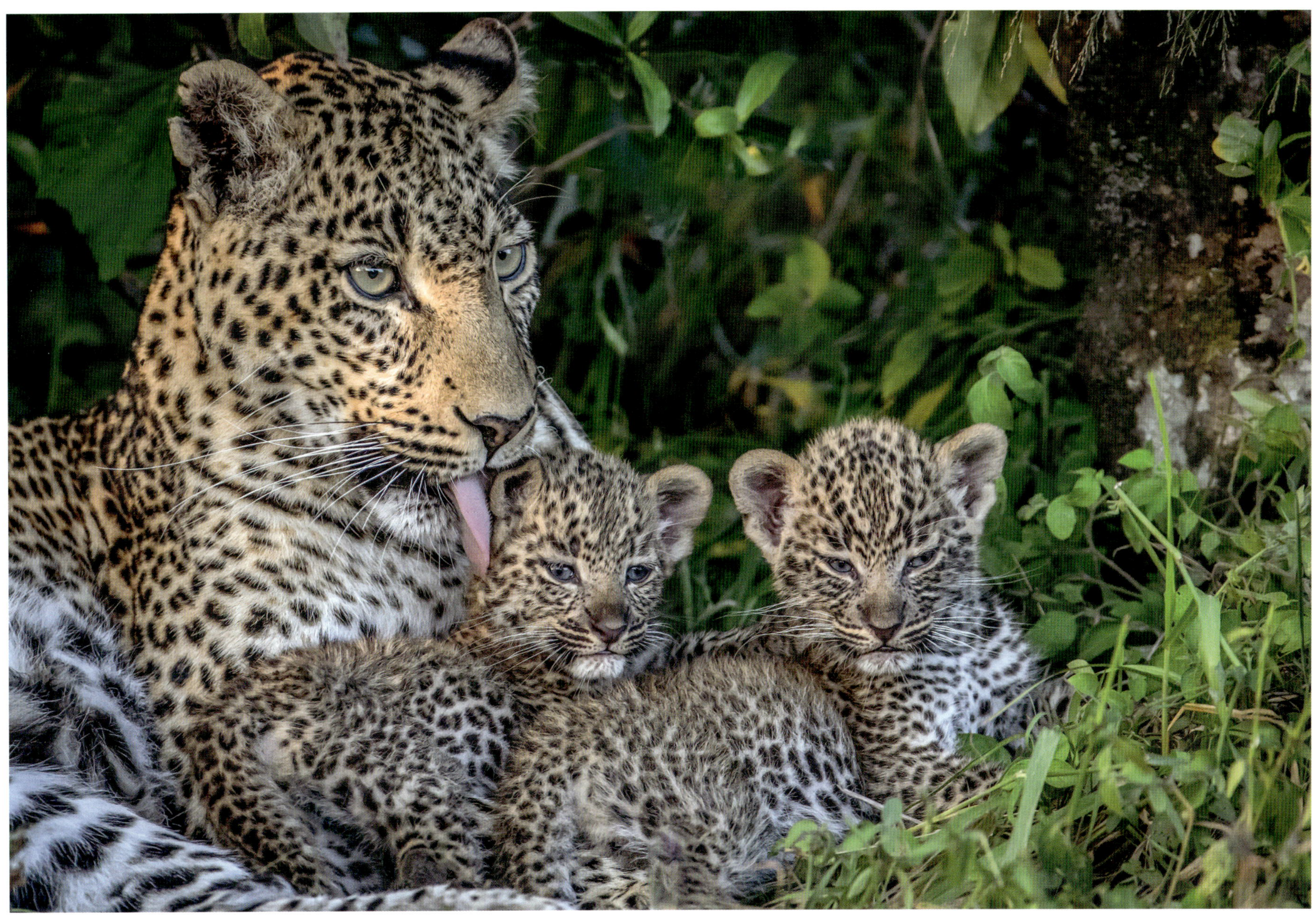

Boxing Day again. Fig again. Single parent family. No skill in pushing the shutter button, all the work is done before. Asante James. Again.

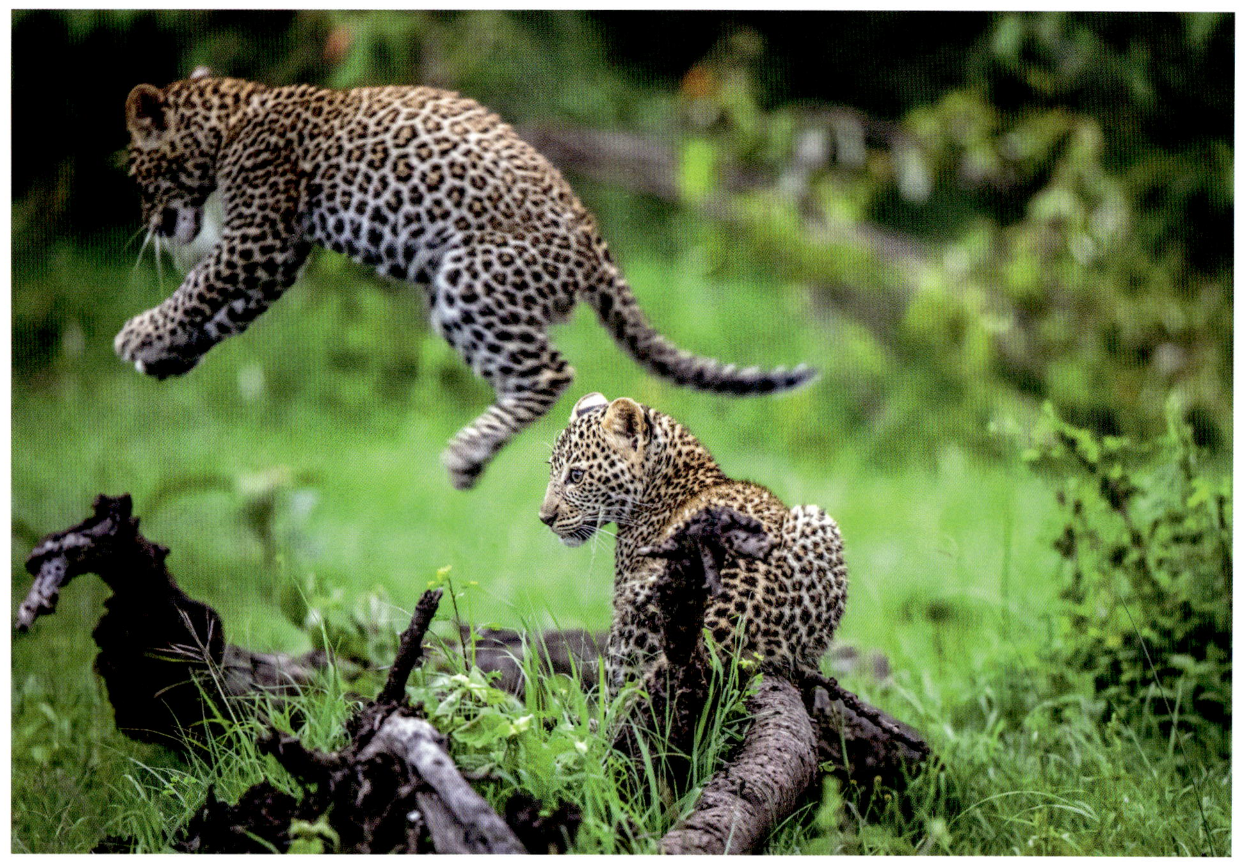

Leap of leopard: when you have sensitivity not cupidity, responsibility not exploitation and largesse not greed, you have a chance, a possibility. I may sound one-eyed but thousands in Kenya agree on conservancies, where every stakeholder benefits. Leopard cubs playing like this is not commonplace, but it is not only more likely in these precious parcels of wildlife nirvana but it is also more enjoyable without monstrous vehicle pressure.

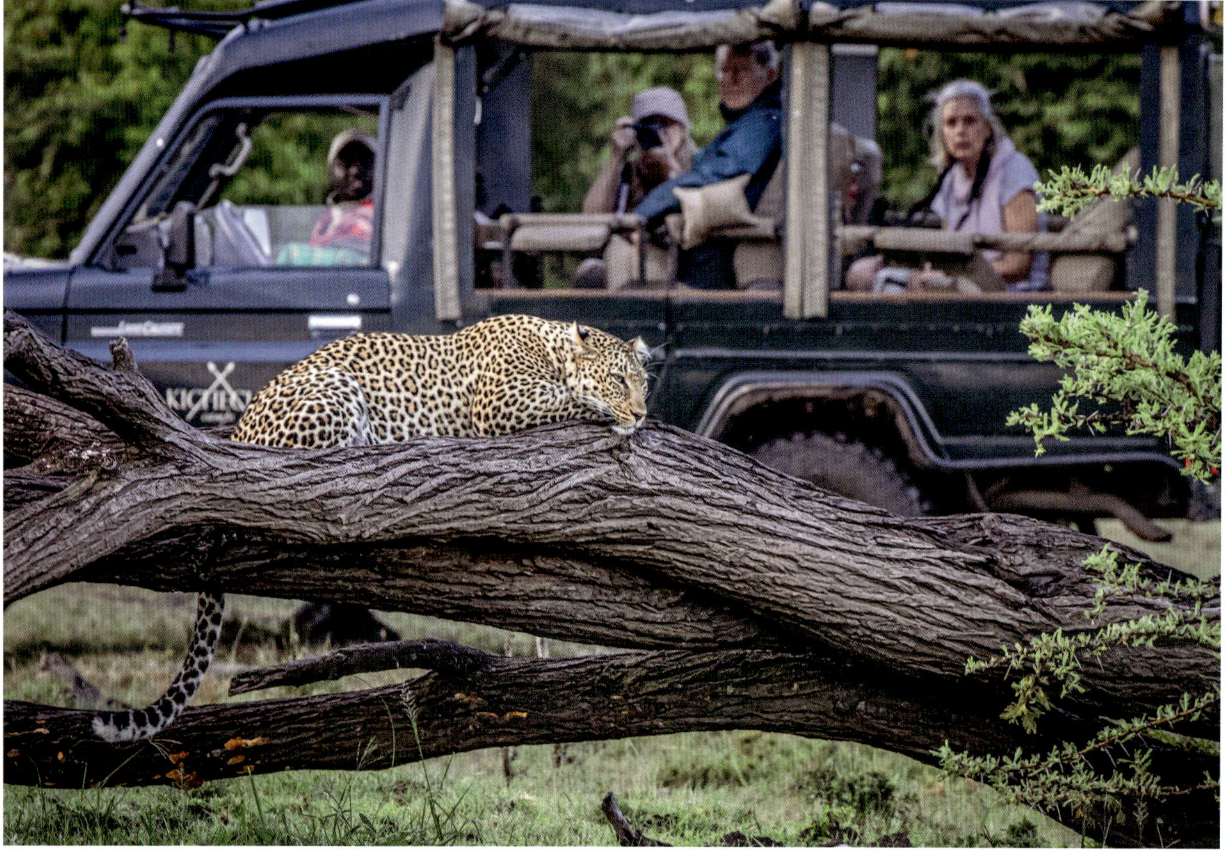

The tourism grail: one leopard moulded into a fallen trunk. One vehicle. Zero stress. Zero crowds. This is why the conservancies were started. To those at the vanguard – particularly Greg, Jake, Mohanjeet and others – I salute you. It was worth the pain.

Little did we know in January 2020 that we would be almost calling time on safaris for two years. So many people work so hard to ensure these animals' security, so when outside factors contribute it hurts. To those travellers who still came and those who arrived hours after nonsensical barriers were lifted, we salute you. Sarah and Andreas, you were two of them and that January we enjoyed the afternoon with this youngster and her mother with utter glee. This was three stops under if anyone really cares.

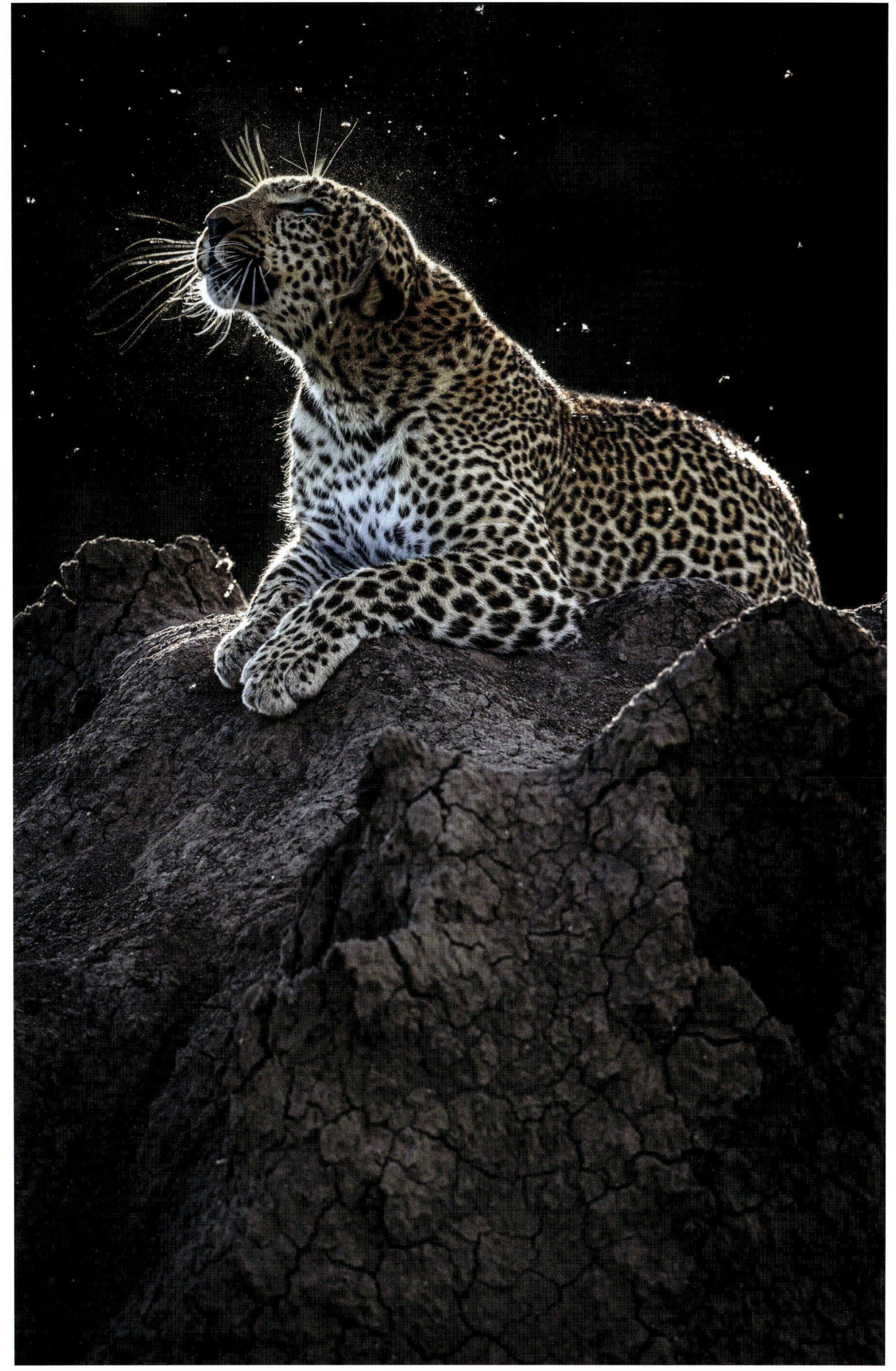

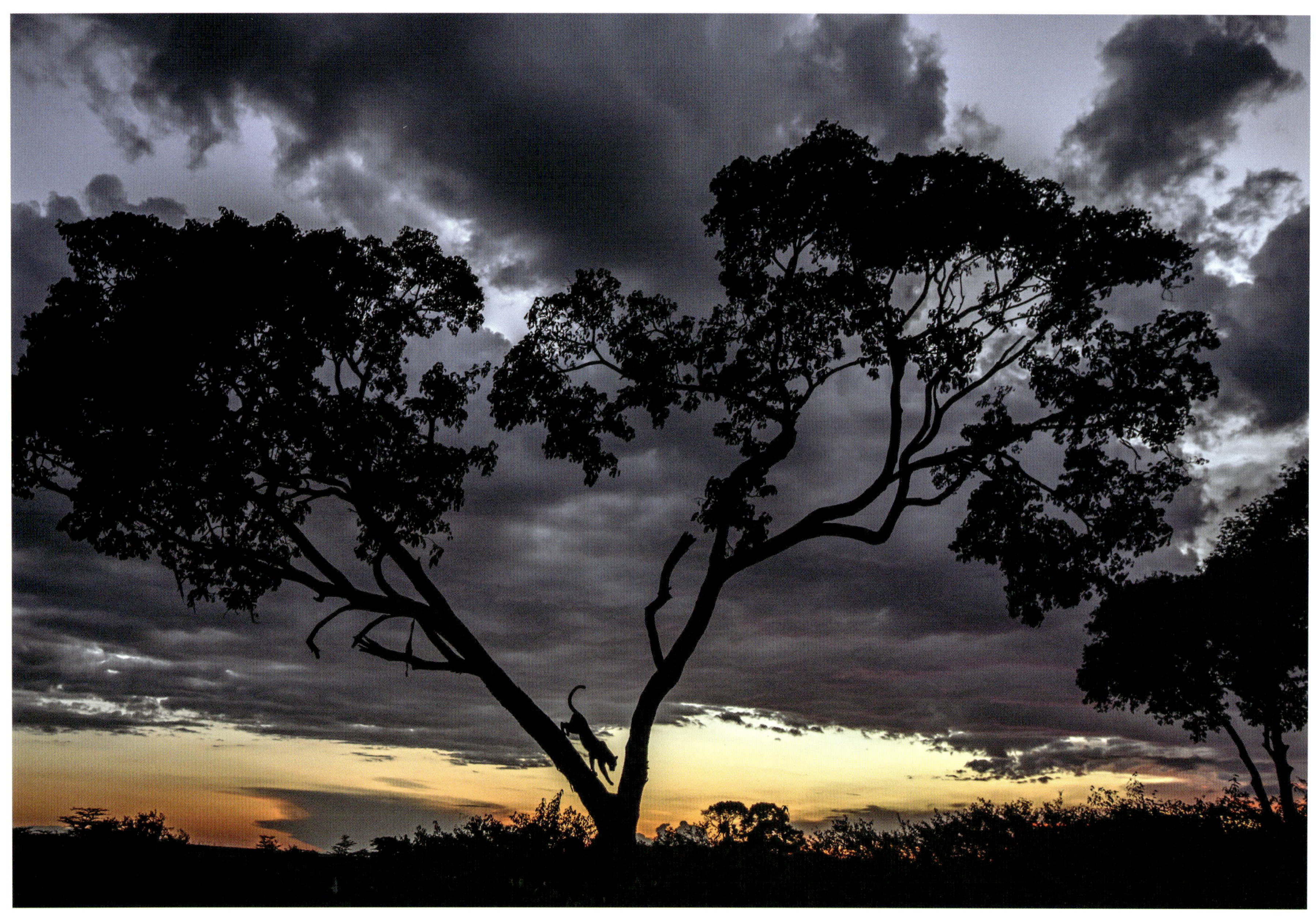

A moment before or a moment after and there is not the critical separation of the (correct) front foot and trunk. Just as I was congratulating myself on a bold gamble with a wide angle, I looked at my son's effort which was far superior.

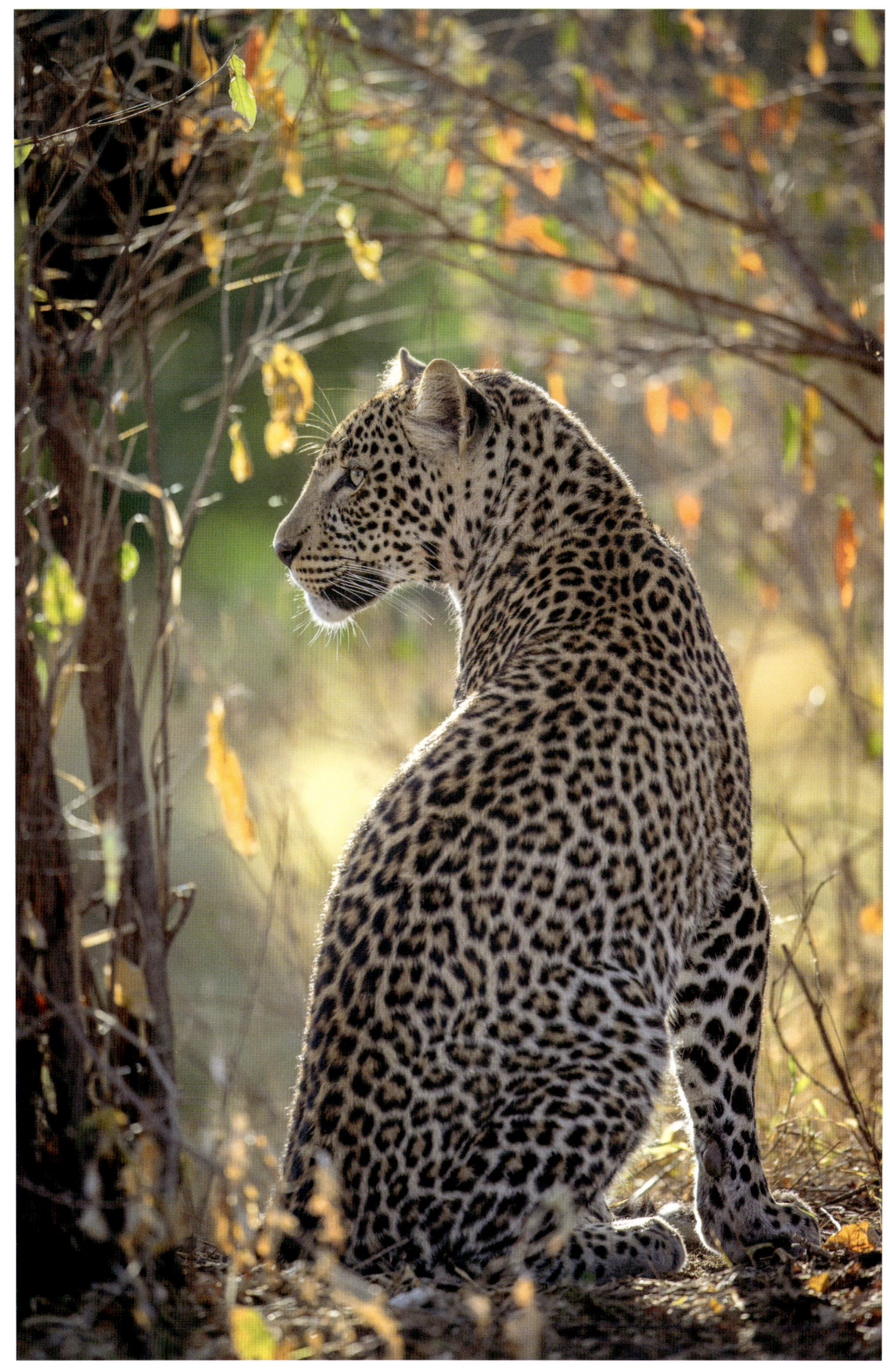

Jackie and Kathryn, this is for you, both hugely supportive of Kicheche Camps but also of all my other often over-ambitious campaigns. It was just one of those mornings and for two leopard obsessives, pretty much nirvana.

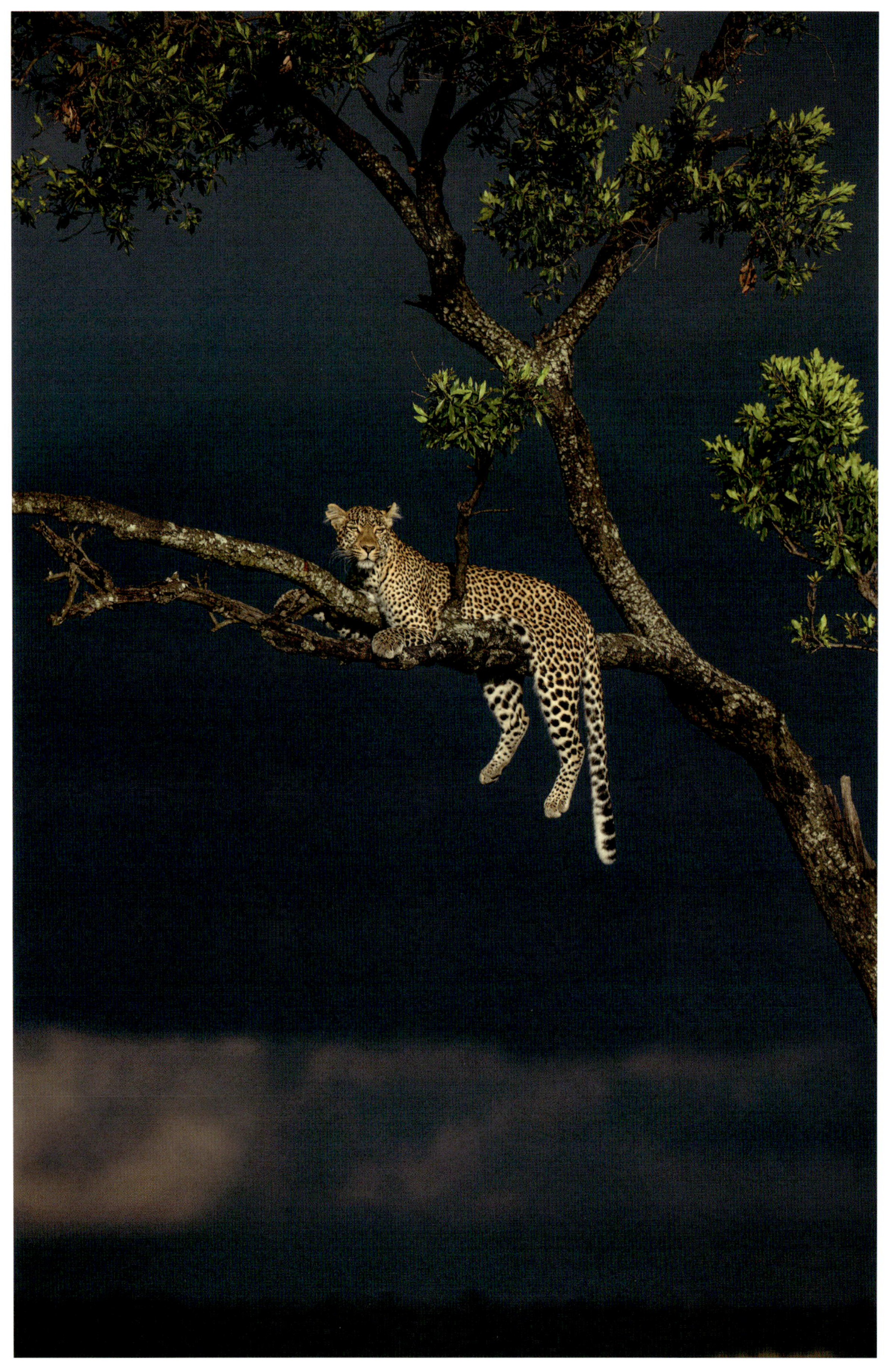

Finding a leopard like this is not hard, as she beams like a beacon in light only the Rift Valley delivers with any sort of meaningful frequency. It's finding her in 4-foot-high oat grass that requires the skill. Thank you mchawi Patrick (magician).

Boscia trees are my favourite, even more so than fever trees. These gnarly, hard-barked sentinels stud the plains with most standing exactly perpendicular to the ground. This one is rare, as it has an appealing lean to it. It is popular with lions and particularly cheetah boys who use it to view the larder. I christened it 'the tree of life'. It is a handle that has stuck. It took me ten years to find a leopard on it; a young one (Akira), frightened by some nearby lions. Yet again my younger son's efforts were better than mine. We've had weddings and other ceremonies there and one day we'll have ashes scattered from it. Mine.

ONE
TWO
THREE
FOUR
FIVE
SIX
SEVEN
EIGHT
NINE

All rhinos are endangered, black ones 'critically'. A disfiguring dehorn has done little to slow the trade. Let's be utterly clear, rhino horn is the same as compressed toenails, with zero medical provenance, yet it carries a street value per gram of more than first cut cocaine. It is consumed in China and Southeast Asia by people trying (and failing) to massage their pitifully flaccid libidos. It is utterly pathetic – of all peccadillos, trimming nails is yet to feature on Pornhub. Deep down, they must know it doesn't work; no one could be that stupid, but just in the same way foie gras is little different to simple pâté, people aren't consuming it because of its validity, they do so because it is so expensive. Gastronomic one-upmanship is both vulgar and destructive, but when it is a sex aid causing the slaughter of a species it is an unspeakable scandal. Whatever their reasons, they are destroying a mammal that will be gone in our lifetime unless drastic and bold measures are taken. You can't just leave it to the heroic but often under-equipped anti-poaching units.

These animals would have been history long ago, but fortunately in the '70s several heroes in Hchuluwi and Umfloxi Reserves recognised the issues and the world was alerted. Sadly, poachers now are far better equipped than their adversaries and the demand is just as great, as is the temptation. However there are darker forces at work: in the most recent CITES gathering, in Panama this time, somehow, *somehow*, the Namibian southern white rhino was demoted from the full protection of Appendix 1 to the far less secure listing of Appendix 2, meaning they are open for trophy hunting and trade. This, again with the WWF's full vocal backing, was done in the name of conservation. Rage doesn't even come close.

There are safe backwaters in areas like Ol Pejeta in Laikipia, Kenya where they have a reliable future; most do not. However, in that same conservancy there is a graveyard where I have shed many tears, whose tombstones herald the individual animals killed and the details of their demise. Sadly, as yet, it does not list the perpetrators.

As ever a live one is worth millions, a dead one nothing like so much. Toenail … Imagine!

▷ Of all the species I've spent time with, the proportion of camera time and observing time is the most imbalanced with the rhino. I'm happy just to watch. However, the view through any sort of precision optic fills me with such rage that photography is secondary. Butchered for their horns, to boost people's sex appeal … how could they?

RHINO

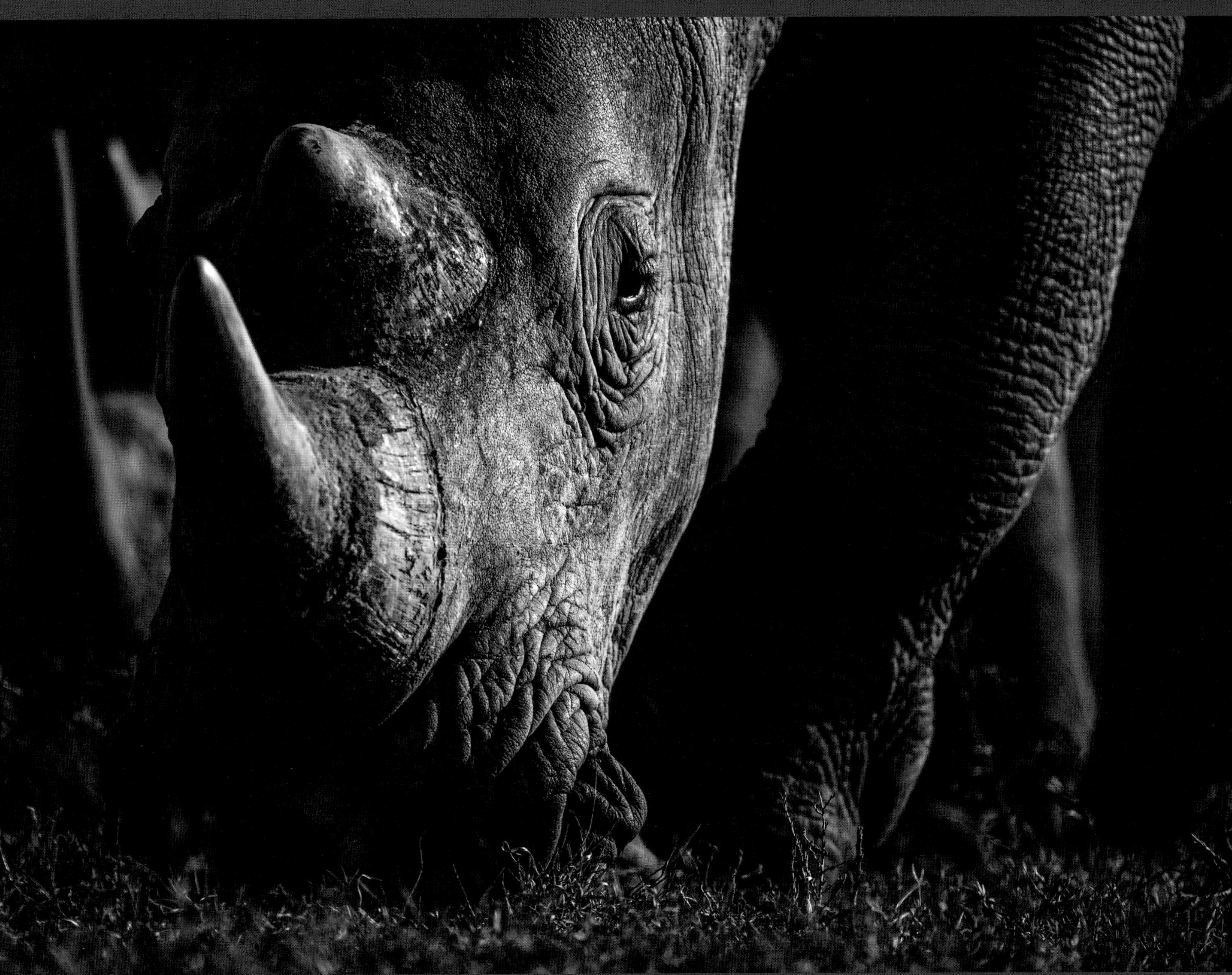

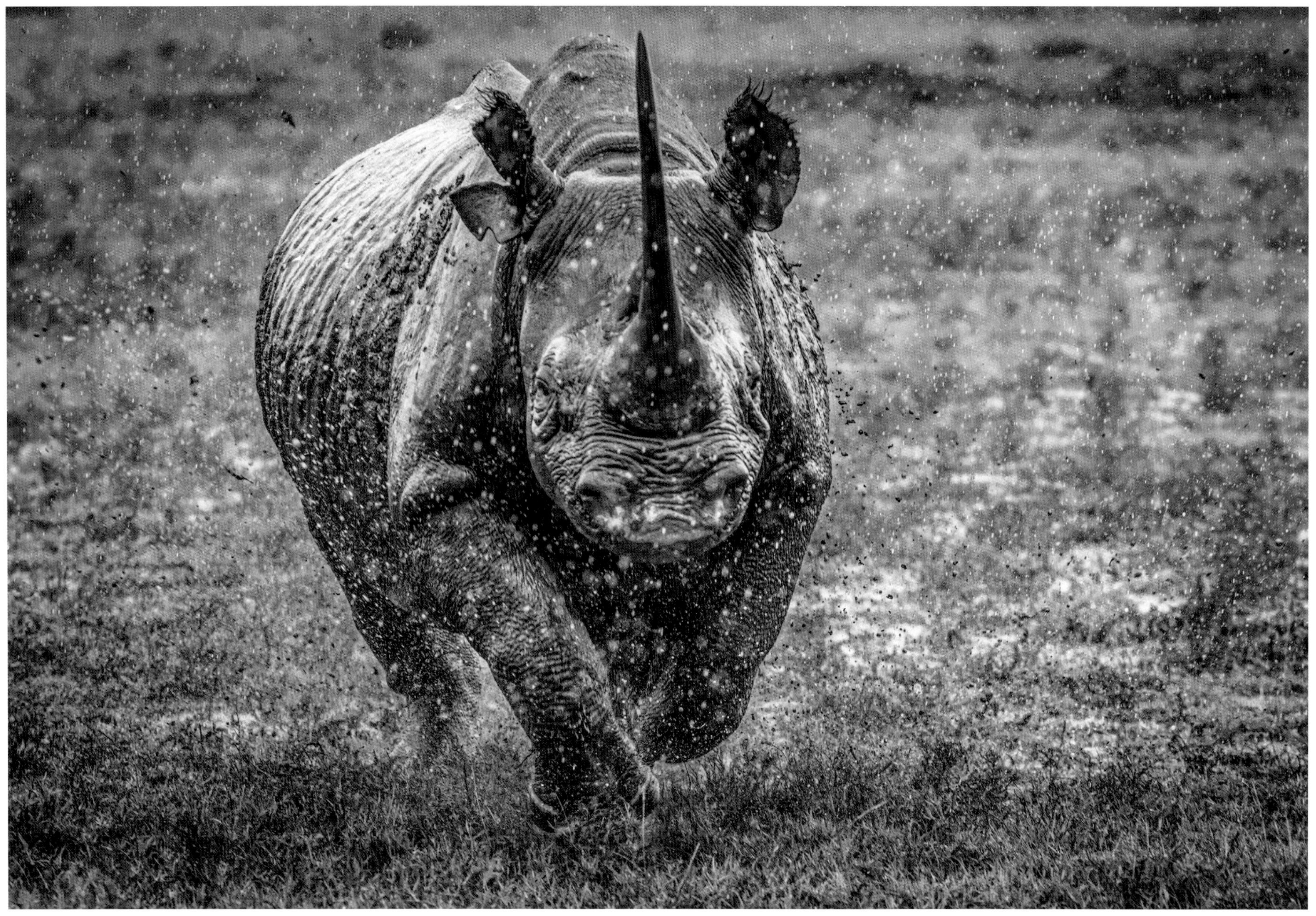

On the charge: I arrived in camp after too long away. It had been dry for months but as Juma, William and Peter and I greeted each other joyfully, I noticed a few billowing cumulus. Around lunchtime these clouds had turned into an angry, threatening nimbus and I needed a vehicle and driver: mechanic Wesley. I have spent months storm-chasing in Mara North, Olare, Naboisho and Ol Pejeta Conservancies, probably years. Nothing excites me more, and not just through a lens. Literally the perfect storm moment is just before it breaks, or indeed as it does when there is still significant light in front of it. Often the moments only last a few minutes, so what is required is a subject – in this case a large black rhino. Thanks Wesley. It was not charging at us, although it may appear that way. The clatter of two buffaloes' bosses irritated it, and, already bothered by the storm it charged after them, never really having eyes on them. It was a magnificent spectacle. From a magnificent animal.

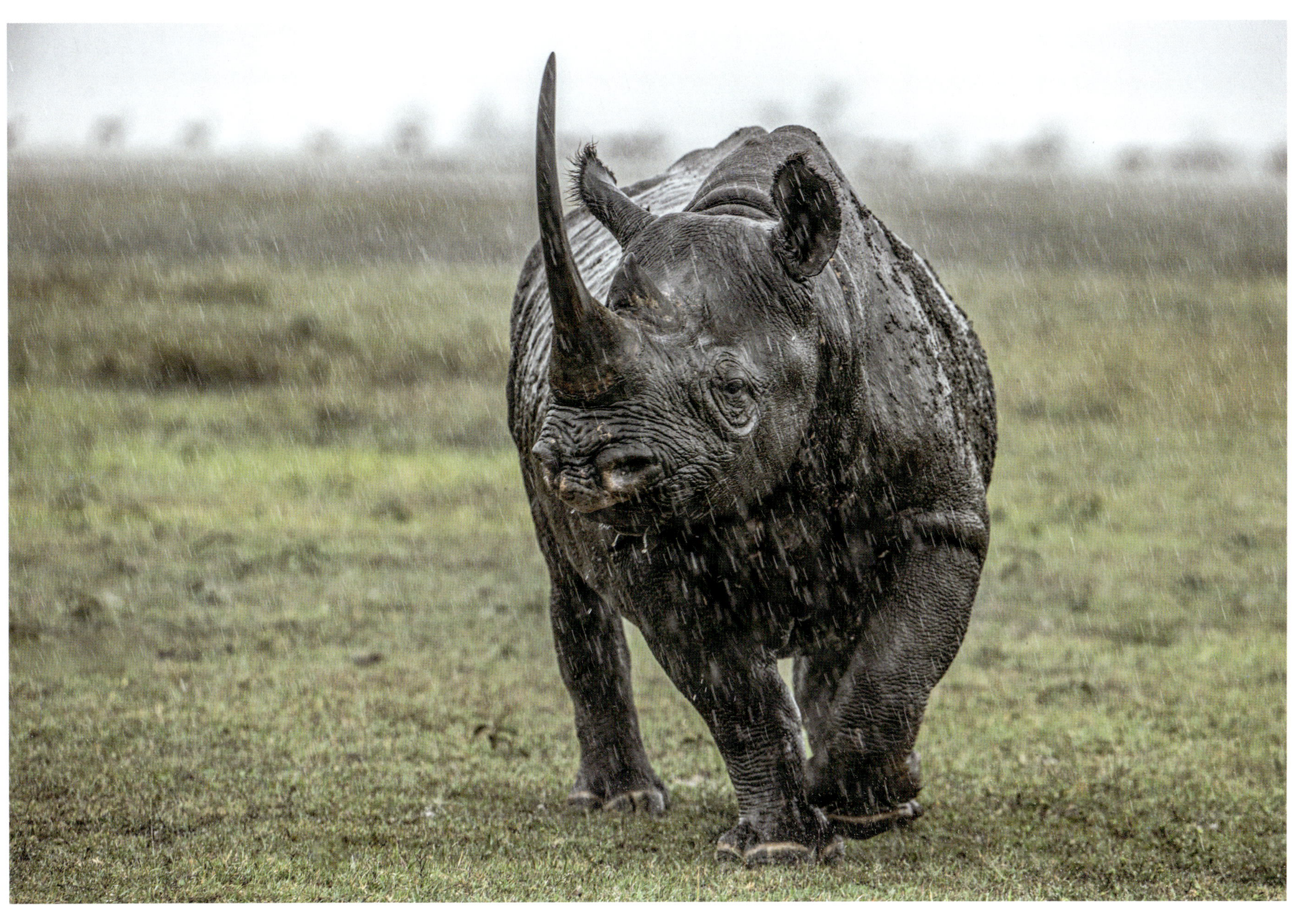

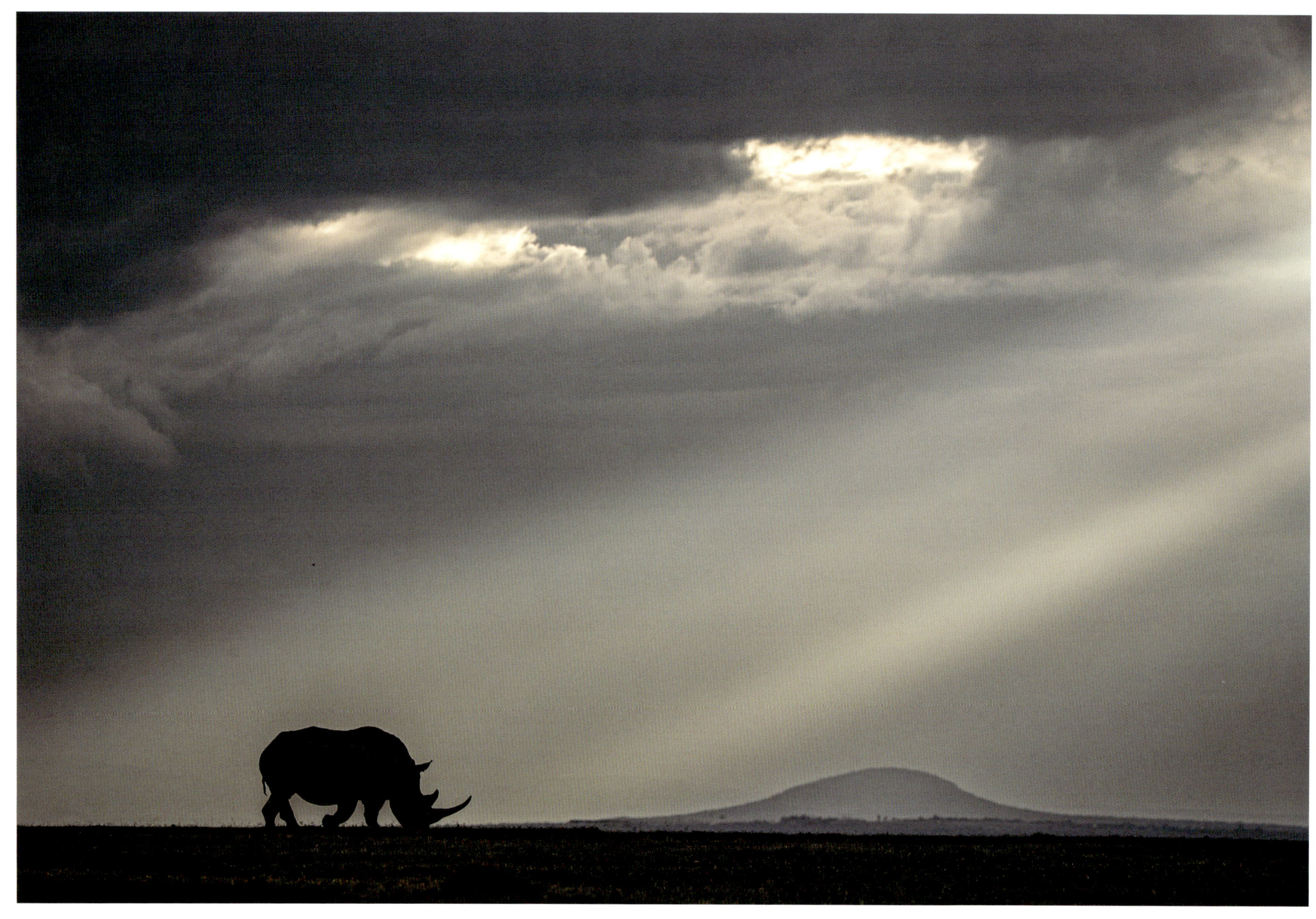

Spotlight on rhino. No-one should ever turn it off.

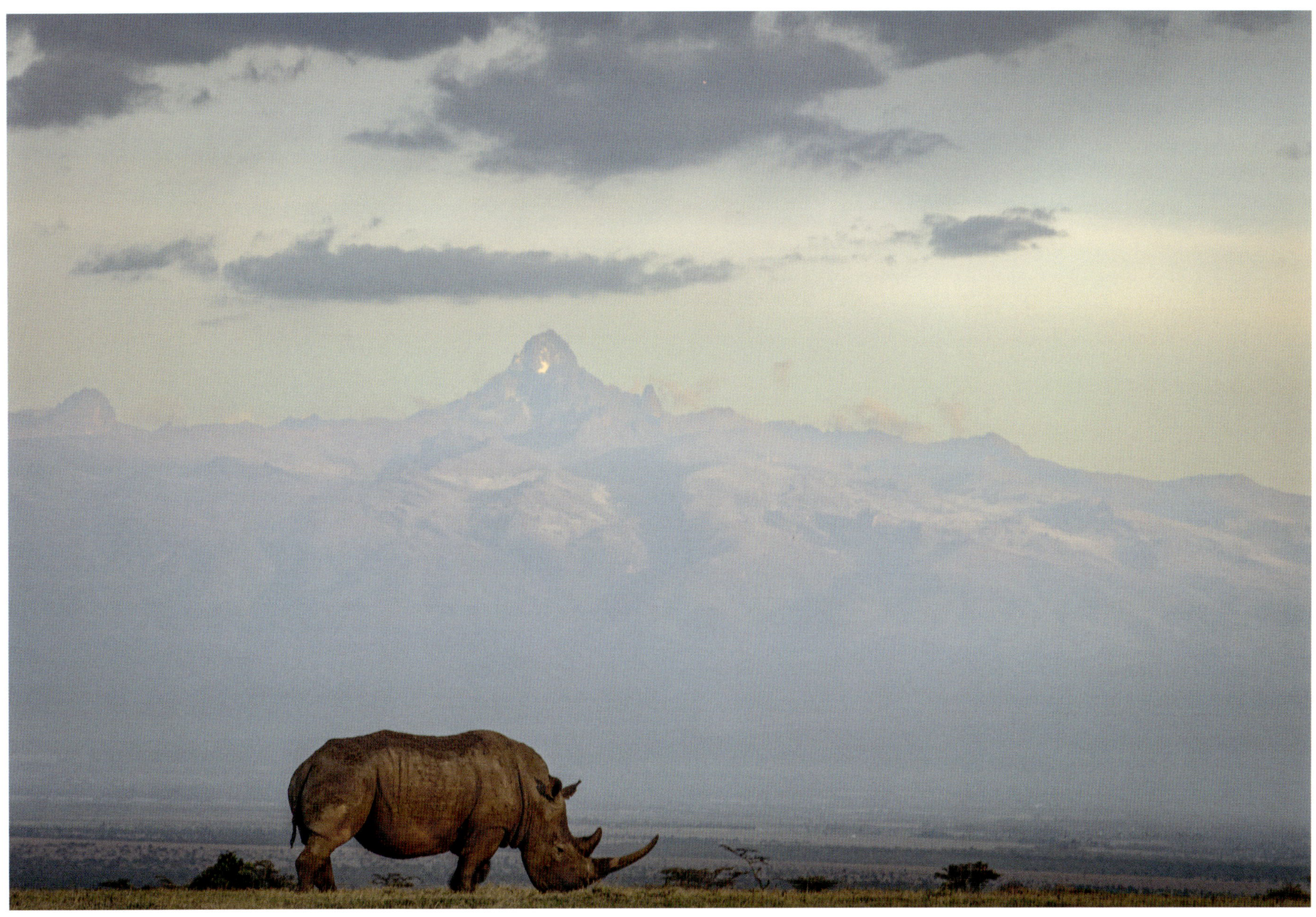

Summit to think about: Ol Pejeta stands in the shadow of Mount Kenya, Africa's second highest mountain and it is almost as if the peak stands guard over these much sought-after mammals as they are protected here. Painted sky, snow-capped summit in full view and a grazing rhino … decent troika, decent afternoon.

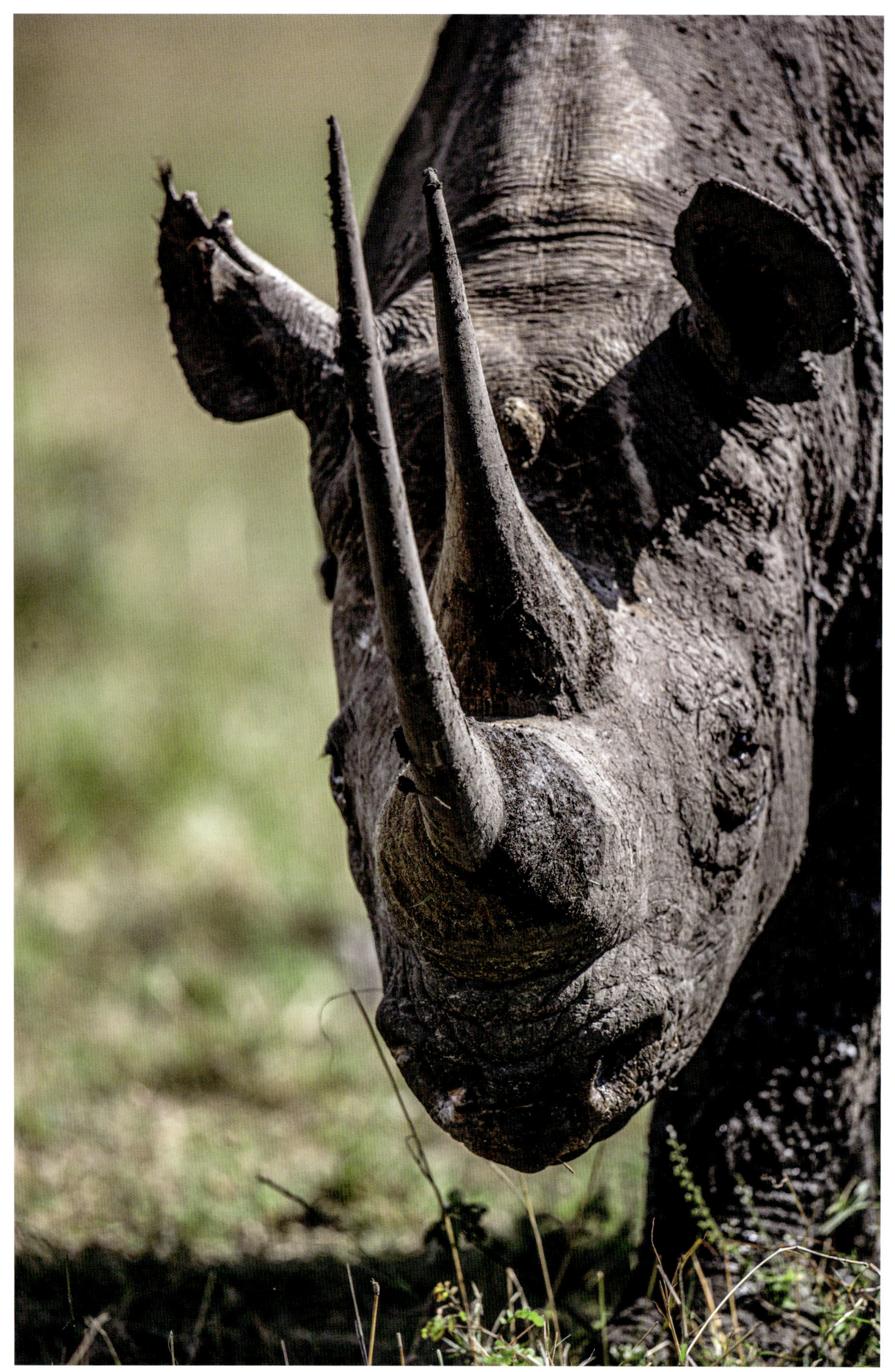

There are some I just doff my cap to. Richard Leakey was one. Wayne Hanssen, feline conservationist of epic levels is another. He forgets more in a weekend about cheetahs and leopards than most of us will ever know. He was with me in 2014, deep in the reserve, and we found this huge old boy: one of the great survivors, one who had lived through the scandalous ravages of the '80s and '90s. It had three horns! No words, only one record shot, but those horns we calculated had a potential street value of around $400,000. He's dead now. Of natural causes. The rhino, not Wayne – that old boy fights on.

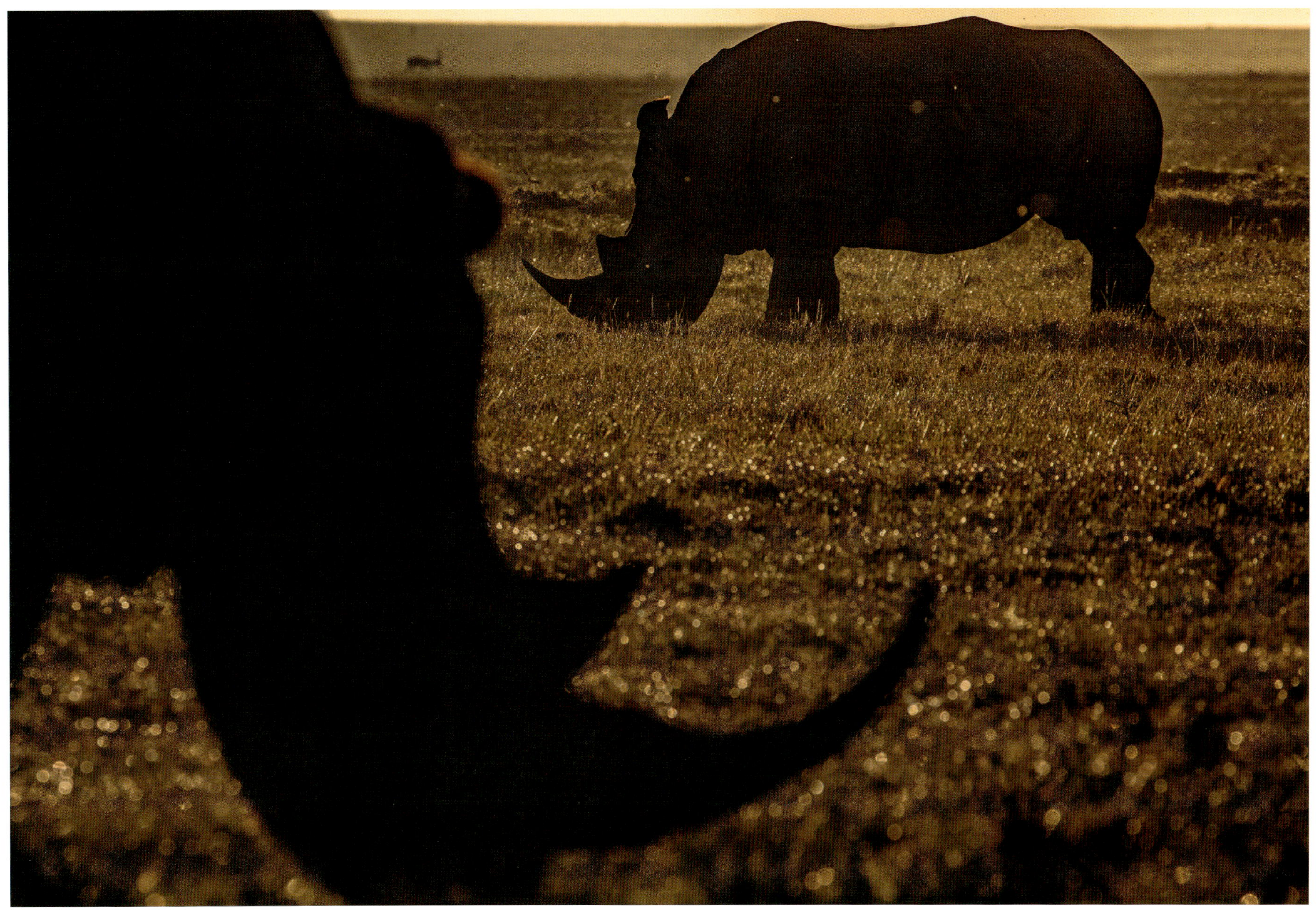

So what for the rhino? Is there a future? They will never roam free across Africa, just as tigers will not over India. Those romantic notions are long past, but conservancies and tourism can save them and hopefully futureproof them for generations. However, if the desire is still there for their bodily parts the problems will not go away. These poachers and purchasers need shaming; they need to squirm. Rhinos don't need meetings and conferences, nor do they need to be relegated off Appendix 1 – this demotion of the Southern white rhino is a staggering recent development encouraged by the WWF. If organisations like them collude with the trophy-hunting business, we have nowhere to go. It appals me. I ran the London Marathon for the rhinos many years ago and throughout all the 26 miles I constantly thought what have they ever done to us?

ONE
TWO
THREE
FOUR
FIVE
SIX
SEVEN
EIGHT
NINE

Feel the need ...

Human animal conflict is never more apparent than with cheetahs. These fleet-footed animals need open county and a plentiful supply of prey. They are a long way below lions, leopards and hyenas in the food chain, so even securing their hard-won meals is problematic. Poaching is still an issue, with the Middle East having developed a both dubious and despicable taste for their cubs as pets.

Richard Adams wrote famously in the remarkable *Watership Down*, 'All the world will be your enemy.' He could have been writing about the cheetah. To see one explode across the plains, its body extended, nostrils flared and rudderlike tail extended, before overhauling a gazelle or impala, is one of the finest sights in nature and one I've never tired of.

There are heroes with cheetahs, what Wayne Hanssen has achieved over thiry years in Namibia is remarkable, but numbers are down. It is simple mathematics. We don't need scientists to endlessly show us their research: cheetahs, with their fragile narrow bloodline, are having their ranges restricted by pastoralists and development, and their cubs killed by hyenas and lions with increasing frequency. It is unsustainable.

Too often sanctimonious documentaries bray about never interfering in nature, desperate for their cute and cloying narrative to remain pristine. They are utterly wrong. We are way beyond that childishly naïve culture. In my opinion, 99 per cent of animals' problems come from humans, so if we can redress the balance sometimes, we should. Cheetahs need monitoring, they need protection, they need space. If it requires intervention to protect them, so be it. The Rift Valley open plains are empirically and geographically designed for the cheetah; the termite mounds seemingly constructed with them in mind. Imagine the savannah without them.

CHEETAH

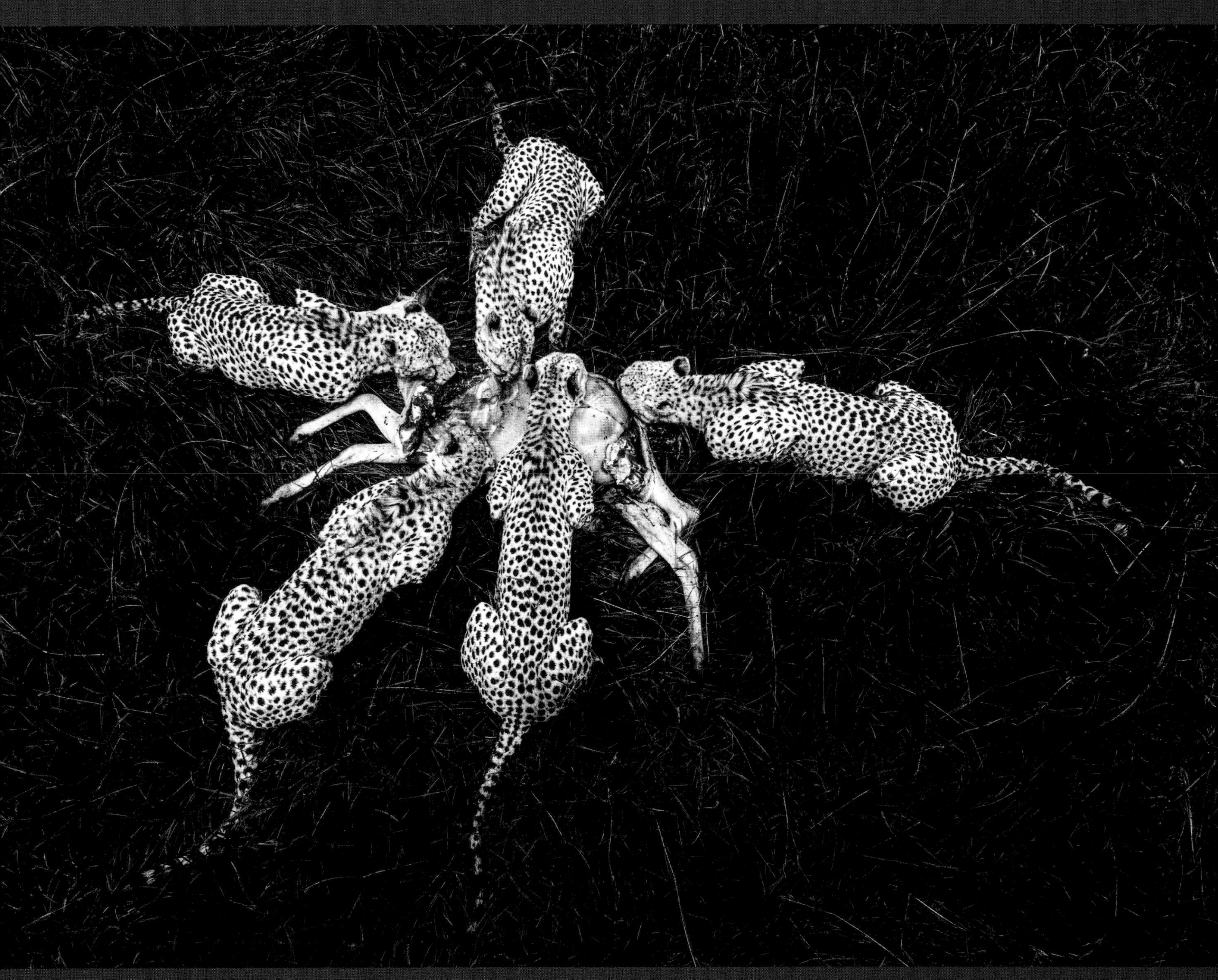

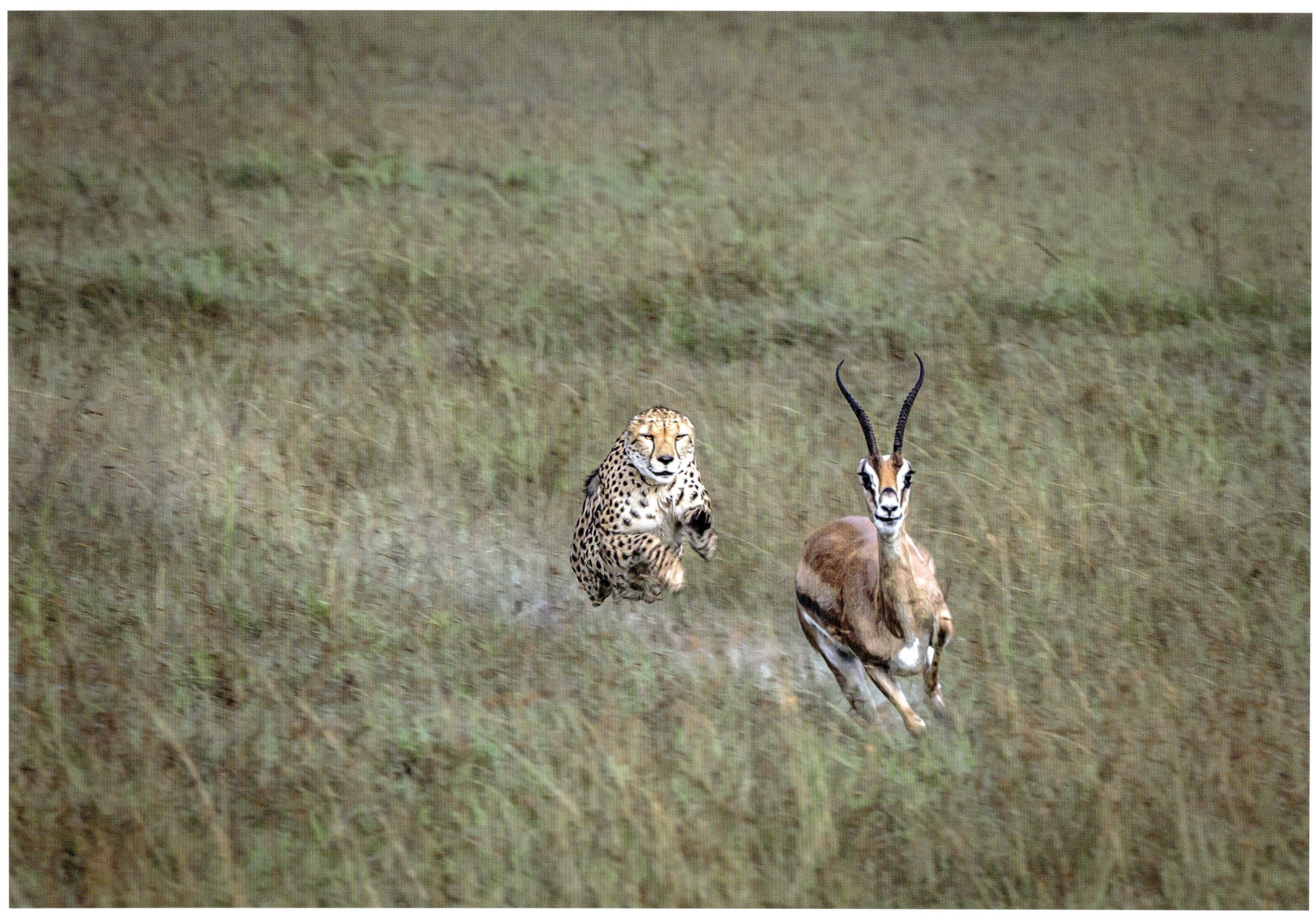

The chase: cheetah numbers are down across Africa and Kenya is no exception. Narrow bloodlines underwrite many of their problems but the proliferation of hyenas and lions is making life desperate at times. This problem only goes away with either culling of hyenas (practical, but will never happen) or sensitive but firm interference from wildlife bodies (would happen, certainly on my watch). They need space and they need prey, and to see one carving through the wet grass, compelled to pursue by its sub-adult family, is one of the greatest sights in nature.

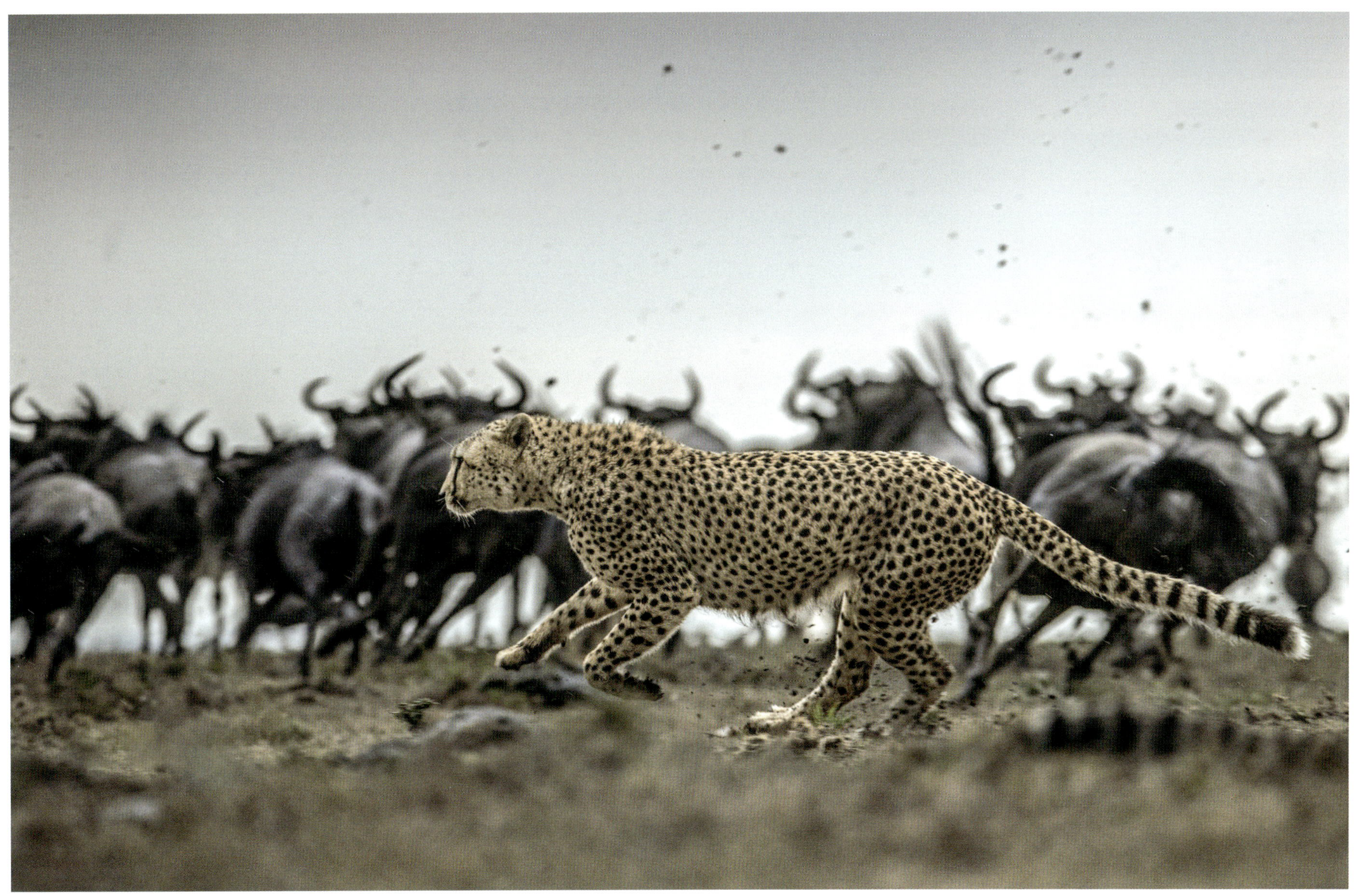

Gnu day: this is one of two huge cheetah brothers. A low angle amplified the drama as he chased off a single hyena whilst his brother tucked into a wildebeest they had just hunted. These two plied their beat across Mara North, Olare and Naboisho Conservancies and were utter Dons. On occasion I've seen them pull down adult topi, wildebeest cows and mature hartebeests. They even chased a leopard up a fever tree once. Magnificent animals. Sadly one has now departed.

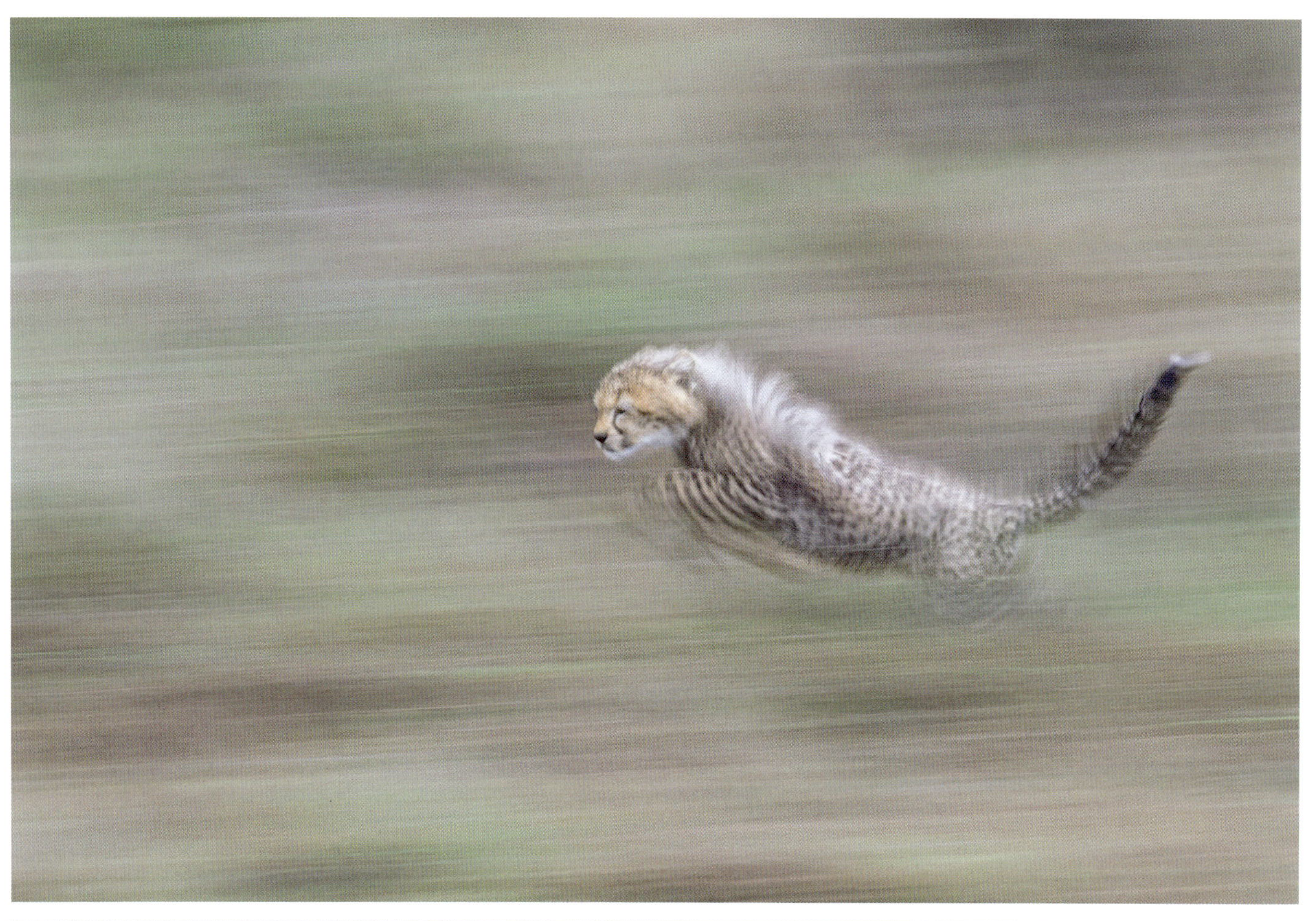

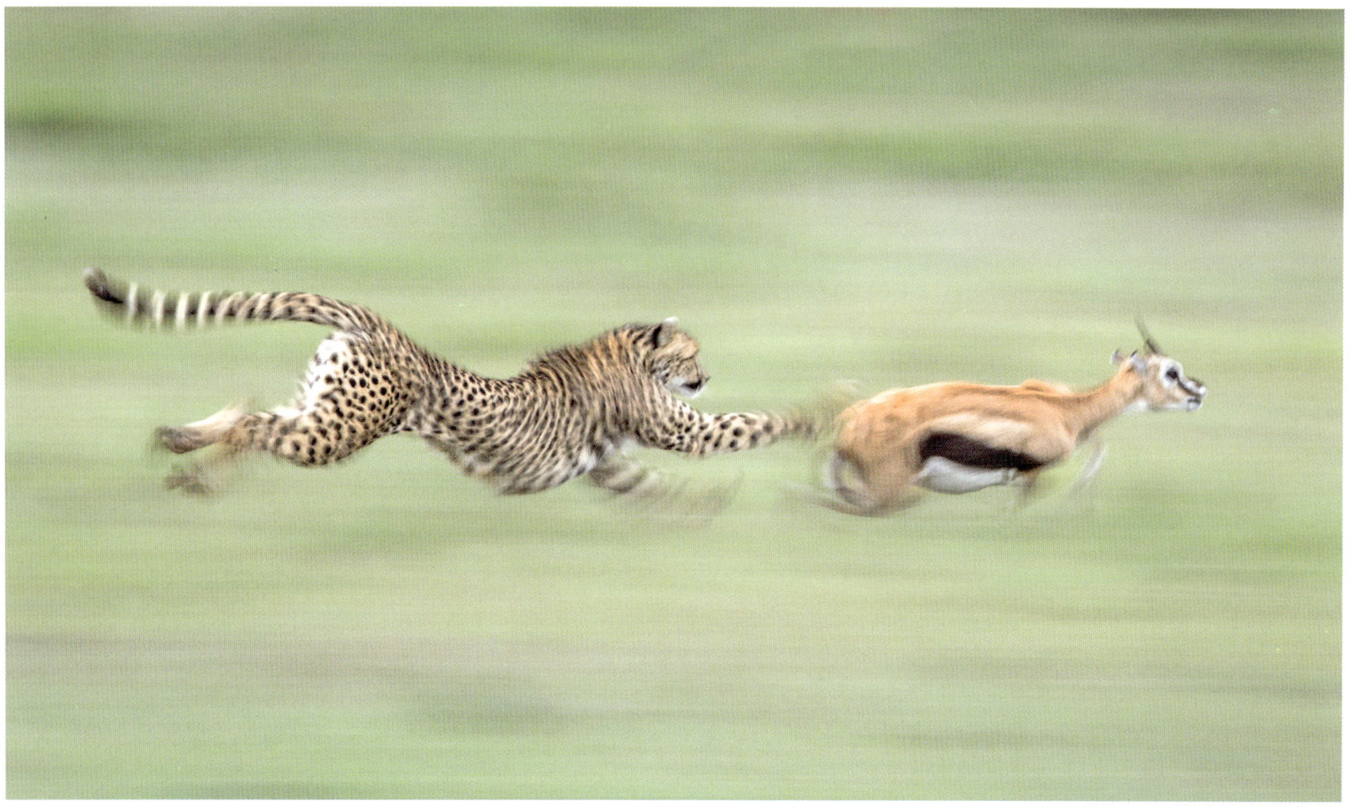

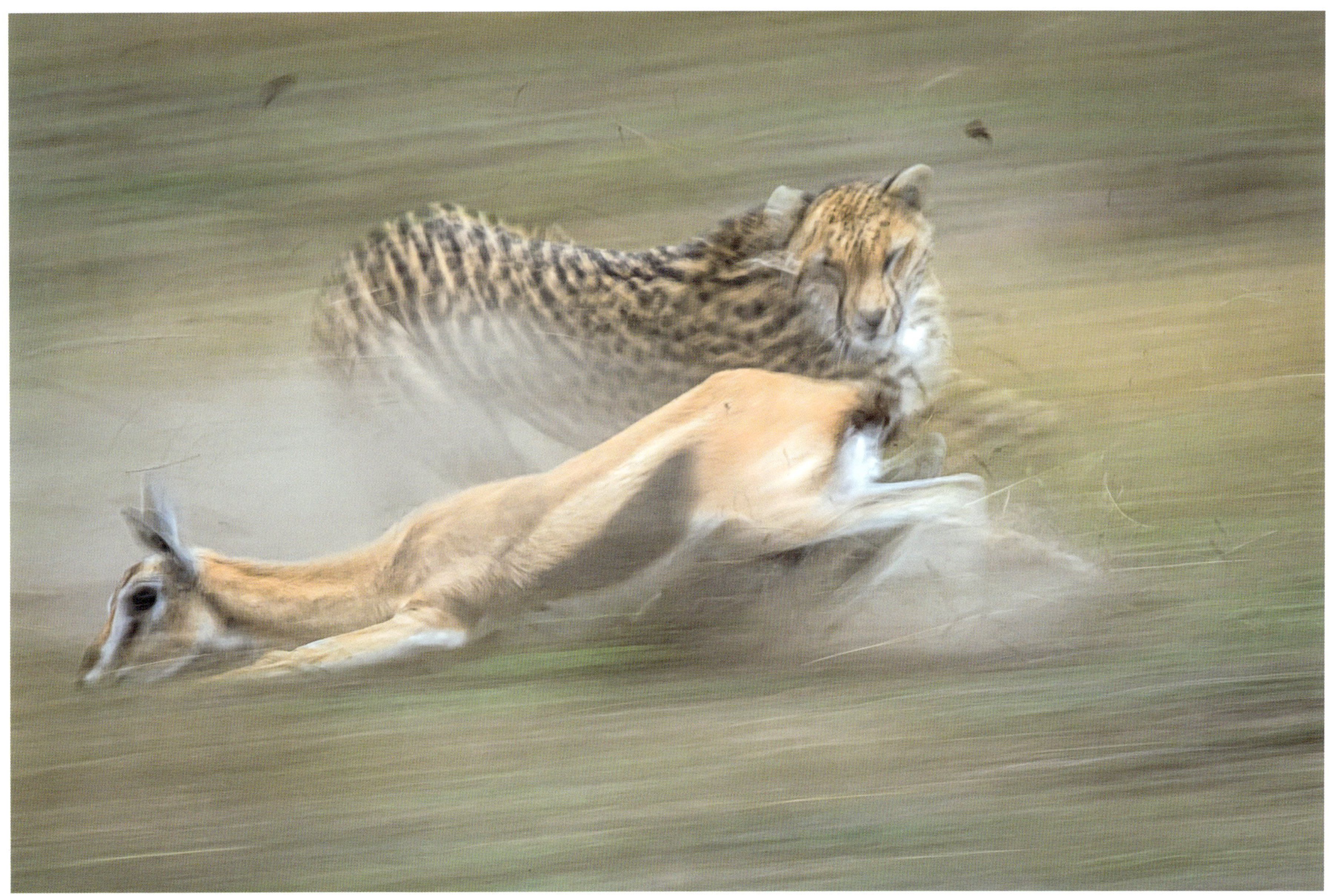

I have been aware not to burden these pages with photographic jargon but slow shutter speeds are my thing, my jam. It took over my life twenty years ago, it still does … as nature intended. It is a huge gamble and frequently fails but this is how I like it, despite the trauma it generates. There is no better creature on the planet anatomically and empirically crafted for a slow speed than a fast cheetah. It is not just the challenge; a fast camera speed just doesn't do justice to this fleet-footed feline. When it is dark and gloomy, it is the only option left. Which is more important, you succeeding with an audacious image or the cheetah feeding her family?

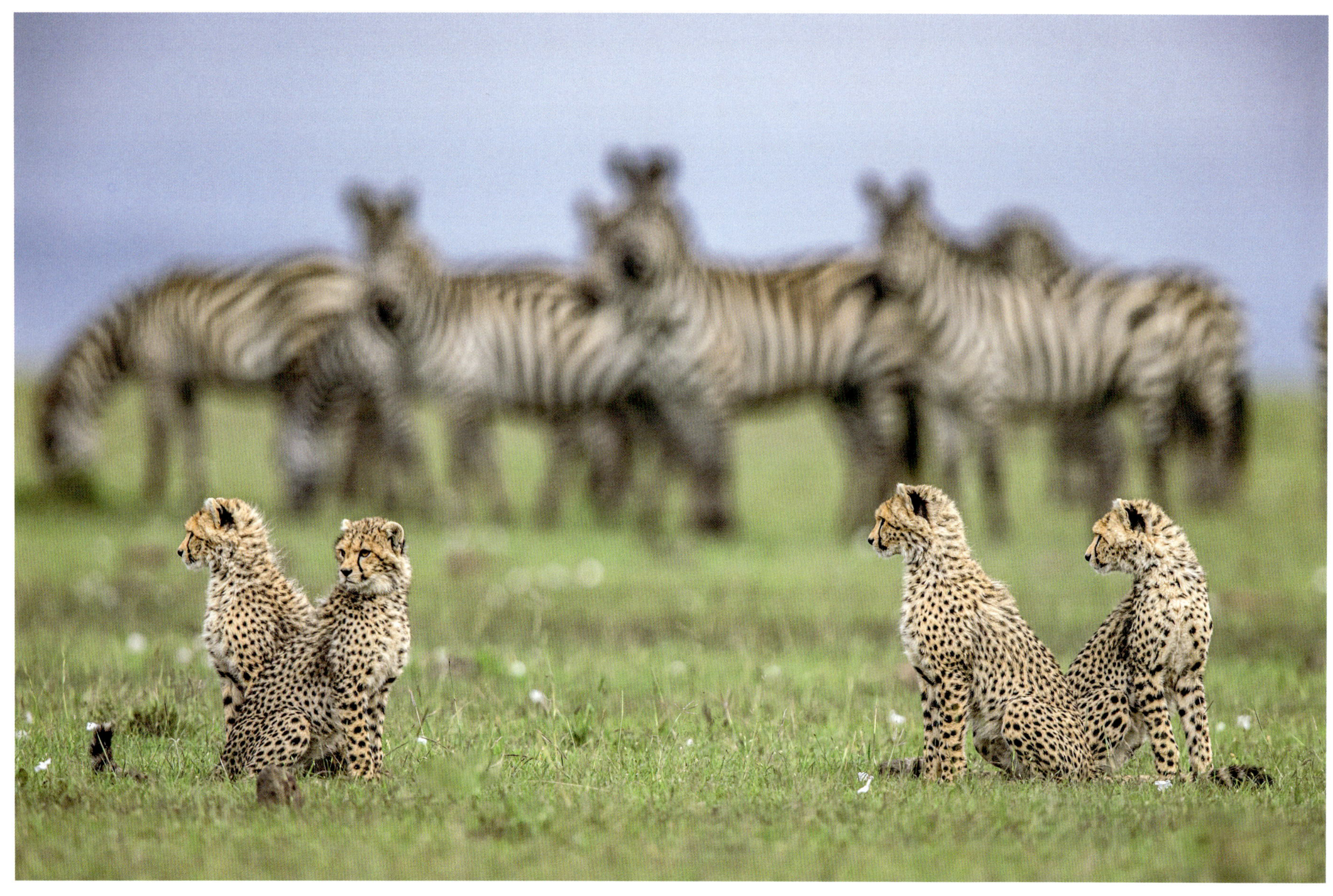

Symmetry, it's everything in photography. Not here.
If there's a group, one will always let you down.

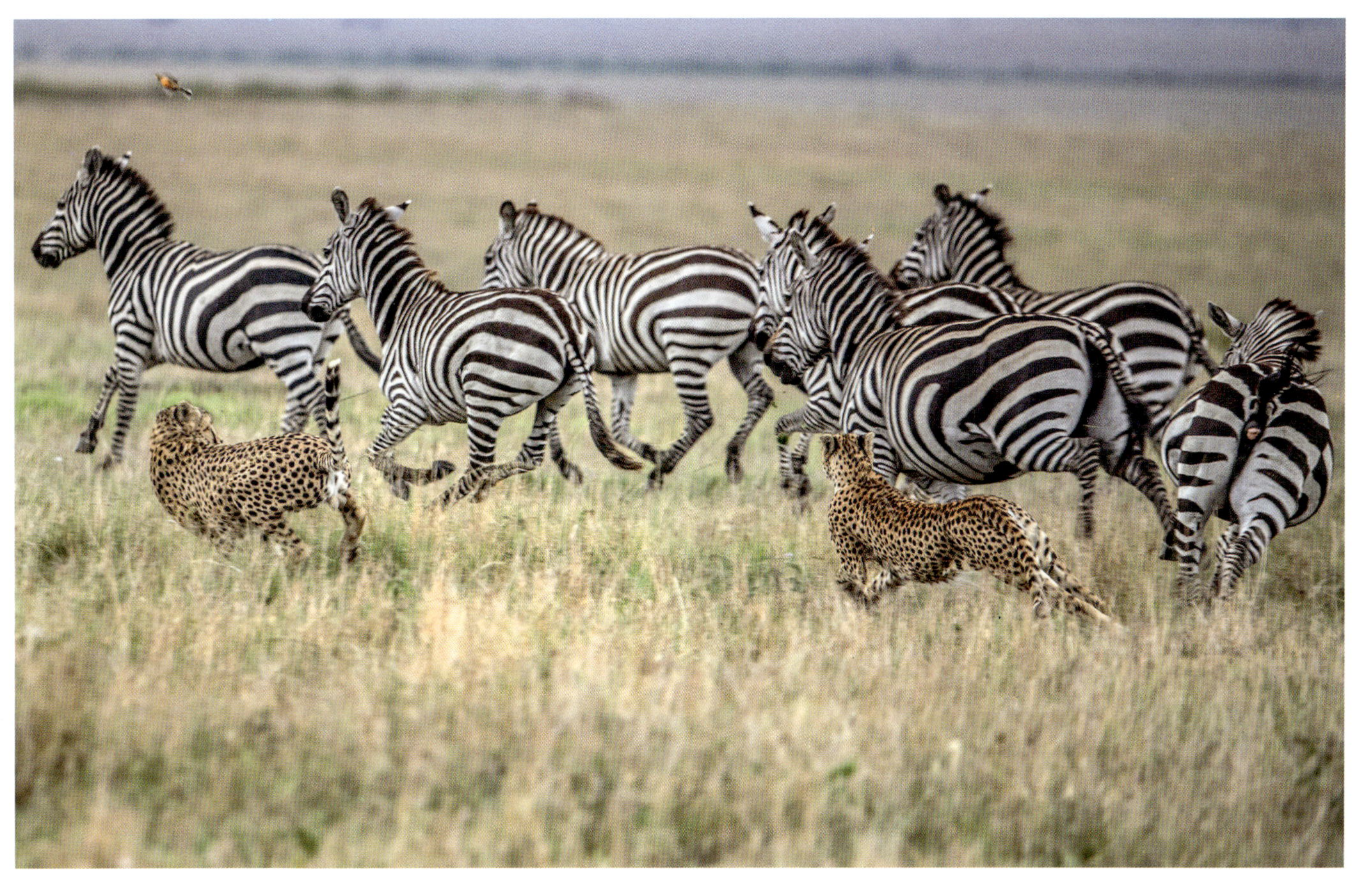

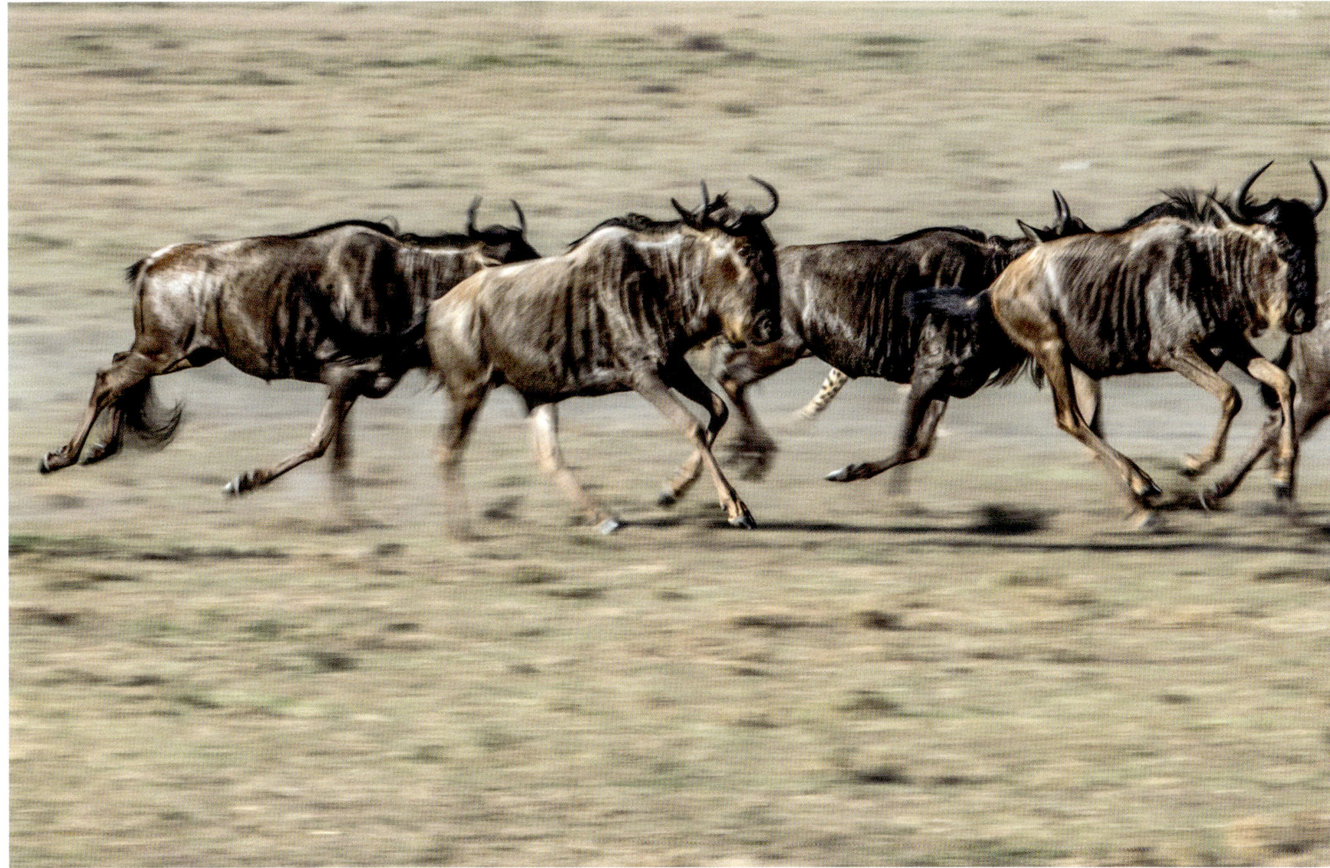

Two chase scenes. Two of the fabled Tano Bora Coalition harass a zebra herd before choosing a sub-adult. Below is for me a more interesting image, as a young cheetah with eyes considerably bigger than stomach tries his luck with a herd of wildebeest stallions. I was not intending to take that image but when there is mystery it often means a better image.

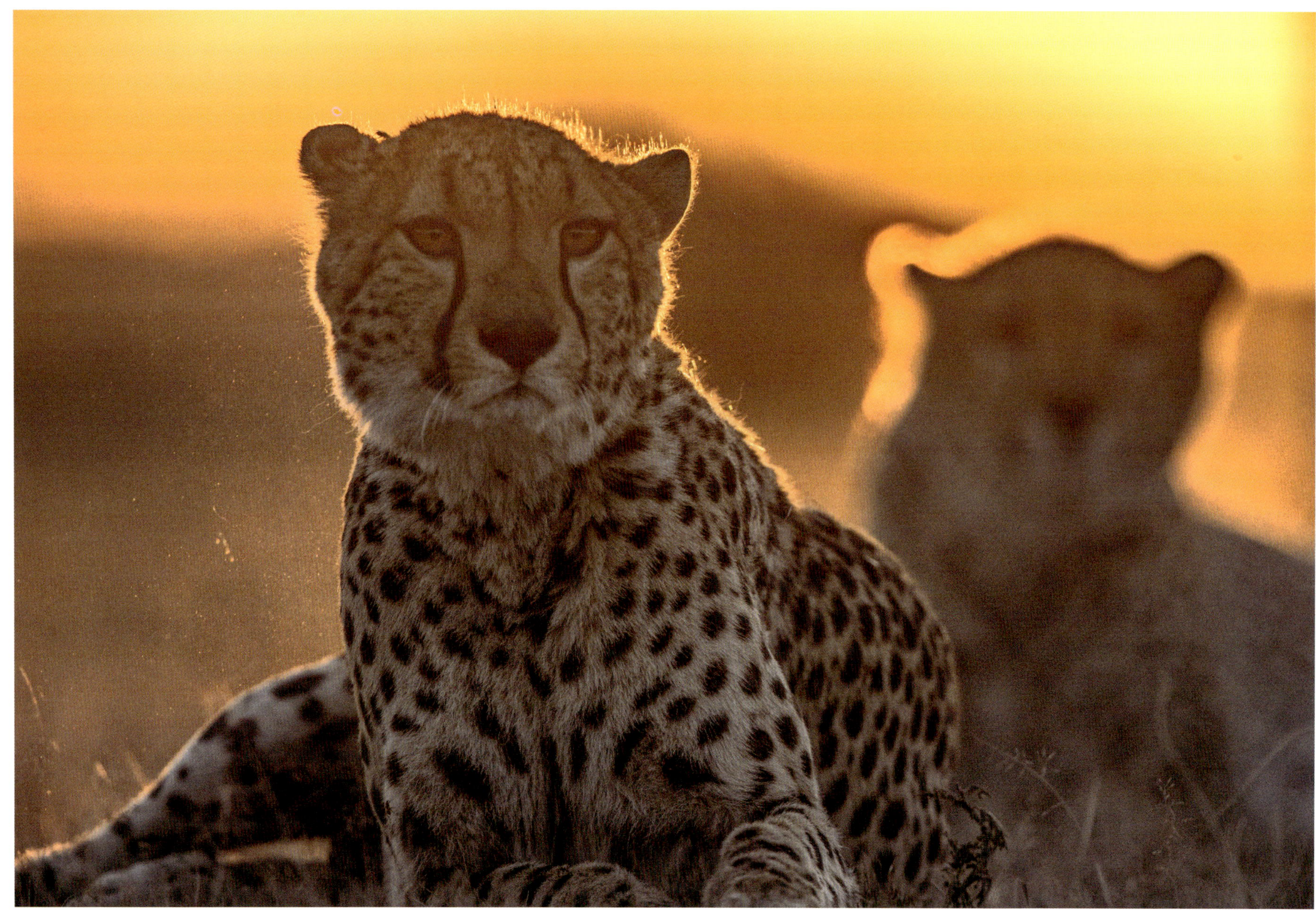

The difference between a photo or a moment a few minutes after sunrise as opposed to half an hour after. Yes, the light is kinder, lasts longer and is more frequent than anywhere in Africa – one of the reasons so many return annually for their Rift Valley fix – but those first few moments demand a subject. Backlit. Marketing clowns (tautology alert) use the phrase 'hero shot', whatever that means; long suffering cheetahs are all heroes to me.

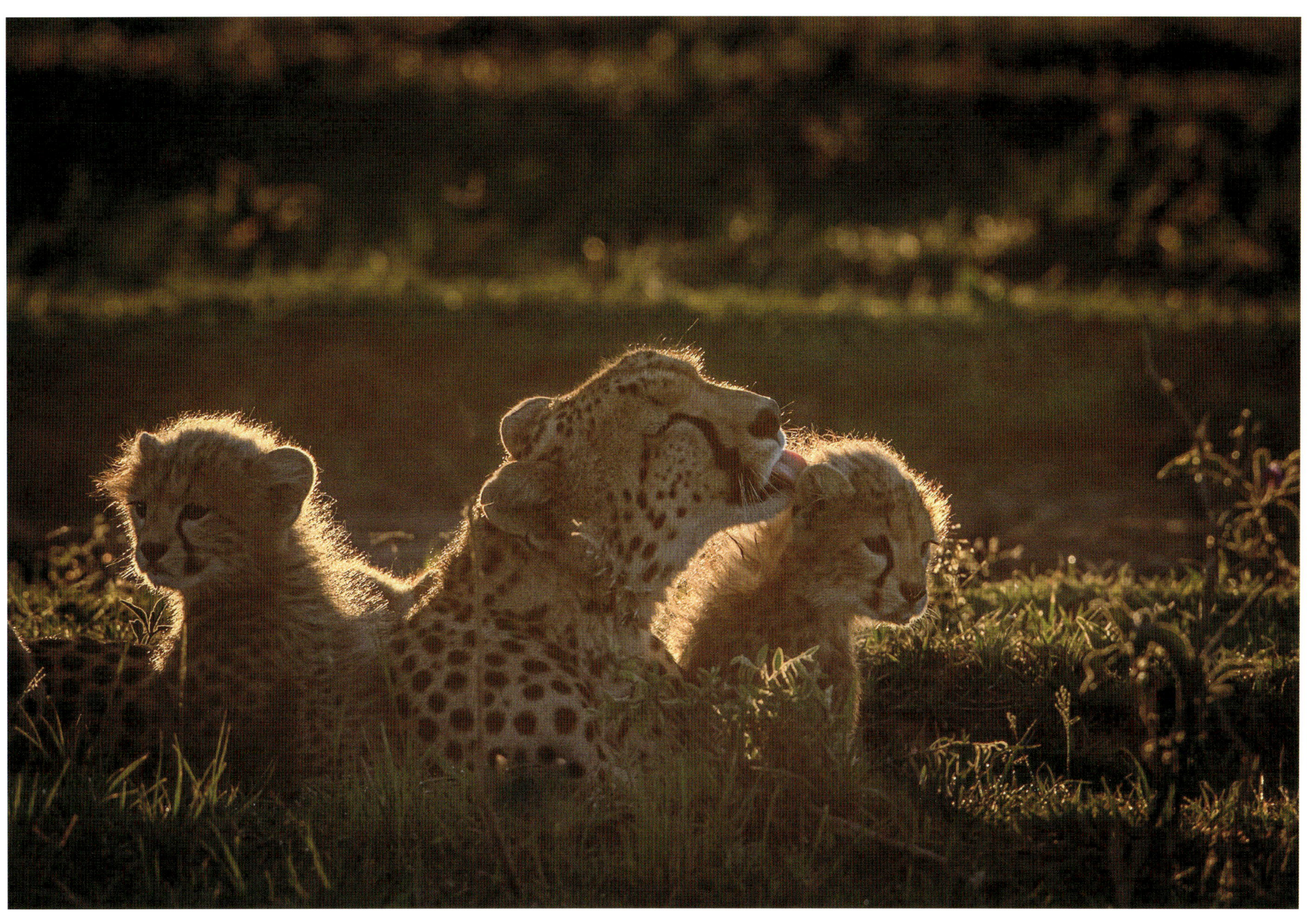

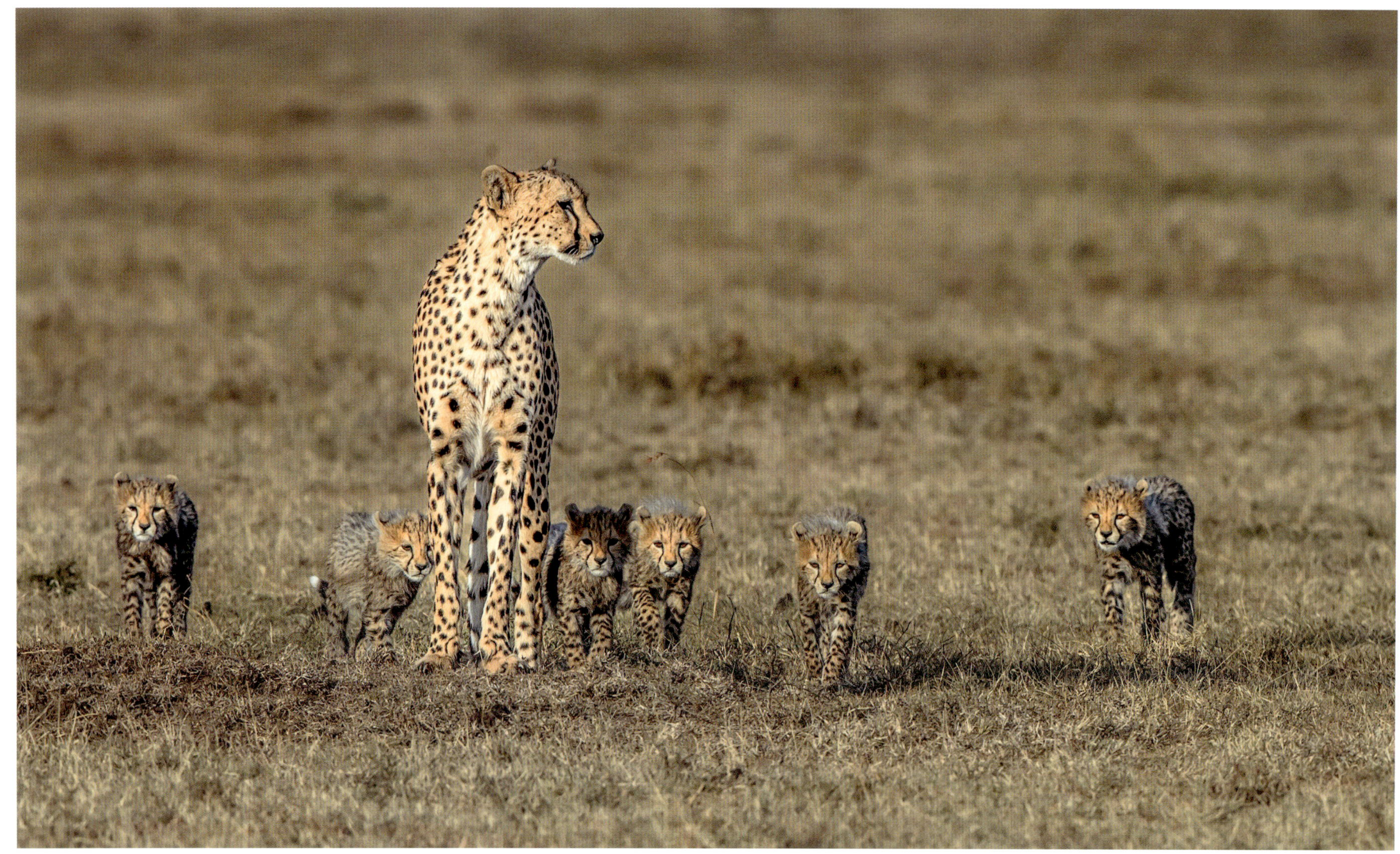

A mother has six cubs. What are their chances of them all making it to adulthood? Almost negligible. These six made it largely down to a conservancy vehicle staying with them from the false dawn to the last blush of sunset. Every day. When hyenas came to investigate or to purloin a hard-earned kill, they were chased off. It worked. It is interference. It is necessary. You ever seen a thin hyena? Exactly. If it bothers you, get over yourselves; this sort of practical pragmatism is the only way now.

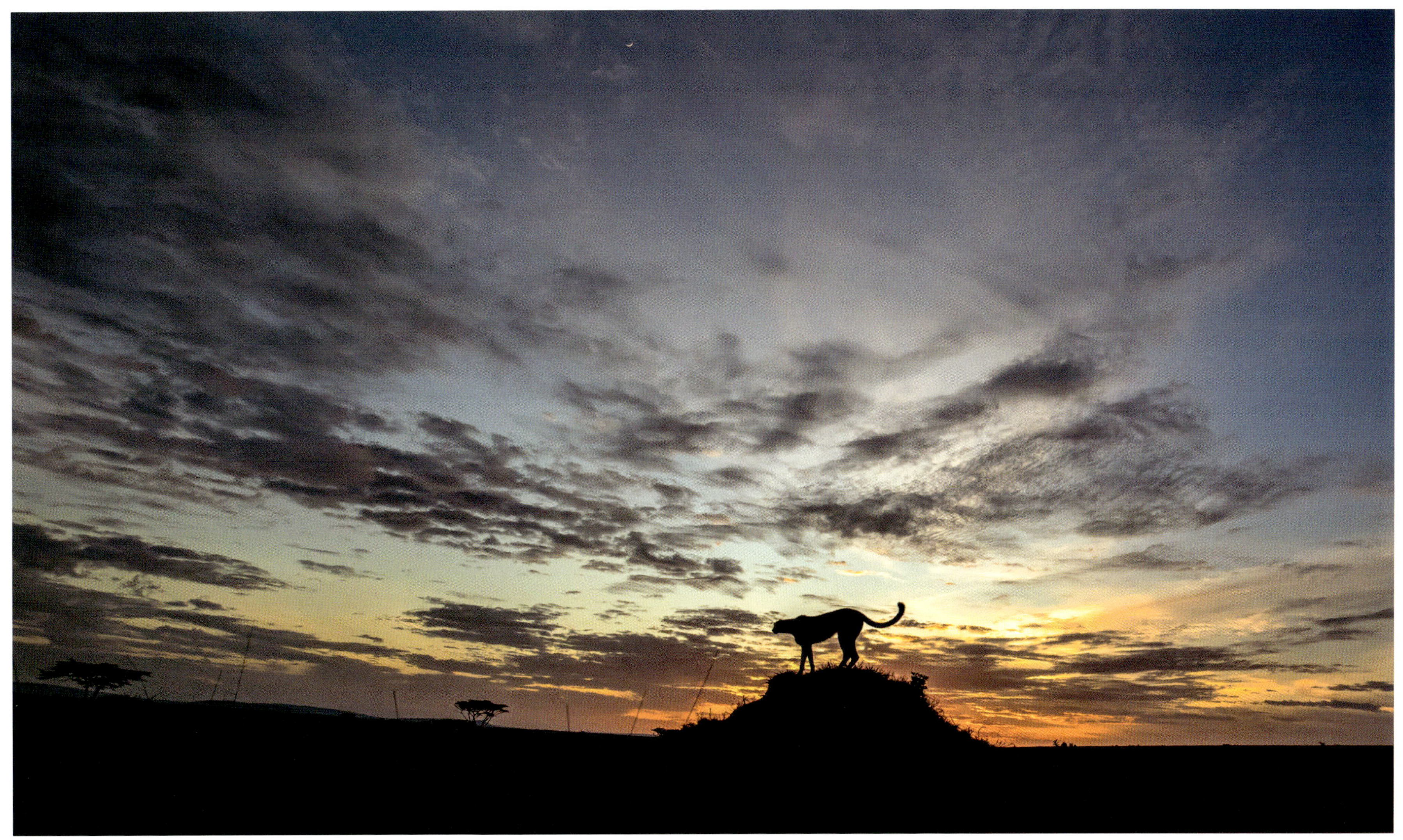

You have to suffer for your craft and despite multiple sit-ups, the stretch down to take this resulted in a flight to Nairobi and a scan to determine the severity of a torn abdominal muscle. My family, with me that morning, sighed collectively. They've been here before. Worth it? Obvs. Think what cheetahs go through.

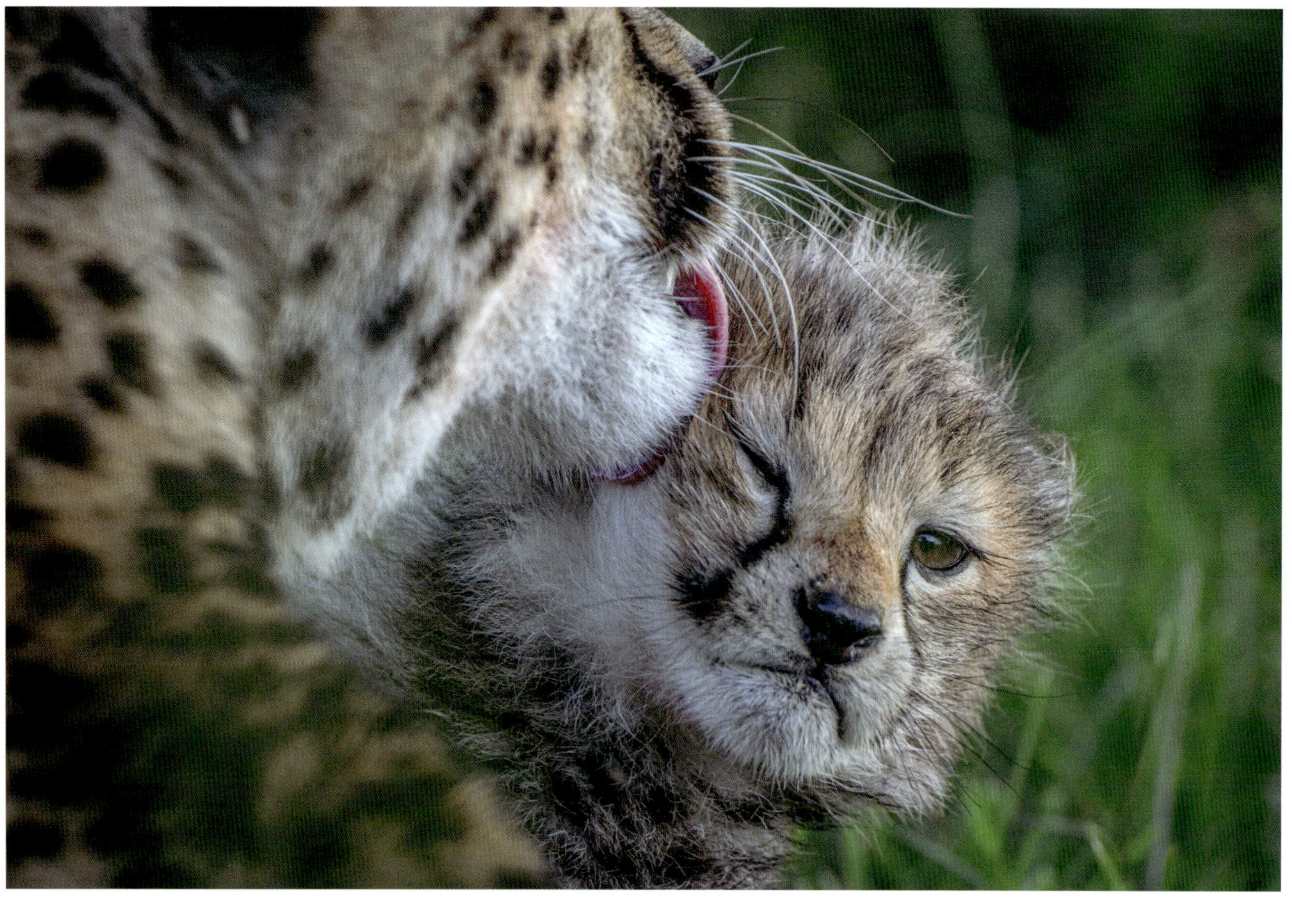

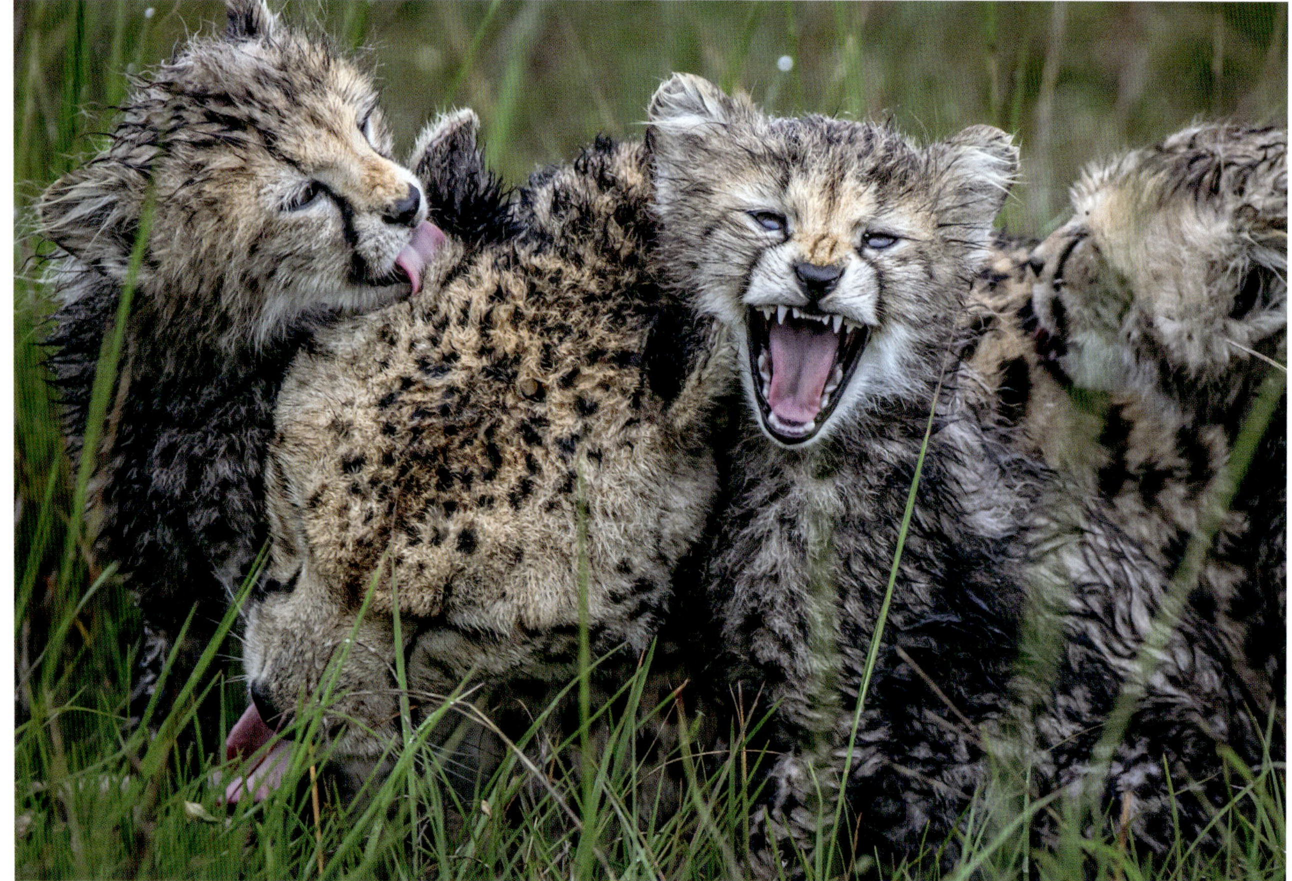

The sandpaper tongue, the intense grooming which is not only affection but also an imperative, as mothers try to deny their mortal enemies – the lions and hyenas – any scent of their precious cargo. Finding them at first light is also priceless.

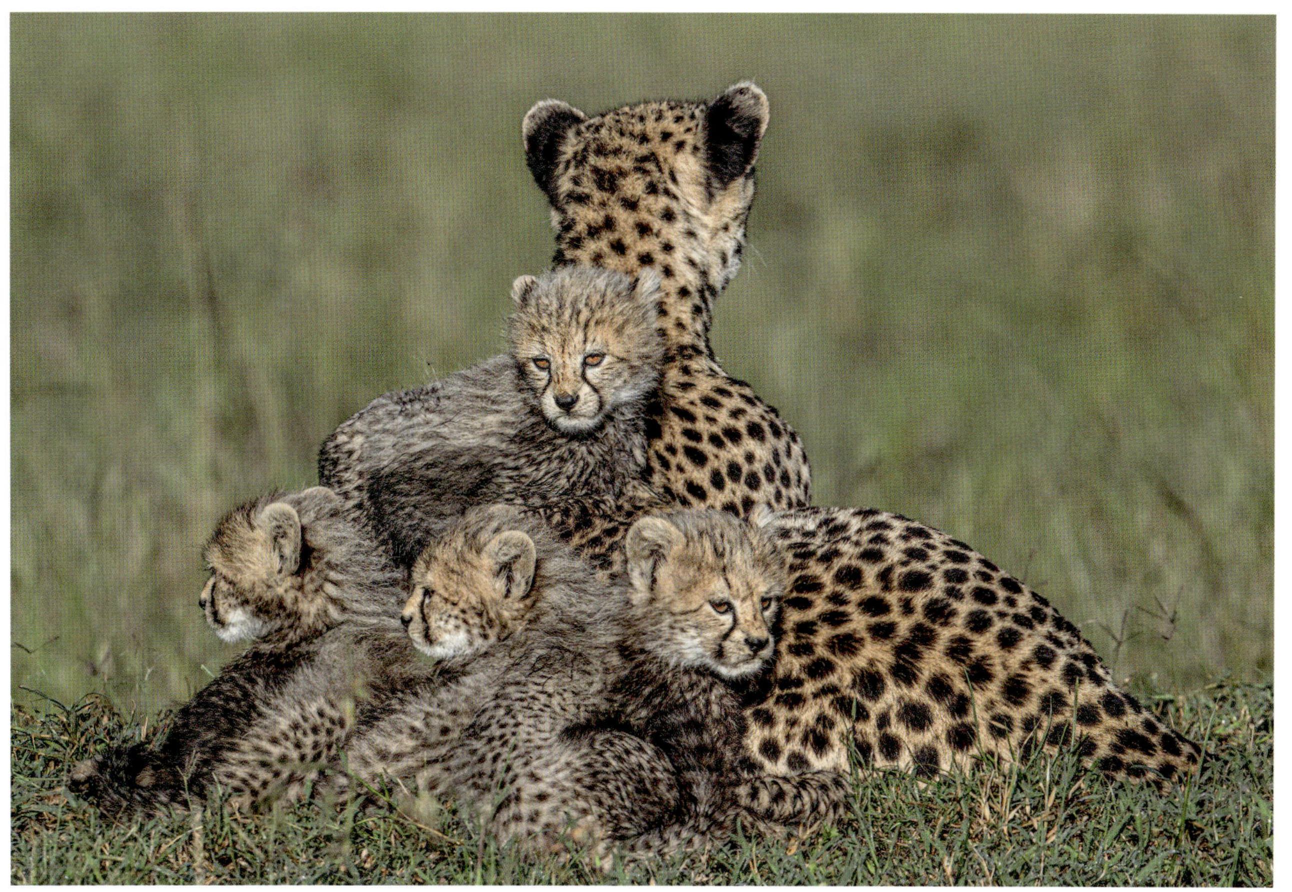

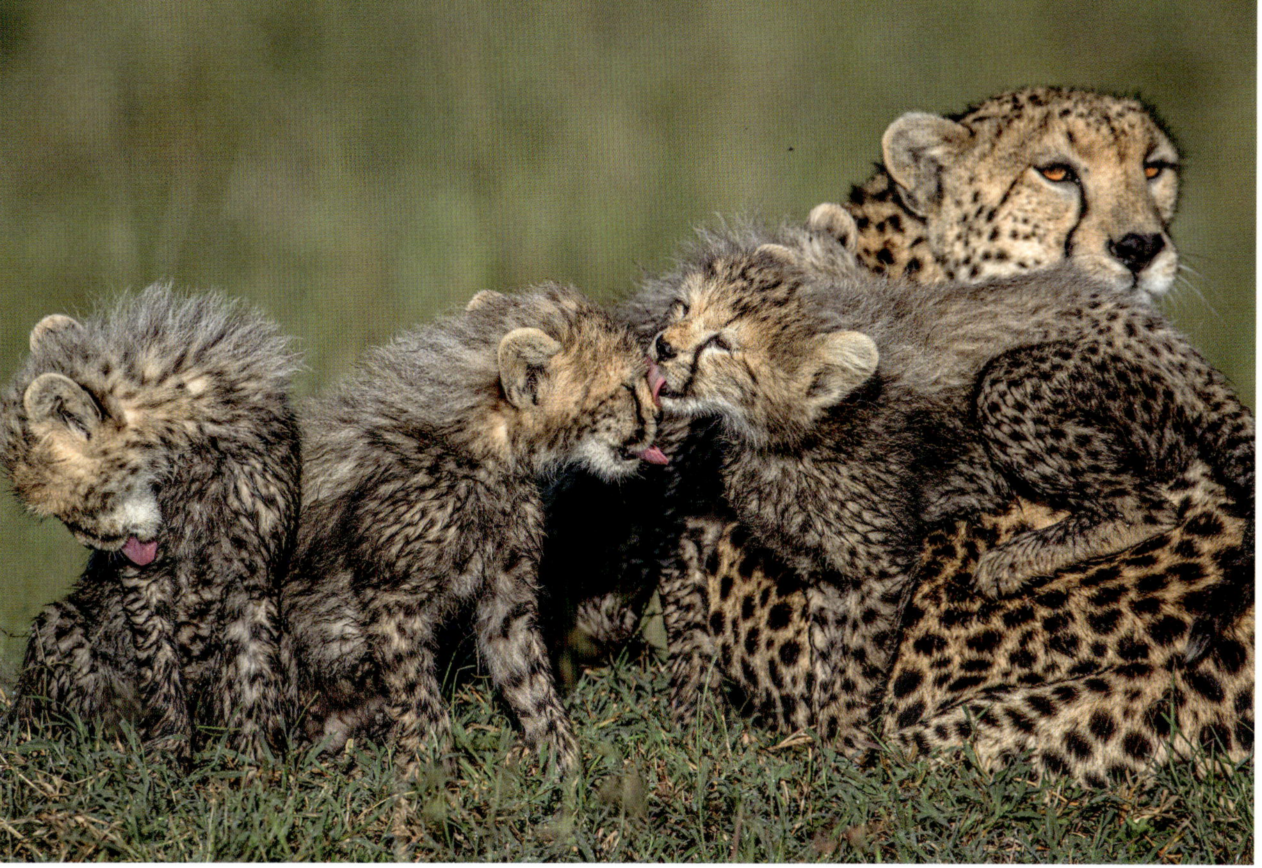

Early morning, Olare Conservancy, a diligent mother with four cubs draped over her at sunrise. There may be better ways of waking up, but I've not found them.

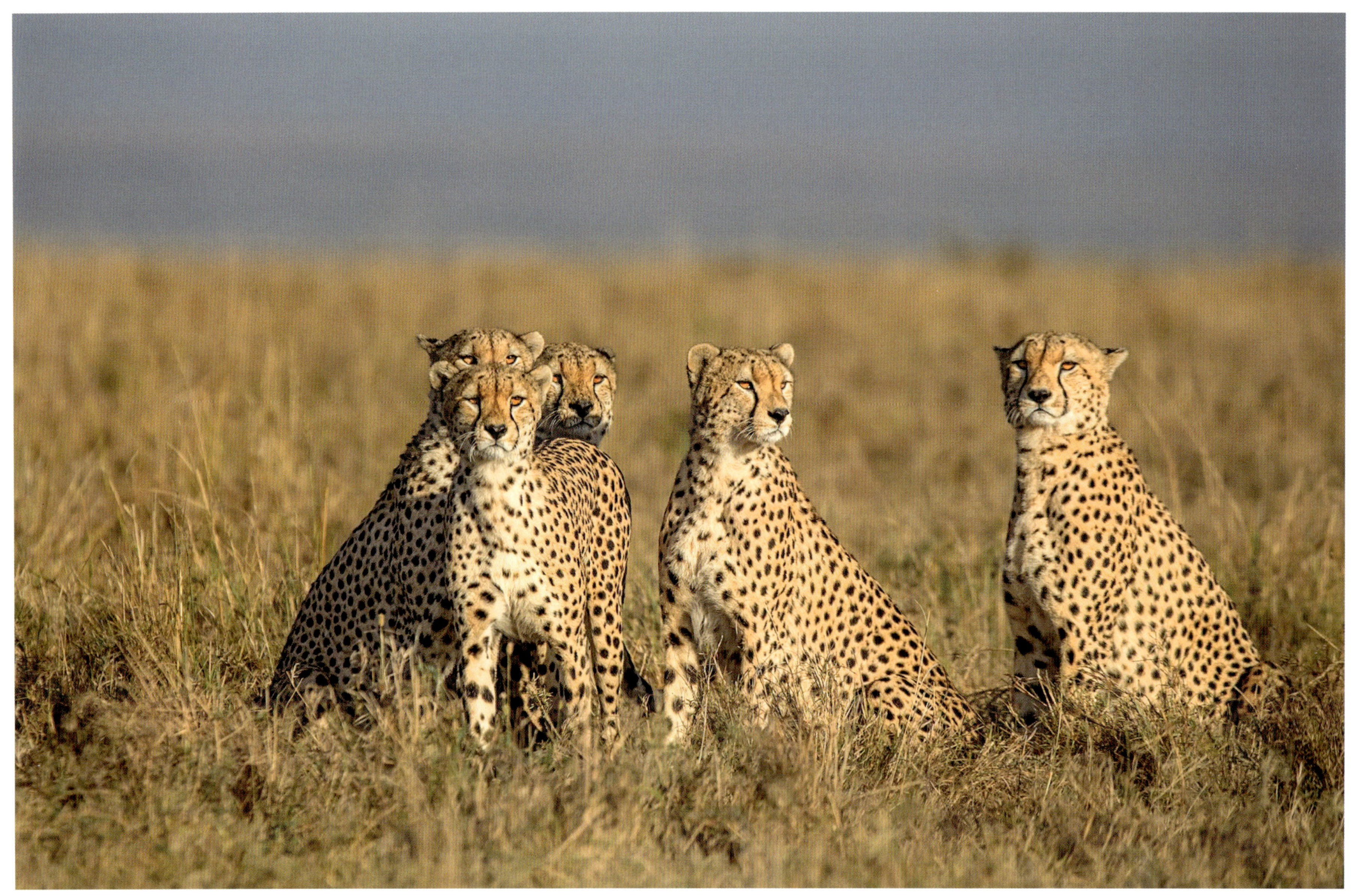

Five star: the fabled Fast Five Coalition posing during a hot September morning. Once they dropped we left them, trying our luck with only two other vehicles on the Mara River, early on during Covid. It turned into a thunderous and prolonged stampede. Sorry about putting your bladder through so much Dan…

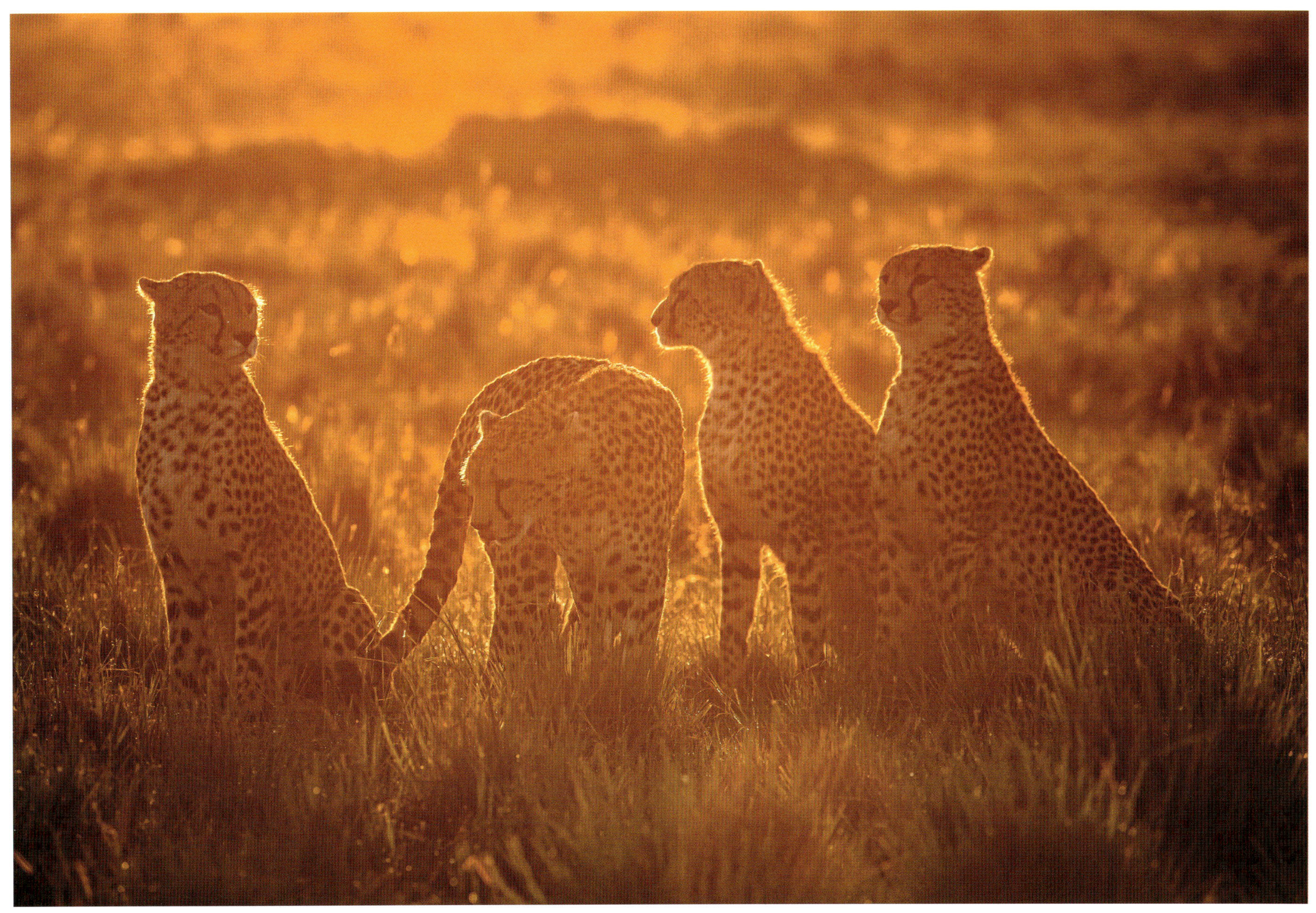

This family took a long time to wake up. Mother knew she had to put a meal on the table but the nearby hyenas put a stop to that. It is just so hard for these cats and it's not getting any easier.

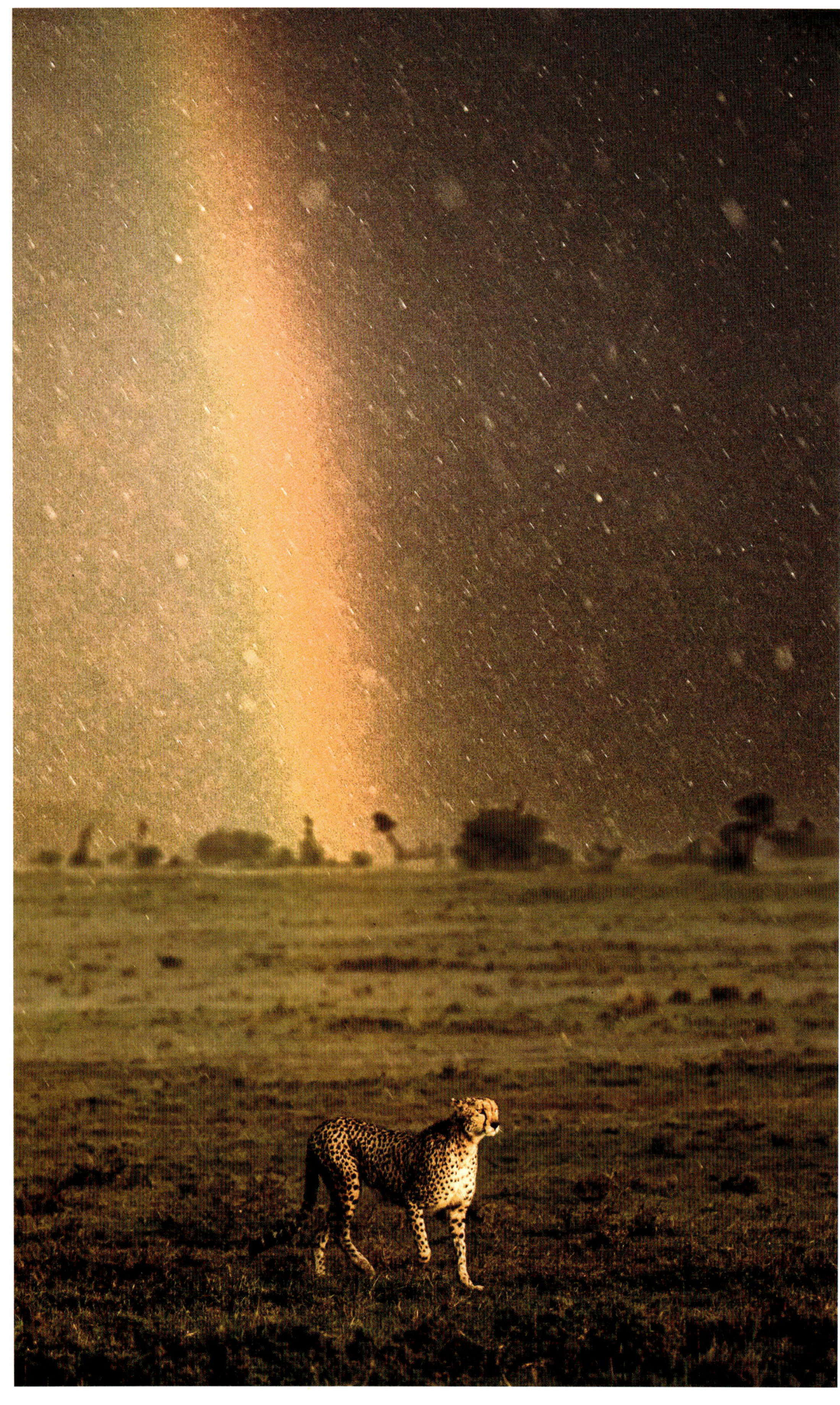

A January storm battered the Naboisho Conservancy to submission in 2023. Almost. Most had turned for home but in the space of a few minutes in a ferocious squall there was both a leopard and cheetah hunting. Storm light, patrolling spotted cat, rain and bow, followed by a burnished sunset… bingo.

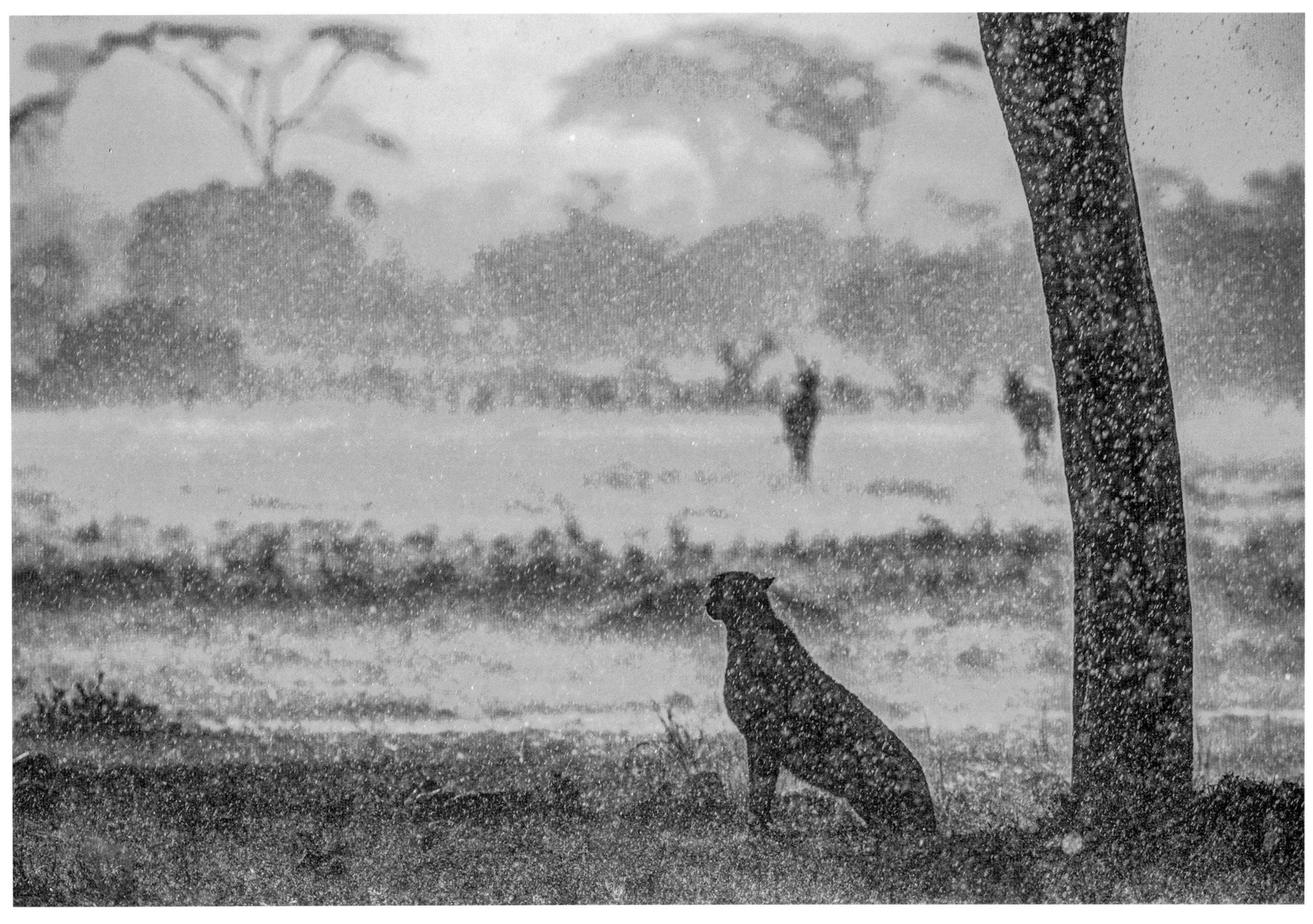

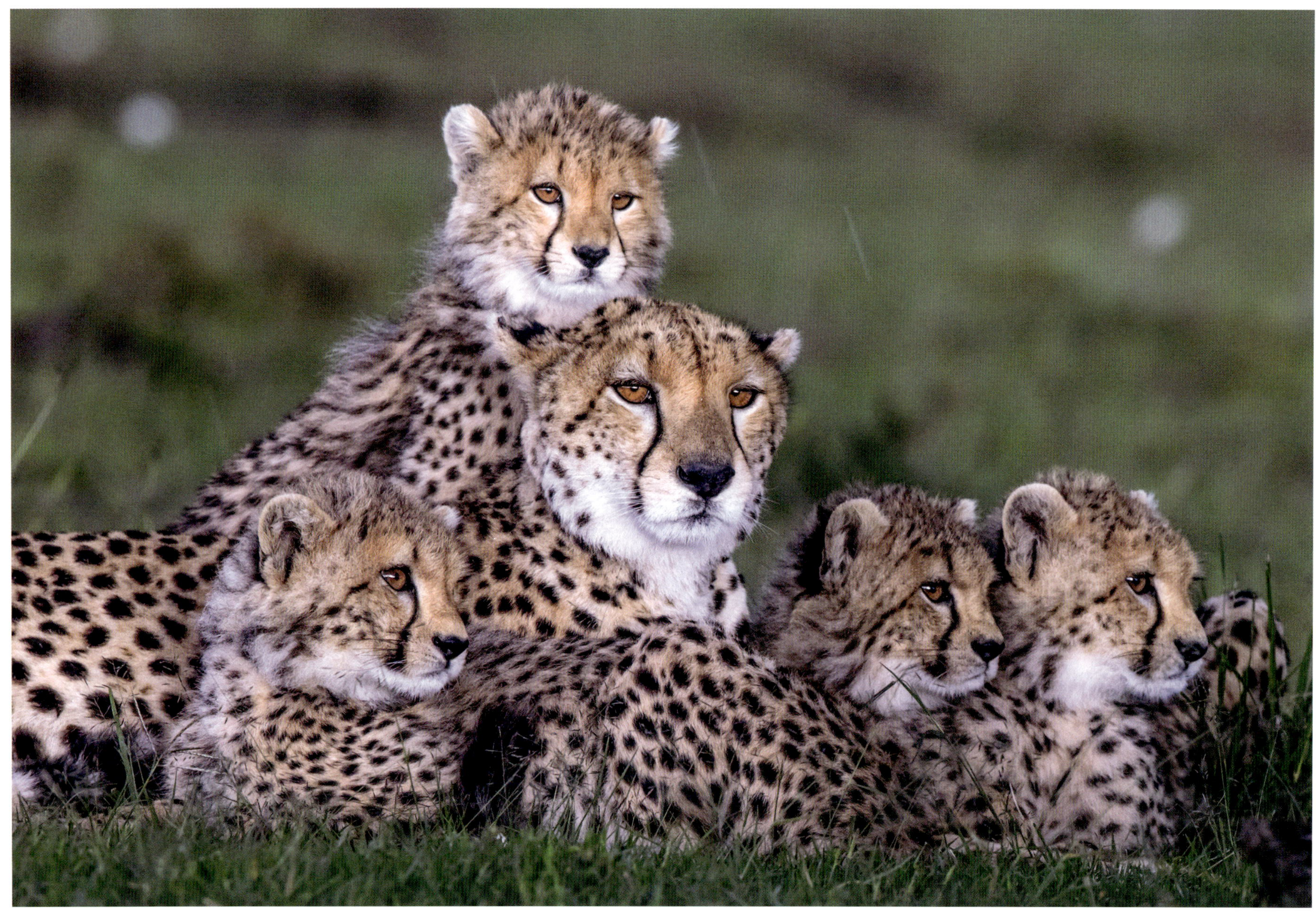

Beauty spots: utterly priceless. If these prosper, they keep tourists entertained and interested for years. If they get slaughtered by the competition, it's another arrow in their birthright. Wringing hand days are over; they need direct protection. If you have a problem with this, safari somewhere else.

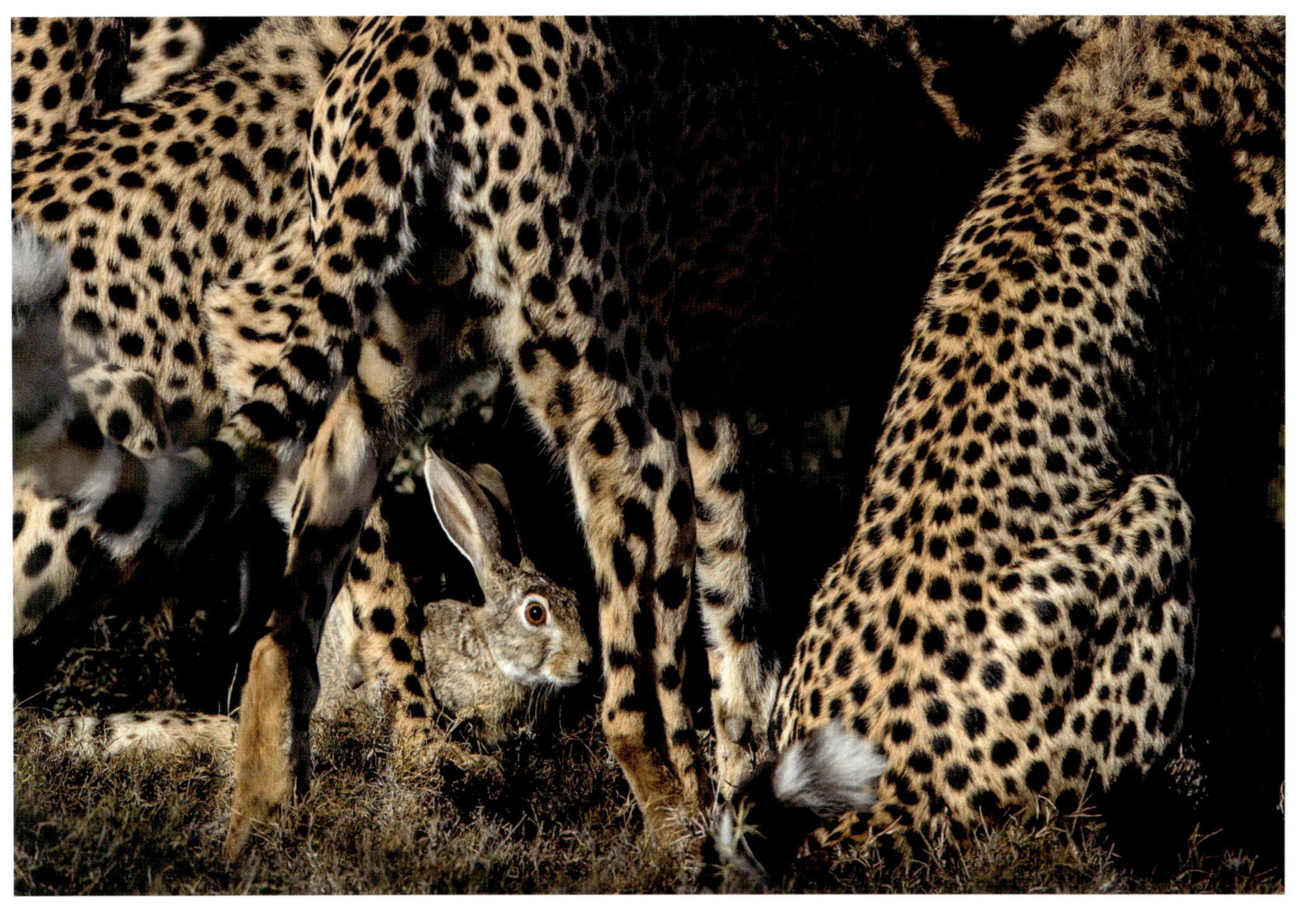

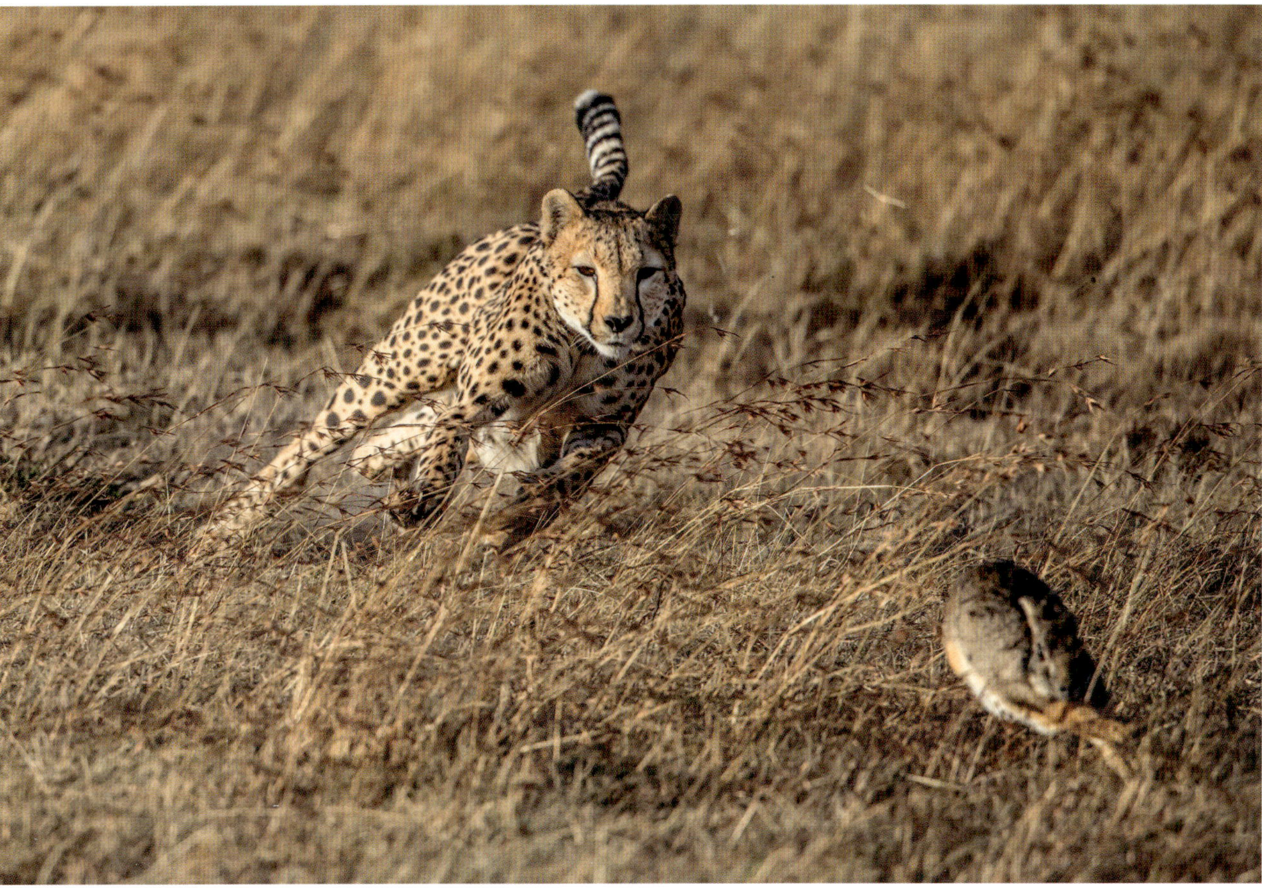

Hare today.

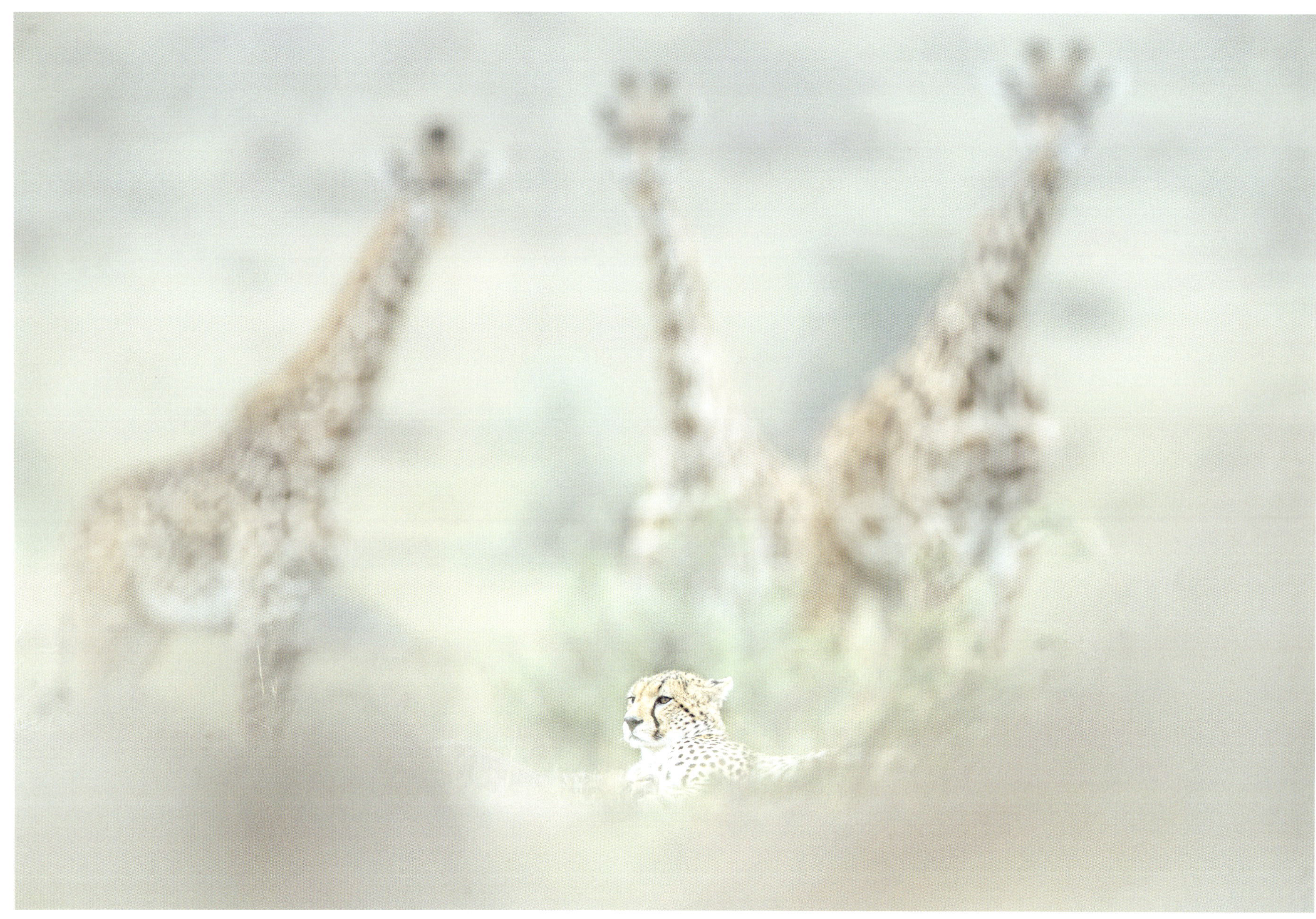

I have seen this before and in my head I remembered distant pikey camera club mantras and closed my aperture right down to get all twelve giraffes and cheetah sharp. Sum of it parts, it wasn't even close, not even a 2/10. When it happened again, an F4 setting taken through granite improved things a little. Mara North at its beautiful, fertile and imperial best.

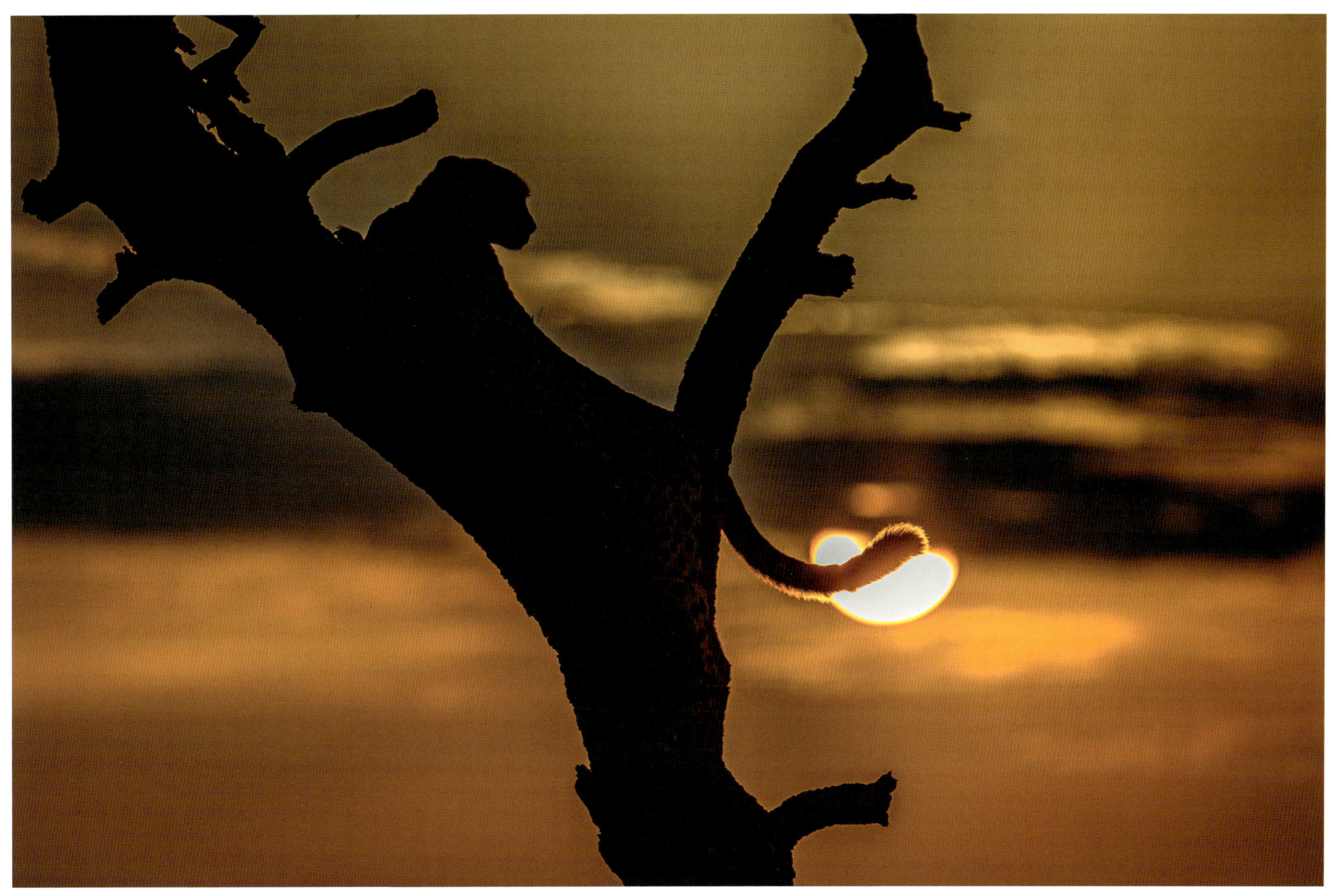

Cheetahs don't climb trees. Oh yes they do. This male woke, stretched, marked and ascended. In the sunrise. Ten minutes from camp. Decent.

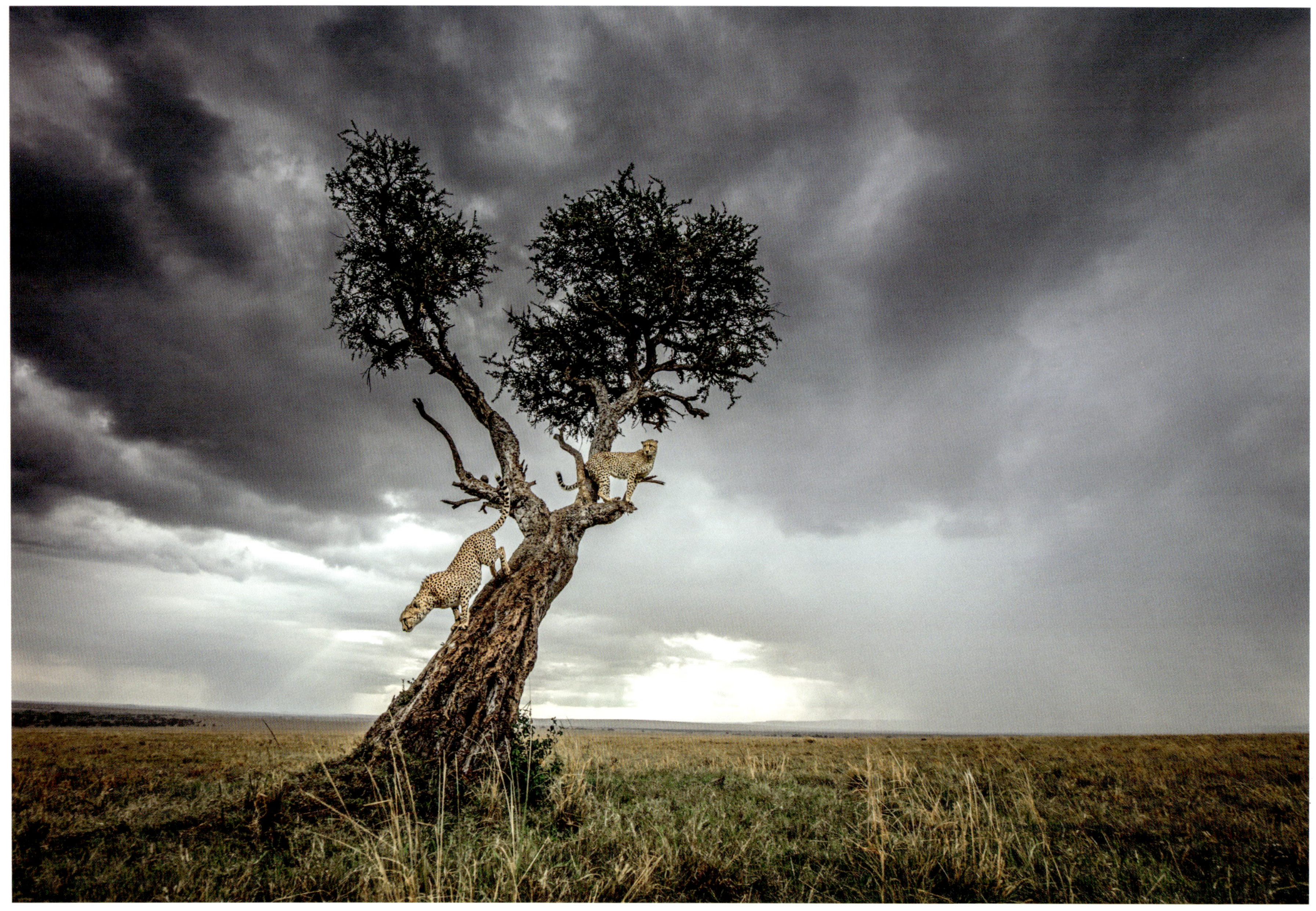

The tree of life: a gnarly landmark which has been popular with cheetahs, particularly male ones. They were a kilometre away, so we waited. And waited. And took chai. And lunch. Then the storm rolled in and they performed.

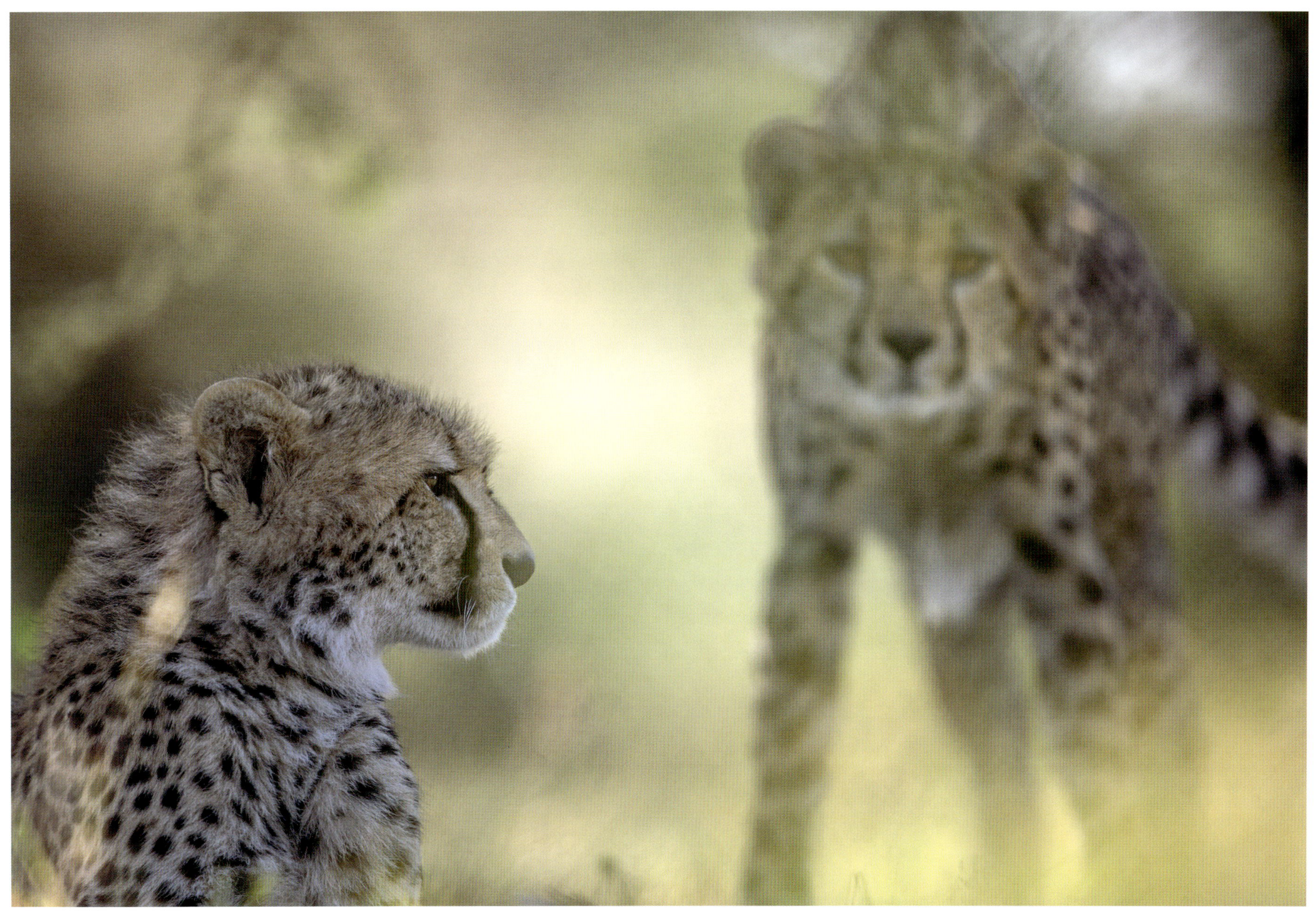

A drop-down side on the cruiser and a fortunate slope
plus a 2.8 aperture and some young and willing subjects.

ONE
TWO
THREE
FOUR
FIVE
SIX
SEVEN
EIGHT
NINE

'Build and they will come,' was the famous line from the Kevin Costner tearjerker *Field of Dreams*. It almost applies to this species which has staged a remarkable recovery. If you stop hunting a species, it will come back. It is pretty simple and there are probably over one million now, migrating through our oceans. To me they are the most impressive of all cetaceans because their antics outstrip any other. Breaching, spy-hopping, tail-slapping and bubble-net feeding make them a joyous quarry for maritime fans.

Traditionally they had been a quarry for commercial whaling which savaged their populations. This does not happen now but they are still imperilled by fishing nets, ship collisions and noise pollution. Then, of course, there is the insidious danger of the drop in fish stocks, something not exclusive just to humpbacks.

These remarkable mammals undertake huge migrations – thousands of miles – between their cold water feeding grounds and warmer breeding areas. This plays a crucial role in transporting nutrients across these vast regions and supporting marine biodiversity. Even their feeding habits help keep an equilibrium in the marine ecosystem.

They were butchered with impunity, almost to extinction. Anyone who has felt the concussion of a breach or tail slap (they do it for fun is the best explanation) would agree that they are better in the water than on a plate. Intelligent, graceful and 30 tons in weight, and now seemingly protected. Sometimes good things do happen.

▷ There is almost something sinister about humpbacks as they surface in a jet black ocean, the millpond surface pierced by their chef's-hat blow. Three stops under takes care of the photograph.

HUMPBACK WHALE

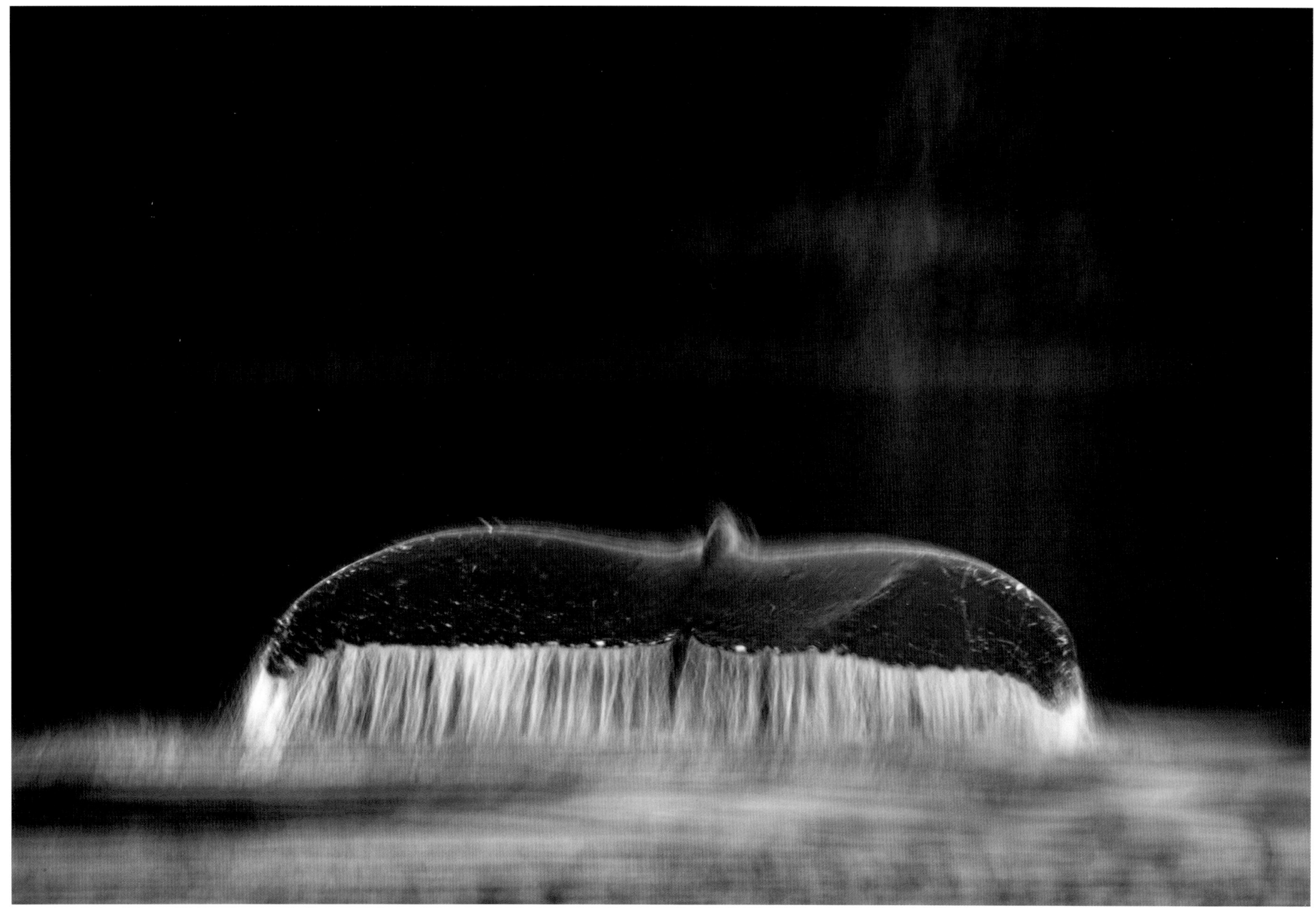

With a small yacht and outstanding crew these sightings are commonplace. The low vantage point and low speed enables images like these to be taken. To think not very long ago these 30 ton leviathans were being butchered. My favourite whale by far, the sound, sight or sometimes even smell never fails to excite me.

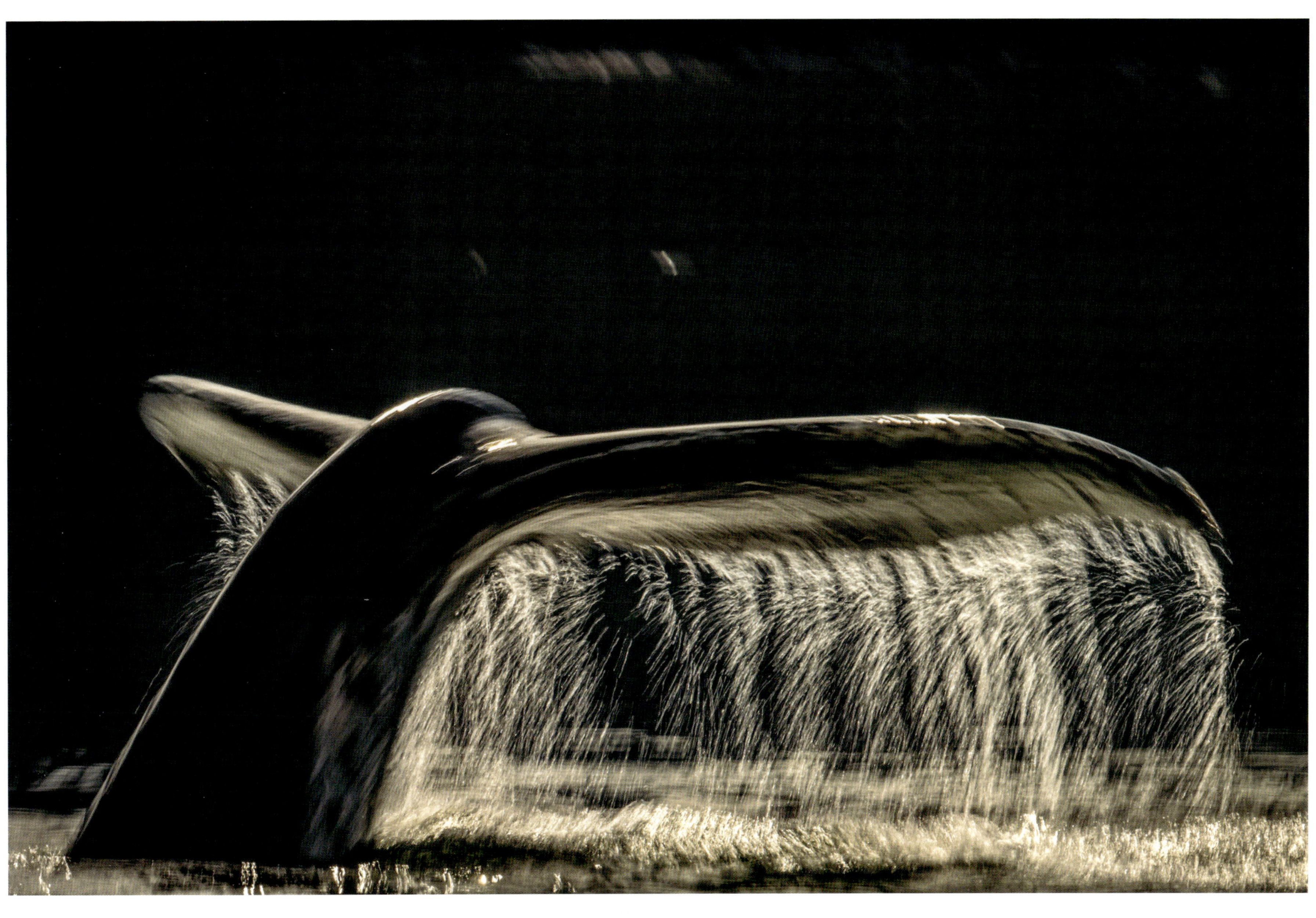

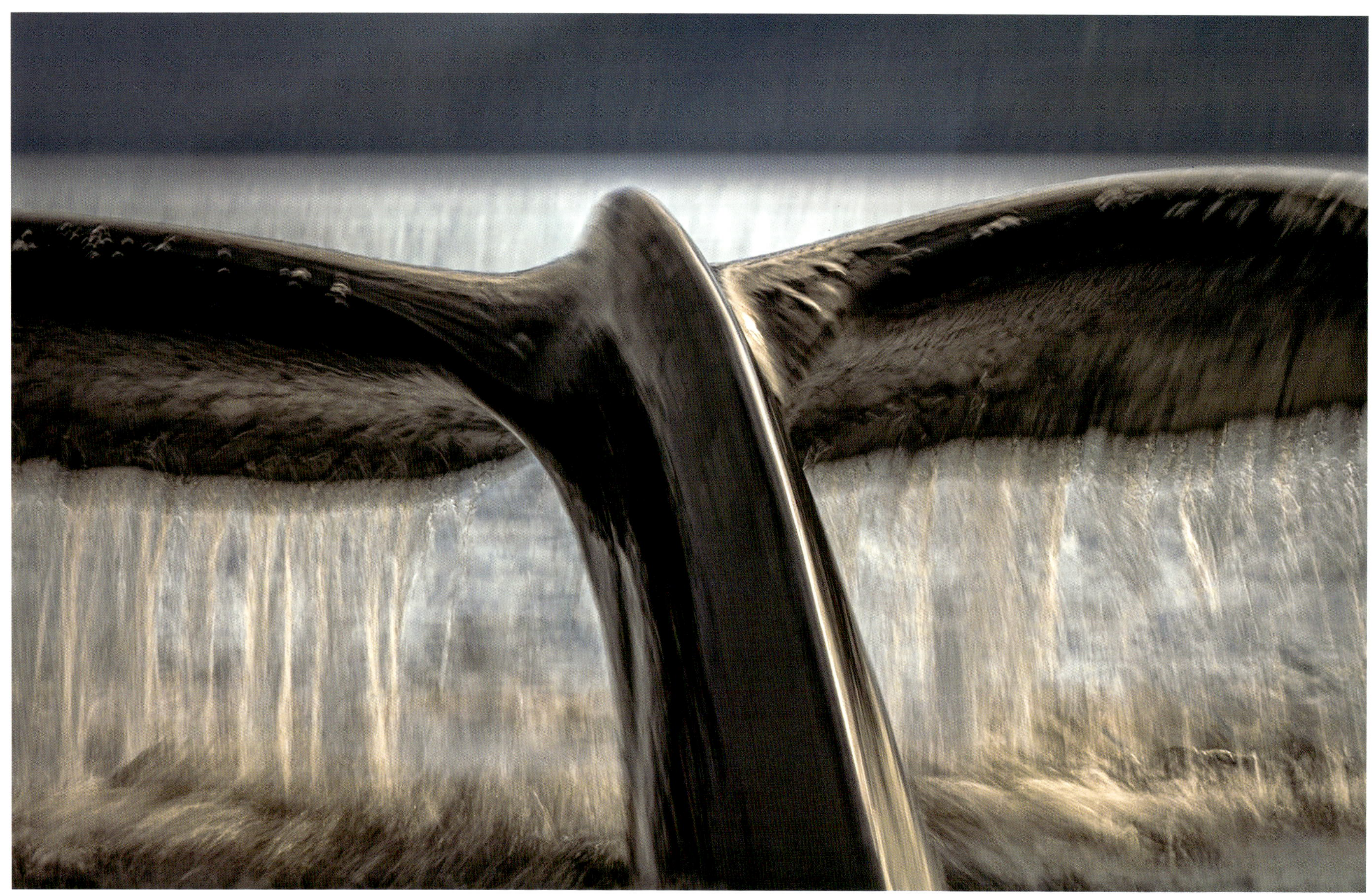

'I'll just take a few fast ("safe") ones first, then I'll try some of these slow ones.' That vanilla approach will hardly gain access into the photography hall of fame. I love trying ludicrously low speeds. What's the worst that can happen? We now have oceans from the Pacific to Antarctica bounteous with these giants; perfect subjects to practise on.

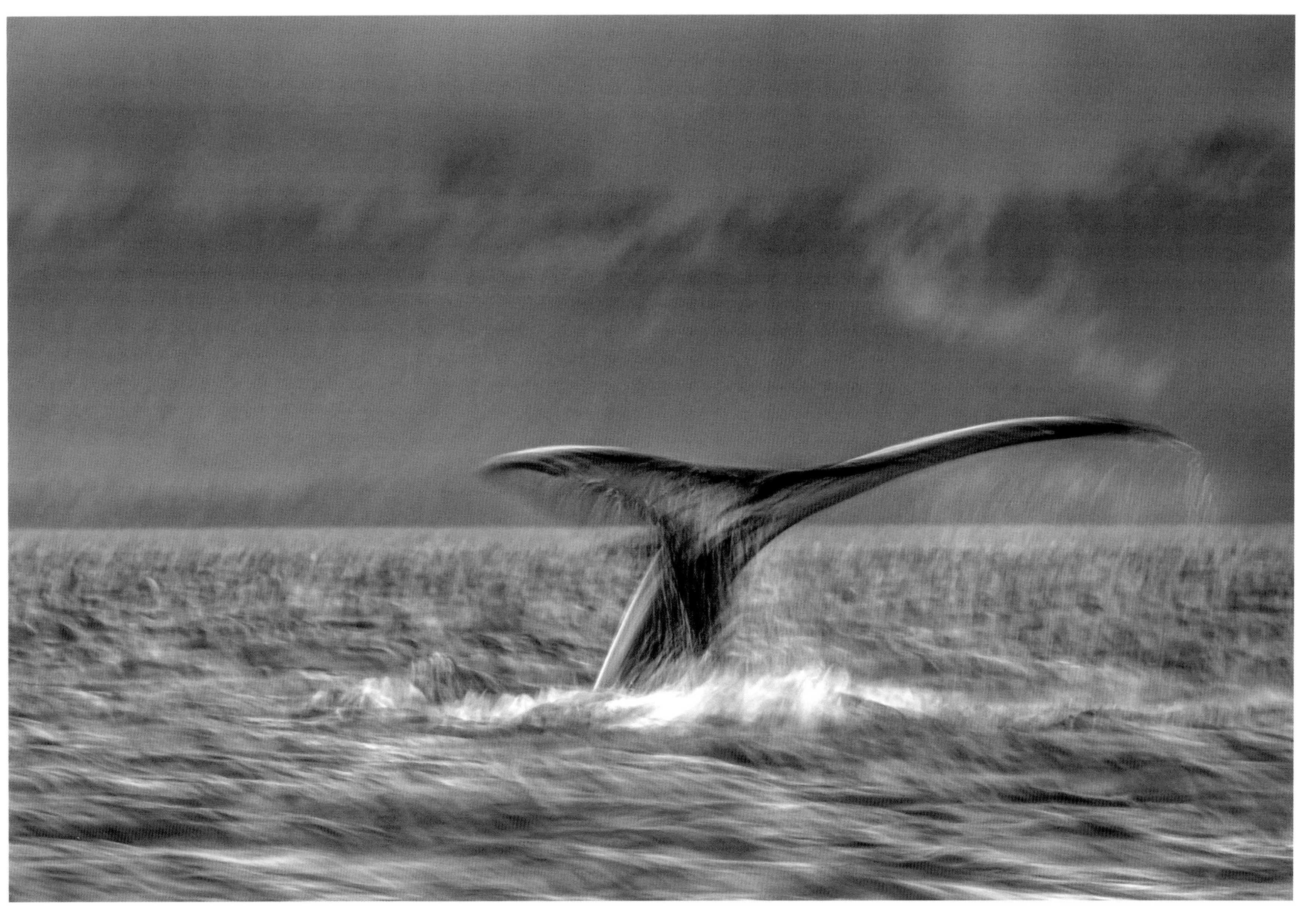

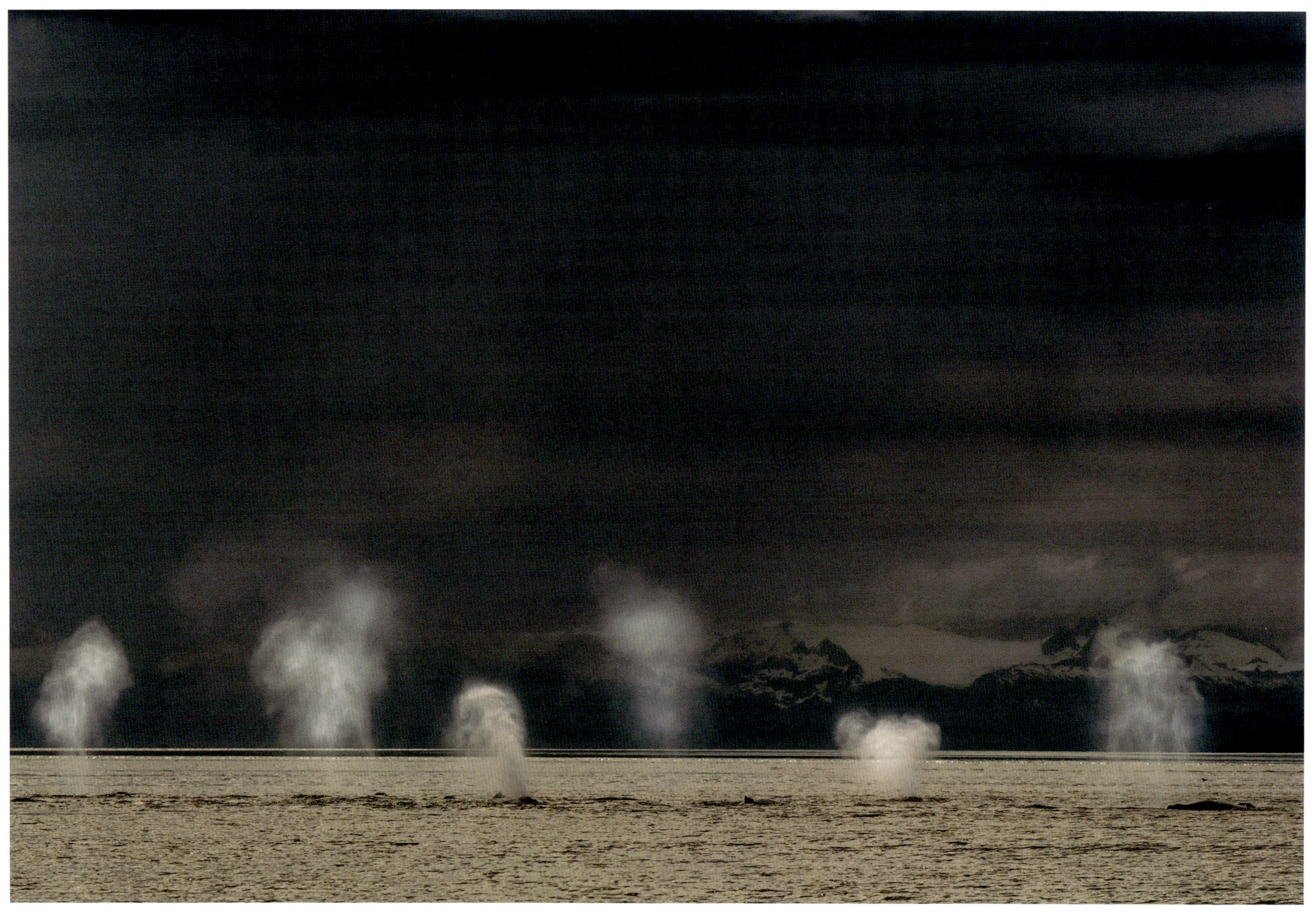

A brooding distant storm, flat water and six humpbacks.

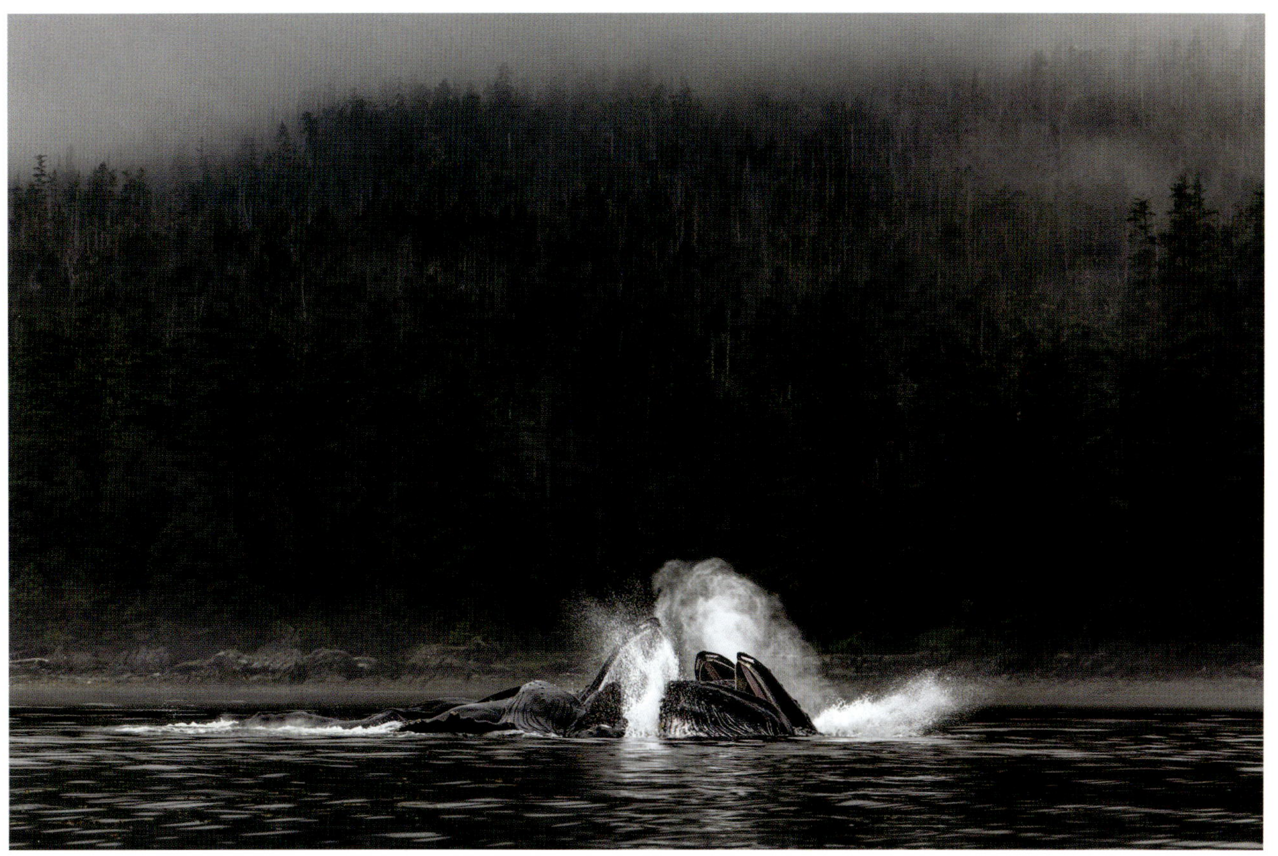

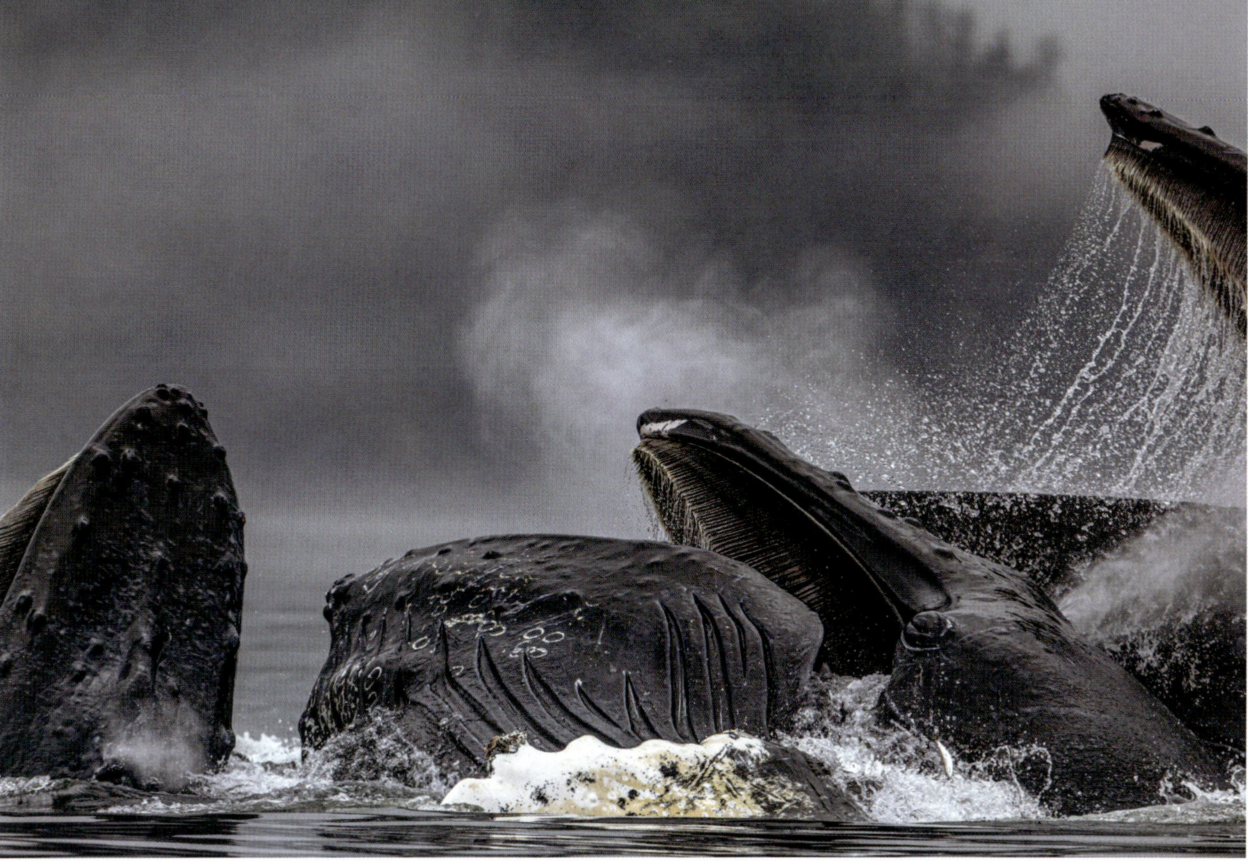

Net gain: when they are in a feeding mood it is ridiculously exciting trying to gauge where they will rise, with a balletic grace, baleens sieving herring, before slipping back into the inky depths.

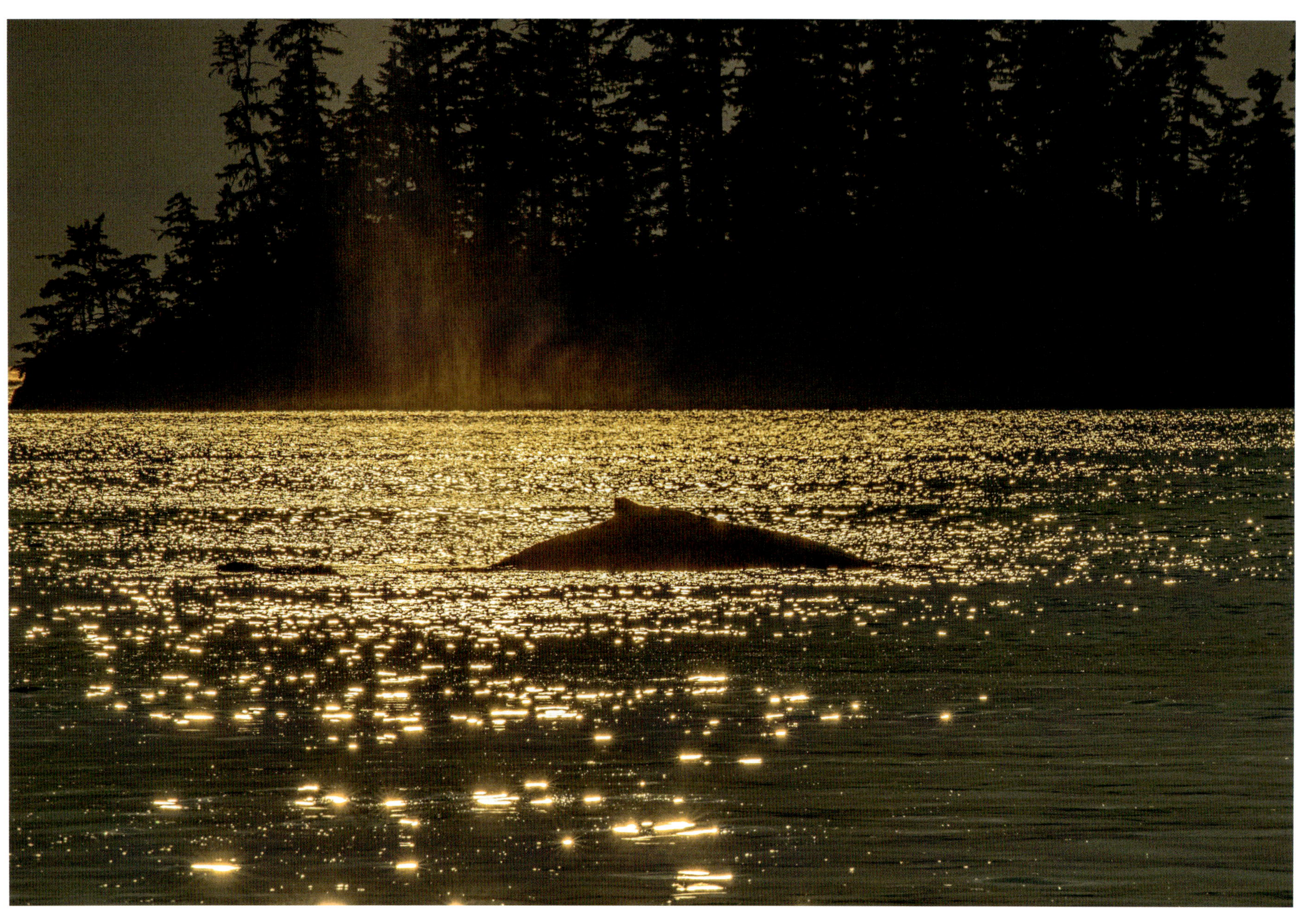

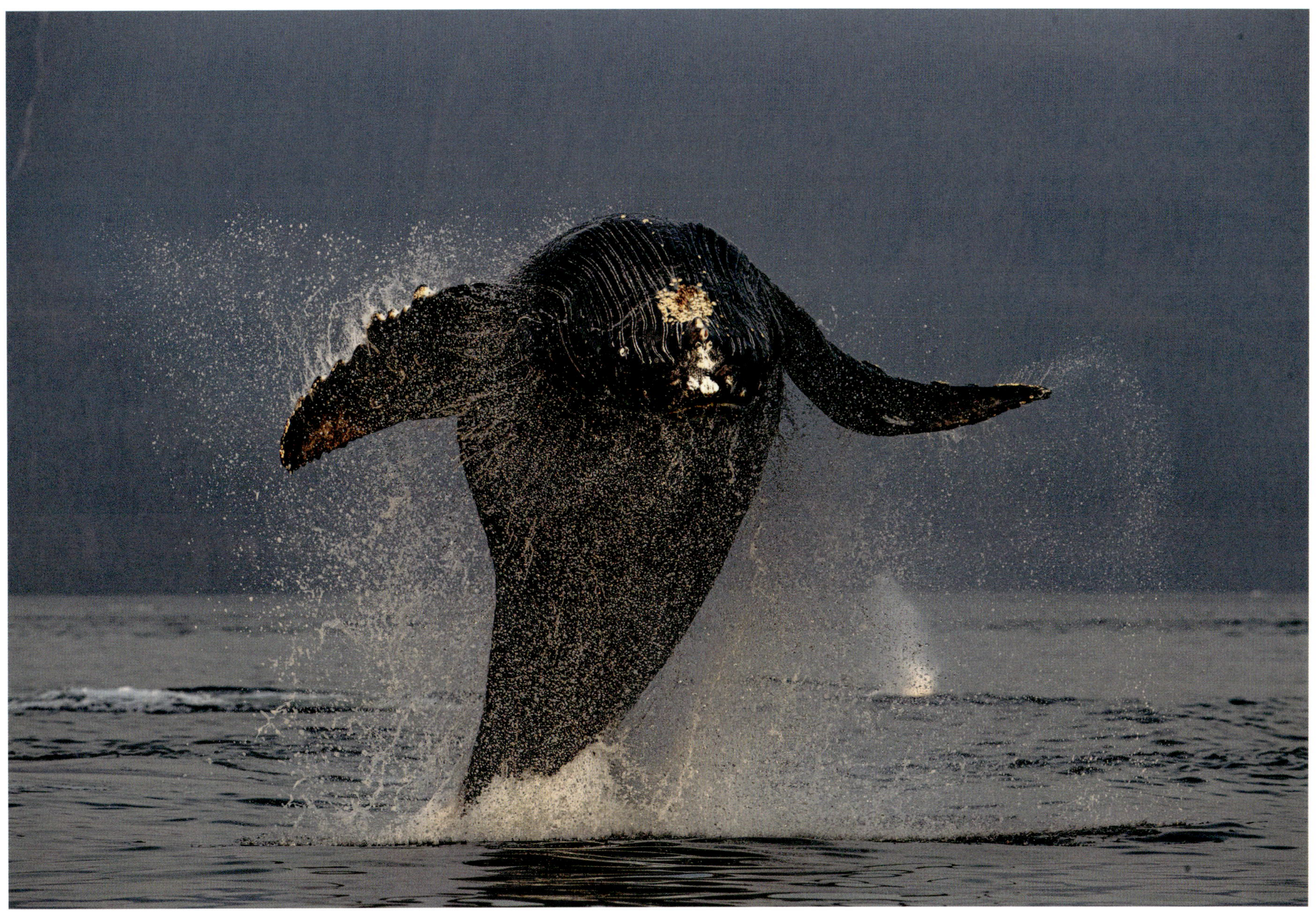

A mere three twitches of the tail is enough to propel 30 cetaceous tons into the air. There is no real science behind breaching, spy-hopping and tail-slapping. Perhaps the best explanation is because they can. Maybe she was trying to impress her young calf behind.

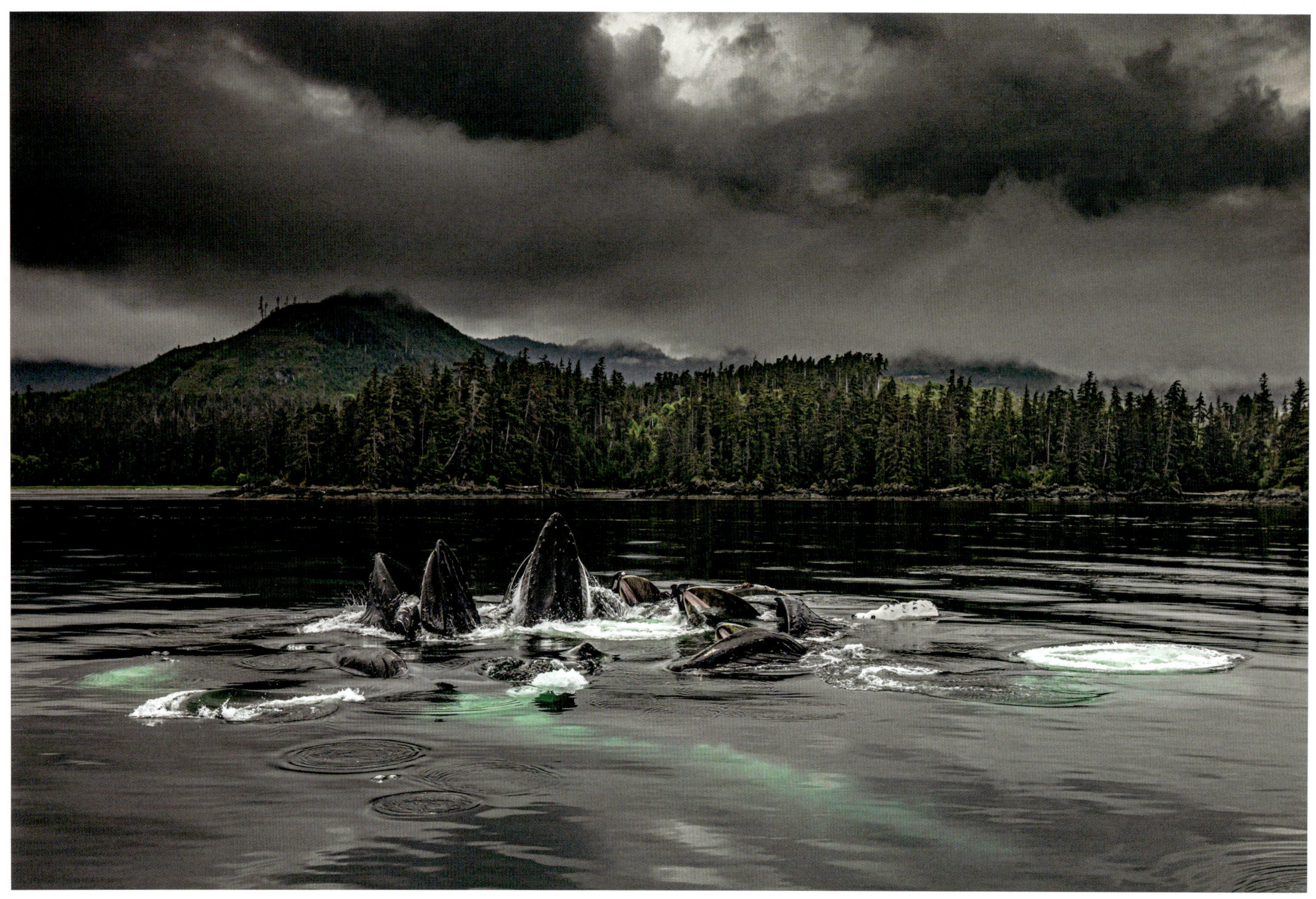

After two days of bubble-netting in Southeast Alaska, we were getting complacent. As a storm approached, these dozen appeared right next to the yacht. It was mesmerising seeing them above, and below, the waterline.

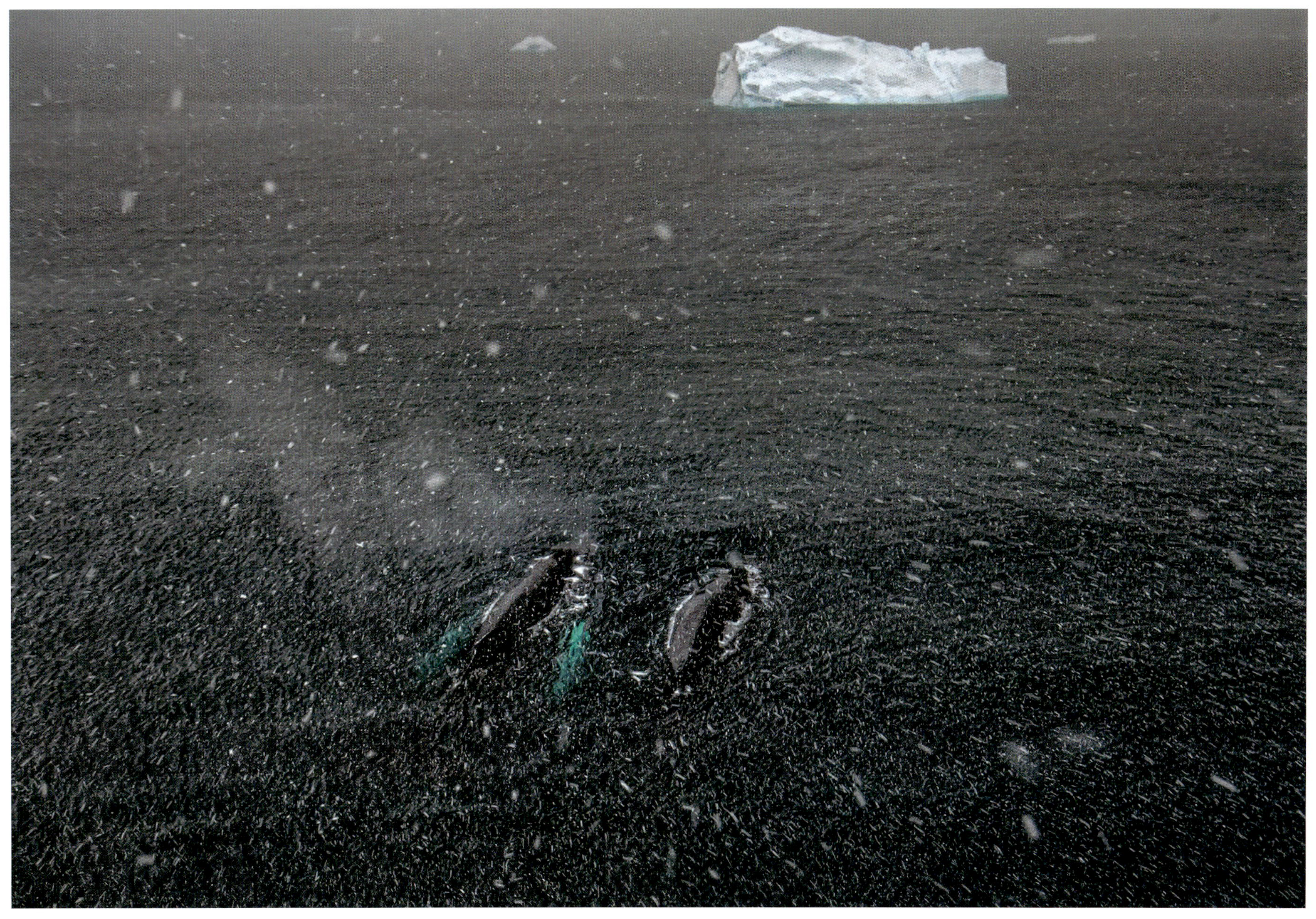

During a gentle flurry of Gerlache Strait snow I gazed out of my cabin, hypnotised by the fluttering flakes and distant berg. I heard their asthmatic blow before I saw them: two humpbacks, peacefully plying their maritime beat before diving.

This section of the book has been optimistic, I wish the other eight were.

SEVEN

EIGHT

NINE

Pantanal jaguars are twice the size of leopards and much bigger than their Central American cousins, mainly due to their diet. Capybara and caiman are not only formidable prey, but also large and rich in protein. Photographing jaguars from their level in a low slung boat is exciting and also physically demanding, just as it should be, but also a seriously exhilarating exercise. This threatened apex predator has been largely wiped out from North America and its population has fallen 30 per cent in the last few years elsewhere, mainly to habitat loss due to agriculture. Each year agricultural fires leave an indelible imprint on their numbers but the Brazilian cat is fairly healthy. Elsewhere, particularly in Central America, the story isn't so rosy. Human-wildlife conflict and hunting for a ghastly trade in domestic markets continues to affect them, particularly in Guatemala and Belize. It has been 'near-threatened' on the IUCN (International Union for Conservation of Nature) Red List since 2002.

Ponder this: jaguars have football and car companies all using their name, without, we are to assume, permission. Tigers show even more largesse to huge companies from breakfast cereals to rugby, football and cricket sides and indeed one vast petrochemical behemoth. Are they footing the bill for this plagiarism?

A British car manufacturer has dined off jaguars for over a hundred years, but I'm not sure how much they have helped this threatened feline. However much machismo and pheromones they try to fuel-inject into their impossibly butch ads, they don't even come close to the real thing.

JAGUAR

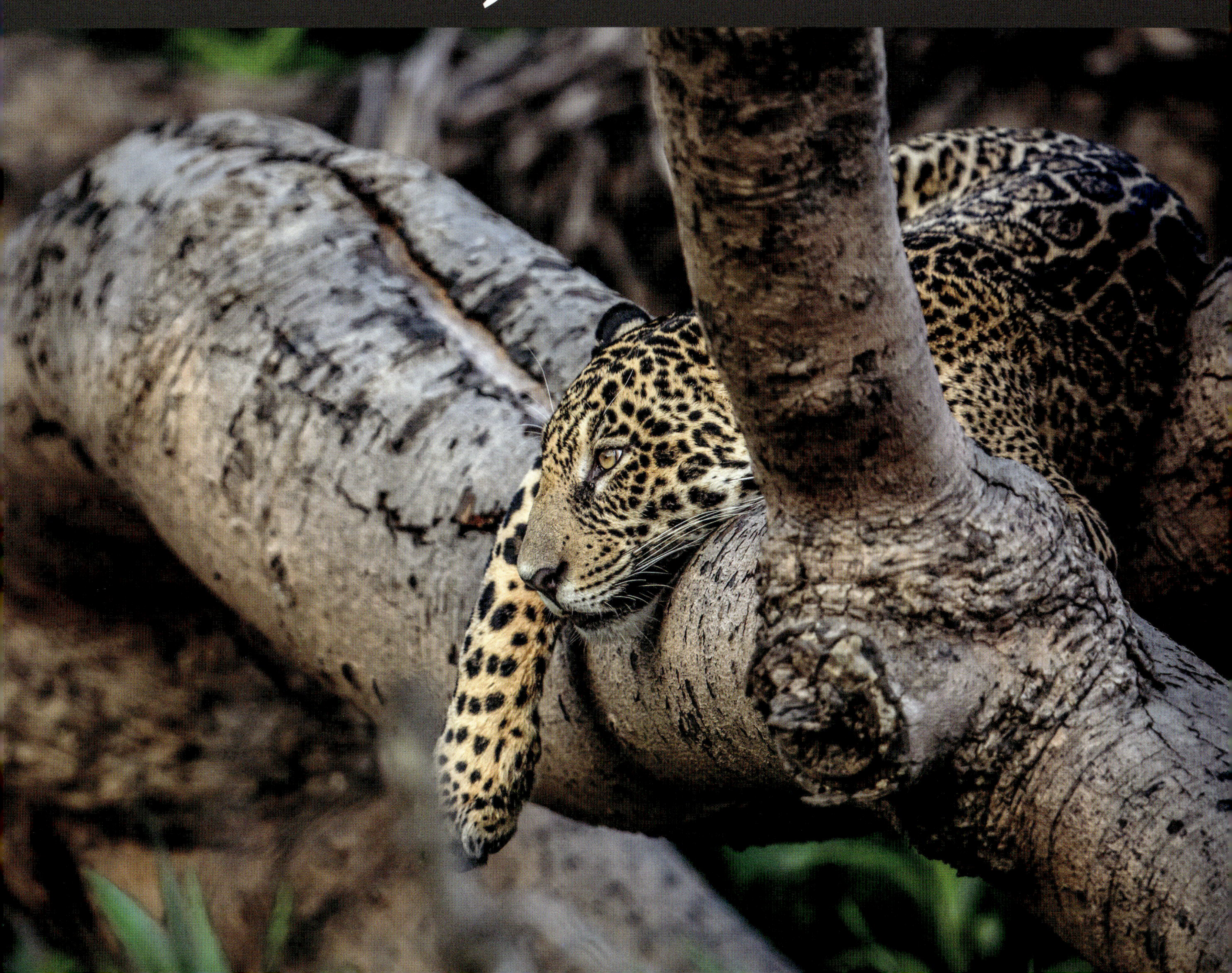

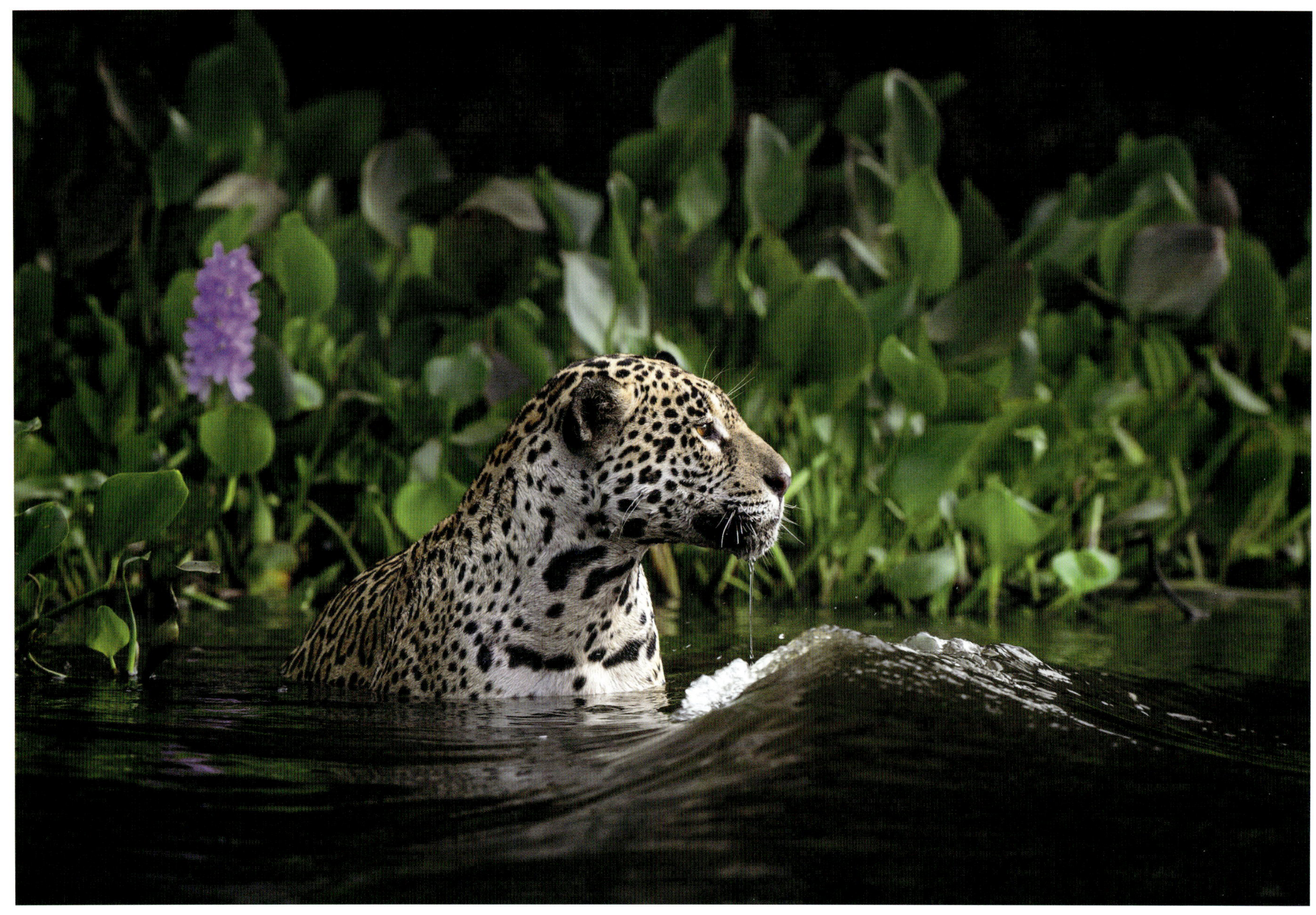

On my first visit guiding in the Pantanal it took a while to comprehend jaguars. Unlike leopards or cheetahs they are alpha predators. They get up when they feel like it and again, unlike most felines, they like water – they actually use it like a road. I will never tire of it.

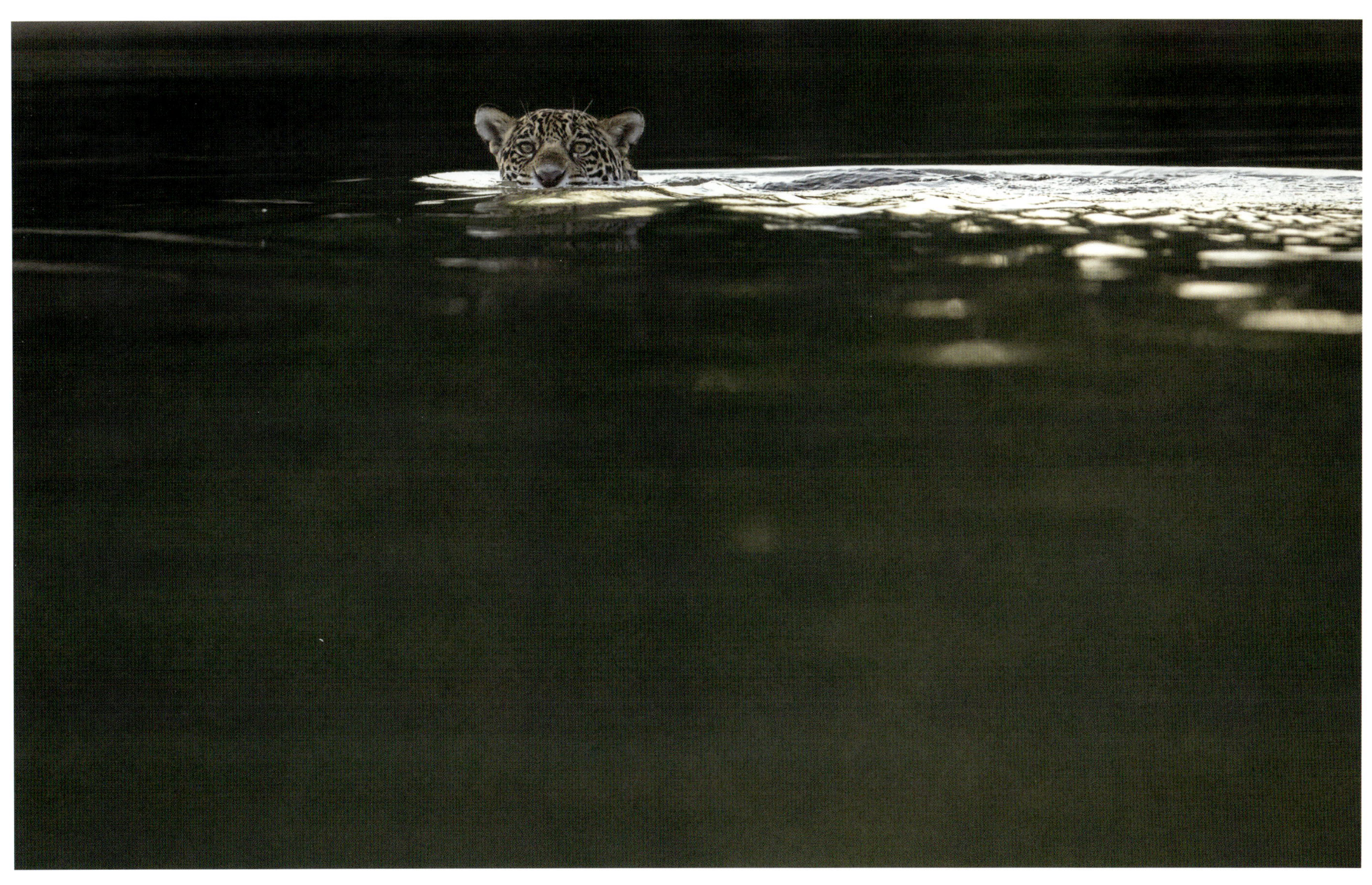

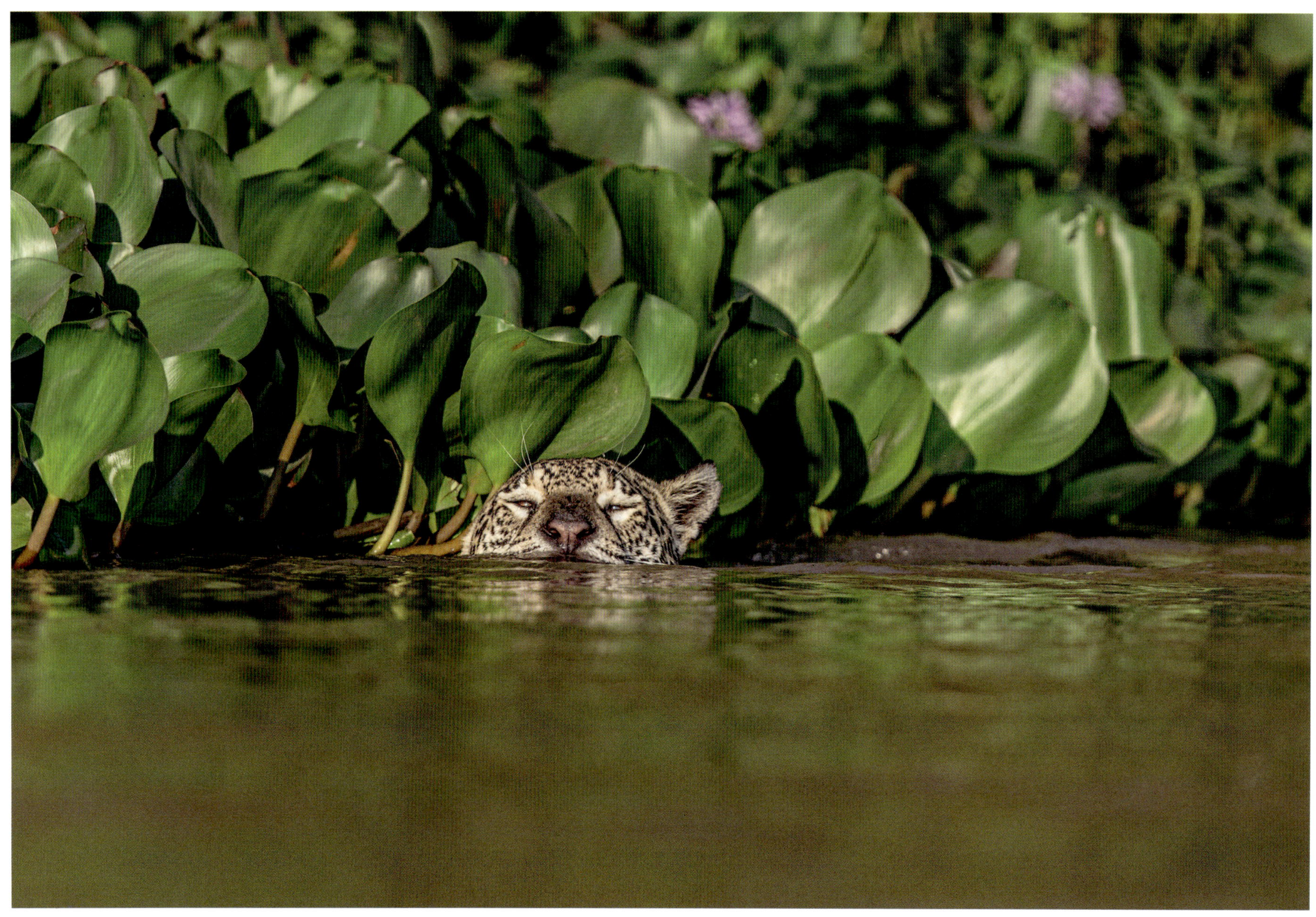

To spend quality time watching jaguars hunt is wildlife viewing from the high table. Seeing the water hyacinth tremble and twitch as they deploy through the undergrowth is tantalising, never knowing when their head will appear.

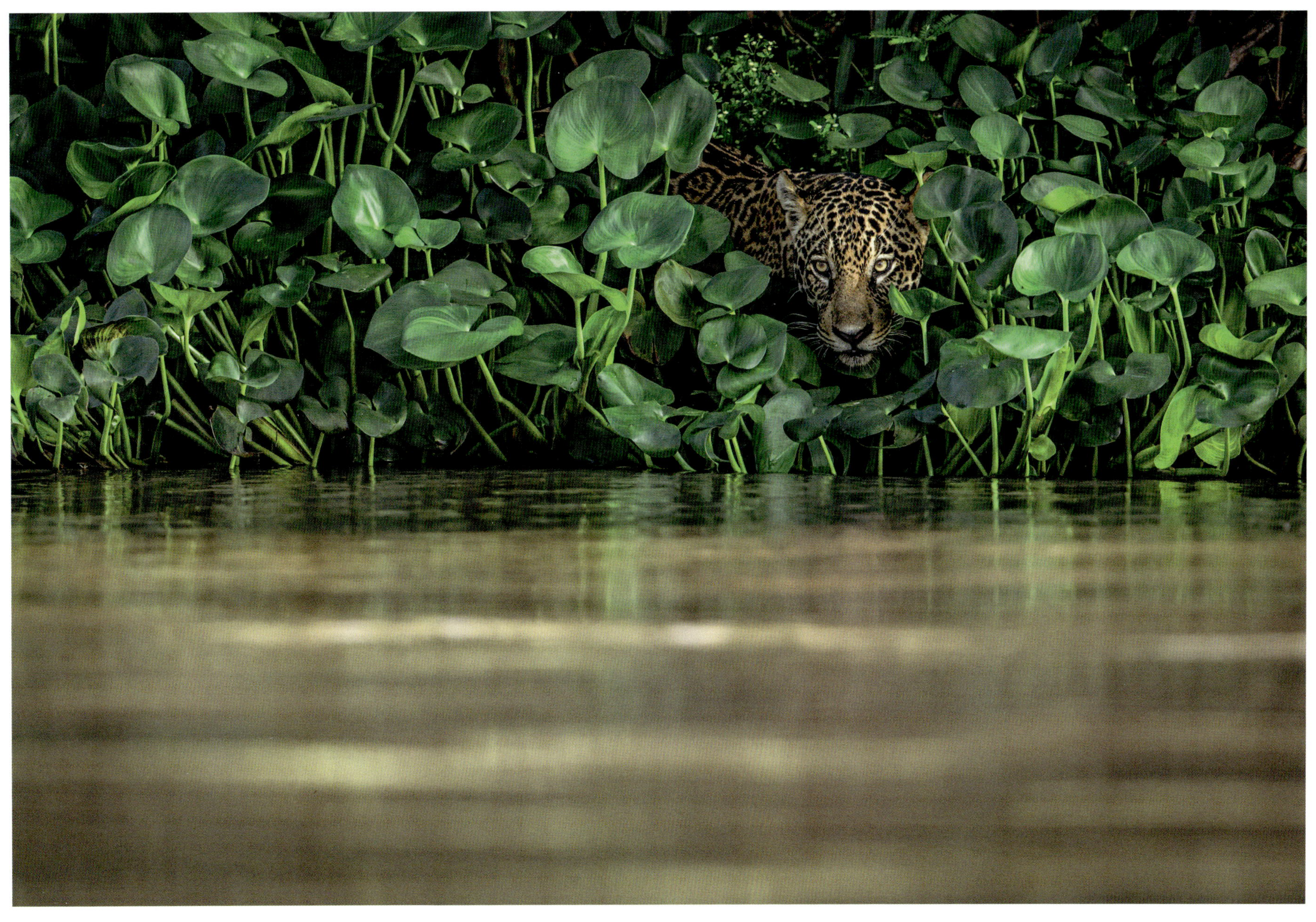

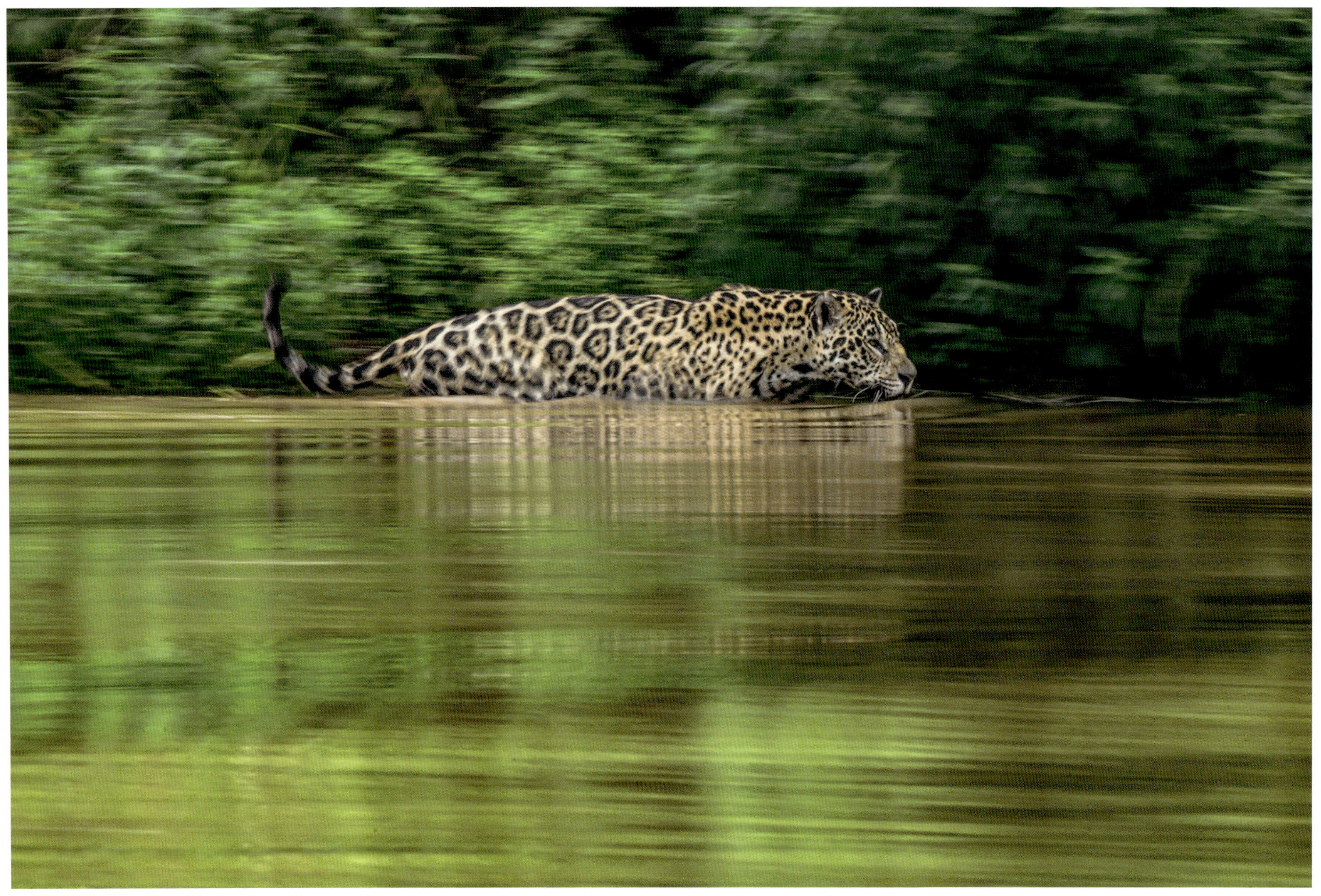

Probably the slowest shutter speed I have ever employed following a female as she hunted upstream. She was struggling against the current but also happier low down away from the smoke of the many agricultural fires that hamper all wildlife in the Pantanal.

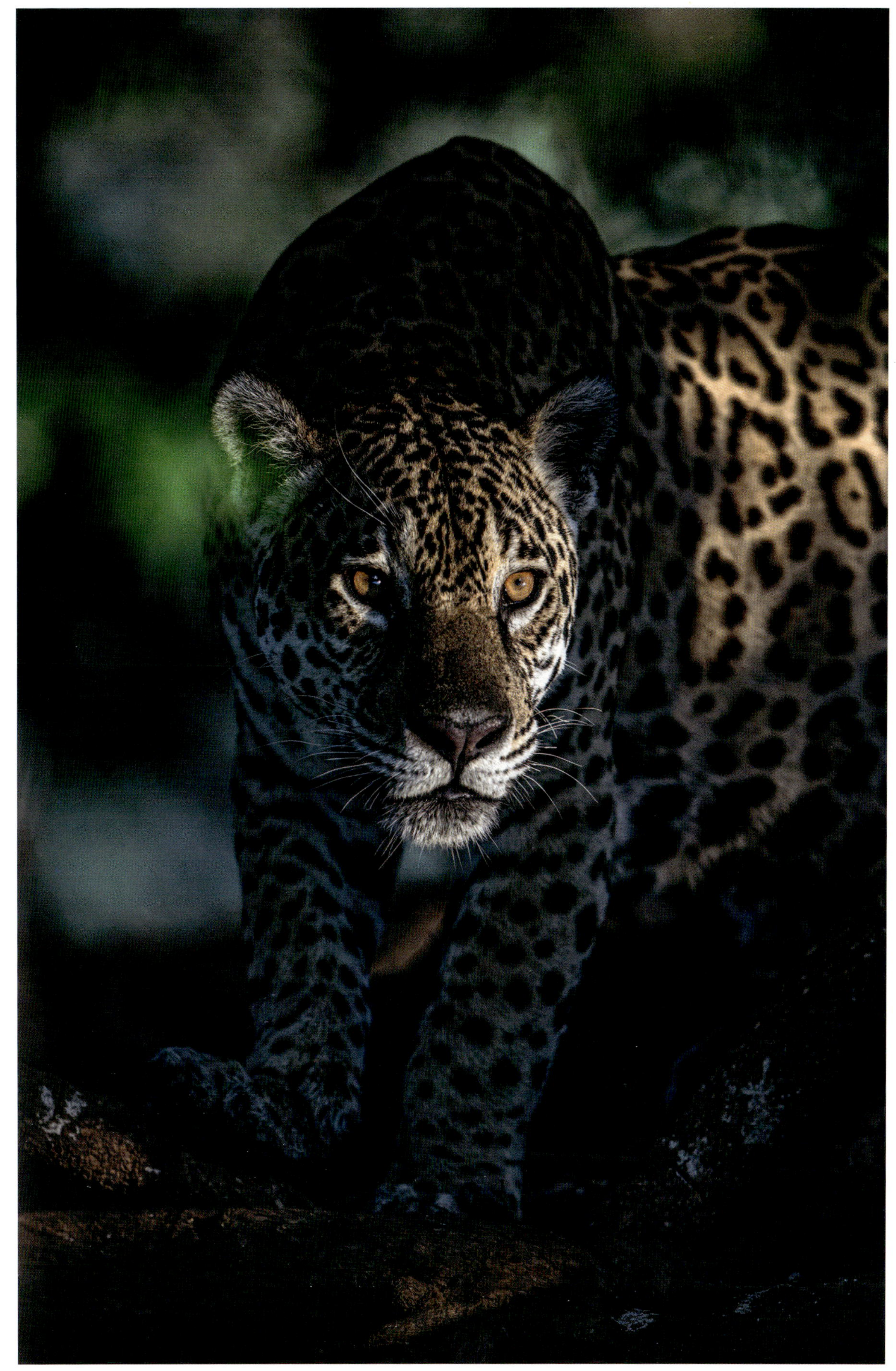

My favourite portrait along the Rio Negro. These predators have been filmed diving off 20-foot-high branches to drop, unsuspecting, onto floating caiman. It was phenomenally hot that afternoon but somehow we got into a superb position as the sun dropped. Background, subject, light – some trinity, some she-type.

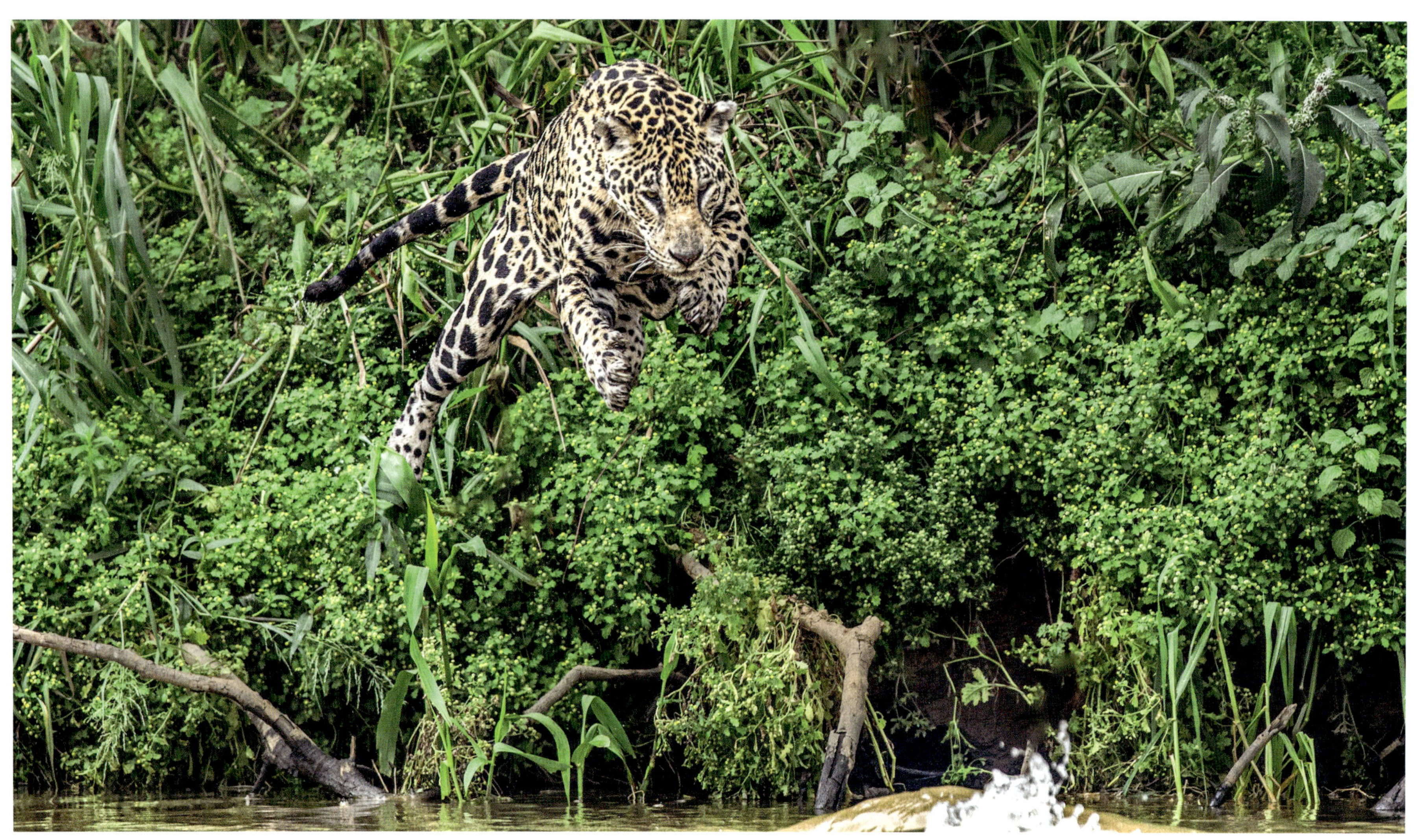

Images like this only happen when all the research, homework and fieldcraft is completed properly. Marcello, Berto and the daddy and mummy of them all, Andre and Akhila – I salute you. Pressing the shutter is the easy bit.

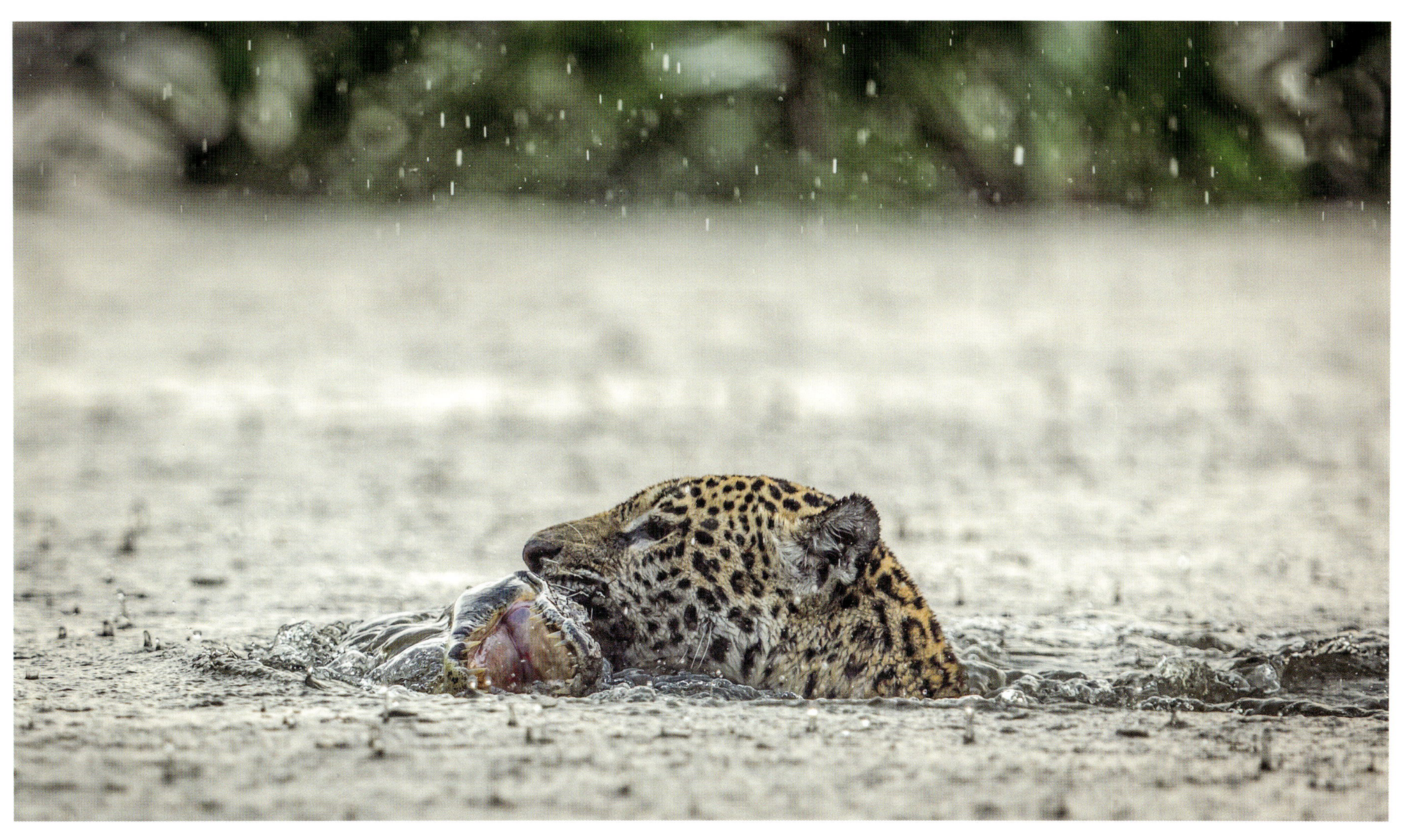

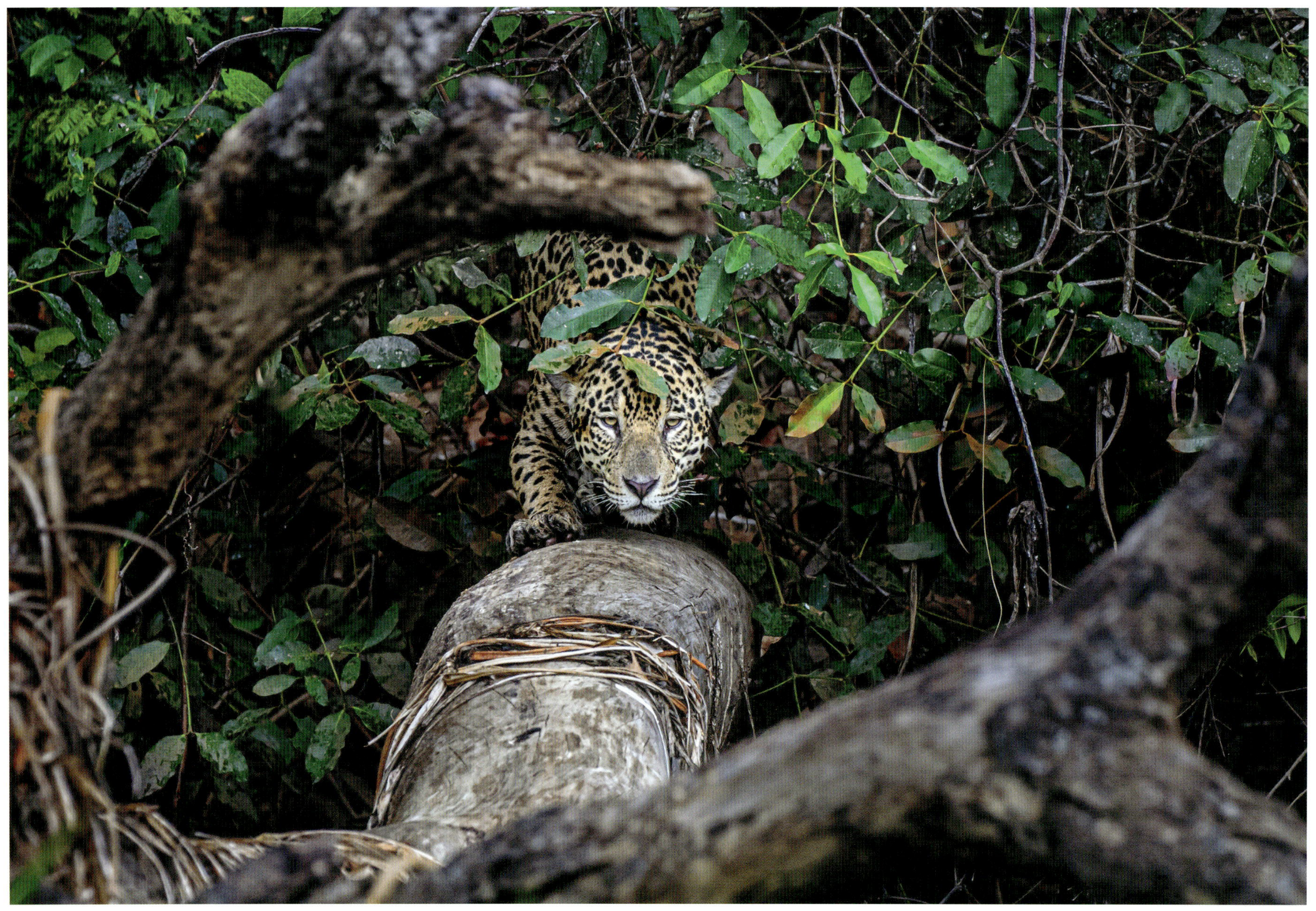

Marcello steered his low slung boat a full 100 metres ahead of this patrolling female and stopped. Then winked. At me. If his gamble fails, so what? It didn't. Never chase the prize. Anywhere. This was fieldcraft from the top drawer.

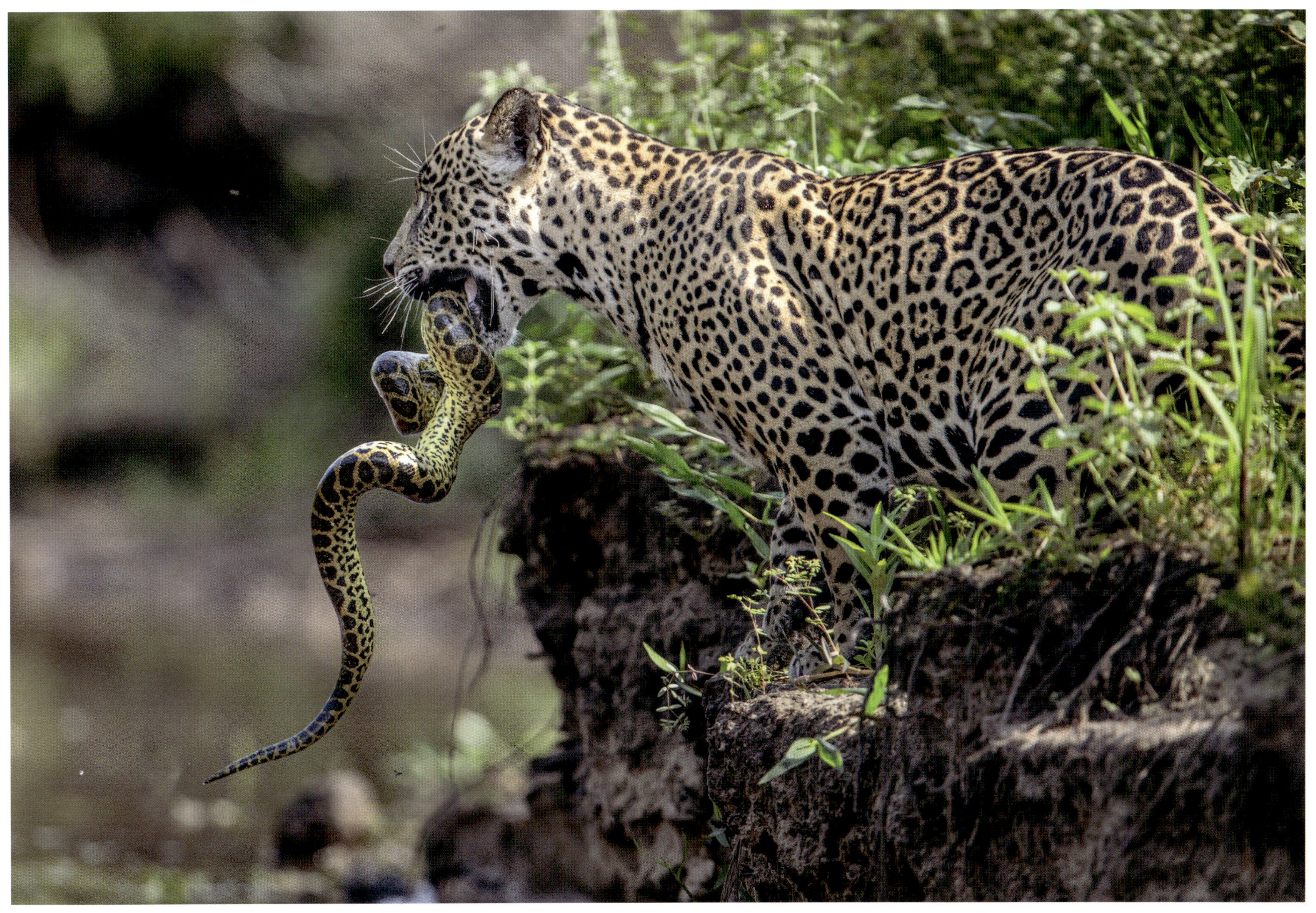

A grab shot: down a tiny tributary with around 5 or 6 inches of draft this female was quartering the banks. Suddenly she dropped and rose with an anaconda in her mouth. Big meal, big moment, obrigado Marcello.

ONE
TWO
THREE
FOUR
FIVE
SIX
SEVEN
EIGHT
NINE

A dusty buffer zone track in Rajasthan many, many years ago was my inauspicious opening game drive, my previous safari having been thwarted by Indian trains. There was little or no chance of anything with a pulse, let alone a Bengal tiger … then, prostrated in the road, a massive, magnificent male. The impact of this literally changed my life, more so when I returned later that year to find out its pelt was residing on the back of someone in China, its other body parts sold as trinkets and medicine. The incandescent rage this elicited is just as potent now.

These animals are safe in national parks, but they will never be allowed to roam over vast ranges as they once did. Census figures apparently tell us their numbers have increased, but we have still lost four subspecies and butchered thousands, all to satiate the cravings of a despicable traditional market in Southeast Asia. Alive, they are worth millions; sliced up on the slab and then parcelled piecemeal to these ghoulish wet stalls, they are worth a few thousand. Angry? You should be.

In all the following years since my striped epiphany I have struggled for photographic satisfaction with tigers. This is unimportant. Byzantine layers of bureaucracy and infuriating and nonsensical decision-making makes it difficult, challenging and frustrating. People often ask me, 'Is the tiger your favourite animal?' The answer is no: faunal favouritism is anthropomorphic bilge and does nothing for any animal's welfare and will certainly not secure its future. Pragmatism, anger and fund-raising might.

A number of years ago an Indian politician decided it would be a good idea to close off 80 per cent of the trails in national parks, looking to augment the sensitive section of his resumé. Some spineless conservationists and marketing lightweights (tautology alert. Again) even agreed with him. This stupid decision has caused more congestion; it also denigrates the tourism opportunities and loses vital eyes on the ground. If this happened elsewhere, it would be an embossed invitation to poachers. The fact that this lunacy cannot be redacted speaks volumes about the smug, bureaucratic and lazy powers that be, masquerading as the heads of wildlife tourism. There are plenty of heroes with tigers, there are thousands who have supported my and others' campaigns, but until the corpulent bodies that reside at the top of the wildlife food chain wake up, the whole tourism experience will continue to languish light years behind that which can be experienced in Africa.

But despite the frustrations, the joy of finding fresh pugmarks, and then the owner of them, will never dim for me or thousands of others.

A tigress that lives a full life, that rears four or five litters, in a National park, with all ancillaries considered and calculated, can be worth as much as $100m. Worth thinking about.

▷ Trying to secure full-day permits is hard enough, the price for them is accompanied by a highwayman, but sometimes that and those Byzantine regulations are forgotten. This is about moments – all wildlife is – and this one I will never forget. Despite the sun being well and truly risen, intransigent restrictions deny entrance until ludicrously late, dictated by protocol rather than the worldwide faunal mantra of getting into position before sunrise. The extra 15 minutes were therefore important.

Pappu's gamble, big one, big reward. A few moments of utter joy.

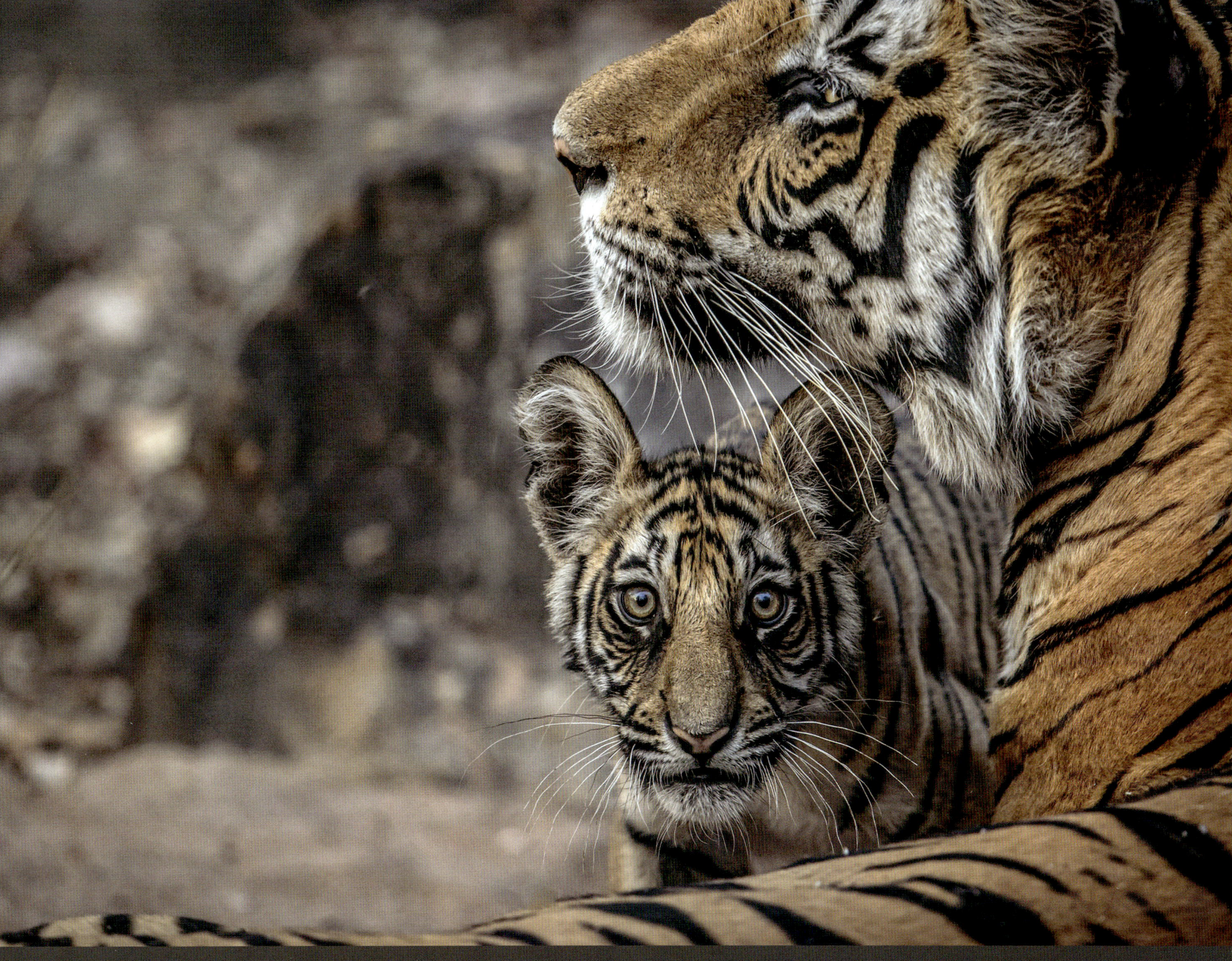

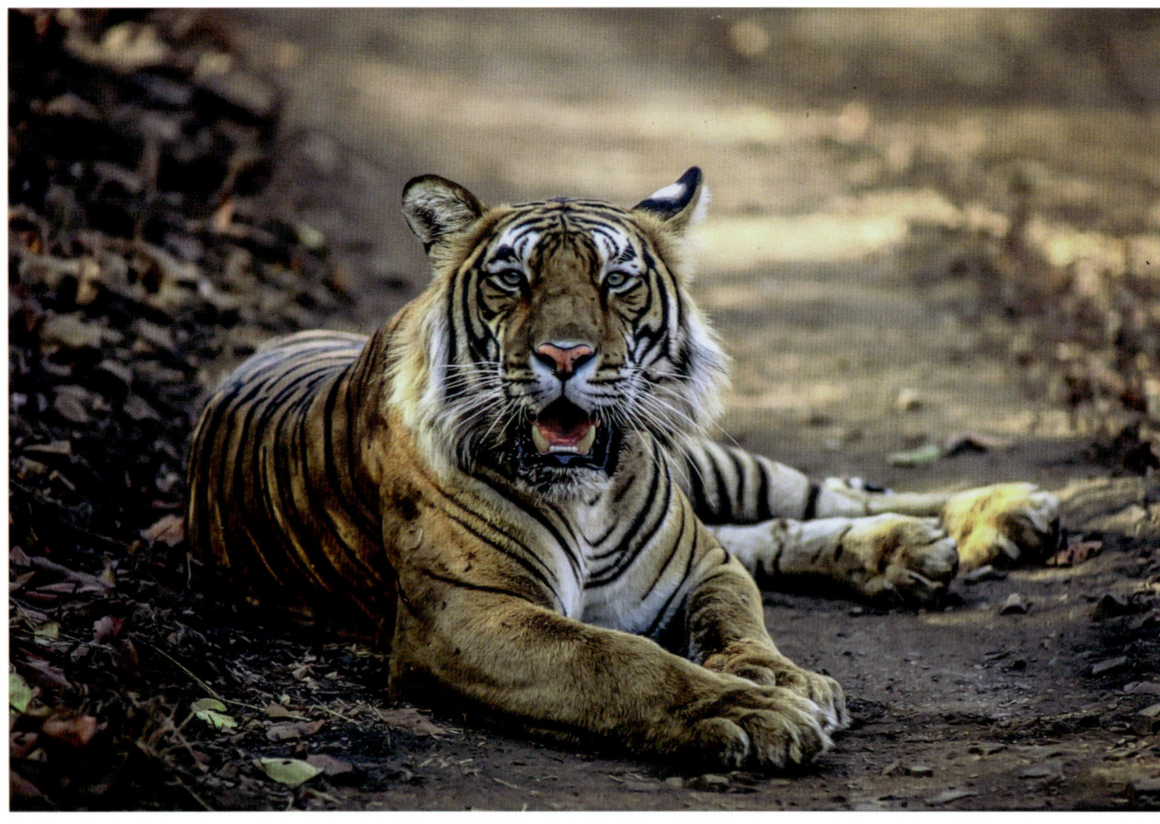

My first tiger. A massive male. I was in bits. A dusty Ranthambore buffer zone track in '98. Just me. It gazed right through me. I managed two photographs. It changed everything. It was poached a few months later. I hope the Chinese degenerate felt butch and brave with the pelt on his back.

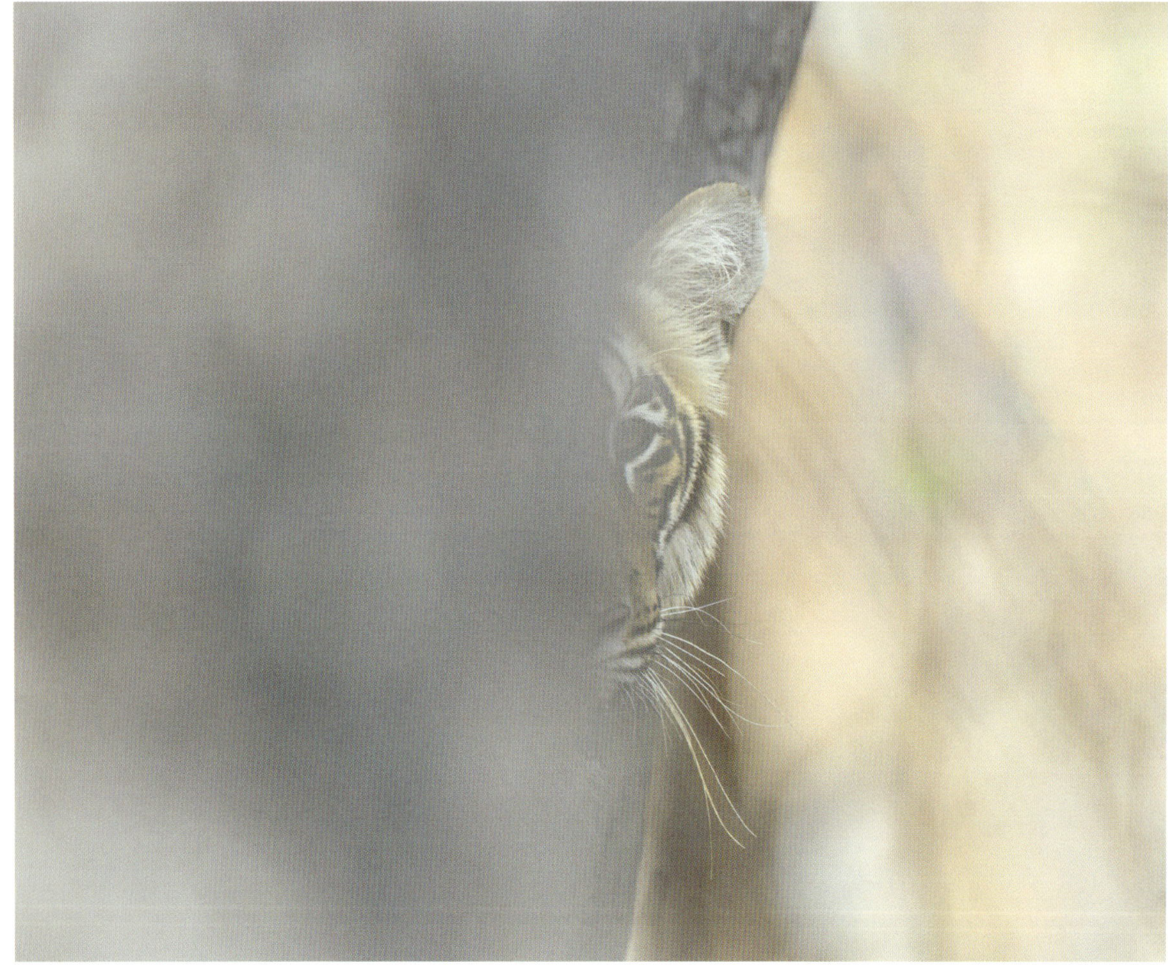

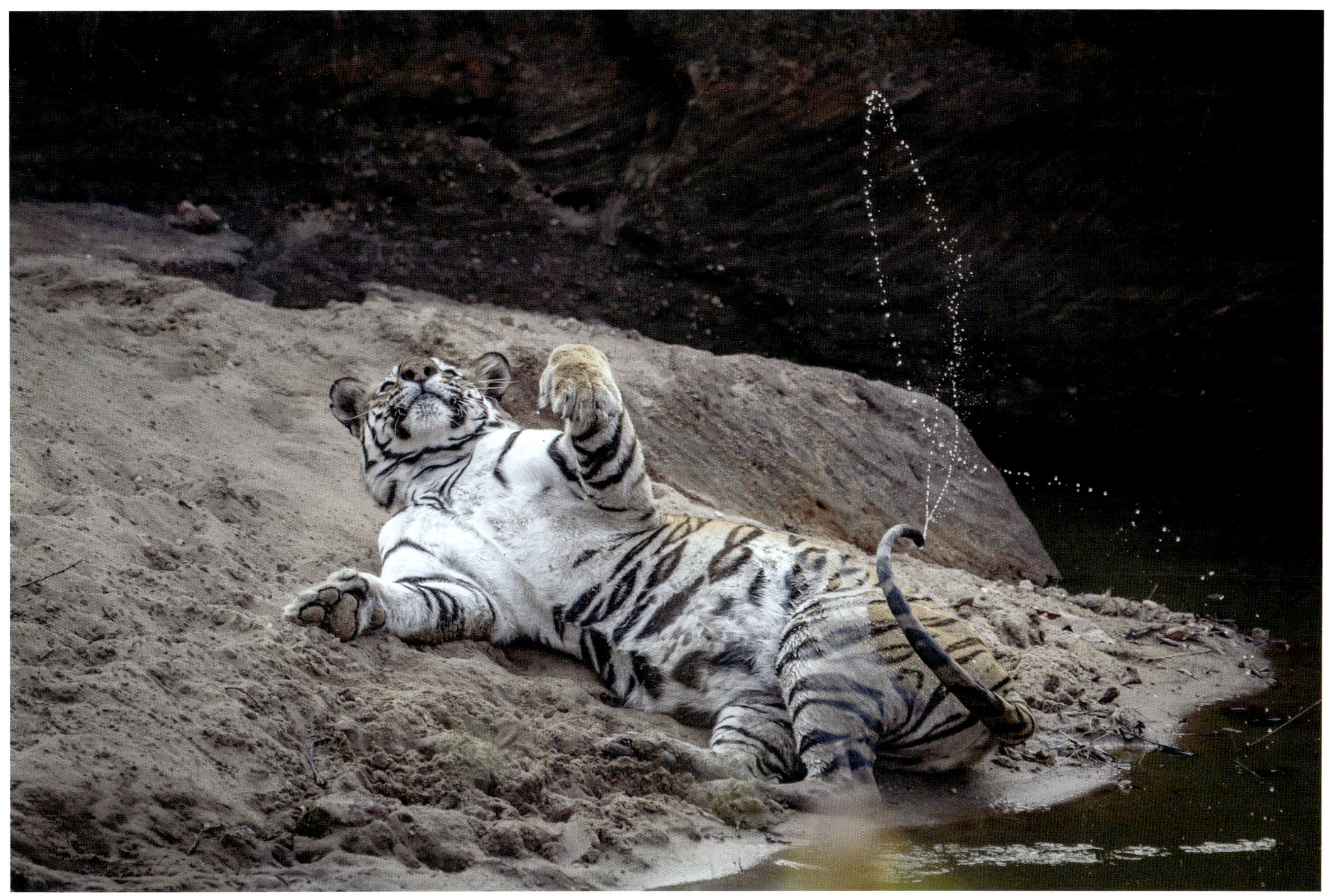

Plenty of heat to make this tigress sleepy, just enough insects to keep her awake. Too much of either would have been a show stopper. I underexposed and concentrated on the tail as it flicked water over its pelt, warding off the many flies.

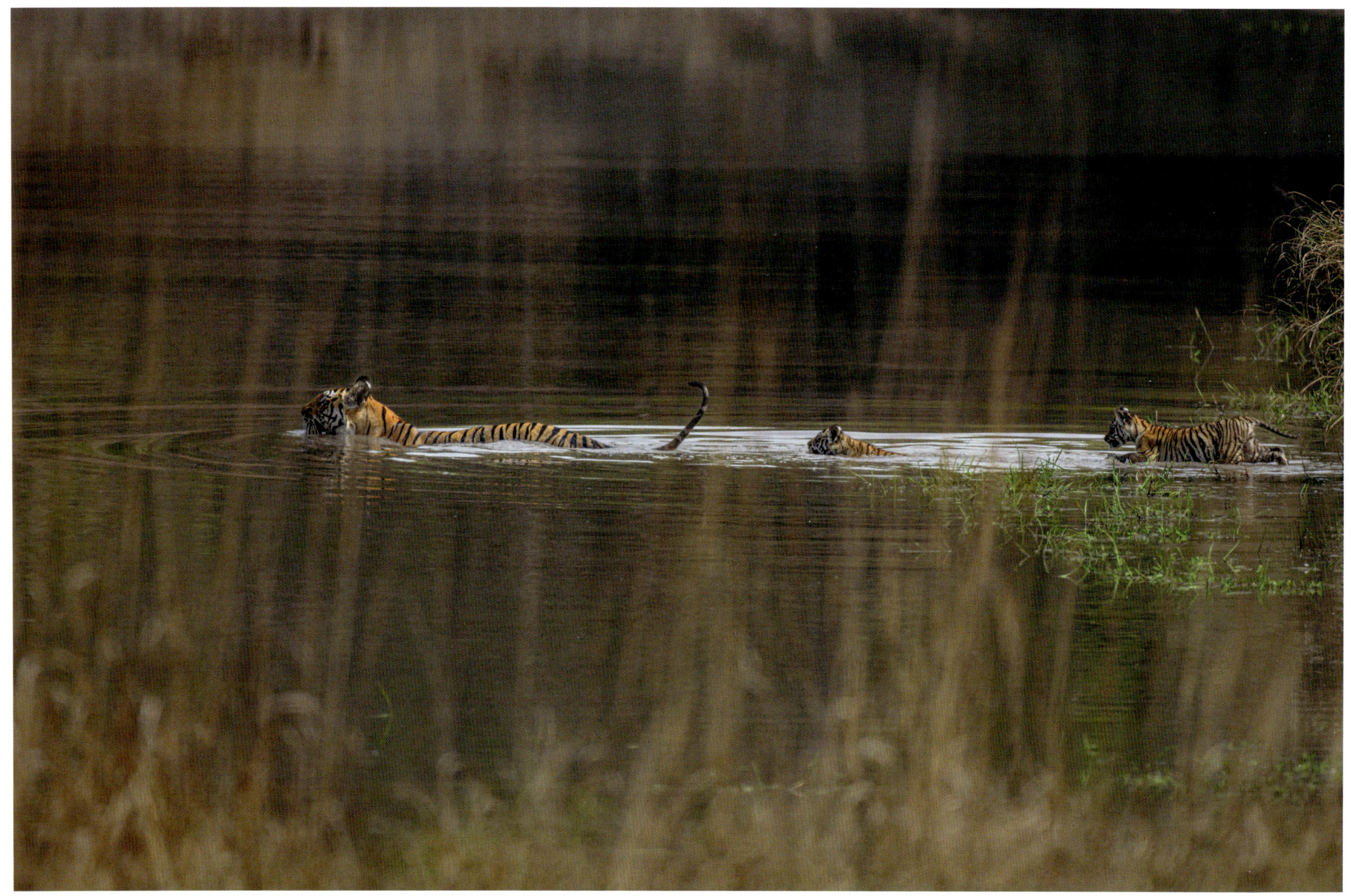

The best tiger moment I've had. On a scorching dry morning, despite the normally advantageous full-day permit, it was quiet in Tala zone. Pappu and I drove across to the nearby Magahdi zone. We knew there was a family there but it was a significant distance away and only the mother had been seen. We sat and waited and eventually the mother appeared. Then two tiny cubs, the smallest I've seen. She took that moment to teach them to swim. In thirty-five years Pappu had never seen this, neither had his equally extraordinary ranger Manjeet. It still brings out goose bumps whenever I think of it.

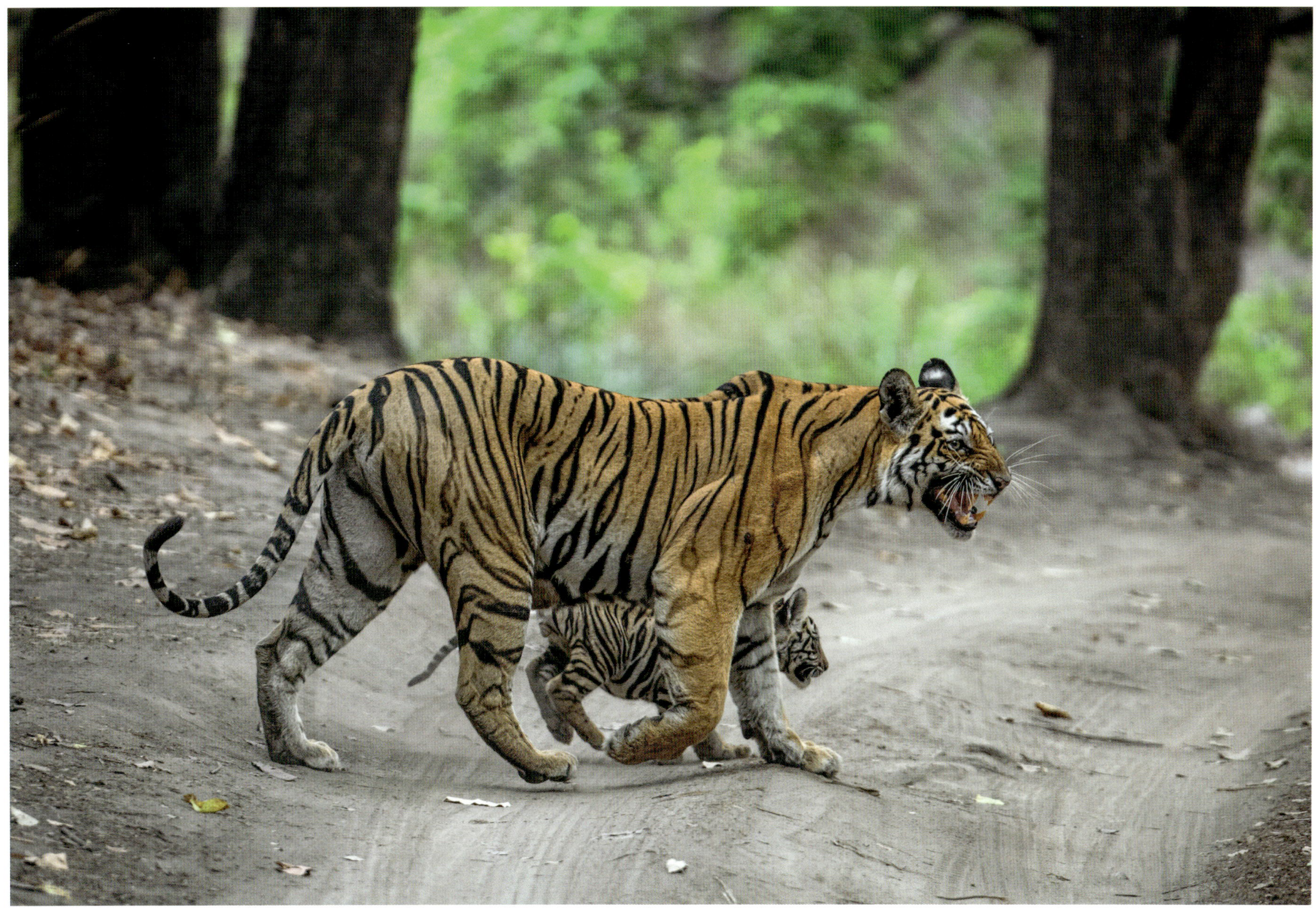

A few days later we waited by the long grass but nothing, not even a single warning call. After driving off we saw freshly sculpted pugmarks, so checked another waterhole and saw them briefly. The cubs were shy and retreated. We had a hunch they may return to their almost impregnable rocky fortress by the gate. It was a good hunch. This whole episode took just under a minute. Utter magic.

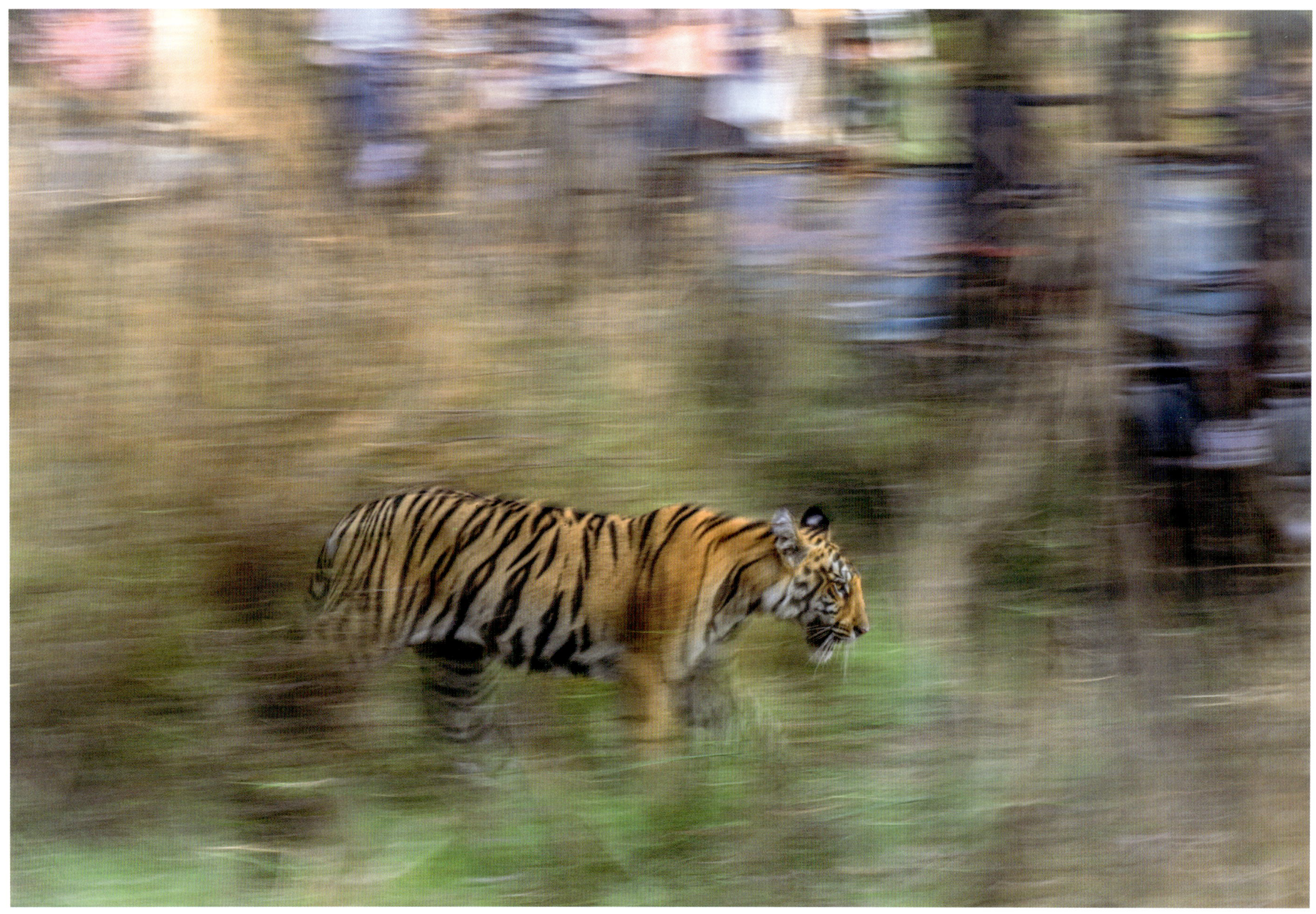

Three yearlings were asleep not far from the road. Slowly vehicles appeared, all (understandably) keen to get a glimpse of this buffer zone triumvirate. Mobile phones have been banned in Tadoba so tourism volume is almost non-existent. There are very few international tourists, which helped the image, as many would have been dressed in khaki or worse still, ludicrous camouflage as opposed to these colourful cottons. I spent a while practising with a slow speed and when the youngster wandered across I was ready. Everyone's cup of tea, I doubt it, but it is mine.

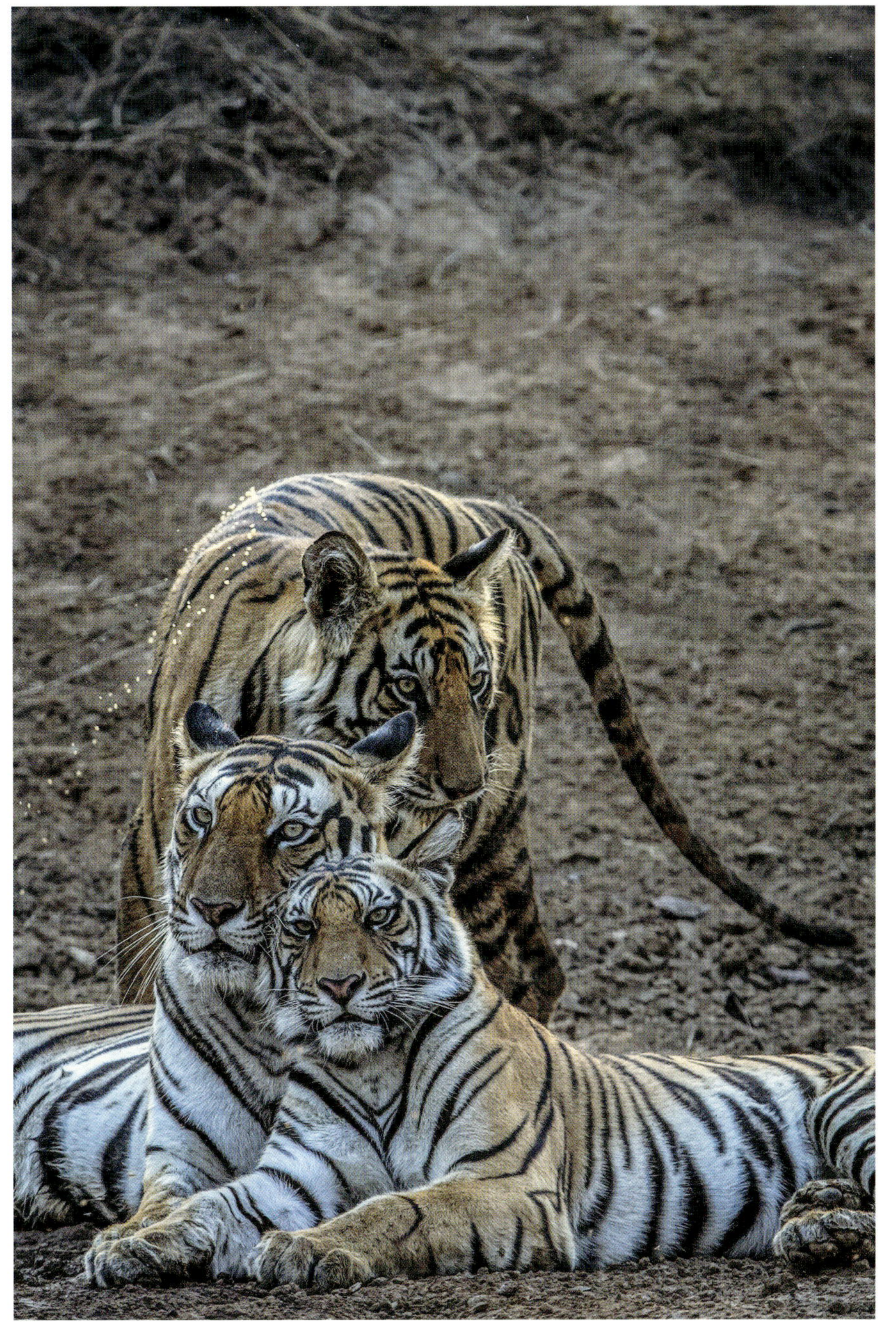

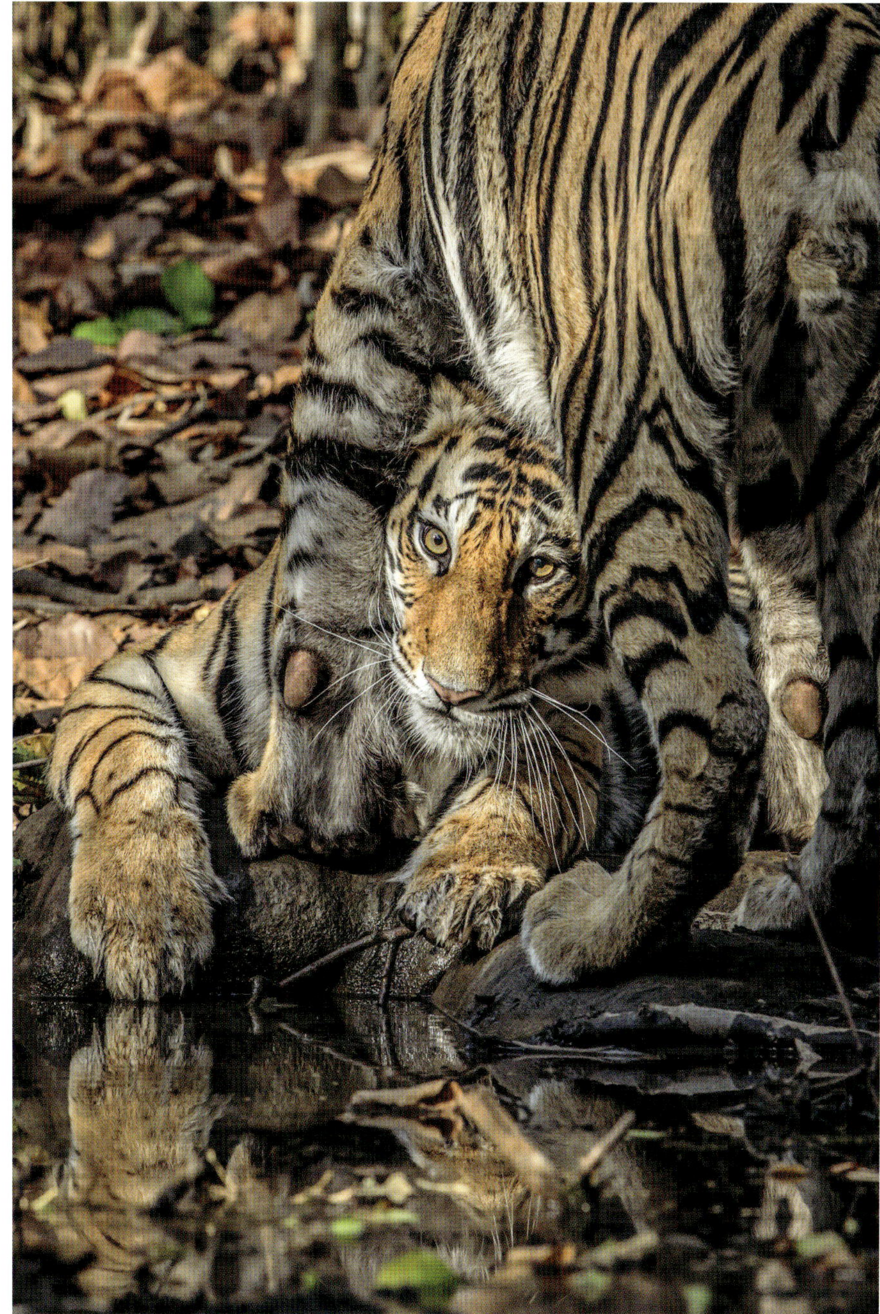

Photographing tigers together is a rarity, especially when the light is kind … patience is never a virtue, it's a must, particularly with tigers.

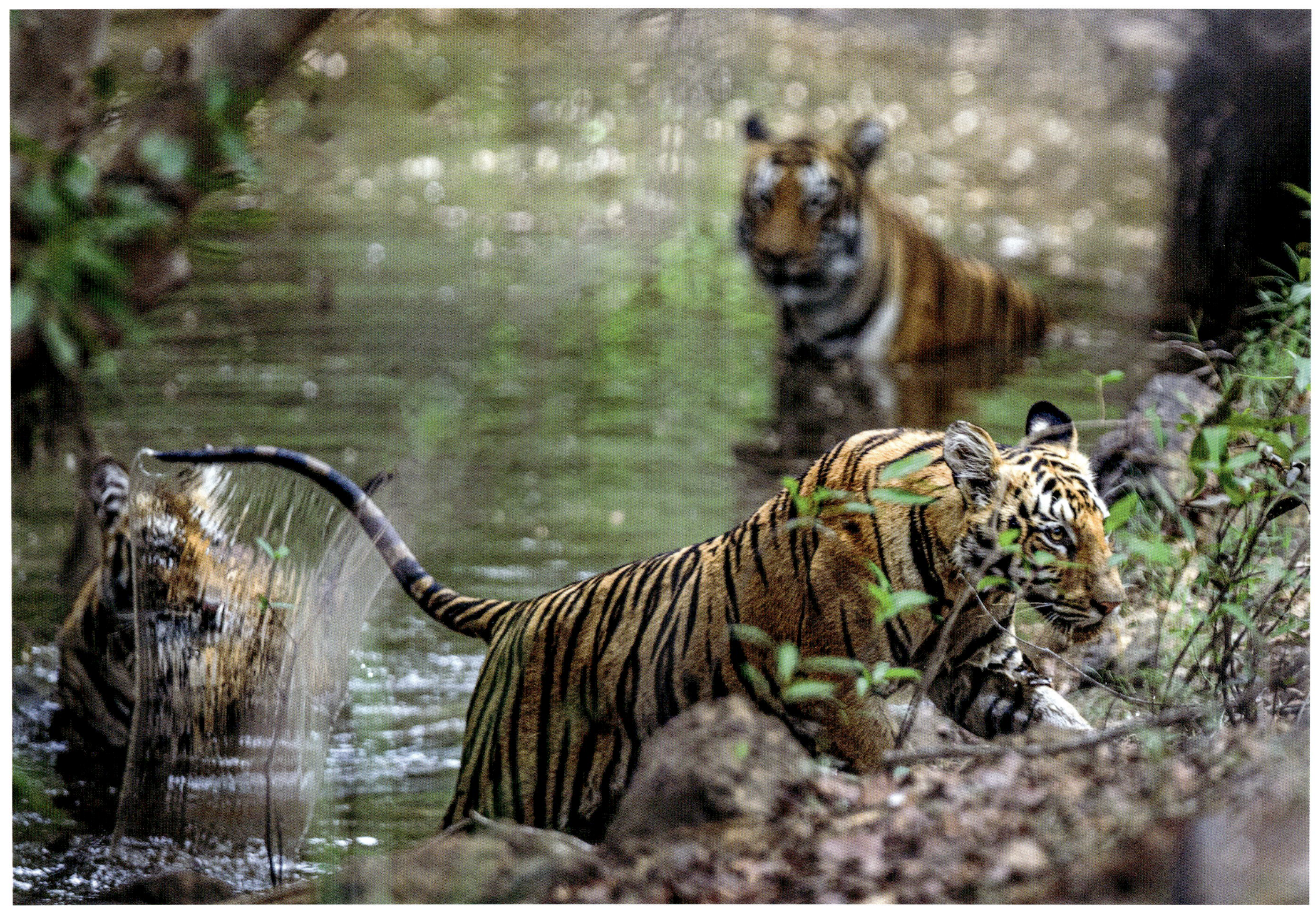

Viraj and Mangesh, I salute you. These two buffer zone alchemists were on it that afternoon, strongly believing that a family of tigers would be hiding in this deep waterhole. It was dark and gloomy but also wonderful.

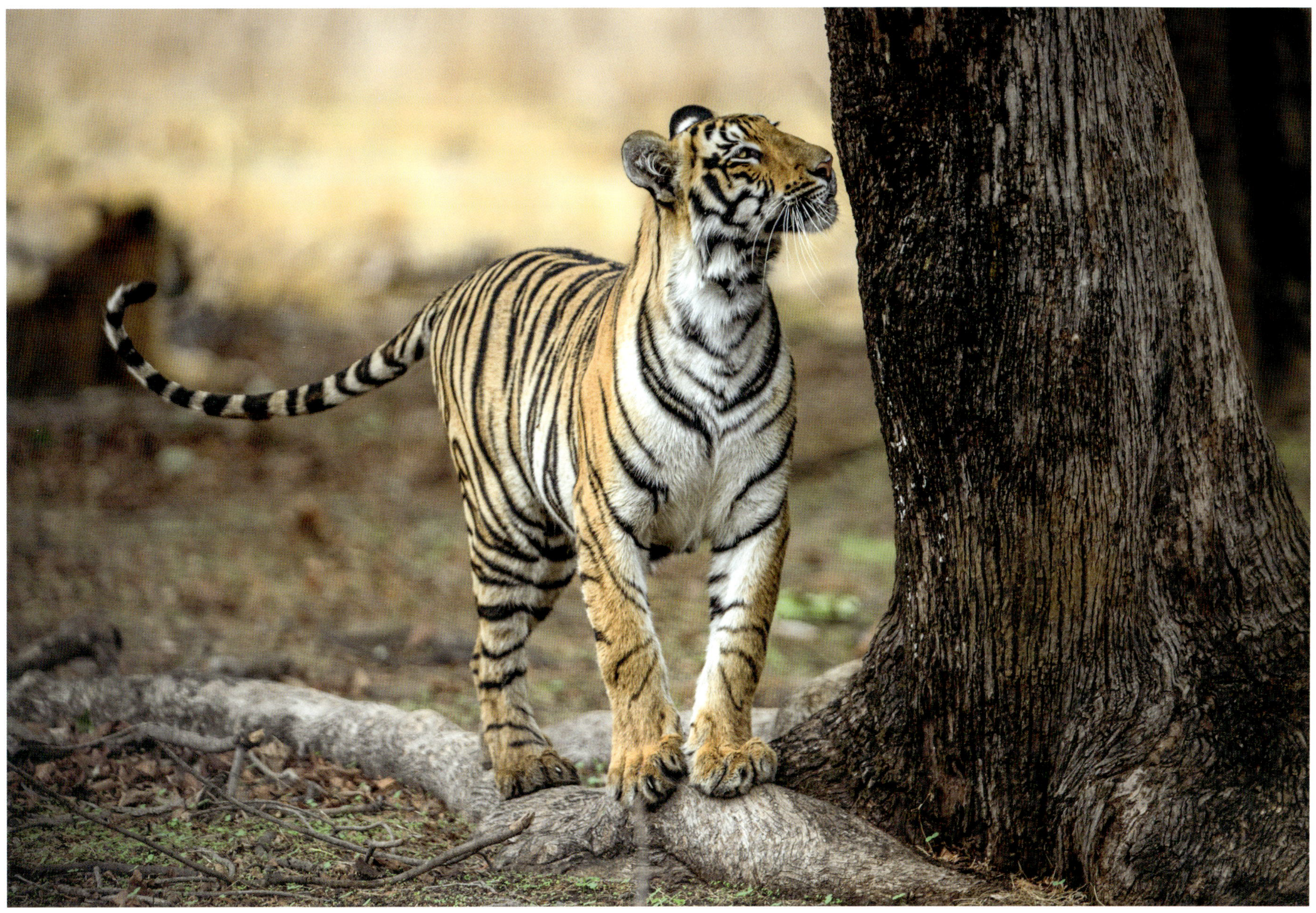

This is a potent area of Tadoba National Park but we waited in sweltering torpor before Himanshu took control. This was an excellent encounter with a youngster and an indifferent parent. However, whenever I enjoy a close-up, I imagine a similar scene when the pursuer has swapped a canon for a rifle … Rage doesn't even come close.

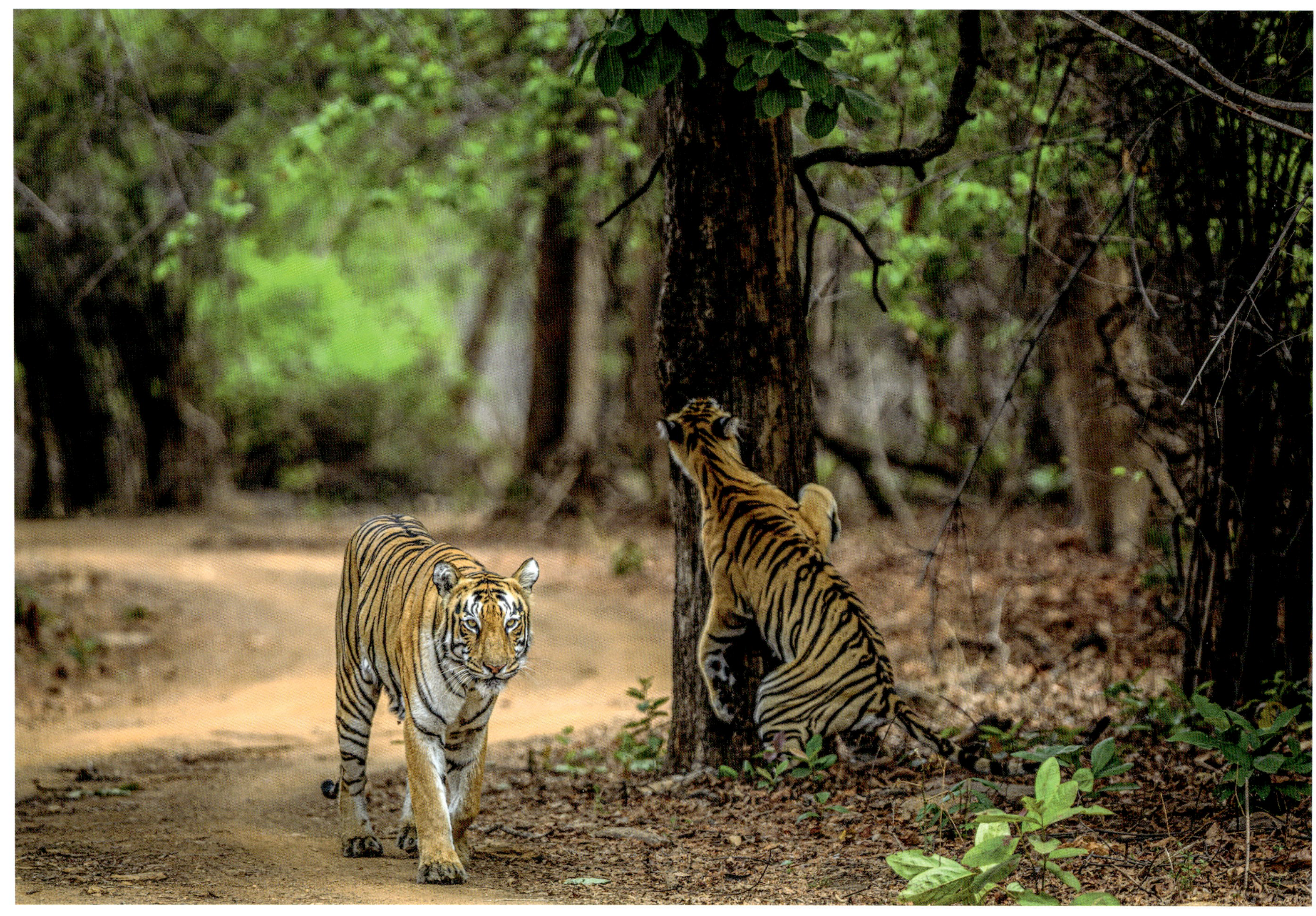

A family following us down a dusty Tadoba track. It didn't take long but it is *never* about time or numbers, but quality, and four tigers following one jeep is quality.

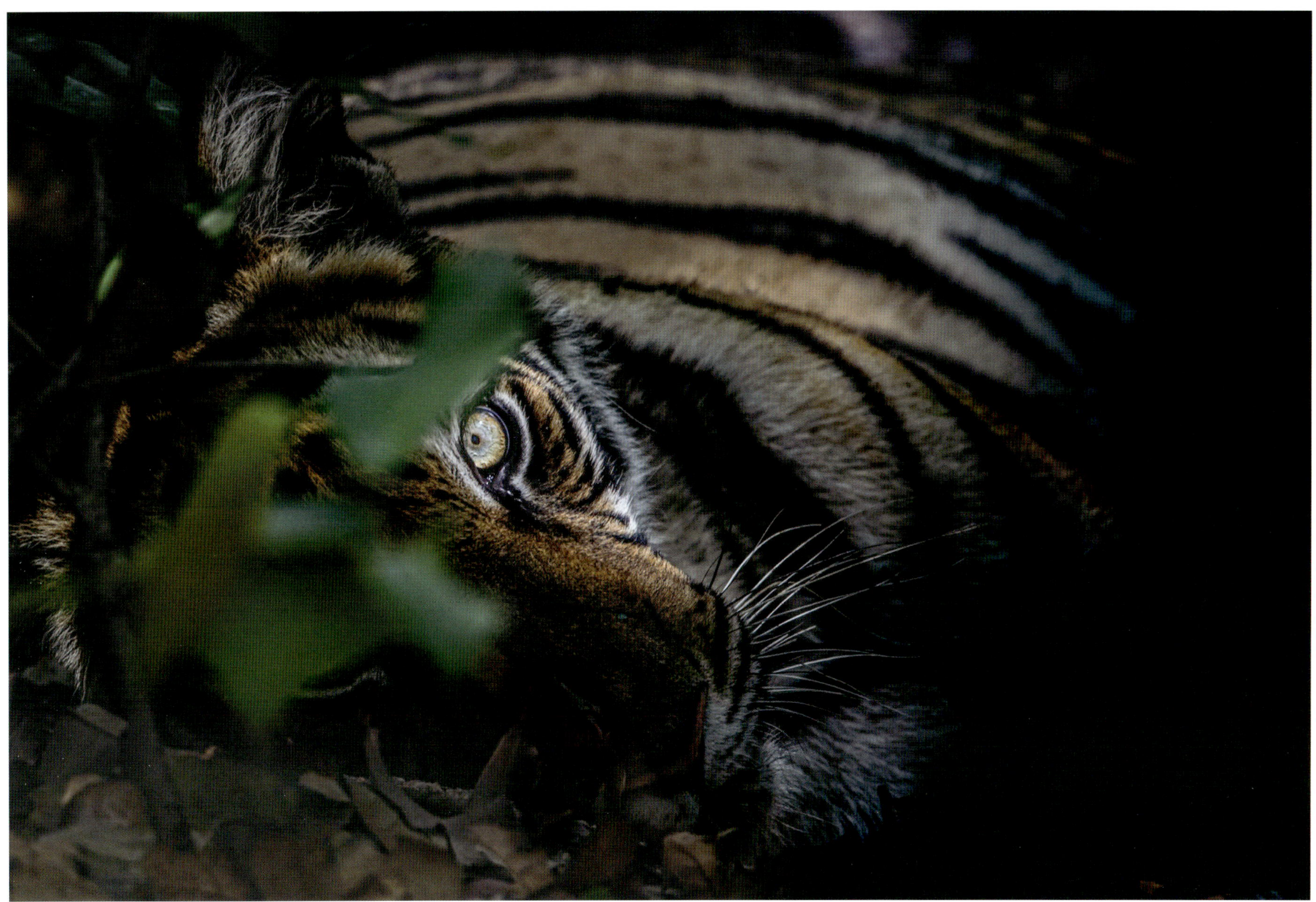

For some reason an idiotic politician wanting to dress up the sensitive side of his CV got 80 per cent of the trails closed in the parks. He knows perfectly well he messed up, but in Asia losing face is everything and he was not prepared to go back on his word. Thankfully, there are still tigers to be had elsewhere. This melancholy close-up was the poster child of many of my marathons.

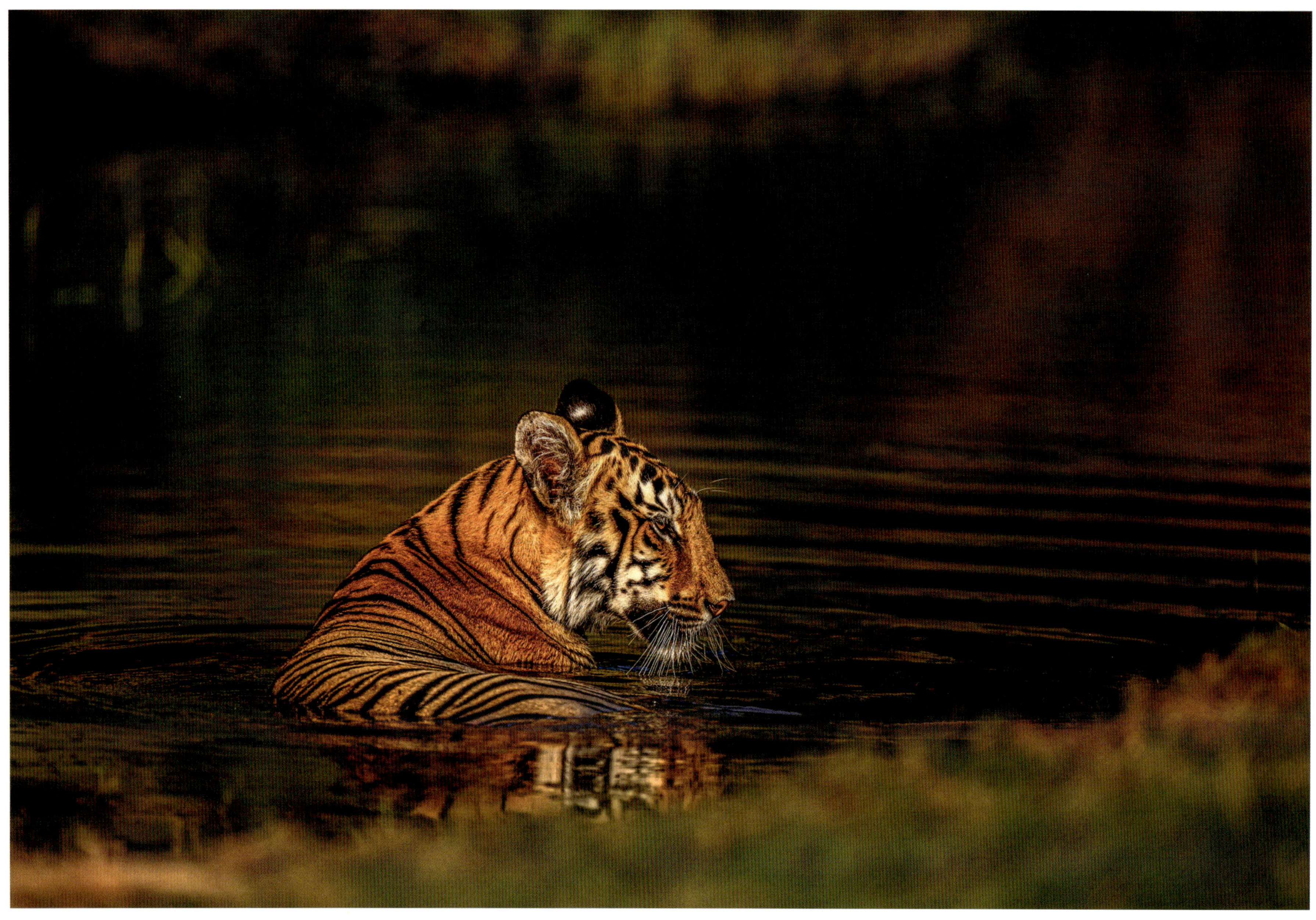

Both images around 20 minutes apart. Cat sightings are rarely doled out evenly. Tadoba buffer zone is a delight and lacks the red tape nonsense that so many officials insist on to ensure most safaris are compromised.

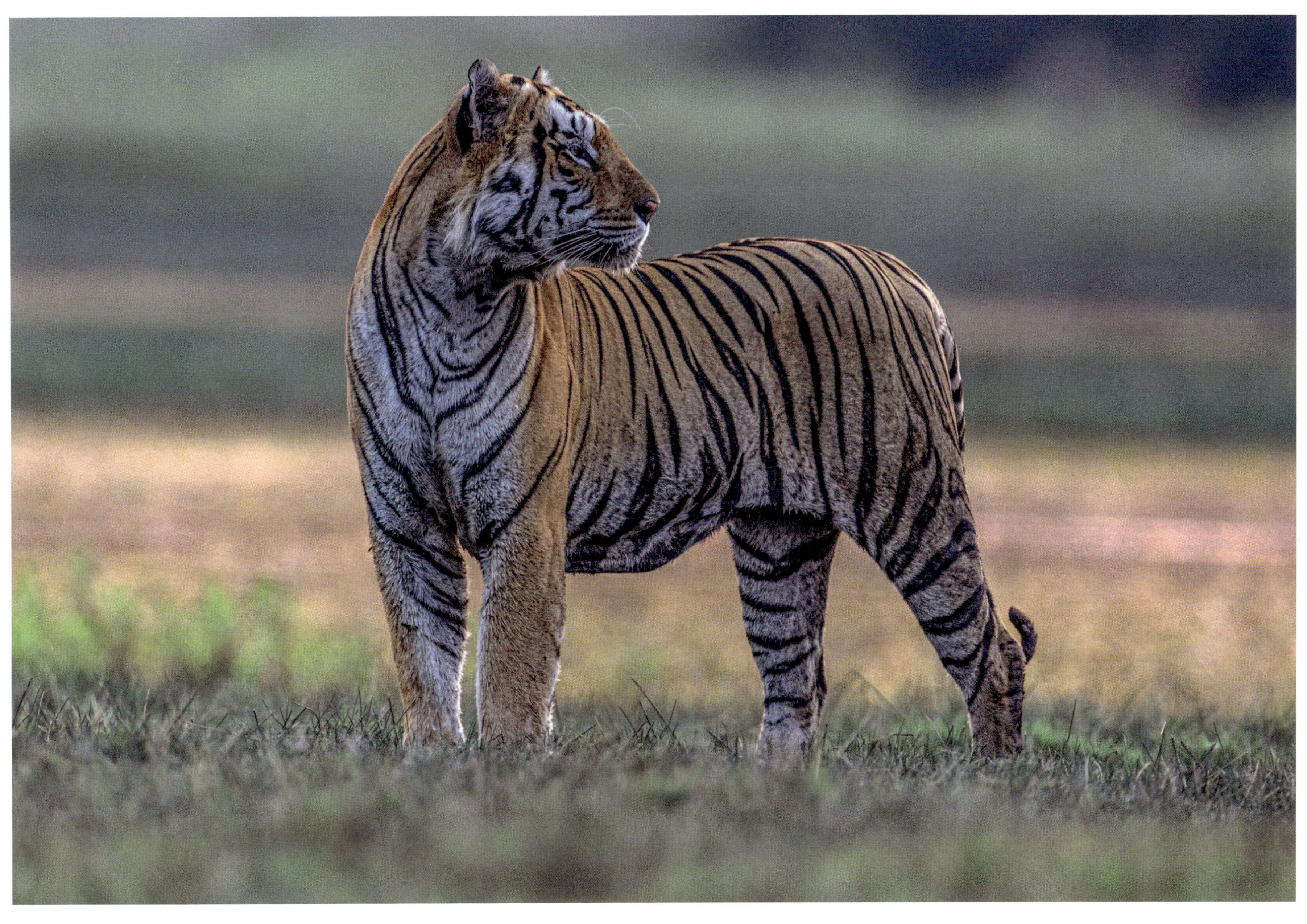

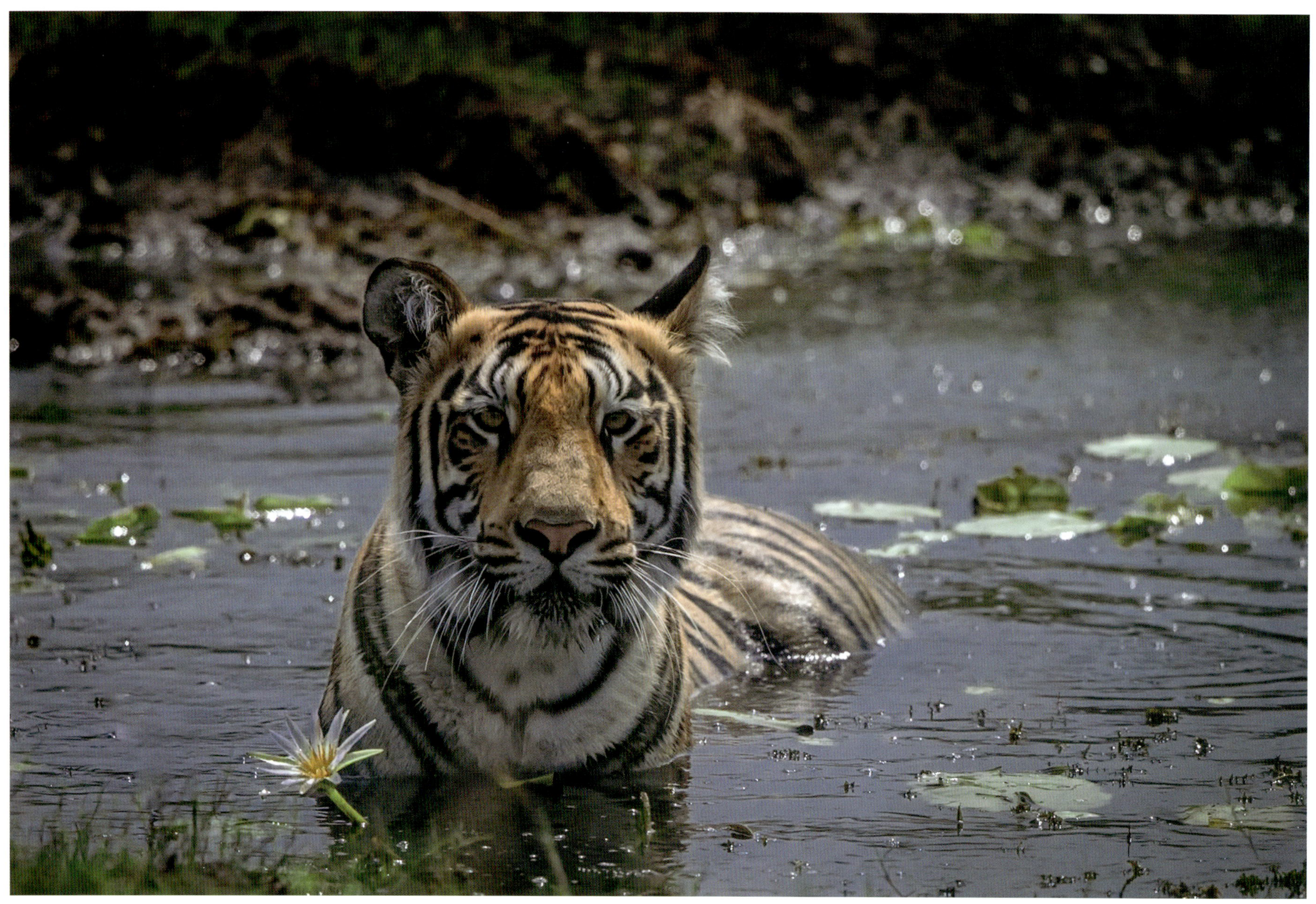

Mid-morning, hot and sultry, cooling-off time
for an adult female, the flower a big bonus.

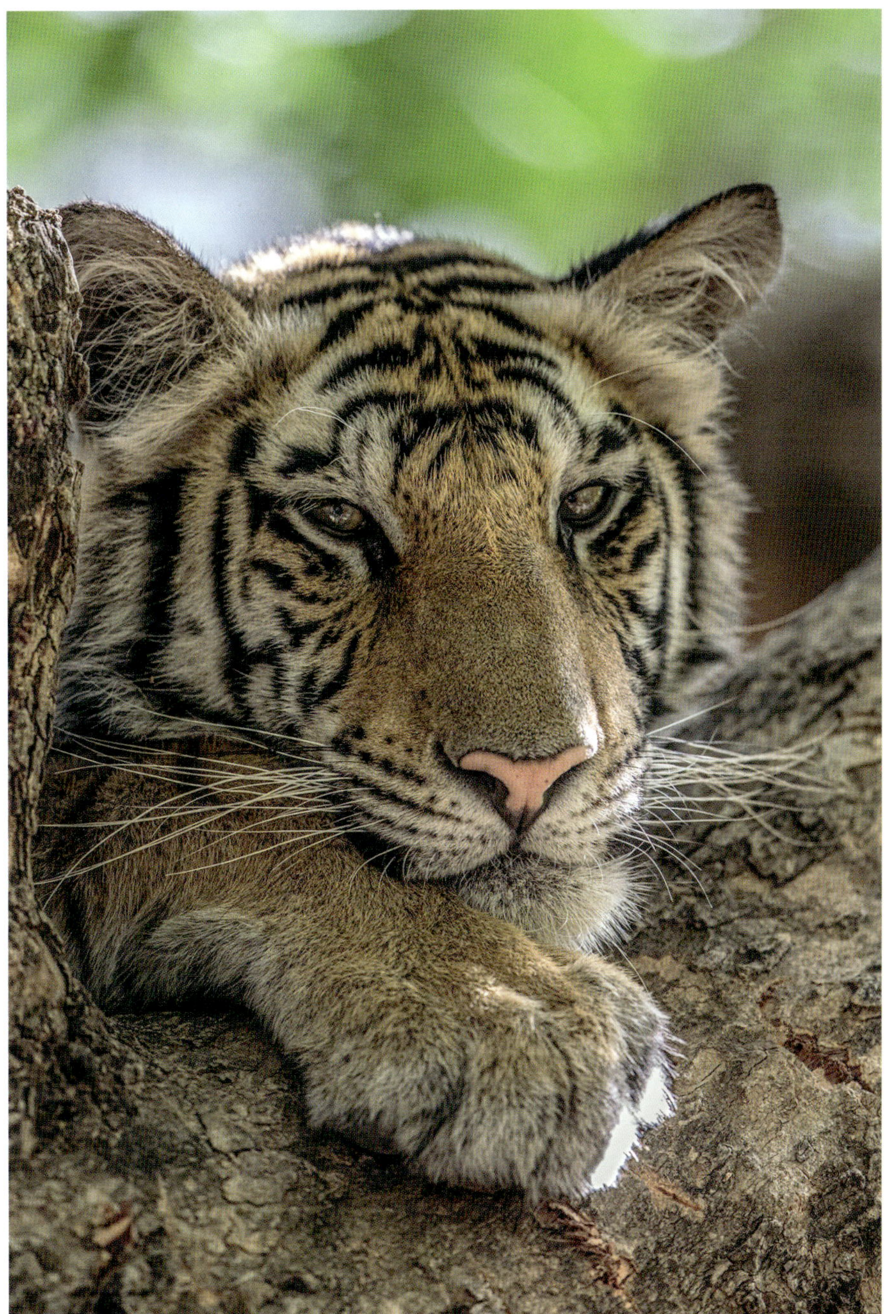

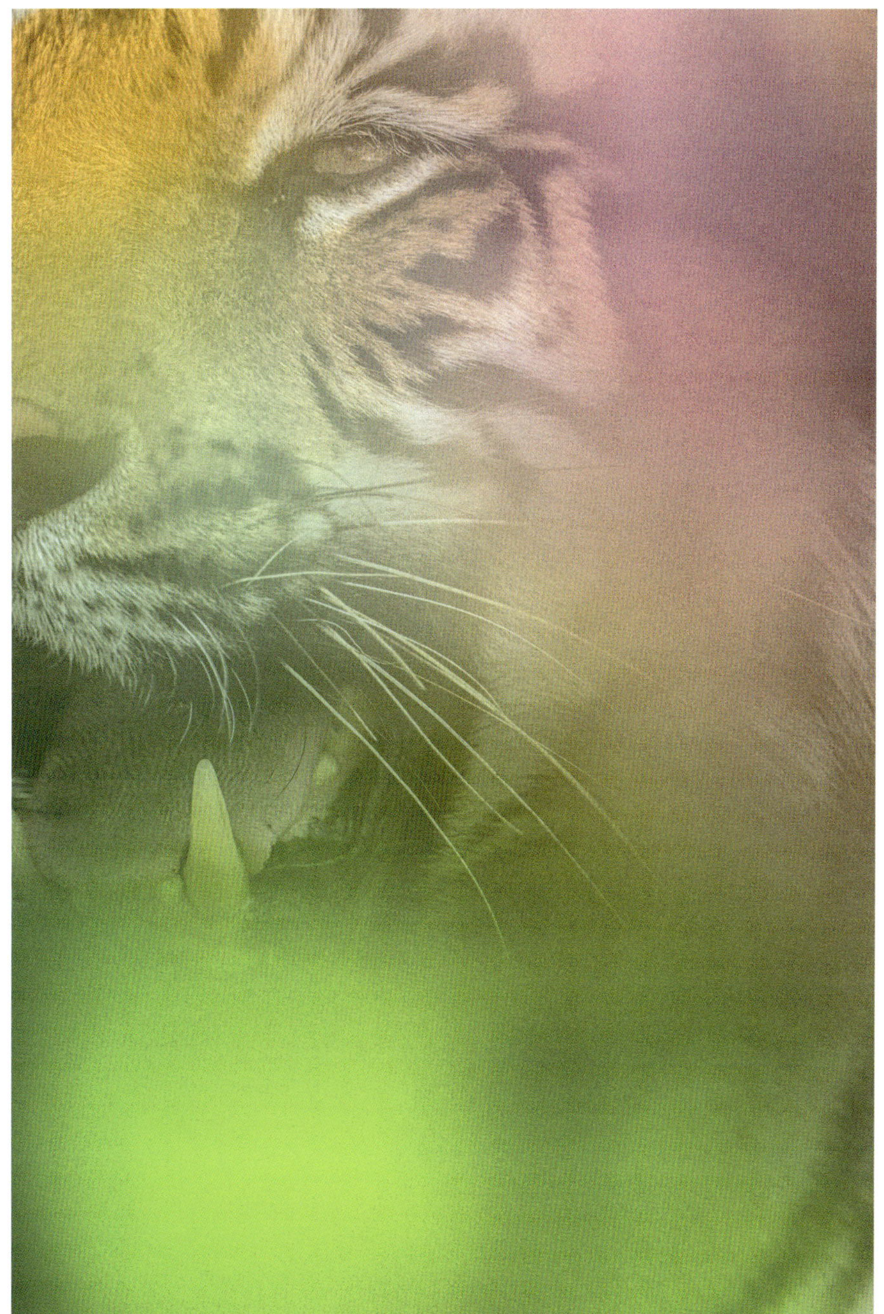

Another climbing youngster – always worthy of a mention. The other looks as though someone has fraudulently messed around with photo software. It wasn't, it was a stationary tiger shot at very shallow aperture through a flowering bush which was closer to me than her.

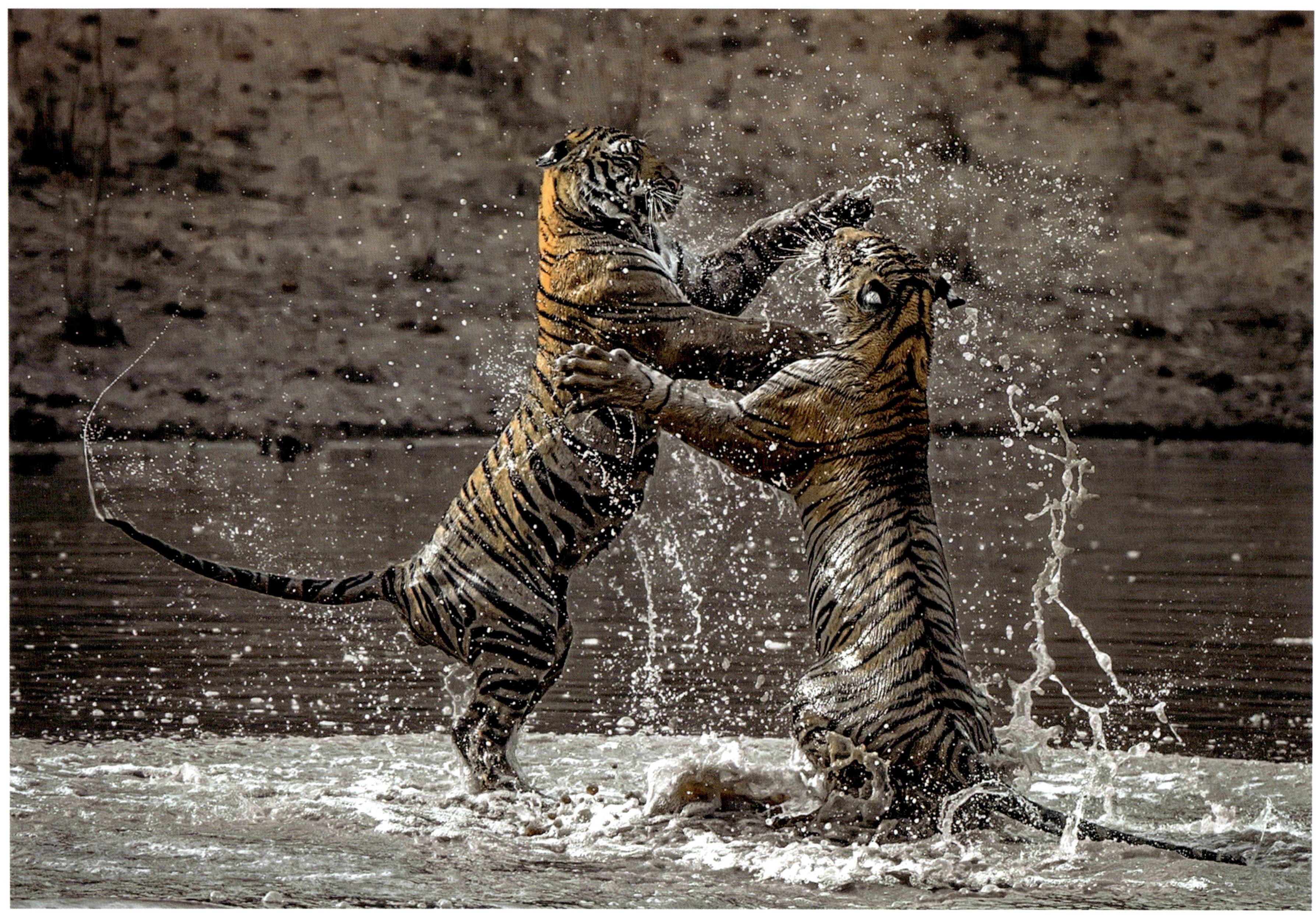

Never mind ducklings in a row, this was the whole flock lined up. The full-day permit was critical, a waterhole that, unlike most which are never landscaped, had decent viewing, water deep enough for drama but not too deep to deny it, two young brothers the same size and their bellies full enough to provide energy but not too replete to garner slothfulness. And then, you had to be there.

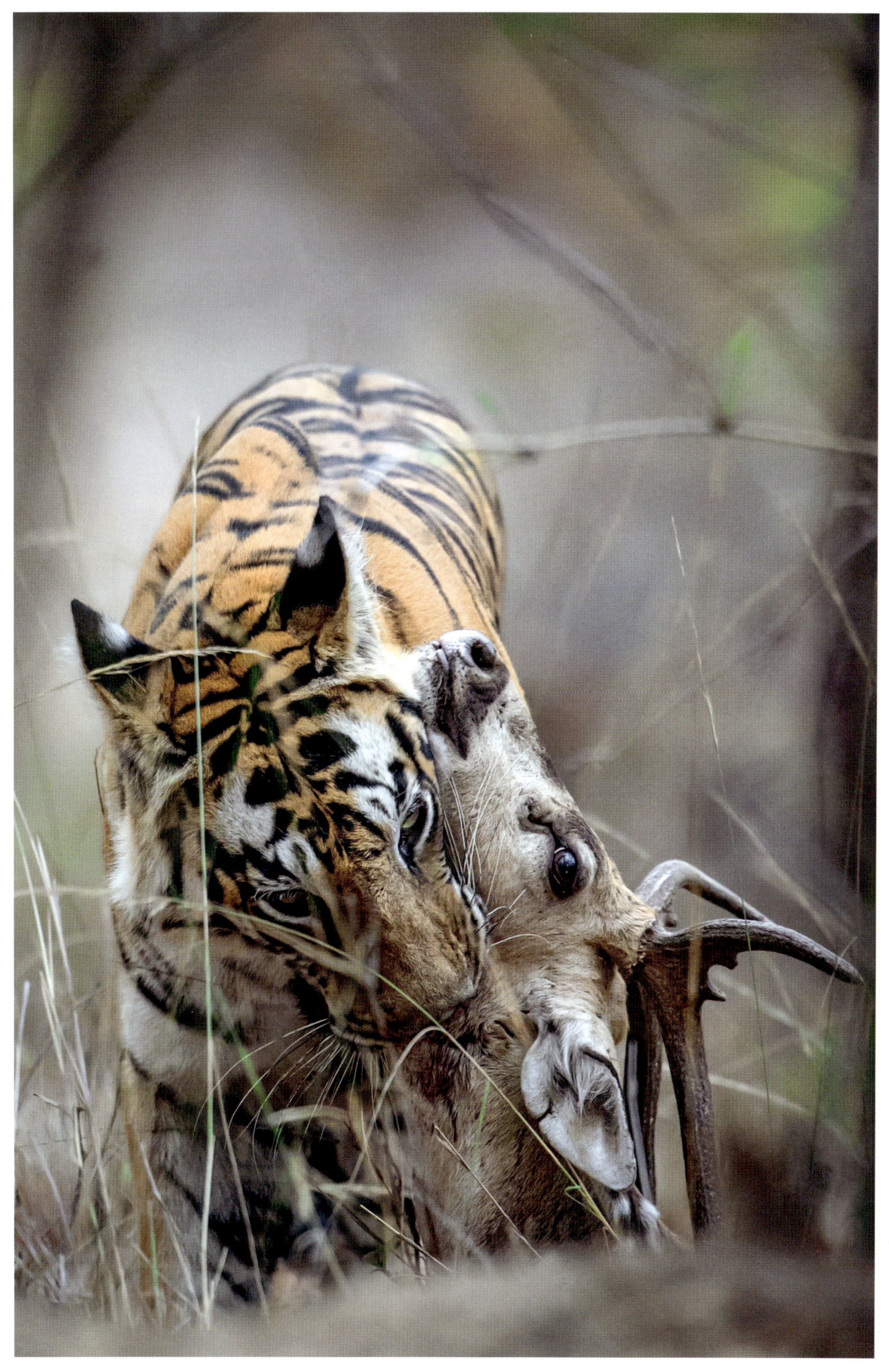

Spotty (ludicrous name – I don't really care for names for wild animals, particularly western ones) had downed a male spotted deer and vanished. Pappu stopped among many vehicles, understandably keen to see her dragging her spoils. We were right in line, he'd done it again.

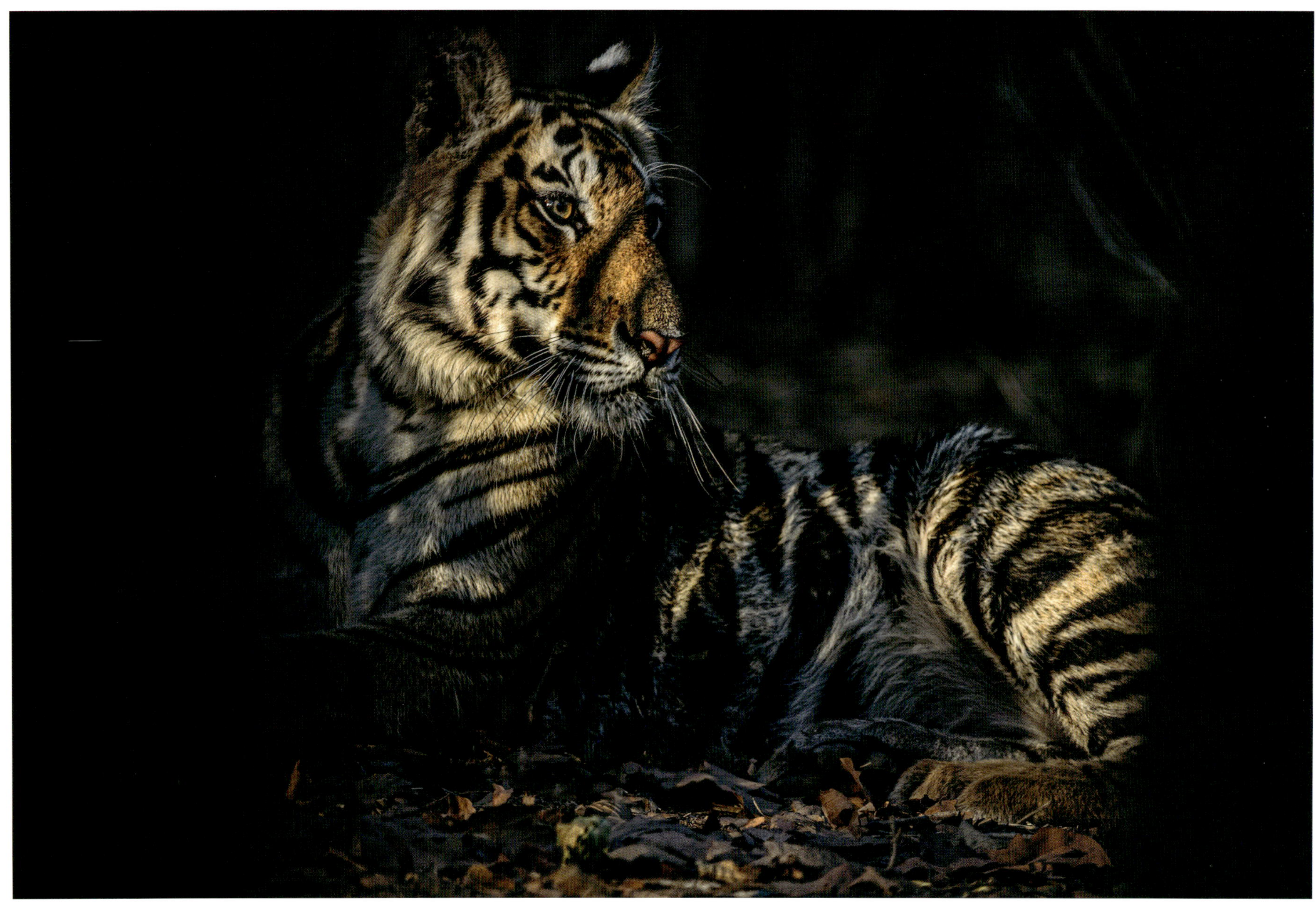

When you have unnecessary restrictions, lazy protagonists and limited time, the beautifully lit images you may expect from properly run African conservancies are not commonplace in India. However, when it does line up there is no better subject. Orange really is the new black.

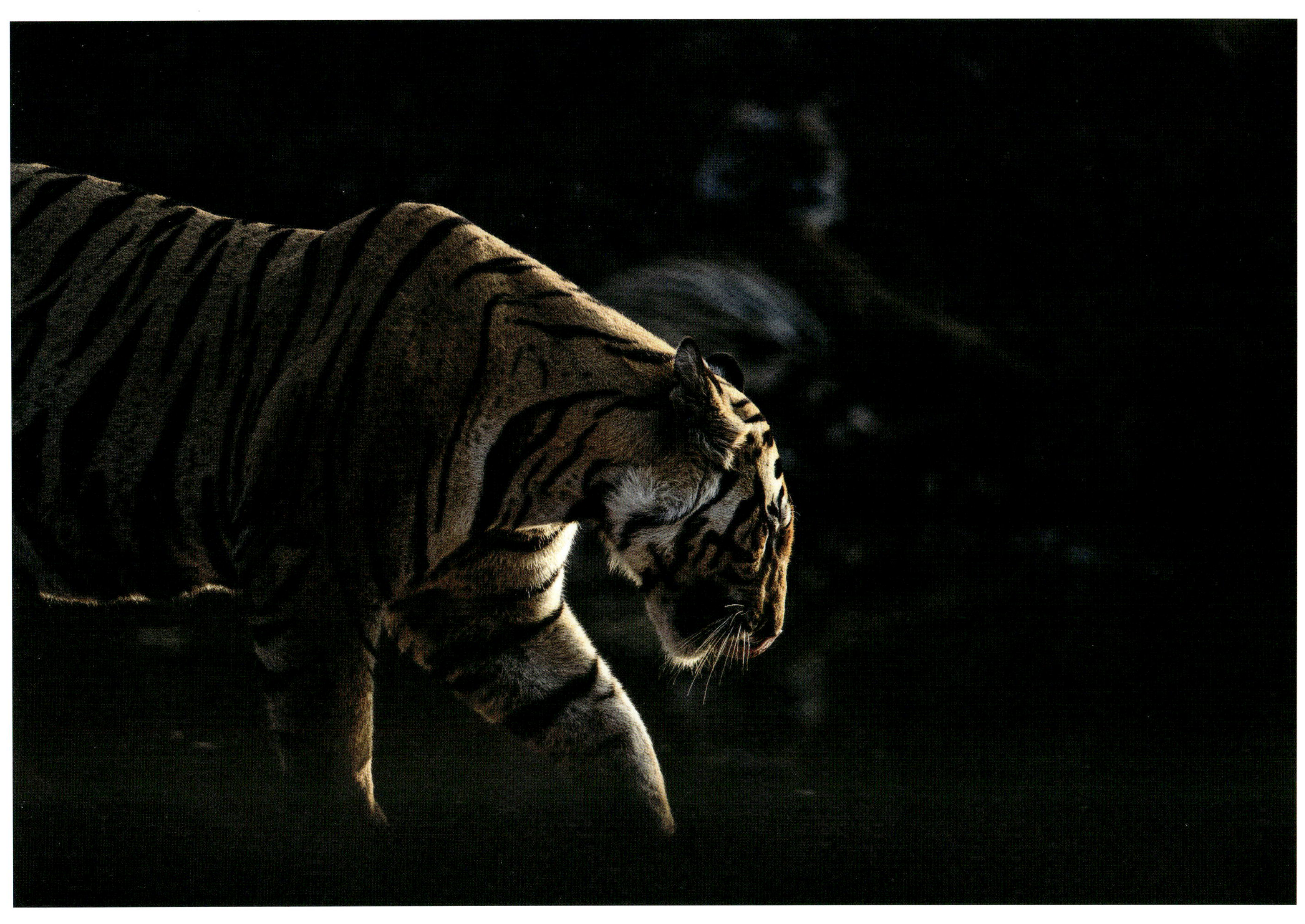

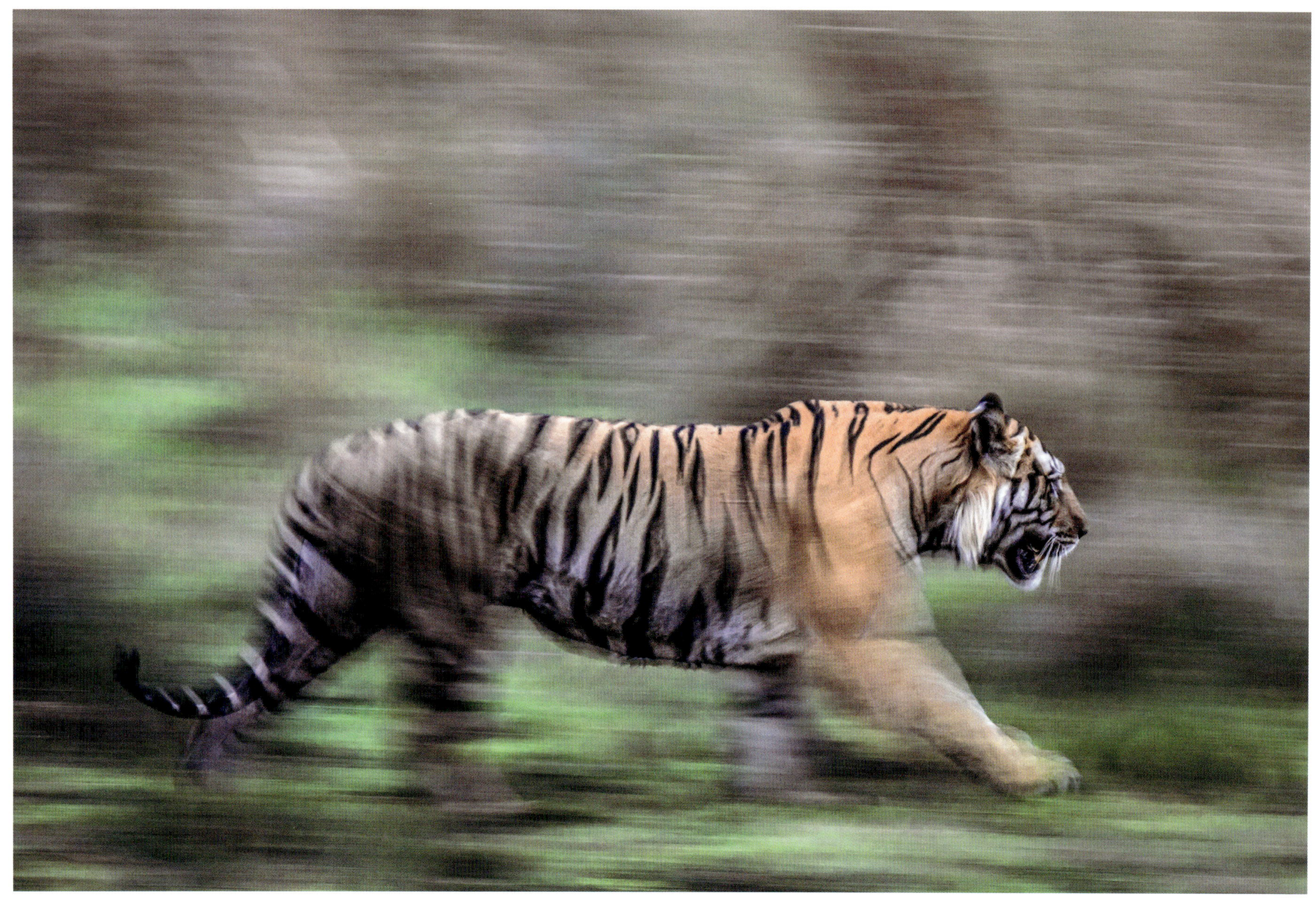

My oft-used slow shutter speed is rare with tigers, as the backgrounds seldom shape up. The main Tala meadow changed all that and 240 kgs of male was a not inconsiderable quarry to target at one quarter of a second.

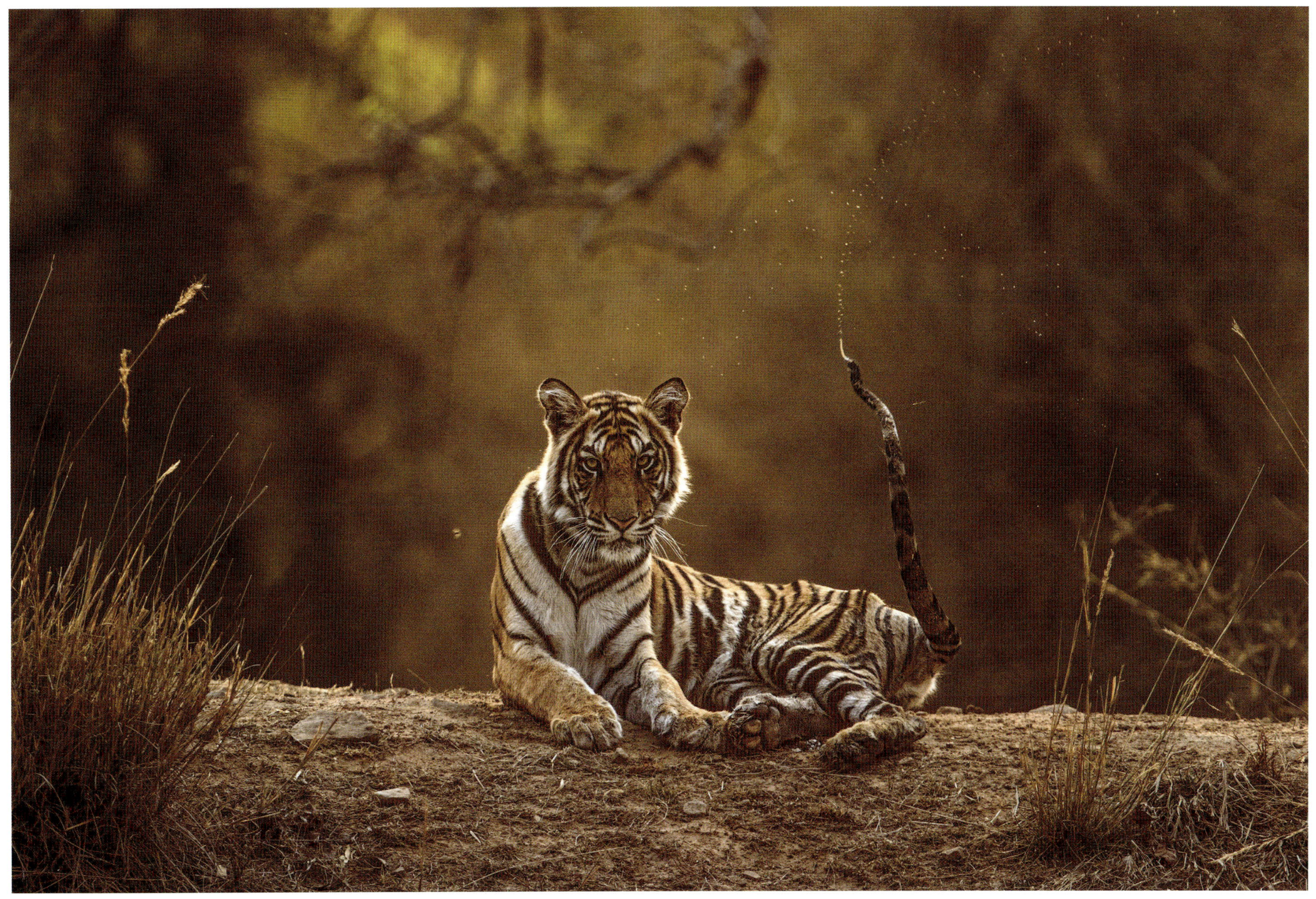

'Paul, I know the reserve is closed on Wednesday afternoon (no, don't ask why, please) but we can get into the buffer zone.' 'Let's do it, Pappu.' Worth the waiting for tickets and paperwork, worth the hours in the 40-degree heat, worth it and more.

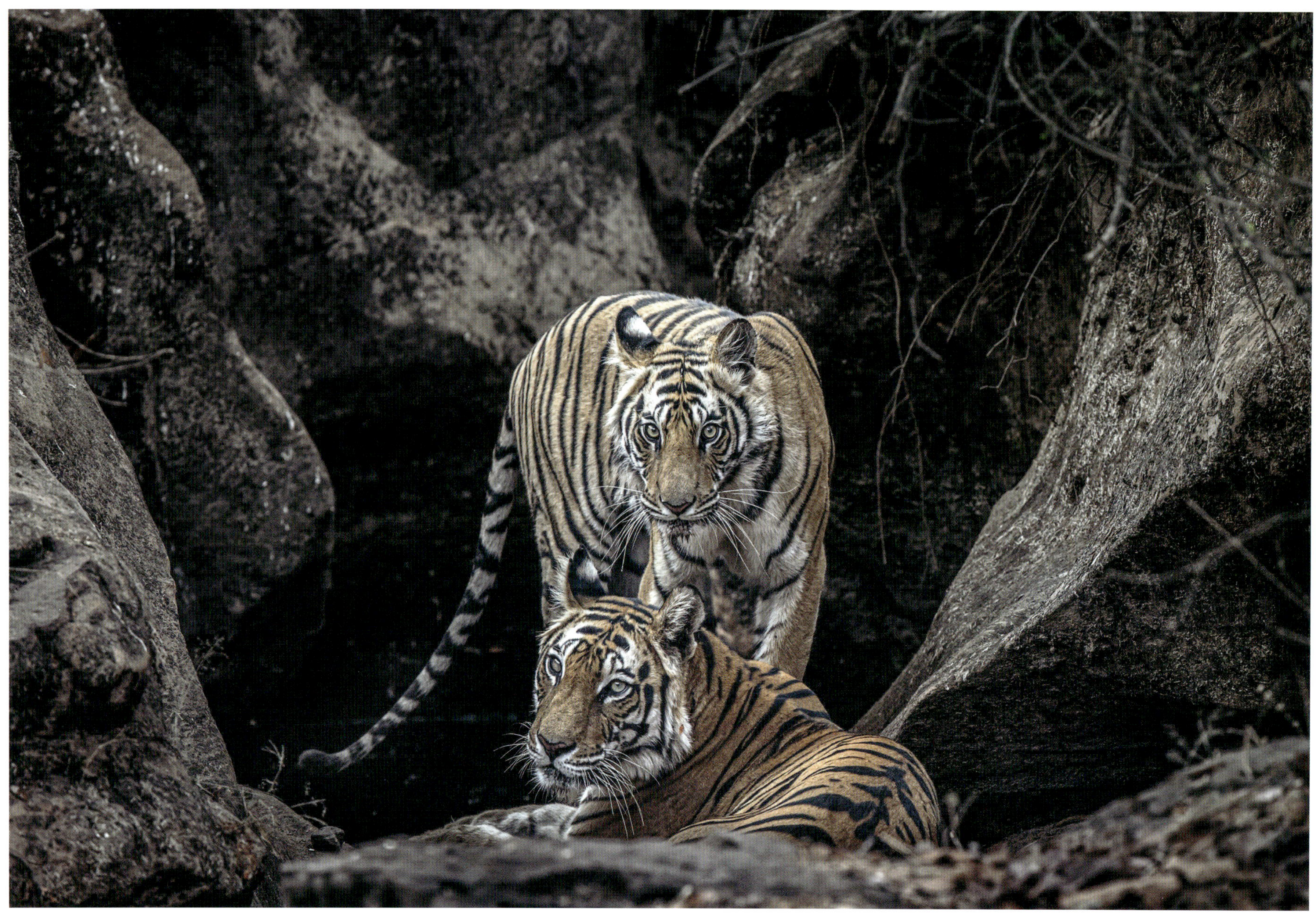

And finally: one mid-afternoon warning call. One three-hour vigil. Nothing. So a return the next morning to try to level out the averages. A small granite waterhole and, for a moment, a mother and yearling posing after slaking their not inconsiderable thirst. It is probably the only tiger photo I'm really happy with, maybe a 6/10. Thanks Pappu, thanks Manjeet, good teamwork. Magical moment. The waterhole is grown over now, why spend 15 minutes clearing it? Shame.

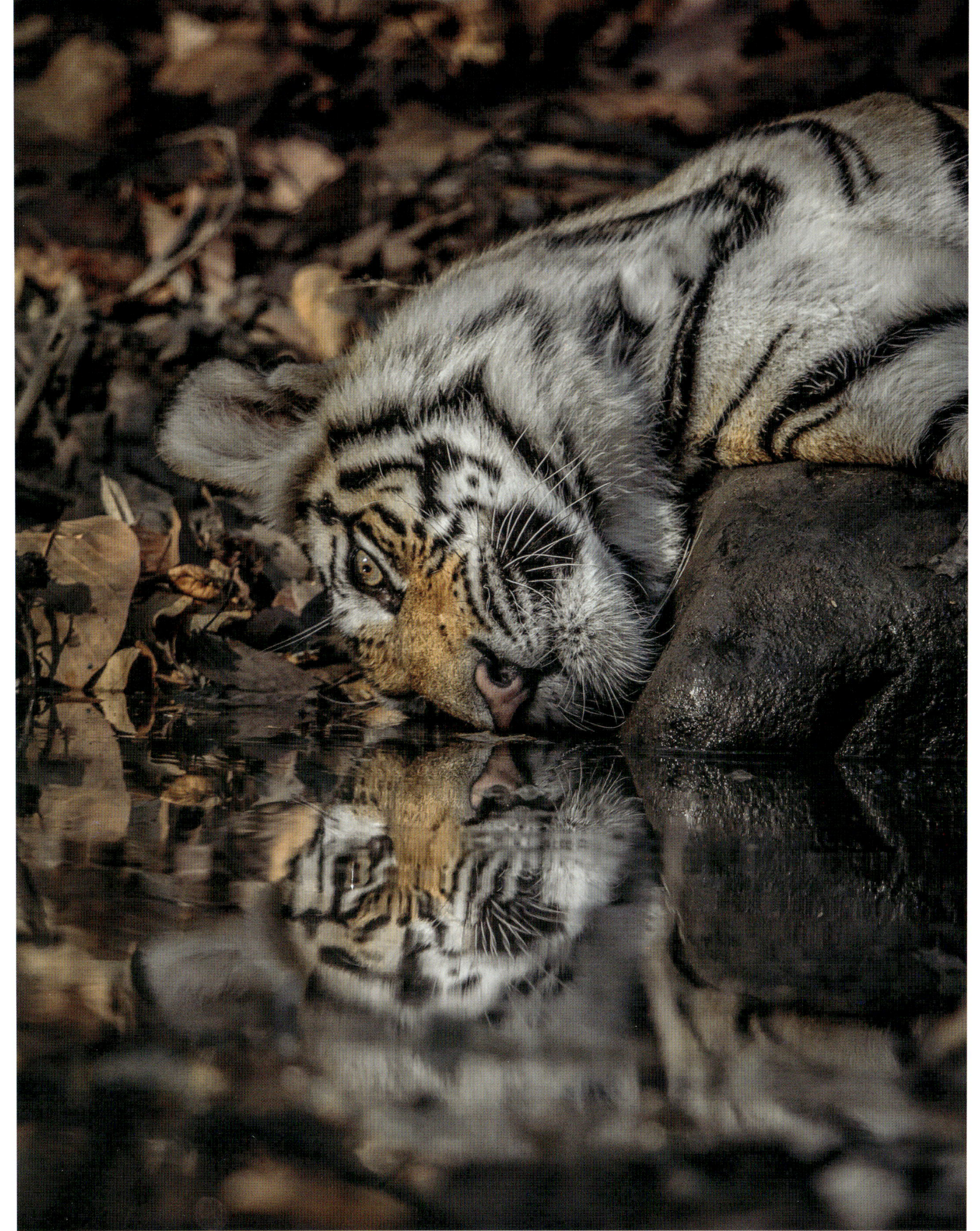

A distant buffer-zone journey and a young tiger prostrated by a small and murky waterhole. The image wasn't difficult, however it makes me smile as the moment the youngster's nose touched the surface it recoiled in shock. Hopefully it lives a full life without many serious shocks.

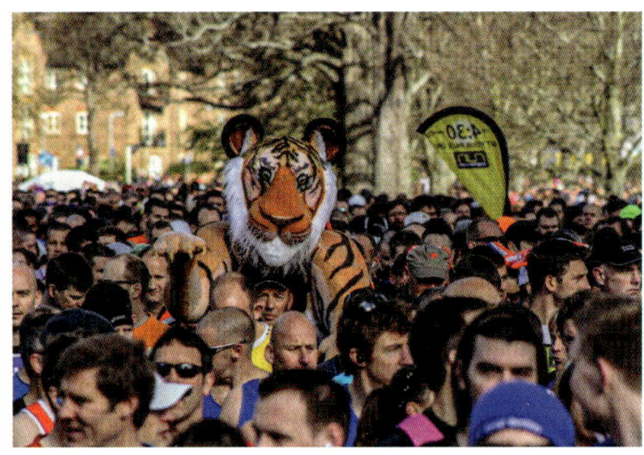

One of Paul's many marathons for tigers.

Published in 2026 by Unicorn
an imprint of Unicorn Publishing Group
Charleston Studio, Meadow Business Centre,
Lewes BN8 5RW
www.unicornpublishing.org

ISBN 978-1-917458-56-6
10 9 8 7 6 5 4 3 2 1

Design by Felicity Price-Smith
Printed in Malta by Gutenberg Press Ltd.

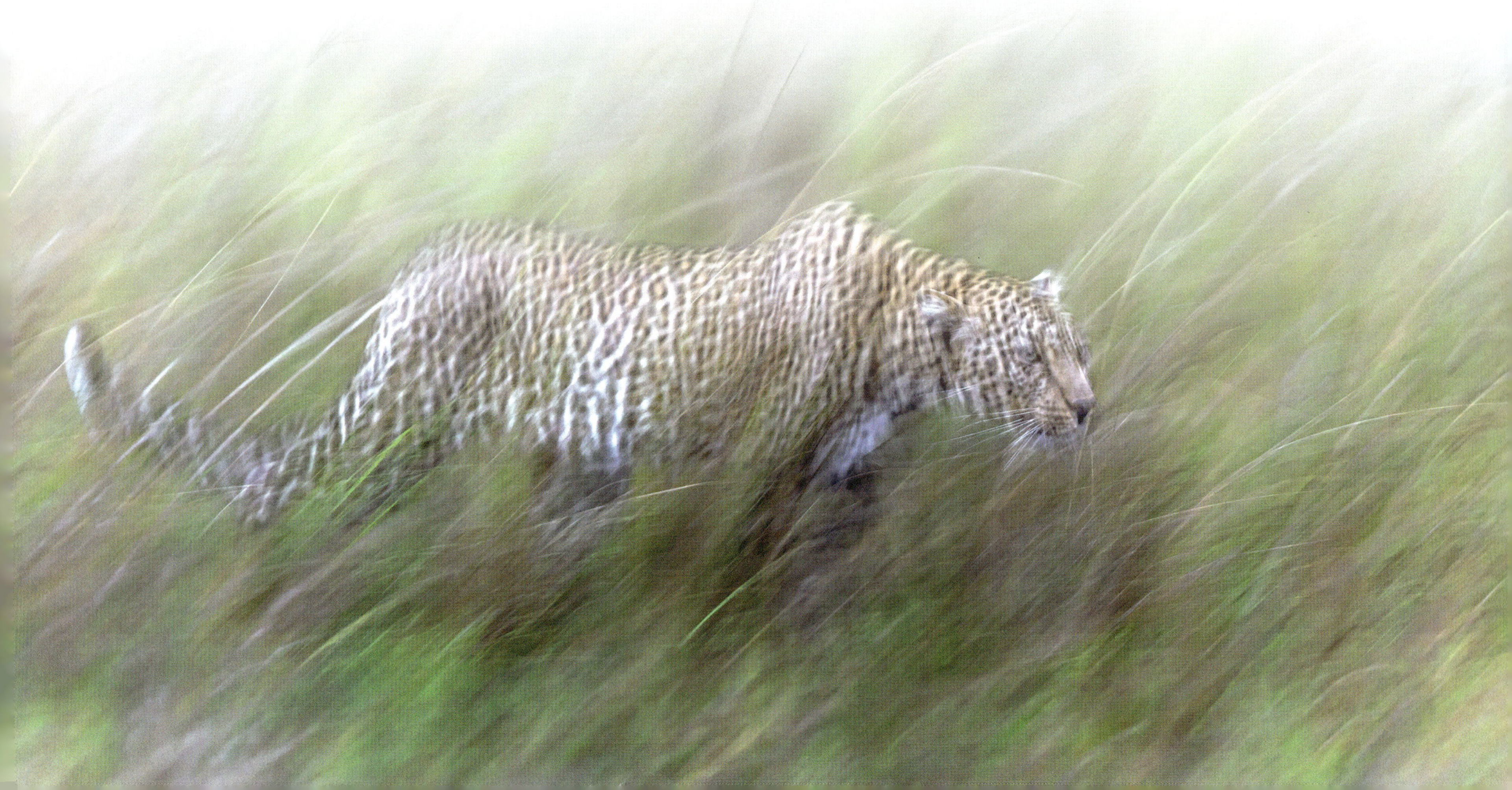